T0211059

Lecture Notes in Computer Science   14676

Founding Editors

Gerhard Goos
Juris Hartmanis

The series Lecture Notes in Computer Science (LNCS), including its subseries Lecture Notes in Artificial Intelligence (LNAI) and Lecture Notes in Bioinformatics (LNBI), has established itself as a medium for the publication of new developments in computer science and information technology research, teaching, and education.

LNCS enjoys close cooperation with the computer science R & D community, the series counts many renowned academics among its volume editors and paper authors, and collaborates with prestigious societies. Its mission is to serve this international community by providing an invaluable service, mainly focused on the publication of conference and workshop proceedings and postproceedings. LNCS commenced publication in 1973.

Ilaria Castellani · Francesco Tiezzi
Editors

Coordination Models and Languages

26th IFIP WG 6.1 International Conference, COORDINATION 2024
Held as Part of the 19th International Federated Conference
on Distributed Computing Techniques, DisCoTec 2024
Groningen, The Netherlands, June 17–21, 2024
Proceedings

 Springer

Editors
Ilaria Castellani 🆔
INRIA Sophia Antipolis
Sophia Antipolis, France

Francesco Tiezzi 🆔
University of Florence
Florence, Italy

ISSN 0302-9743 ISSN 1611-3349 (electronic)
Lecture Notes in Computer Science
ISBN 978-3-031-62696-8 ISBN 978-3-031-62697-5 (eBook)
https://doi.org/10.1007/978-3-031-62697-5

This Springer imprint is published by the registered company Springer Nature Switzerland AG
The registered company address is: Gewerbestrasse 11, 6330 Cham, Switzerland

If disposing of this product, please recycle the paper.

Foreword

The 19th International Federated Conference on Distributed Computing Techniques (DisCoTec) took place in Groningen, The Netherlands, during June 17–21, 2024. It was organized by the Bernoulli Institute of Mathematics, Computer Science, and Artificial Intelligence at the University of Groningen, The Netherlands.

The DisCoTec series is one of the major events sponsored by the International Federation for Information Processing (IFIP). It comprises three main conferences:

- COORDINATION, the IFIP WG6.1 26th International Conference on Coordination Models and Languages – Program Chairs: Ilaria Castellani (Inria Sophia Antipolis, France) and Francesco Tiezzi (University of Florence, Italy).
- DAIS, the IFIP WG6.1 24th International Conference on Distributed Applications and Interoperable Systems – Program Chairs: Rolando Martins (University of Porto, Portugal) and Mennan Selimi (South East European University, North Macedonia).
- FORTE, the IFIP WG6.1 44th International Conference on Formal Techniques for Distributed Objects, Components and Systems – Program Chairs: Valentina Castiglioni (Eindhoven University of Technology, The Netherlands) and Adrian Francalanza (University of Malta, Malta).

Together, these conferences cover a broad spectrum of distributed computing subjects—from theoretical foundations and formal description techniques, testing and verification methods, to language design and system implementation approaches.

Following recent developments in the research community, all conferences included an Artifact Evaluation track, whose goal is to improve and reward research reproducibility and to increase visibility of the effort of tool developers. Each conference implemented this track independently, in close coordination with Roberto Casadei (University of Bologna, Italy) who served as Artifact Evaluation chair.

In addition to the individual sessions of each conference, the event included several plenary sessions that gathered attendants from the three conferences. In coordination with the General Chair, the three DisCoTec conferences selected the plenary keynote speakers. The three keynote speakers and the title of their talks are listed below:

- Prof. Laura Kovács (Vienna University of Technology, Austria) – *Automated Reasoning in BlockChain Security*
- Prof. Paulo Veríssimo (KAUST, CEMSE, RC3 - Resilient Computing and Cybersecurity Center, Saudi Arabia) – *Platform Resilience? Beware of Threats from the "basement"*
- Prof. Marieke Huisman (University of Twente, The Netherlands) – *VerCors: Inclusive Software Verification*

As traditional in DisCoTec, the program included an additional joint session with the best papers from each conference. The best papers were:

- *A Probabilistic Choreography Language for PRISM*, by Marco Carbone and Adele Veschetti;
- *Compact Storage of Data Streams in Mobile Devices*, by Rémy Raes, Olivier Ruas, Adrien Luxey-Bitri, Romain Rouvoy;
- *Weak Simplicial Bisimilarity for Polyhedral Models and SLCSη*, by Nick Bezhanishvili, Vincenzo Ciancia, David Gabelaia, Mamuka Jibladze, Diego Latella, Mieke Massink and Erik De Vink.

The federated event was further enriched with the following three satellite events:

- DiDiT: The 1st International Workshop on Distributed Digital Twins, organized by Victoria Degeler (University of Amsterdam, The Netherlands), Dilek Dustegor (University of Groningen, The Netherlands), Heerko Groefsema (University of Groningen, The Netherlands), and Elena Lazovik (TNO, The Netherlands).
- ICE: 17th Interaction and Concurrency Experience, organized by Clément Aubert (Augusta University, USA), Cinzia Di Giusto (Université Côte d'Azur, France), Simon Fowler (University of Glasgow, UK), and Violet Ka I Pun (Western Norway University of Applied Sciences, Norway).
- PLNL: The Fourth Workshop on Programming Languages in The Netherlands, organized by Daniel Frumin (University of Groningen, The Netherlands) and Wouter Swierstra (Utrecht University, Netherlands) on behalf of VERSEN, the Dutch National Association for Software Engineering.

I would like to thank the Program Committee chairs of the different events for their cooperation during the preparation of the federated event, the Artifact Evaluation chair for his dedicated coordination work, and the Steering Committee of DisCoTec and their conferences for their guidance and support. Moreover, I am grateful to the keynote speakers and all conference attendees for joining us in Groningen.

The organization of DisCoTec 2024 was only possible thanks to the hard work and dedication of the Organizing Committee, including Bas van den Heuvel (publicity chair), Daniel Frumin and Claudio Antares Mezzina (workshop co-chairs), Magda Piekorz and Ineke Schelhaas (logistics and finances), as well as all the colleagues and students who volunteered their time to help.

Finally, I would like to thank IFIP WG6.1 for sponsoring this event, Springer's Lecture Notes in Computer Science team for their support and sponsorship, EasyChair for providing the reviewing infrastructure, the Dutch Research Council (NWO) for financial support (file number 21382), and the Faculty of Science and Engineering of the University of Groningen for providing meeting rooms and administrative support.

June 2024   Jorge A. Pérez

Preface

This volume contains the proceedings of the 26th International Conference on Coordination Models and Languages (COORDINATION 2024), held on June 18–20, 2024, at the University of Groningen, The Netherlands, as part of the 19th International Federated Conference on Distributed Computing Techniques (DisCoTec 2024).

Modern information systems rely increasingly on combining concurrent, distributed, mobile, adaptive, reconfigurable, and heterogeneous components. New models, architectures, languages, and verification techniques are necessary to cope with the complexity induced by the demands of today's software development. Coordination languages have emerged as a successful approach, in that they provide abstractions that cleanly separate behaviour from communication, thereby increasing modularity, simplifying reasoning, and ultimately enhancing software development. Building on the success of the previous editions, COORDINATION 2024 provides a well-established forum for the growing community of researchers interested in models, languages, architectures, and implementation techniques for coordination.

COORDINATION 2024 solicited contributions in four different categories: (1) regular papers describing thorough and complete research results and experience reports; (2) short papers describing research in progress, calls for action, or opinions on past COORDINATION research, on the current state of the art, or on prospects for the years to come; (3) survey papers describing important results and success stories related to the topics of COORDINATION; and (4) tool papers describing technological artefacts in the scope of the research topics of COORDINATION, and requiring the submission of the associated artefact via a separate procedure.

There were 28 paper submissions distributed over the different categories: 15 regular papers, 2 short papers, 1 survey paper, and 10 tool papers. The selection of the papers was entrusted to the Programme Committee (PC), consisting of 31 members from 14 different countries (with gender balance F/M = 15/16). The selection of the papers was done electronically, in two phases. In the first phase, which lasted five weeks, each submission was single-blind reviewed by at least three PC members, in some cases with the help of external reviewers. During the second phase, which lasted slightly less than one week, the papers were thoroughly discussed. The decision to accept or reject a paper was based not only on the reviews and scores but also on these in-depth discussions. In the end, 17 papers were selected to be presented at the conference: 8 regular papers, 1 short paper, 1 survey paper, and 7 tool papers.

The authors of the submitted tool papers were requested to participate in the EAPLS artefact badging, which instead was optional for all the other paper categories. There were 15 artefact submissions. The 12 members of the Artefact Evaluation Committee (AEC), chaired by Rumyana Neykova, awarded the Available and Reusable Badge to 6 artefacts, the Available and Functional Badge to 3 artefacts, and the Available Badge to 1 artefact.

As Programme Chairs, we actively contributed to the selection of the three keynote speakers of DisCoTec 2024:

– Prof. Marieke Huisman (University of Twente, The Netherlands);
– Prof. Laura Kovács (Vienna University of Technology, Austria);
– Prof. Paulo Veríssimo (KAUST, Kingdom of Saudi Arabia).

We are most grateful to Prof. Huisman for accepting our invitation as COORDI-NATION-related keynote speaker. This volume includes the abstract of her keynote talk: "VerCors: Inclusive Software Verification".

As is traditional in DisCoTec, a joint session with the best papers from each main conference was organised. The best paper of COORDINATION 2024 was "A Probabilistic Choreography Language for PRISM" by Marco Carbone and Adele Veschetti.

We are grateful to all the persons involved in COORDINATION 2024. In particular, we thank the authors for their submissions, the attendees of the conference for their participation, the PC members and external reviewers for their work in reviewing submissions and participating in the discussions, the AEC chair Rumyana Neykova and the AEC members for their effort in the evaluation of the artefacts, the Publicity chair Saverio Giallorenzo for taking care of the announcements, and the Steering Committee, chaired by Mieke Massink, for their guidance and support. We are also grateful to the Organising Committee, chaired by Jorge A. Pérez, for their excellent job. We also thank the providers of the EasyChair Conference Management System, which was of great help in the submission and reviewing process and in the preparation of the proceedings. We would also like to acknowledge the prompt and professional support from Springer, which published these proceedings in printed and electronic volumes as part of their LNCS book series.

June 2024   Ilaria Castellani
                                                                  Francesco Tiezzi

Organisation

Programme Committee

Giorgio Audrito	University of Turin, Italy
Laura Bocchi	University of Kent, UK
Chiara Bodei	University of Pisa, Italy
Marcello Bonsangue	Leiden University, The Netherlands
Silvia Crafa	University of Padua, Italy
Cinzia Di Giusto	Université Côte d'Azur, France
Paola Giannini	University of Eastern Piedmont, Italy
Hannah Gommerstadt	Vassar College, USA
Heerko Groefsema	University of Groningen, The Netherlands
Thomas Hildebrandt	University of Copenhagen, Denmark
Sung-Shik Jongmans	Open University of the Netherlands, The Netherlands
Dimka Karastoyanova	University of Groningen, the Netherlands
Jean Krivine	IRIF, CNRS, France
Eva Kühn	Vienna University of Technology, Austria
Roland Kuhn	Actyx AG, Germany
Alberto Lluch Lafuente	Technical University of Denmark, Denmark
Antónia Lopes	University of Lisbon, Portugal
Michele Loreti	University of Camerino, Italy
Mieke Massink	CNR-ISTI, Pisa, Italy
Hernan Melgratti	University of Buenos Aires, Argentina
Maurizio Murgia	Gran Sasso Science Institute, Italy
Anna Philippou	University of Cyprus, Cyprus
José Proença	CISTER & University of Porto, Portugal
Violet Ka I Pun	Western Norway University of Applied Sciences, Norway
Barbara Re	University of Camerino, Italy
Marjan Sirjani	Mälardalen University, Sweden
Meng Sun	Peking University, China
Carolyn Talcott	SRI International, USA
Peter Thiemann	University of Freiburg, Germany
Mirko Viroli	University of Bologna, Italy
Franco Zambonelli	Università di Modena e Reggio Emilia, Italy

Artefact Evaluation Committee

Nour Ali	Brunel University London, UK
Tiago Cogumbreiro	UMass Boston, USA
Saverio Giallorenzo	University of Bologna, Italy
Arwa Hameed Alsubhi	University of Glasgow, UK
Keigo Imai	DeNA, Japan
Omar Inverso	Gran Sasso Science Institute, Italy
Doriana Medic	University of Turin, Italy
Mário Pereira	NOVA School of Science and Technology, Portugal
Lorenzo Rossi	University of Camerino, Italy
Cristina Seceleanu	Mälardalen University, Sweden
Felix Stutz	University of Luxembourg, Luxembourg
Fangyi Zhou	Amazon, UK

Additional Reviewers

Gianluca Aguzzi	Diego Latella
Alessandro Bocci	Majid Lotfian Delouee
Hao Bu	Dalia Papuc
Valerio De Caro	Zeinab Sharifi
Davide Domini	Andrés Tello
Nicolas Farabegoli	Xiaoyong Xue
Stefano Forti	

VerCors: Inclusive Software Verification (Keynote Talk)

Marieke Huisman

University of Twente, The Netherlands

VerCors supports deductive verification of concurrent software, written in multiple programming languages, where the specifications are written in terms of pre-/postcondition contracts using permission-based separation logic. Work on the VerCors verifier started more than a decade ago. In this decade, the focus of the work on VerCors has shifted from verification of (concurrent) Java programs only to the development of a verifier that can support different programming languages, by exploiting their commonalities for developing efficient verification support.

In this talk, I will first give an overview of the VerCors verifier:

- how it is set up as a program transformation tool that translates an annotated program into input for the Viper framework, which is then used as verification back-end,
- how it supports different programming languages and features, and
- how it has been used on different case studies (and how this has further improved VerCors).

In the last part of my talk, I will sketch my ideas and plans to further increase the inclusiveness of VerCors, so that it becomes easier to support new programming languages and to reuse the existing verification infrastructure in new settings.

Contents

Regular Papers

Choreographic Automata: A Case Study in Healthcare Management

Sourabh Pal[1]([⊠]) [ID], Ivan Lanese[1] [ID], and Massimo Clo[2]

[1] Olas Team, University of Bologna/INRIA, Bologna, Italy
{sourabh.pal2,ivan.lanese}@unibo.it
[2] Area ICT e Transizione digitale dei servizial cittadino - Direzione Generale Cura della Persona, Salute e Welfare, Emilia Romagna, Italy
massimo.clo@regione.emilia-romagna.it

Abstract. Choreographic models in general, and Choreographic Automata (CA) in particular, can be used to analyze and validate communicating systems. We applied CAs to a case study in healthcare management, the procedure for accreditation and authorization of public and private healthcare structures in the Emilia Romagna region (Italy). We formalized the procedure first using a BPMN collaboration diagram as intermediate step, and then using CAs. The tool Corinne showed a few issues in the formalized model, but it turned out that such issues were due to too strict requirements posed by the theory underlying Corinne. This gave us useful feedback for future improvements of Corinne and its underlying theory.

Keywords: Choreographies · Healthcare management · Modeling · Communicating systems

1 Introduction

Choreographic models (see, e.g., the survey in [24]) are gaining popularity in the design and implementation of distributed systems in different domains [9] e.g., healthcare systems [7]. Choreographic approaches are used to holistically describe the interactions among components in message-passing systems, and enable to enforce relevant communication properties such as deadlock-freedom by construction. Choreographies provide two complementary views, i.e., the *global view* and the *local view*. The global view is the abstract description of the entire system, i.e., it consists of all the participants and describes their interactions from a global viewpoint. On the contrary, the local view represents the behavior of a specific participant and the message exchanges involving this participant.

The work has been partially supported by French ANR project SmartCloud ANR-23-CE25-0012, by INdAM – GNCS 2024 project MARVEL, code CUP_E53C23001670001 and by European Union - NextGenerationEU PNRR Mission 4, Component 1, Investment 4.1 (DM 351/2022) - Public Administration. The authors thank the anonymous reviewers for their useful comments and suggestions.

I. Castellani and F. Tiezzi (Eds.): COORDINATION 2024, LNCS 14676, pp. 3–19, 2024.
https://doi.org/10.1007/978-3-031-62697-5_1

The global view is useful to design a system, while local views are more relevant in the implementation phase. Given a global view, it is possible to automatically generate local views enacting the global behavior.

In this paper, we use Choreographic Automata (CAs) [3], which combine the choreographic approach with the visual representation and the mathematical theory of finite state automata. We apply CAs to a case study from health-care administration, namely the procedure for accreditation and authorization of public and private healthcare structures in the Emilia Romagna region (Italy).

Since our case study is defined in natural language, in form of a regional law, formalising it directly as CA is not easy. We found a suitable intermediate step as a collaboration diagram in the Business Process Modelling Notion (BPMN) [4]. BPMN is a semi-formal graphical notation for describing business processes, and it is more flexible than CAs. Such flexibility allows for easier modeling and interaction with domain experts. Then, one can refine the BPMN collaboration diagram to derive a CA, more suitable for the automatic analysis of communication properties.

For the analysis, we exploit the tool Corinne [28,30], which allows one to analyze CAs represented in the DOT format [12]. On the one hand, this allows us to verify that the protocol considered in the case study satisfies relevant communication properties. On the other hand, this allows us to verify also whether the expressive power of CAs and the related analysis techniques are suitable for applications in such a setting. Actually, our analysis showed that the theory implemented in Corinne (and aligned with most of the theories for choreographies in the literature, such as the ones surveyed in [24]) is too rigid, signaling as errors behaviors that are not problematic in practice. Indeed, it requires that if a participant is involved in some branch of a protocol, then it should be involved in all the branches. The rationale for this is that if a branch in which the participant is not involved is taken, then the participant is left waiting, possibly forever. However, in practice, participants are not waiting for interaction, but just react if they receive a request. In order to support and recognize as correct such behaviors, we would need to extend Corinne with support for *late join* (also called selective participation) [15], which allows a participant to enter a conversation only if required to do so, e.g., only in some branch of a choice. The feedback provided by this case study will drive the development of Corinne and of the underlying theory in the following years.

Structure of the paper. Section 2 gives an informal introduction to the case study. We then model the case study as BPMN collaboration diagram in Sect. 3 and as choreographic automaton in Sect. 4. We analyze the choreographic automaton using Corinne in Sect. 5 and we discuss the lessons learned from the modeling and validation in Sect. 6. Section 7 concludes the paper and discusses related and future work.

2 Case Study: Natural Language Description

Design and development of distributed communication systems is very complex. Researchers and practitioners consider the choreography approach suitable to verify the communication properties of distributed systems to avoid issues such as deadlocks at the design level of the software development [2, 5, 22, 25]. The key purpose of choreographies is to enact the principle of correctness-by-construction [22], which ensures that choreographies satisfying suitable conditions are free from communication errors such as deadlocks. We apply the choreographic approach to a case study on healthcare management. Health is a fundamental right of the individual. The Emilia-Romagna region provides regional health care services to protect the fundamental rights of their citizens. It also ensures the quality, safety, and transparency of health services through the process for authorization and accreditation of public and private health structures [19], turned on in 1998 and nowadays regulated by the Regional Law of 6 November 2019, n. 22 [26].

The healthcare authorization procedure aims at ensuring the quality of healthcare services and assistance to the citizens. The authorization guarantees the structural, organizational, technological, and safety requirements of the patients in the public and private healthcare facilities in the Emilia-Romagna region in Italy. The authorization to operate the healthcare infrastructure is issued by the Mayor of the municipality. In contrast, the accreditation gives organizations, healthcare structures, and professionals, already in possession of healthcare authorization, the status of "subject suitable for providing services on behalf of the National Health Service". It provides for the possession of additional requisites that refer to the quality of health care and the related evaluation methods. It is granted by the *Regional Coordinator of Authorization and Accreditation* with subsequent verification of the *Technical Accreditation Body* aimed at ascertaining the possession or maintenance of the requirements. We have identified three protocols in this process, namely regional coordination for authorization and accreditation, authorization of health services, and accreditation of health services. In this case study, we will focus on the regional coordination for authorization and accreditation which assists in providing consistency and homogeneity in the exercise of the functionalities of authorization and accreditation processes. Ten participants are involved in this protocol, described below. In order to simplify the match between our models, which use English names for participants, and the original document, which is in Italian, we report the translations in Table 1.

- General Directorate of Health (GDH): The highest authority in the process of authorization and accreditation, it instructs the other sub-ordinate participants to perform their tasks to ensure consistency within the authorization and accreditation, to maintain the organization rationalization, and to maintain the homogeneity to perform the functions.
- Regional Coordinator (RCOO): It is the main authority to conduct the different functions to issue authorization and accreditation to healthcare structures.

Table 1. Participant Name in Italian and Corresponding English Translation

Participants Name (Italian)	Participants Name (English)
Direzione Generale Competente in Materia di Sanità,	General Directorate of Health (GDH)
Giunta Regionale	Regional Council (RC)
Coordinatore Regionale per l'Autorizzazione e l'Accreditamento	Regional Coordinator (RCOO)
Commissioni per l'Autorizzazione	Authorization Commission (AC)
Aziende Usl	Local Health Authority (LHA)
Anagrafe Regionale delle Strutture Sanitarie	Registry of Healthcare Structures (RHS)
Organismo Tecnicamente Accreditante	Technically Accrediting Body (OTA)
Responsabile dell'OTA	OTA Manager (OTAM)
Elenco dei Valutatori	Evaluators (EV)
Tecnici Esperti	Expert Technicians (ET)

- Authorization Commission (AC): It establishes itself in the public health departments of the local health unit to ensure the homogeneity in the assessment of authorization and it also identifies the priority of criteria to carry out checks for the authorization.
- Local Health Authority (LHA): It is the healthcare organization that is seeking authorization and accreditation.
- Registry of Healthcare Structures (RHS): It stores the data for the accreditation and it provides the data upon request of RCOO.
- Technically Accrediting Body (OTA): It performs the accreditation checks to ensure impartiality, transparency, and autonomy in the activities of the management.
- OTA Manager (OTAM): It is a manager expert in assessing the quality of the healthcare management system.
- Evaluators (EV): They are qualified and trained professionals from the public and private national health services that are situated within the OTA to pursue the technical assessment of the accreditation.
- Expert Technicians (ET): They perform further technical investigations on the LHA.
- Regional Council (RC): It identifies the RCOO among the managers of its own services to ensure homogeneity and consistency in the process. It also decides how to manage the EV on the proposal of the OTAM.

In a distributed communicating system, all the participants interact through message passing. In our case study, the RCOO will grant accreditation to the public or private LHA based on the verification of the OTA. The GDH notifies the RC to identify the RCOO among the managers of its own services. Subsequently, the GDH provides resources to the RCOO to perform their functions and it also instructs the RCOO to pursue verification of specific functions to evaluate the LHA for further continuation of the accreditation. The RCOO formulates proposals on which data the RHS needs to collect, and on how it should work, to the RC. Then, the RC sends the criteria established for the topics above to the RHS. The RCOO coordinates with the AC to check whether existing authorized LHA maintain prerequisites and satisfy additional criteria to maintain the quality of healthcare. It also prepares plans for issuing, renewing, and monitoring accreditation and proposes them to the GDH. The RCOO maintains relations with the services of the GDH in order to guarantee the connection between its own functions and the policies and skills of the area. Moreover, it mandates the OTA to conduct verification to check whether existing authorized LHA are maintaining the prerequisites to provide safe health facilities. Besides, the OTA delegates the actual checks to an OTAM. The OTAM prepares the verification report of the LHA and it also conducts further technical investigation with support from the experts, such as EV and ET. Thereafter, the OTAM sends the report to the RCOO. The RCOO prepares the proposal for renewal, refusal, or issuing of the accreditation based on that report and submits it to the GDH to take the necessary action on the LHA.

3   Case Study: BPMN Collaboration Diagram

Since the specification of our case study, briefly described in the previous section, is given in natural language and hence necessarily informal, transforming it directly into a choreographic model is complex and error-prone. Therefore, we decided to model the protocol first using a BPMN collaboration diagram [4], which is closer to the informal specification since they both focus on participants, activities and processes, while choreographies focus on message passing. However, moving to a BPMN collaboration diagram allows one to move from an informal to a semi-formal specification, and to explicitly introduce choices and message passing communications, key to then move to choreographies. The fact that the representation of the BPMN collaboration diagram is graphical and closer to the specification also allows an easier interaction with domain experts to ensure that the model actually captures the intended protocol. As a second step, we then converted the BPMN collaboration diagram into a CA to enable the verification of the correctness of its structure and behavior using the Corinne tool [28,30]. We transformed the natural language description of the healthcare system into a BPMN collaboration diagram manually.

A BPMN collaboration diagram is a semi-formal specification with a wide variety of expressive and flexible features to ease the representation of complex systems. In this section, we present a fragment of our case study, available in Fig. 1, to give to the reader an intuition about the transformation of our case study from natural language to BPMN specification. The whole case study model is available in [29]. The BPMN collaboration diagram consists of different participants [1] that represent a specific role or entity that is involved in a business process. Each participant has its own internal processes, and participants collaborate through the message passing. In our example in Fig. 1, we present six participants, namely RC, RCOO, OTA, OTAM, EV, and ET. The process diagram describes the details of a business process involving them. Notably, it provides a visual representation that gives a clear understanding of the flow of information and the sequence of activities of the business process. In Fig. 1, for compactness, we detail the process diagram of the participant OTAM, while leaving not specified the behavior of other participants. Below, we will describe the different BPMN features and symbols when they occur in our description of the case study, while referring to [4] for a more comprehensive description.

The participants communicate among themselves through message passing. Therefore, the *message event* (double circle containing an envelope) indicates the sending or receiving of a message to/from another process or participant. A dashed line connects the send and the receive. The OTAM is first involved in the protocol when the OTA appoints it for carrying out the authorization and accreditation checks. Therefore, the OTA notifies the OTAM to conduct checks on existing authorizations through the message event on the left.

A process is a collection of multiple tasks: in BPMN a single activity within a process is called a *task*. The OTAM, after receiving notification from the OTA, performs the task **Request for Resources**, where the OTAM requires the RCOO to provide resources to perform its functions. Note that the dashed arrow from the activity denotes that as part of the activity a message is sent. Thereafter, the RCOO provides the required resources to the OTAM via a **Provide Resources** message. In BPMN, an *Exclusive Gateway or XOR Gateway* (diamond containing an X) is a decision gateway used to model a point in the process where the flow can take one of several mutually exclusive paths. The decision about which path to take is based on the evaluation of conditions associated with each outgoing sequence flow. The OTAM, after getting resources from the RCOO, checks whether the list of EVs exists. If not, then it first creates the list of EVs. Otherwise, the OTAM needs to **Perform Technical Investigation** for accreditation or needs to **Update Evaluators List** for assistance with the technical investigation. Here, we use an exclusive gateway to represent the choice of the path. The detailed explanations of the two paths are as follows:

– **Perform Technical Investigation:** The OTAM carries out the technical investigations, and expresses the technical judgment of competence by verifying the possession and maintenance of the accreditation requirements.
– **Update Evaluators List:** The OTAM holds and updates the list of EVs.

For the technical investigation for the checks of authorization and accreditation, the OTAM may need assistance from experts such as EV and ET sequentially, as follows:

1. The OTAM performs the checks by making use of the EVs. The OTAM **Notify to Assist Investigation** to the EVs. The EVs perform the technical investigation and submit to the OTAM the technical **Investigation Report**.

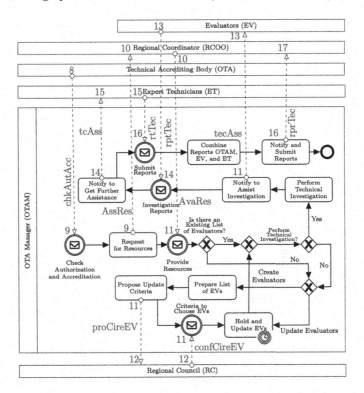

Fig. 1. BPMN Collaboration Diagram: A Fragment of Our Case Study.

2. The OTAM, after receiving the investigation report from the EVs, needs to perform further investigation with the assistance of the ETs. Therefore, it **Notify to Get Further Assistance** to the ETs. The ETs assist and **Submit Report** to the OTAM.

The OTAM **Combine Reports of OTAM, EVs, and ETs** after performing all necessary checks for authorization and accreditation. Thereafter, (s)he **Notify and Submit Report** to the RCOO and terminates the process. To **Create and Update Evaluators List**, the OTAM performs the tasks sequentially i.e., **Prepare List of Evaluators, Propose Update Criteria, Update Evaluator List**. Moreover, the list of EVs gets updated periodically.

4 Case Study: Choreographic Automaton

We use Choreographic Automata (CAs) [3] to model the message-passing behavior of our case study. This will allow us to verify the correctness of such behavior. The key concept of choreographic approaches is to describe the interactions among participants from a global viewpoint. In CAs, finite state automata are used, and a transition of the automaton models a message passing communication. More precisely, the interaction among two participants is represented as

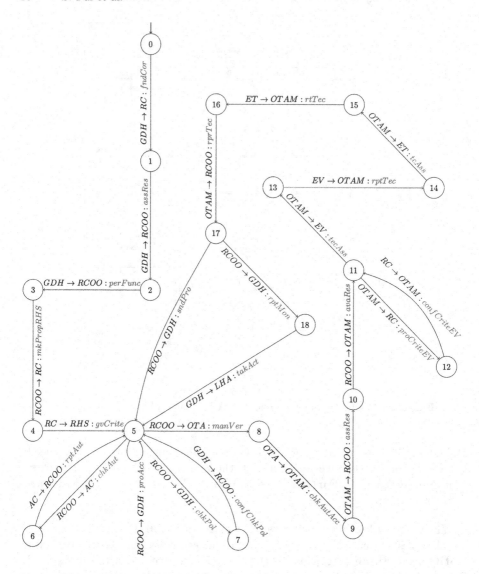

Fig. 2. Choreographic Automaton for Regional Coordination for Authorization and Accreditation.

a label $A \to B : m$, where participant A sends message m to participant B, which in turn receives it [3]. In this section, we will discuss the transformation of our case study from BPMN collaboration diagram to CA. We transformed the BPMN collaboration diagram into a CA manually. Note that we have a correspondence between dashed arrows representing message flow in the BPMN Collaboration Diagram and interactions in the corresponding CA.

We present the choreographic automaton of our case study in Fig. 2. To ease the comparison with the BPMN collaboration model, identifiers of states from the CA as well as labels of the transitions are also reported in the BPMN collaboration diagram, in red. Remember however that only part of the BPMN model is in Fig. 1, while the whole model is in [29]. Let us start the description from the initial state (state 0 in the top-left). GDH proposes RC to identify a RCOO with transition $GDH \rightarrow RC : fndCor$, to maintain consistency, organizational rationalization, and homogeneity of authorization and accreditation. Further, the GDH notifies the RCOO that resources have been assigned $GDH \rightarrow RCOO : assRes$ to execute the authorization and accreditation procedure. Moreover, the GDH requires the RCOO to perform the required functions $GDH \rightarrow RCOO : perFunc$ for accreditation. The RCOO requires adequate information to perform the tasks for accreditation and authorization, which will be managed by the RHS. Hence, the RCOO proposes to the RC with message $RCOO \rightarrow RC : mkPropRHS$ which data the RHS should manage and how it should work. As a result, the RC gives the criteria to the RHS with message $RC \rightarrow RHS : gvCrite$ on which data to manage and how. Afterward, the RCOO may take 4 alternative actions:

1. (loop involving state 6) to ask the AC to check an existing authorization $RCOO \rightarrow AC : chkAut$ of some LHA for further continuation. The AC will respond with the authorization report $AC \rightarrow RCOO : rptAut$ message to the RCOO;
2. (loop involving state 7) to request the GDH for consultation to prepare a monitoring policy $RCOO \rightarrow GDH : chkPol$, which will trigger a reply from the GDH confirming the consultation, $GDH \rightarrow RCOO : confChkPol$;
3. (self-loop at state 5) to propose to the GDH the regional planning for issuing, renewing and monitoring accreditation $RCOO \rightarrow GDH : proAcc$;
4. (transition to state 8) to ask the OTA to start the actual procedure for accreditation, $RCOO \rightarrow OTA : manVer$.

In this last case, the OTA notifies the OTAM to check authorization and accreditation $OTA \rightarrow OTAM : chkAutAcc$ for checking the quality of the healthcare management systems of some LHA (this starts the part represented in BPMN in Fig. 1). The OTAM requests the RCOO to assign the corresponding resources $OTAM \rightarrow RCOO : assRes$, and the RCOO makes such resources available $RCOO \rightarrow OTAM : avaRes$ to the OTAM. Afterward, the OTAM may take 2 alternative paths: (1) (loop involving state 12) To manage the list of EVs: while this procedure is quite complex it is mostly local to the OTAM, hence we only have a loop composed by a pair of interactions, where the OTAM sends to the RC the proposal $OTAM \rightarrow RC : proCriteEV$ message about the criteria to manage the EVs, and the RC answers to the OTAM with message $RC \rightarrow OTAM : confCriteEV$ to confirm the proposed evaluation criteria; or else (2) the OTAM asks the EVs for technical assistance with message $OTAM \rightarrow EV : tecAss$ and the EVs reply with a technical report $EV \rightarrow OTAM : rptTec$.

In the last case, after receiving the technical report from the EVs, the OTAM performs a similar message exchange with the ETs (messages $OTAM \rightarrow ET : tcAss$ and $ET \rightarrow OTAM : rtTec$). Note that from the informal specification it is not clear whether the two message exchanges should be sequential as in our model or concurrent. We will come back to this topic in the discussion. Further, the OTAM sends to the RCOO the results of the investigation with message $OTAM \rightarrow RCOO : rprTec$. The RCOO may react in 2 ways (from left to right): (a) It sends to the GDH with message $RCOO \rightarrow GDH : sndPro$ a proposal for grant, renew, refusal, suspension, or revocation of the accreditation, based on the report received from the OTA, and it ends the protocol, or (b) It sends to the GDH with message $RCOO \rightarrow GDH : rptMon$ the report on the monitoring of the LHA, based on the OTA report. Upon further analysis, and based on the seriousness of the violation of the requisites of the LHA, the GDH notifies the LHA with message $GDH \rightarrow LHA : takAct$ the outcome of the evaluation. This may involve to revoke or suspend the accreditation, or to take necessary actions to fix some violations.

5   Validation

As a result of the modeling exercise above, we represented our case study in the form of CA. CAs are equipped with a theory [3] ensuring that systems obtained from their projection are well-behaved, provided that the CA is well-formed. Well-formedness can be automatically checked using the tool Corinne [28]. Below we introduce well-formedness, which is composed of well-sequencedness and well-branchedness, and we discuss its application to our case study. The following definitions are taken from [3].

Definition 1 (Well-sequencedness). *A c-automaton CA is well-sequenced if for each two consecutive transitions* $q \xrightarrow{A \rightarrow B : m} q' \xrightarrow{C \rightarrow D : n} q''$ *either*

- *They share a participant, that is* $\{A, B\} \cap \{C, D\} \neq \emptyset$, *or*
- *They are concurrent, i.e. there is* q''' *such that* $q \xrightarrow{C \rightarrow D : n} q''' \xrightarrow{A \rightarrow B : m} q''$

Intuitively, two transitions that share no participant are independent, hence can be executed in any order, and well-sequencedness requires that both orders are explicitly represented.

In order to define well-branchedness we need some preliminary definitions.

Definition 2 (Candidate q-branch). *A pre-candidate q-branch is a path in the automaton starting from state q and such that each cycle has at most one occurrence within the path. A candidate q-branch is a maximal pre-candidate q-branch with respect to prefix order.*

Definition 3 (q-span). *A pair* (π, π') *of pre-candidate q-branches of CA is a q-span if*

1. *either* π *and* π' *are cofinal, with no common node but q and the last one;*
2. *or* π *and* π' *are candidate q-branches with no common node but q;*
3. *or* π *and* π' *are a candidate q-branch and a loop on q with no other common nodes.*

We can now define well-branchedness. Well-branchedness is defined only on deterministic CAs, but our case study is deterministic hence this restriction has no impact.

Definition 4 (Well-branchedness) *A deterministic CA is well-branched if for each state q and participant A sender in a transition from q, all of the following conditions hold:*

1. *all transitions from q involving A, have sender A;*
2. *for each transition t from q whose sender is not A and each transition t' from q whose sender is A, t and t' are concurrent;*
3. *for each q-span (π, π') where A is the sender of the first transition in both paths and each participant $B \neq A$, consider the first pair of different transitions involving B in π and in π': they are both receive, with a different sender or a different message.*

Intuitively, well-branchedness ensures that when a participant A makes a choice between two branches π and π', it makes the choice between all the available options (condition 1) unless they are concurrent actions (condition 2). Also, each other participant B, if it has to make different transitions in the two branches, it is notified of the outcome of the choice by either receiving different messages, or receiving messages from different participants (condition 3).

Such conditions should hold on any pair of paths starting with a common node, but actually it is enough to make the check only on maximal pairs, which form what we call q-spans. To simplify the analysis, we slightly extended Corinne. Indeed, Corinne has been conceived to iteratively improve a CA till it becomes well-formed, hence, in case the CA contains many violations of the conditions, Corinne only showed the first one. We are more interested in getting full feedback on a protocol to then discuss with domain experts about the issues. Thus, we extended the tool so that all the violations of the well-formedness conditions were shown in a single execution. We also did other minor improvements, and the updated version of Corinne is available on the Corinne repository [30].

By using the Corinne tool, we first checked well-sequencedness. A number of pairs of transitions were flagged as violating the condition, but interestingly they can be categorized in two classes, both involving state 5. On the one hand, transition from 4 to 5 with label $RC \rightarrow RHS : gvCrite$ (let us call it t_g) has no participant in common with any of the transitions exiting from state 5. On the other hand, transition from 18 to 5 with label $GDH \rightarrow LHA : takAct$ (let us call it t_a) has no participant in common with transitions from state 5 to either 8 or 6. The intuition behind the issue is similar in both the cases. State 5 is a state where participant $RCOO$ decides which actions to take, but the two incoming transitions t_g and t_a do not involve him, hence the issue. There are two ways to fix the diagram, if we deem that it is important that the $RCOO$ is notified about the end of t_g and/or t_a, then notification transitions should be added. E.g., in the case of t_g, RHS should send a message to $RCOO$ notifying him that criteria have been received. Vice versa, one can decide that transitions t_g and t_a should be concurrent to the following actions. In CA, this is done by explicitly duplicating transitions t_g and t_a so that copies of them could occur at any point in the following. This will represent them as concurrent actions, but would make the diagram unreadable. We will come back to this issue in Sect. 6.

We then tested well-branchedness. Here a much larger set of issues is raised, always related to condition 3. We describe one of the issues raised in detail, and then briefly comment on the others which are similar. Let us consider as an example the cycles from state 11: the one via 13, 14, 15, 16, 17, 18, 5, 8, 9, 10 involves multiple participants, while the one via state 12 only involves $OTAM$ and RC. This is flagged as an error of well-branchedness, since other participants, say EV, are left waiting if the choreography always takes the cycle via 12. This is not a real issue here, since in practice the small cycle is taken a small number of times, and more importantly since the other participants are not actively waiting that the choreography involves them, but just react when invoked. Taking into account that participants may only be involved in some branches of the choreography takes the name of *late join* (or selective participation), and it has been studied in the literature [15], but it is not yet supported by Corinne. We will come back to this issue in Sect. 6.

Actually, all the other issues raised by Corinne are also related to late join, since the same issue happens in many other cases, e.g., between different cycles originating from state 5, or between the two paths from state 17 to 5. Notably, the main reason behind well-branchedness is to ensure that when there is a choice, participants which need to act differently in different branches are notified of the outcome of a choice. This always happens in our case study. Consider for instance participant GDH. It is involved in different branches of the choice from 5, and the sub-choice from 11. Indeed, at 7 it receives a message chkPol from $RCOO$ and then needs to react with message confChkPol, at 17 it receives a message sndPro but no reaction is expected from him, and at state 18 it receives a message rptMon and it is expected to react by sending message takAct to LHA. The GDH is not directly participating to the choice of which path to take from 5 and from 17, but it is always informed of the outcome by $RCOO$, which is in charge of deciding the path to be taken, and sends different messages to GDH in all the paths, hence GDH always knows how to react.

6   Lessons Learned

We discuss below a few lessons we learned from the modeling exercise and analysis above. They will probably apply to other case studies in the same area, and possibly also in other areas, but this will need to be confirmed by further studies.

Gap between laws and choreographies: Laws describe protocols in terms of roles, responsibilities of each role, and activities performed by each role. There are some mentions of message passing, but it is frequently implicit and not detailed. Explicit mentions are, e.g., "The global results are sent to $RCOO$ to proceed with the relevant obligations" (translated from [26, Art. 13, paragrpah 3.b], resulting in the transition from state 13 to 14). Implicit mentions are, e.g., "The organizational methods, human and instrumental resources to be assigned to the $RCOO$, for performing the functions referred to in paragraph 3, are defined by the GDH." (translated from [26, Art. 3, paragraph 2]), which we modeled as the transition from state 1 to state 2. In order to better match the activities described by the laws, and the message passing modeled by the choreography, it makes sense to use an intermediate model such as a BPMN collaboration diagram, which describes both the activities and the message exchanges. This will be even more needed if multiparty session types [22,24] were used instead of CAs, since they impose more constraints on the model than CAs.

Importance of late join: the only issues raised by Corinne related to well-branchedness are due to the missed support for late join in Corinne. While historically approaches in the area of choreographies and session types assume that all the participants are aware of when the choreography starts and how it progresses, in reality, as already mentioned in [15], most of the participants simply react by taking action when involved by other participants, and do not care if they are not involved in some execution. Hence, we believe that late join [15] is fundamental to reason on real life protocols, and would deserve more attention by the community. In our case, supporting late join in Corinne is a main item for future work. We mention that there are also approaches [18, 23] that allow for late join, but they require special actions for joining a protocol. In our case study, it seems joining as a result of receiving a normal message more closely matches reality.

Parallel protocols: in practice, many actors carry on multiple protocols at the same time. This is the case of $RCOO$ in our case study, where each activity corresponds to one of the loops from state 5. We modeled these activities using a choice, but in practice these activities can happen together, hence our model does not fully capture the actual behavior. However, such a model would require in CAs to explicitly represent all the possible interleavings, what would make the model very difficult to manage and reason about, due to the combinatorial explosion of states. In order to avoid such problem one could allow for an explicit representation of parallel composition, as for instance in g-choreographies [32] and BPMN collaboration or choreography diagrams.

Creation of new participants: somehow surprisingly, creation of new participants occurs quite often in our case study, in the sense that persons are given some role that they then use in the protocol. For instance, the RC nominates the $RCOO$, and then GDH interacts with the newly appointed $RCOO$. Currently, explicit creation of new roles is not supported by CAs (and the same holds for most formalisms in the area), hence errors such as a participant having to interact before its creation are not highlighted.

7   Conclusion, Related and Future Work

In this paper, we have modeled the protocol for accreditation and authorization of healthcare structures in the Emilia Romagna region, Italy, using first a BPMN collaboration diagram and then a CA. We also used the tool Corinne to check the well-formedness properties of the resulting CA.

The analysis gave interesting feedback on how to extend Corinne and the underlying theory to better support the analysis of such a kind of protocols, as discussed in the previous section. While not highlighting any real issue in the protocol, the modeling exercise has been useful to give a more precise specification of the protocol, and highlighting its message passing aspect.

Related Work. We have used both BPMN collaboration diagrams and CAs as tools for our modeling and analysis. We remark here that BPMN also allows for BPMN choreographies [5], which, like CAs, focus on interactions. However, they do not have a formal semantics, what makes the analysis not grounded on a precise theory. For instance, a single BPMN choreography interaction may represent any number of message passing communications between the same participants, in any order, making unclear who starts and who ends such an interaction. While BPMN choreographies could be used as a further intermediate step between BPMN collaboration diagrams and CAs, we considered this step not valued the effort. Indeed, we preferred BPMN collaboration diagrams since they are closer to the natural language specification, making them more suitable than BPMN choreographies as intermediate step. One could perform verification directly on the BPMN collaboration diagrams, but available techniques are based essentially on model checking. However, model checking suffers from state-space explosion [8,13], hence also statistical model checking, which is a form of simulation, is used. However, the latter cannot provide full guarantees. We instead focus on specific communication properties, and our dedicated techniques are more effective in this specific setting.

Many models focusing on the correctness of message passing in distributed systems also exist, see, e.g., the survey in [24]. Among the various approaches, conversation protocols [14], which are non-deterministic Büchi automata whose labels resemble our interactions, are one of the closest to CAs. Also conversation protocols require well-formedness conditions, however the comparison between the two sets of well-formedness conditions is not easy, as also mentioned in [3]. However, broadly speaking, the conditions on conversation protocols are more global, hence when they are not satisfied it is not easy to get feedback about which part of the automaton makes the condition fail. In CAs, feedback is instead local and one can exploit it to update the protocol to fix the issue.

As mentioned in the discussion, it would be good to extend CAs with support for parallel composition. Parallel composition was supported originally in multiparty asynchronous global types [21,22], but there parallel branches were required to have disjoint sets of participants. This is not enough in our case study, where for instance we would like to specify that the $RCOO$ participates to different subprotocols in parallel. Also, multiparty session types (see, e.g., the survey in [24]) need to satisfy many syntactic conditions on the protocol. While these conditions are useful to enforce good communication properties, they make it impossible to model not well-behaved systems. This is an issue in our case, where we want to get feedback on existing, possibly not well-behaved, protocols. Parallel composition where the same participant can act in multiple parallel branches can be specified for instance in g-choreographies [16,32]. Conditions in [32] are close to the ones of conversation protocols, while the ones in [16] are closer to ours. Analysis could be automated by relying on the PomCho tool suite [17]. However, the approaches above focus on asynchronous communication, while we believe that synchronous communication sometimes better matches human-based synchronizations. However, this last point requires further investigation.

DCR graphs [10,20] are also a model to represent and analyze distributed systems while avoiding explosion of the representation due to concurrency, but they focus on events and dependencies among them instead of on communications, hence they are less suitable to analyze properties related to message passing.

Beyond parallel composition, other features of protocols have been studied in the literature, such as having a variable number of participants play a given role in the choreography [11] (multirole), or the possibility of having protocols where the number of some messages is parametric on a previously transmitted integer [31]. While the latter behavior never occurred in our case study, the former could be used to better model roles such as EVs or ETs. However, in our case study EVs or ETs always act as a single participant, hence it is not clear whether the added complexity of multiroles provides any more insight on the correctness of the protocol. This question is left for future work.

While in the present paper we have not stressed the projection from CA to local descriptions so to enable a correct by construction implementation, we recall here that [3] proves that a simple homomorphic projection allows one to generate such local descriptions. However, as showed in [27], there are cases where a correct implementation exists, but in order to generate it more refined techniques are needed. Such cases never occur in our case study, hence the simple projection in [3] would be fine, once the well-formedness issues discussed in Sect. 5 are solved.

Future Work. The main motivation for our work is to verify whether CAs are suitable to analyze scenarios from healthcare management, and whether CAs can bring added value to healthcare management. While initial results are promising, as we discussed in the previous section, we believe the current theory of CAs and the Corinne tool need to be improved to support late join and dynamic creation of participants to better analyze this kind of case studies. Also, right now well-formedness checks of Corinne are assuming a synchronous communication framework. This has not emerged as a main limitation for our case study, where communications are mostly human-based, however adding checks for an asynchronous implementation [3] would be interesting, to pave the way to the use of the projection operation of CAs (which generates Communicating Finite State Machines [6]) to generate correct-by-construction support to execute the protocol.

Beyond working on those improvements, and considering additional case studies, we plan to improve on the feedback provided by Corinne. Indeed, Corinne raises many issues which are similar as distinct errors, e.g., issues of late join related to a same loop and many other paths in the CA. While adding support for late join would at least mitigate this issue, it would be interesting to automatically group highlighted issues which rely on the same or similar causes. This would allow to provide better feedback to the user.

References

1. Adamo, G., Borgo, S., Di Francescomarino, C., Ghidini, C., Guarino, N., Sanfilippo, E.M.: Business processes and their participants: an ontological perspective. In: Esposito, F., Basili, R., Ferilli, S., Lisi, F. (eds.) AI*IA 2017 Advances in Artificial Intelligence. AI*IA 2017. LNCS, vol. 10640, pp. 215–228 Springer, Cham (2017). https://doi.org/10.1007/978-3-319-70169-1_16
2. Autili, M., Inverardi, P., Tivoli, M.: Automated synthesis of service choreographies. IEEE Softw. **32**(1), 50–57 (2015)
3. Barbanera, F., Lanese, I., Tuosto, E.: Choreography automata. In: Bliudze, S., Bocchi, L. (eds.) COORDINATION 2020. LNCS, vol. 12134, pp. 86–106. Springer, Cham (2020). https://doi.org/10.1007/978-3-030-50029-0_6
4. Barjis, J.: The importance of business process modeling in software systems design. Sci. Comput. Program. **71**(1), 73–87 (2008)
5. BPMN choreography diagrams documentation. https://www.ibm.com/docs/en/rational-soft-arch/9.7.0?topic=diagrams-bpmn-choreography
6. Brand, D., Zafiropulo, P.: On communicating finite-state machines. J. ACM **30**(2), 323–342 (1983)
7. Bravetti, M., et al.: Towards global and local types for adaptation. In: Counsell, S., Núñez, M. (eds.) SEFM 2013. LNCS, vol. 8368, pp. 3–14. Springer, Cham (2014). https://doi.org/10.1007/978-3-319-05032-4_1
8. Corradini, F., Fornari, F., Polini, A., Re, B., Tiezzi, F., Vandin, A.: A formal approach for the analysis of BPMN collaboration models. J. Syst. Softw. **180**, 111007 (2021)
9. Coto, A., Barbanera, F., Lanese, I., Rossi, D., Tuosto, E.: On formal choreographic modelling: a case study in EU business processes. In: Margaria, T., Steffen, B. (eds.) Leveraging Applications of Formal Methods, Verification and Validation. Verification Principles. ISoLA 2022. LNCS, vol. 13701, pp. 205–219. Springer, Cham (2022). https://doi.org/10.1007/978-3-031-19849-6_13
10. Debois, S., Hildebrandt, T.T., Slaats, T.: Replication, refinement & reachability: complexity in dynamic condition-response graphs. Acta Informatica **55**(6), 489–520 (2018)
11. Deniélou, P.-M., Yoshida, N.: Dynamic multirole session types. In: Ball, T., Sagiv, M. (eds.), Proceedings of the 38th ACM SIGPLANSIGACT Symposium on Principles of Programming Languages, POPL 2011, Austin, TX, USA, 26–28 January 2011, pp. 435–446. ACM (2011)
12. DOT. https://graphviz.org/doc/info/lang.html
13. Fu, X., Bultan, T., Su, J.: Analysis of interacting BPEL web services. In: Feldman, S.I., Uretsky, M., Najork, M., Wills, C.E. (eds.), Proceedings of the 13th International Conference on World Wide Web, WWW 2004, New York, NY, USA, May 17-20, 2004, pp. 621–630. ACM (2004)
14. Xiang, F., Bultan, T., Jianwen, S.: Conversation protocols: a formalism for specification and verification of reactive electronic services. Theor. Comput. Sci. **328**(1–2), 19–37 (2004)
15. Gheri, L., Lanese, I., Sayers, N., Tuosto, E., Yoshida, N.: Design-by-contract for flexible multiparty session protocols. In: Ali, K., Vitek, J. (eds.), 36th European Conference on Object-Oriented Programming, ECOOP 2022, 6–10 June 2022, Berlin, Germany, volume 222 of *LIPIcs*, pp. 8:1–8:28. Schloss Dagstuhl - Leibniz-Zentrum für Informatik (2022)

16. Guanciale, R., Tuosto, E.: Realisability of pomsets. J. Log. Algebraic Methods Program. **108**, 69–89 (2019)
17. Guanciale, R., Tuosto, E.: Pomcho: a tool chain for choreographic design. Sci. Comput. Program. **202**, 102535 (2021)
18. Harvey, P., Fowler, S., Dardha, O., Gay, S.J.: Multiparty session types for safe runtime adaptation in an actor language. In: Møller, A., Sridharan, M. (eds.), 35th European Conference on Object-Oriented Programming, ECOOP 2021, 11–17 July 2021, Aarhus, Denmark (Virtual Conference), volume 194 of *LIPIcs*, pp. 10:1–10:30. Schloss Dagstuhl - Leibniz-Zentrum für Informatik (2021)
19. Healthcare authorization and accreditation protocol. https://salute.regione.emilia-romagna.it/ssr/strumenti-e-informazioni/autorizzazione-e-accreditamento/autorizzazione-e-accreditamento-sanitario
20. Hildebrandt, T.T., Slaats, T., López, H.A., Debois, S., Carbone, M.: Declarative choreographies and liveness. In: Pérez, J.A., Yoshida, N. (eds.) FORTE 2019. LNCS, vol. 11535, pp. 129–147. Springer, Cham (2019). https://doi.org/10.1007/978-3-030-21759-4_8
21. Honda, K., Yoshida, N., Carbone, M.: Multiparty asynchronous session types. In: Necula, G.C., Wadler, P. (eds.), Proceedings of the 35th ACM SIGPLAN-SIGACT Symposium on Principles of Programming Languages, POPL 2008, San Francisco, California, USA, 7-12 January 2008, pp. 273–284. ACM (2008)
22. Honda, K., Yoshida, N., Carbone, M.: Multiparty asynchronous session types. J. ACM **63**(1), 9:1–9:67 (2016)
23. Hu, R., Yoshida, N.: Explicit connection actions in multiparty session types. In: Huisman, M., Rubin, J. (eds.) FASE 2017. LNCS, vol. 10202, pp. 116–133. Springer, Heidelberg (2017). https://doi.org/10.1007/978-3-662-54494-5_7
24. Hüttel, H., et al.: Foundations of session types and behavioural contracts. ACM Comput. Surv. **49**(1), 3:1–3:36 (2016)
25. Kavantzas, N., Burdett, D., Ritzinger, G., Fletcher, T., Lafon, Y., Barreto, C.: Web services choreography description language version 1.0. 3C Candidate Recommendation **9**, 290–313 (2005)
26. Legge Regionale 06 Novembre 2019. https://demetra.regione.emilia-romagna.it/al/articolo?urn=er:assemblealegislativa:legge:2019;22
27. Li, E., Stutz, F., Wies, T., Zufferey, D.: Complete multiparty session type projection with automata. In: Enea, C., Lal, A. (eds.) Computer Aided Verification. CAV 2023, LNCS, Part III, vol. 13966, pp. 350–373. Springer, Cham (2023). https://doi.org/10.1007/978-3-031-37709-9_17
28. Orlando, S., Pasquale, V.D., Barbanera, F., Lanese, I., Tuosto, E.: Corinne, a tool for choreography automata. In: Salaün, G., Wijs, A. (eds.) FACS 2021. LNCS, vol. 13077, pp. 82–92. Springer, Cham (2021). https://doi.org/10.1007/978-3-030-90636-8_5
29. Pal, S., Lanese, I., Clo, M.: BPMN collaboration diagram of the Regional Coordination for Healthcare Authorization and Accreditation protocol. https://drive.google.com/file/d/1i10iTBZ_kvOcwSrRyTQZ_qEJHUsCB3dz/view
30. Pal, S., Lanese, I., Tuosto, E.: Corinne-3. https://github.com/lanese/corinne-3
31. Thiemann, P., Vasconcelos, V.T.: Label-dependent session types. Proc. ACM Program. Lang. **4**(POPL), 67:1–67:29 (2020)
32. Tuosto, E., Guanciale, R.: Semantics of global view of choreographies. J. Log. Algebraic Methods Program. **95**, 17–40 (2018)

A Probabilistic Choreography Language for PRISM

Marco Carbone[1(✉)] and Adele Veschetti[2]

[1] IT University of Copenhagen, Copenhagen, Denmark
`maca@itu.dk`
[2] Technische Universität Darmstadt, Darmstadt, Germany
`adele.veschetti@tu-darmstadt.de`

Abstract. We present a choreographic framework for modelling and analysing concurrent probabilistic systems based on the PRISM model-checker. This is achieved through the development of a choreography language, which is a specification language that allows to describe the desired interactions within a concurrent system from a global viewpoint. Employing choreographies provides a clear and comprehensive view of system interactions, enabling the discernment of process flow and detection of potential errors, thus ensuring accurate execution and enhancing system reliability. We equip our language with a probabilistic semantics and then define a formal encoding into the PRISM language and discuss its correctness. Properties of programs written in our choreographic language can be model-checked by the PRISM model-checker via their translation into the PRISM language. Finally, we implement a compiler for our language and demonstrate its practical applicability via examples drawn from the use cases featured in the PRISM website.

1 Introduction

Understanding and programming distributed systems present significant challenges due to their inherent complexity, and the possibility of obscure edge cases arising from their complex interactions. Unlike monolithic systems, distributed programs involve multiple nodes operating concurrently and communicating over networks, introducing a multitude of potential failure scenarios and nondeterministic behaviours. One of the primary challenges in understanding distributed systems lies in the fact that the interactions between multiple components can diverge from the sum of their individual behaviours. This emergent behaviour often results from subtle interactions between nodes, making it difficult to predict and reason about the system's overall behaviour.

PRISM [2] is a probabilistic model checker that offers a specialised language for the specification and verification of probabilistic concurrent systems. PRISM has been used in various fields, including multimedia protocols [19], randomised distributed algorithms [16,18], security protocols [17,22], and biological systems [11,14]. At its core, PRISM provides a declarative language with a set of constructs for describing probabilistic behaviours and properties within a system.

© IFIP International Federation for Information Processing 2024
Published by Springer Nature Switzerland AG 2024
I. Castellani and F. Tiezzi (Eds.): COORDINATION 2024, LNCS 14676, pp. 20–37, 2024.
https://doi.org/10.1007/978-3-031-62697-5_2

Given a distributed system, we can use PRISM to model the behaviour of each of its nodes, and then verify desired properties for the entire system. However, this approach can become difficult to manage as the number of nodes increases.

Choreographic programming [20] is an emerging programming paradigm in which programs, referred to as choreographies, serve as specifications providing a global perspective on the communication patterns inherent in a distributed system. In particular, instead of relying on a central orchestrator or controller to dictate the behavior of individual components, choreographic languages focus on defining communication patterns and protocols that govern the interactions between entities. In essence, choreographies abstract away the internal details of individual components and emphasise the global behaviour as a composition of decentralised interactions. Although, this approach can be used for a proper subset of distributed systems, choreographies have proven to be very useful in many use cases since they facilitate the automatic generation of decentralised implementations that are inherently correct-by-construction.

This paper presents a choreographic language designed for modelling concurrent probabilistic systems. Additionally, we introduce a compiler capable of translating protocols described in this language into PRISM code. This choreographic approach not only simplifies the modelling process but also ensures integration with PRISM's powerful analysis capabilities.

As an example, we consider a simplified version of the thinkteam example, a three-tier data management system [6], presented in the PRISM documentation[1]. The protocol aims to manage exclusive access to a single file, controlled by the CheckOut process. Users can request access, which can be granted based on the file's current status. The goal is to ensure that only one user possesses the file at any given time while allowing for efficient access requests and retries in case of denial. Users move between different states (0, 1, or 2) based on the granted or denied access to the file with corresponding rates (λ, μ, θ); the CheckOut process transitions between two states (0 or 1):

```
1     ctmc
2     module User
3         User_STATE : [0..2] init 0;
4
5         [alpha_1] (User_STATE=0) → lambda : (User_STATE'=1);
6         [alpha_2] (User_STATE=0) → lambda : (User_STATE'=2);
7         [beta] (User_STATE=1) → mu : (User_STATE'=0);
8         [gamma_1] (User_STATE=2) → theta : (User_STATE'=1);
9         [gamma_2] (User_STATE=2) → theta : (User_STATE'=2);
10    endmodule
11
12    module CheckOut
13        CheckOut_STATE : [0..1] init 0;
14
15        [alpha_1,alpha_2] (CheckOut_STATE=0) → 1 : (CheckOut_STATE'=1);
16        [beta] (CheckOut_STATE=1) → 1 : (CheckOut_STATE'=0);
17        [gamma_1,gamma_2] (CheckOut_STATE=1) → 1 : (CheckOut_STATE'=1);
18    endmodule
```

In PRISM, modules are individual processes whose behaviour is specified by a collection of commands, in a declarative fashion. Processes have a local state, can

---

[1] https://www.prismmodelchecker.org/casestudies/thinkteam.php.

interact with other modules and query each other's state. Above, the modules User (lines 2-10) and CheckOut (lines 12-18) can synchronise on different labels, e.g., alpha_1. On line 5, (User_STATE=0) is a condition indicating that this transition is enabled when User_STATE has value 0. The variable lambda is a rate, since the program models a Continuous Time Markov Chain (CTMC). The command (User_STATE'=1) is an update, indicating that User_STATE changes to 1 when this transition fires.

Understanding the interactions between processes in this example might indeed be challenging, especially without additional context or explanation. Alternatively, when formalised using our choreographic language, the same model becomes significantly clearer.

```
C0 := CheckOut → User : (+["1*lambda"] ; C1 +["1*lambda"] ; C2)
C1 := CheckOut → User : (+["1*theta"] ; C0)
C2 := CheckOut → User : (+["1*mu"] ; C1 +["1*mu"] ; C2)
```

In this model, we define three distinct choreographies, namely C0, C1, and C2. These choreographies describe the interaction patterns between the modules CheckOut and User. The state updates resulting from these interactions are not explicitly depicted as they are not relevant for this particular protocol, but necessary in the PRISM implementation. As evident from this example, the choreographic language facilitates a straightforward understanding of the interactions between processes, minimizing the likelihood of errors. In fact, we can think of the choreography representation of this example as the product of the two PRISM modules seen above.

Through our contributions, we aim to provide a smooth workflow for modeling, analyzing, and verifying concurrent probabilistic systems, ultimately increasing their usability in various application domains. In particular, by employing choreographies, we gain a clear and comprehensive view of the interactions occurring within the system, allowing us to discern the flow of processes and detect any potential sources of error in the modelling phase.

Contributions and Overview. We summarise our contributions as follows:

- we propose a choreographic language equipped with well-defined syntax and semantics, tailored specifically for describing concurrent systems with probabilistic behaviours (§ 2). To the best of our knowledge, this is the first probabilistic choreography language that is not a type abstraction;
- we introduce a semantics for the minimal fragment of PRISM needed for code generation from choreographies (§ 3), which follows PRISM's original semantics [2];
- we establish a rigorous definition for a translation function from choreographies to PRISM (§ 4), and address its correctness. This translation serves as a crucial intermediary step in transforming models described in our choreographic language into PRISM-compatible representations;
- we give a compiler implementation that executes the defined translation function (§ 5), enabling users to utilise PRISM's robust analysis features while benefiting from the expressiveness of choreographies;
- we show some use cases in order to demonstrate the applicability of our language (§ 6).

2   Choreography Language

In the introduction, we showed our choreography language via an example. We now formalise our language by giving its syntax and semantics. For the sake of clarity, we slightly change the syntax with respect to the syntax of our tool.

Syntax. Let p range over a (possibly infinite) set of module names $\mathcal{R}$, x over a (possibly infinite) set of variables Var, and v over a (possibly infinite) set of values Val. Choreographies, the key component of our language, are defined by the following syntax:

$$C ::= p \to \{p_1, \ldots, p_n\} : \Sigma_{j \in J} \lambda_j : u_j;\ C_j \ \mid\ \text{if } E@p \text{ then } C_1 \text{ else } C_2 \ \mid\ X \ \mid\ 0$$

$$u ::= (x' = E)\ \&\ u \ \mid\ (x' = E) \qquad\qquad E, g ::= f(\tilde{E}) \ \mid\ x \ \mid\ v$$

The syntactic category C denotes choreographic programs. The interaction term $p \to \{p_1, \ldots, p_n\} : \Sigma\{\lambda_j : x_j = E_j. C_j\}_{j \in J}$ denotes an interaction initiated by module p with modules p_i's (for p and all p_i distinct). A choreography specifies what interaction must be executed next, shifting the focus from what can happen to what must happen. When the interaction happens, one of the j branches is selected as a continuation. Branching is a random move: the number $\lambda_j \in \mathbb{R}$ denotes either a probability or a rate. This will depend on the language we wish to use. In the case of probabilities, it must be the case that $0 \le \lambda_j \le 1$ and $\Sigma_j \lambda_j = 1$. Once a branch j is taken, the choreography will execute some assignments u_j. A single assignment has the syntax $(x' = E)$ meaning that the value obtained by evaluating expression E is assigned to variable x; assignments can be concatenated with the operator $\&$. Note that x' is used for an assignment to x: here, we follow the syntax adopted in PRISM (see § 3). Expressions are obtained by applying some unspecified functions to other expressions or, as base terms, i.e., variables and values (denoted by v).

The term $\text{if } E@p \text{ then } C_1 \text{ else } C_2$ denotes a system where module p evaluates the guard E (which can contain variables located at other modules) and then (deterministically) branches accordingly. The term X is a (possibly recursive) procedure call: in the semantics, we assume that such procedure names are defined separately. The term 0 denotes the system finishing its computation.

Semantics. In the sequel, we define a state, denoted by S, as a mapping from variables to values, i.e., $S : \mathsf{Var} \to \mathsf{Val}$. Given a value v and a variable x, a substitution $[v/x]$ is an update on a state, i.e., $S[v/x](y) = \begin{cases} v & \text{if } y = x \\ S(y) & \text{otherwise} \end{cases}$ Then, the update $S[u]$ is such that $S[x' = E\ \&\ u] = S[E \downarrow_S /x][u]$ and $S[x' = E] = S[E \downarrow_S /x]$, where $E \downarrow_S$ is an unspecified (decidable) evaluation of the expression E in the state S.

Given the set of all possible states $\mathcal{S}$ and a set of definitions $\mathcal{D}$ of the form $X \overset{\text{def}}{=} C$, we can define the operational semantics of choreographies as the minimal relation $\longrightarrow^{\mathcal{D}} \subseteq \mathcal{S} \times C \times \mathbb{R} \times \mathcal{S} \times C$ such that (we omit $\mathcal{D}$ if not relevant):

(Interact) $(S, \mathsf{p} \rightarrow \{\mathsf{p_1}, \ldots, \mathsf{p_n}\} : \Sigma_{j \in J} \lambda_j : u_j; \; C_j) \longrightarrow_{\lambda_j} (S[u_j], C_j)$

(IfThenElseT) $E{\downarrow}_S = \mathsf{tt} \;\; \Rightarrow \;\; (S, \mathtt{if}\ E@\mathsf{p}\ \mathtt{then}\ C_1\ \mathtt{else}\ C_2) \longrightarrow_1 (S, C_1)$

(IfThenElseF) $E{\downarrow}_S = \mathsf{ff} \;\; \Rightarrow \;\; (S, \mathtt{if}\ E@\mathsf{p}\ \mathtt{then}\ C_1\ \mathtt{else}\ C_2) \longrightarrow_1 (S, C_2)$

(Call) $X \stackrel{\mathrm{def}}{=} C \in \mathcal{D} \;\; \Rightarrow \;\; (S, X) \longrightarrow_1 (S, C)$

The transition relation is a Discrete Time Markov Chain (DTMC) or a Continuous Time Markov Chain (CTMC) depending on whether we use probabilities or rates in the branching construct. Note that states of the Markov chain are the pairs (S, C), while the transitions are given by the relation $\longrightarrow$.

Example 1. Consider the following choreography:

$$C = \mathsf{p} \rightarrow \{\mathsf{q}\}\ \lambda_1 : (x' = 1); \quad \mathsf{p} \rightarrow \{\mathsf{q}\}\ \lambda_2 : (x' = 1); \mathbf{0}$$

The semantics of C starting from a state in which $S(x) = S(y) = 0$ can be depicted as follows (for $C' = \mathsf{p} \rightarrow \{\mathsf{q}\}\ \lambda_1 : (x' = 1); \mathbf{0}$):

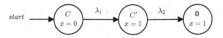

Example 2. Consider the following definition:

$$C \stackrel{\mathrm{def}}{=} \mathsf{p} \rightarrow \{\mathsf{q}\} \begin{cases} \lambda_1 : (x' = 1)\&(y' = 2); \; C \\ \lambda_2 : (x' = 3)\&(y' = 1); \; C \end{cases}$$

The semantics of C starting from a state in which $S(x) = S(y) = 0$ can be depicted as follows:

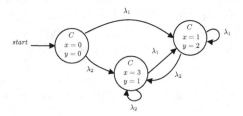

3   The PRISM Language

We now give a formal definition of a fragment of the PRISM language by introducing its formal syntax and semantics.

Syntax. We reuse some of the syntactic terms used for our choreography language, including assignments and expressions. In the sequel, let a range over a (possibly infinite) set of labels $\mathcal{L}$. We define the syntax of (a subset of) the PRISM language as follows:

$$
\begin{array}{llll}
\text{(Networks)} & N, M ::= & \mathbf{0} & \text{empty network} \\
& & \mid \mathbf{p} : \{F_i\}_i & \text{module} \\
& & \mid M\|[A]\|M & \text{parallel composition}
\end{array}
$$

$$
\text{(Commands)} \quad F ::= [\alpha]\, g \;\rightarrow\; \Sigma_{i \in I} \lambda_i : u_i \quad (\alpha \in \{\epsilon\} \cup \mathcal{L})
$$

Networks are the top syntactic category for system of modules composed together. The term $\mathbf{0}$ represent an empty network. A module is meant to represent a process running in the system and is denoted by its name and its commands, formally written as $\mathbf{p} : \{F_i\}_i$, where $\mathbf{p}$ is the name and the F_i's are commands. Networks can be composed in parallel, in a CSP style: a term like $M_1\|[A]\|M_2$ says that networks M_1 and M_2 can synchronise using labels in the finite set A. In this work, we omit PRISM's hiding and substitution constructs as they are irrelevant for our current choreography language. Commands in a module have the form $[\alpha]g \rightarrow \Sigma_{i \in I}\{\lambda_i : u_i\}$. The character α can either be the empty string ϵ or a label a, i.e., $\alpha \in \{\epsilon\} \cup \mathcal{L}$. If ϵ then no synchronisation is required. On the other hand, if there is label a then there will be a synchronisation with other modules that must synchronise on a. The term g is a guard on the current variable state. If both label and guard are enabled, then the command executes a branch i with probability/rate λ_i. As for choreographies, if the λ_i's are probabilities, we must have that $0 \leq \lambda_i \leq 1$ and $\Sigma_{i \in I}\lambda_i = 1$.

Semantics. To give a probabilistic semantics to the PRISM language, we follow the approach given in the PRISM documentation [2]. Hereby, we do that by defining two relations: one with labels for networks and one on states. Our relation on networks is the minimum relation $\rightsquigarrow$ satisfying the rules given in Fig. 1. Rule (M) just exposes a command at network level. Rule (P$_1$) propagates a command through parallel composition if α is empty or if the label a is not part of the set A. When the label a is in A, we apply rule (P$_2$). In this case, the product of the probabilities/rates must be taken by extending the two different branches to every possible combination. This also includes the combination of the associated assignments.

$$
\frac{F \in \{F_k\}_k}{\mathbf{p} : \{F_k\}_k \;\rightsquigarrow\; F} \; (\mathsf{M}) \qquad \frac{\exists j \in \{1,2\}.\; M_j \;\rightsquigarrow\; [\alpha]\, g \rightarrow \Sigma_{i \in I}\lambda_i : u_i \quad \alpha \notin A}{M_1\|[A]\|M_2 \;\rightsquigarrow\; [\alpha]\, g \rightarrow \Sigma_{i \in I}\lambda_i : u_i} \; (\mathsf{P_1})
$$

$$
\frac{M_1 \;\rightsquigarrow\; [a]\, g \rightarrow \Sigma_{i \in I}\lambda_i : u_i \qquad M_2 \;\rightsquigarrow\; [a]\, g' \rightarrow \Sigma_{j \in J}\lambda'_j : u'_j \qquad a \in A}{M_1\|[A]\|M_2 \;\rightsquigarrow\; [a]\, g \wedge g' \rightarrow \Sigma_{i,j}\, \lambda_i * \lambda'_j : u_i \& u'_j} \; (\mathsf{P_2})
$$

Fig. 1. Semantics for PRISM networks

Based on the relation above, given $M \;\rightsquigarrow\; [\alpha]\, g \rightarrow \Sigma_{i \in I}\lambda_i : u_i$ and two states S and S', we define the function

$$
\mu([\alpha]\, g \rightarrow \Sigma_{i \in I}\lambda_i : u_i,\; S,\; S'\,) = \Sigma_{S[u_i]=S', i \in I}\lambda_i
$$

which gives the probability/rate for the system to go from state S to state S' after executing command $[\alpha]\, g\ \rightarrow \Sigma_{i \in I} \lambda_i : u_i$, for some α. If the λ_i are probabilities, then the function must be a probability distribution. Note that $\mu(F, S, S')$ only denotes the probability/rate for the system to move from state S to state S' after executing command F. However, there can be other commands derived from a given network M through the relation $\rightsquigarrow$ that would cause a transition from S to S'. Therefore, we define the transition relation on states $M \vdash S \longrightarrow_\lambda S'$ as

$$\frac{\forall j, \alpha.\ M\ \rightsquigarrow\ F_j \qquad\qquad S \vdash F_j}{M \vdash S\ \longrightarrow_{\Sigma_j \mu(F_j, S, S')}\ S'}\ \text{(Transition)}$$

where $S \vdash [\alpha]\, g\ \rightarrow \Sigma_{i \in I} \lambda_i : u_i$ is defined as $g{\downarrow}_S$. Note that since PRISM is declarative, a term M never changes while the state of the system evolves.

It is important to point out that, in general, the transition rule above does not give the exact probability of a transition in case of a Markov chain (DTMC), since the sum $\sum_j \mu(F_j, S, S')$ could be a value greater than 1. In order to get the right probability, the value has to be normalised for all reachable S'. In the next section, we will show that this is not an issue for networks that are obtained from our translation from choreography to PRISM.

Example 3. Consider the following network M:

$$\mathsf{p} : \{\quad [] \ x = 0\ \rightarrow 1 : (x' = 1)$$
$$[a]\ y < 1\ \rightarrow 0.4 : (x' = x + 1)\ +\ 0.6 : (x' = x)\quad \}$$

$$\mathsf{q} : \{\quad [] \ y = 0\ \rightarrow 1 : (y' = 1)$$
$$[a]\ x < 1\ \rightarrow 0.5 : (y' = y + 1)\ +\ 0.5 : (y' = y)\quad \}$$

above, the two modules p and q can both do independent actions, as well as synchronising on label a. Applying the semantics, we can easily derive $M\ \rightsquigarrow$ $[]\ x = 0\ \rightarrow 1 : (x' = 1)$, $M\ \rightsquigarrow\ []\ y = 0\ \rightarrow 1 : (y' = 1)$, and $M\ \rightsquigarrow\ F$, such that

$$F = [a]\ x < 1\ \&\ y < 1\ \rightarrow 0.2 : (x' = x + 1)\ \&\ (y' = y + 1)$$
$$+\ 0.2 : (x' = x + 1)\ \&\ (y' = y)$$
$$+\ 0.3 : (x' = x)\ \&\ (y' = y + 1)$$
$$+\ 0.3 : (x' = x)\ \&\ (y' = y)$$

Let $s_0 = (x = 0, y = 0)$, $s_1 = (x = 1, y = 0)$, $s_2 = (x = 0, y = 1)$, and $s_0 = (x = 1, y = 1)$ be all possible states, with s_0 a starting state. Then,

$$\mu([]\ x = 0\ \rightarrow 1 : (x' = 1), s_0, s_1) = 1 \qquad \mu(F, s_0, s_1) = 0.2$$
$$\mu([]\ y = 0\ \rightarrow 1 : (y' = 1), s_0, s_2) = 1 \qquad \mu(F, s_0, s_2) = 0.3$$
$$\mu(F, s_0, s_0) = 0.3 \qquad\qquad\qquad\qquad \mu(F, s_0, s_3) = 0.2$$

Now, by (Transition), we have that $M \vdash s_0 \rightarrow_{1.2} s_1$, $M \vdash s_0 \rightarrow_{1.3} s_1$. Clearly, both transitions should be normalised, finally yielding the following DTMC:

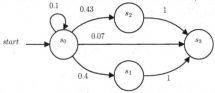

Example 4. The choreography presented in Example 2 can be described by the following PRISM network M (for $\lambda_i = \mu_i * \gamma_i$):

$$\mathsf{p}:\{ \quad [a]\ s_\mathsf{p} = 0 \ \rightarrow \mu_1 : (x' = 1)\ \&\ (s_\mathsf{p}' = 1) \qquad []\ s_\mathsf{p} = 1 \ \rightarrow 1 : (s_\mathsf{p}' = 0)$$
$$[b]\ s_\mathsf{p} = 0 \ \rightarrow \mu_2 : (x' = 3)\ \&\ (s_\mathsf{p}' = 2) \qquad []\ s_\mathsf{p} = 2 \ \rightarrow 1 : (s_\mathsf{p}' = 0) \quad \}$$

$$\mathsf{q}:\{ \quad [a]\ s_\mathsf{q} = 0 \ \rightarrow \gamma_1 : (y' = 2)\ \&\ (s_\mathsf{q}' = 1) \qquad []\ s_\mathsf{q} = 1 \ \rightarrow 1 : (s_\mathsf{q}' = 0)$$
$$[b]\ s_\mathsf{q} = 0 \ \rightarrow \gamma_2 : (y' = 1)\ \&\ (s_\mathsf{q}' = 2) \qquad []\ s_\mathsf{q} = 2 \ \rightarrow 1 : (s_\mathsf{q}' = 0) \quad \}$$

The two modules p and q synchornize on the labels a and b. Applying the semantics, the global state can evolve according to F_1 or F_2, defined as follows:

$$F_1 = [a]\ s_\mathsf{p} = 0\ \&\ s_\mathsf{q} = 0 \ \rightarrow \quad \mu_1 * \gamma_1 : (x' = 1)\ \&\ (y' = 2)\ \&\ (s_\mathsf{p}' = 1)\ \&\ (s_\mathsf{q}' = 1)$$
$$F_2 = [b]\ s_\mathsf{p} = 0\ \&\ s_\mathsf{q} = 0 \ \rightarrow \quad \mu_2 * \gamma_2 : (x' = 3)\ \&\ (y' = 1)\ \&\ (s_\mathsf{p}' = 2)\ \&\ (s_\mathsf{q}' = 2)$$

4   Projection

Our next task is to provide a mapping that can translate choreographies into the PRISM language. This section addresses projection formally.

Mapping Choreographies to PRISM. The operation of generating endpoint code from a choreography is known as *projection*. We observe that to simulate a choreography interaction in PRISM, we need to use labels on which each involved module can synchronise. Therefore, without loss of generality, we make a slight abuse of notation and assume that each interaction in a choreography is annotated with a unique label (which will be used by the projection). We call such a choreography an *annotated choreography*. For example, the choreography $\mathsf{p} \rightarrow \{\mathsf{q}\} + \lambda_1 : \mathbf{0} + \lambda_2 : \mathtt{if}\ E@\mathsf{p}\ \mathtt{then}\ \mathbf{0}\ \mathtt{else}\ \mathbf{0}$ is going to be annotated as $\mathsf{p} \rightarrow^a \{\mathsf{q}\} + \lambda_1 : \mathbf{0} + \lambda_2 : \mathtt{if}\ E@\mathsf{p}\ \mathtt{then}\ \mathbf{0}\ \mathtt{else}\ \mathbf{0}$. We now separate the definition of projection based on whether we are dealing with rates or probabilities. We start with choreographies with rates:

Definition 1 (Projection, CTMC). *Given an annotated choreography with rates C, a module p, and a natural number ι, we define the function* proj *as:*

$$\mathsf{proj}(\mathsf{q}, \mathsf{p} \rightarrow^a \{\mathsf{p}_1, \ldots, \mathsf{p}_n\} : \Sigma_{j \in J} \lambda_j : u_j;\ C_j, \iota) = \qquad \boxed{\textit{if } \mathsf{q} = \mathsf{p}}$$
$$\left\{ [a_j]\ s_\mathsf{q} = \iota \ \rightarrow \lambda_j :\ s_\mathsf{q} = s_\mathsf{q} + 1 + \textstyle\sum_{k=1}^{j-1} \mathsf{nodes}(C_k)\ \&\ u_j \downarrow_\mathsf{q} \right\}_{j \in J}$$
$$\cup\ \textstyle\bigcup_j \mathsf{proj}(\mathsf{q}, C_j, \iota + 1 + \textstyle\sum_{k=1}^{j-1} \mathsf{nodes}(C_k))$$

$$\mathsf{proj}(\mathsf{q}, \mathsf{p} \rightarrow^a \{\mathsf{p}_1, \ldots, \mathsf{p}_n\} : \Sigma_{j \in J} \lambda_j : u_j;\ C_j, \iota) = \qquad \boxed{\textit{if } \mathsf{q} \in \{\mathsf{p}_1, \ldots, \mathsf{p}_n\}}$$
$$\left\{ [a_j]\ s_\mathsf{q} = \iota \ \rightarrow 1 :\ s_\mathsf{q} = s_\mathsf{q} + 1 + \textstyle\sum_{k=1}^{j-1} \mathsf{nodes}(C_k)\ \&\ u_j \downarrow_\mathsf{q} \right\}_{j \in J}$$
$$\cup\ \textstyle\bigcup_j \mathsf{proj}(\mathsf{q}, C_j, \iota + 1 + \textstyle\sum_{k=1}^{j-1} \mathsf{nodes}(C_k))$$

$$\mathsf{proj}(\mathsf{q}, \mathsf{p} \rightarrow^a \{\mathsf{p}_1, \ldots, \mathsf{p}_n\} : \Sigma_{j \in J} \lambda_j : u_j;\ C_j, \iota) = \qquad \boxed{\textit{if } \mathsf{q} \notin \{\mathsf{p}, \mathsf{p}_1, \ldots, \mathsf{p}_n\}}$$
$$\textstyle\bigcup_j \mathsf{proj}(\mathsf{q}, C_j, \iota + \textstyle\sum_{k=1}^{j-1} \mathsf{nodes}(C_k))$$

$$\text{proj}(q, \texttt{if } E@\texttt{p then } C_1 \texttt{ else } C_2, \iota) = \qquad \boxed{if \; \mathsf{q} = \mathsf{p}}$$

$$\left\{ \begin{array}{l} [] \; s_q = \iota \; \& \; E \; \rightarrow \; 1 : s_q' = \iota + 1, \\ [] \; s_q = \iota \; \& \; \text{not}(E) \; \rightarrow \; 1 : s_q' = \iota + \text{nodes}(C_1) + 1 \end{array} \right\}$$
$$\cup \quad \text{proj}(\mathsf{p}, C_1, \iota + 1) \quad \cup \quad \text{proj}(\mathsf{p}, C_2, \iota + \text{nodes}(C_1) + 1)$$

$$\text{proj}(q, \texttt{if } E@\texttt{p then } C_1 \texttt{ else } C_2, \iota) = \qquad \boxed{if \; \mathsf{q} \neq \mathsf{p}}$$

$$\text{proj}(\mathsf{p}, C_1, \iota) \quad \cup \quad \text{proj}(\mathsf{p}, C_2, \iota + \text{nodes}(C_1))$$

$$\text{proj}(q, \mathbf{0}, \iota) = \emptyset$$

$$\text{proj}(q, X, \iota) = [] \; s_q = \iota \; \rightarrow \; 1 : s_q' = \iota' \qquad where \; \text{defs}(X) = \iota'$$

We go through the various cases of the definition above. The first three cases handle the projection of an interaction. If we project the first module p, then we create one command per branch, assigning the corresponding rate. Note that this is possible since we are dealing with rates. The additional variable s_q is the counter for this module and we identify uniquely this interaction. In order to do it consistently for follow up statements of the subterm choreographies, we use the function $\text{nodes}(C)$ which returns the number of nodes of C, i.e., the number of steps of the projection function. Obviously, when projecting the next branch we need to consider all other possible branches that may have been already projected. Intuitively, a label and an integer (ranged by ι) identify a node in the abstract syntax tree of a choreography. Also, note that we assume that from a label a we can generate distinct sublabels a_j just by adding some index j. For the sake of space, we do not define the function precisely, but we observe that this could also be easily defined via the label annotations. The second case defines the projection of an interaction for one of the modules $\{\mathsf{p}_1, \ldots, \mathsf{p}_n\}$. Similarly to the previous case, we define a command for each branch of the interaction. However, the rate of each command is going to be 1, making sure that each branch synchronises with probability $\lambda_j * 1$ (see rule (P$_2$) in Fig. 1). The third case is the one when we are projecting a module that is not in the set $\{\mathsf{p}, \mathsf{p}_1, \ldots, \mathsf{p}_n\}$. The if-then-else construct is only interesting for module p where the module makes an internal choice based on the evaluation of the guard E. For recursive calls, we generate a command that resets the counter to a distinct value given by the auxiliary function defs. As an example, we can apply the projection function to Example 2 and obtain the PRISM modules from Example 4.

As hinted above, the projection in Definition 1 would be incorrect if instead of using rates we used probabilities. This is simply because we cannot force both p and $\{\mathsf{p}_1, \ldots, \mathsf{p}_n\}$ to take the same branch with the probability distribution of the λ_i's. To fix this problem, we have the following definition instead:

Definition 2 (Projection, DTMC). *Given an annotated choreography with probabilities C, a module p, and a natural number ι, we define* proj *as:*

$$\mathsf{proj}(\mathsf{q}, \mathsf{p} \to \{\mathsf{p}_1, \ldots, \mathsf{p}_n\} : \Sigma_{j \in J} \lambda_j : u_j; \, C_j, \iota) = \qquad \boxed{if \; \mathsf{q} = \mathsf{p}}$$

$$\left\{ \begin{array}{l} [] \; s_q = \iota \; \to \; \Sigma_{j \in J} \lambda_j : s'_q = \iota + 1 + j, \\ \{[l_j] \; s_q = \iota + 1 + j \; \to \; 1 : s'_q = \iota + 1 + \Sigma_{k=1}^{j-1} \mathsf{nodes}(C_k) \; \& \; u_j \downarrow_q\}_{j \in J} \end{array} \right\}$$
$$\cup \; \bigcup_j \mathsf{proj}(\mathsf{q}, C_j, s + 1 + \Sigma_{k=1}^{j-1} \mathsf{nodes}(C_k))$$

The other cases of the definition are equivalent to those in Definition 1.

The fix is immediate: module p takes a (probabilistic) internal decision on the jth branch and then synchronises on label l_j with $\{\mathsf{p}_1, \ldots, \mathsf{p}_n\}$.
Correctness. Our projection operations are correct with respect to the semantics of choreographies and PRISM. In the sequel, S_+ is a state S extended with the extra variables s_q (for each module in a choreography) used by the projection. In the projection, we utilize alphabetized parallel composition $\|$, wherein modules synchronise solely on labels that appear in both modules. Additionally, a choreography is *strongly connected*, if (i) subsequent interactions share some modules [9] and, (ii) in every branch of a probabilistic choice or an if-then-else involving modules $\mathsf{p}_1, \ldots, \mathsf{p}_n$, the fist action (if any) of every other module q must be an interaction with $\mathsf{p}_1, \ldots, \mathsf{p}_n$ (up to unfolding of recursive calls). For example, the choreography

$$X \overset{\text{def}}{=} \mathsf{p} \to \{\mathsf{q}\} : \begin{pmatrix} \lambda_1 : u_1; \; \mathsf{q} \to \{\mathsf{r}\} : \lambda'_1 : u'_1; \; X \\ \lambda_2 : u_2; \; X \end{pmatrix}$$

is strongly connected while $\mathsf{p} \to \{\mathsf{q}\} : \left(\lambda_1 : u_1; \; \mathsf{r}_1 \to \{\mathsf{r}_2\} : \lambda'_1 : u'_1; \; \mathbf{0}. \right)$ is not.

Theorem 1 (EPP). *Given an annotated strongly connected choreography C, we have that $(S, C) \longrightarrow_\lambda (S', C')$ iff $\|_\mathsf{q} \mathsf{proj}(\mathsf{q}, C, \iota) \vdash S_+ \longrightarrow_\lambda S'_+$.*

Proof (Sketch). The proof must be separated into whether we deal with rates or probabilities. For Definition 1, the proof proceeds by induction on the term C. For $C = \mathsf{p} \to \{\mathsf{p}_1, \ldots, \mathsf{p}_n\} : \Sigma_{j \in J} \lambda_j : u_j; \, C_j$, the key case, we clearly have that, for any state S there exists S' such that $(S, C) \longrightarrow_{\lambda_j} (S', C_j)$. We need to show two things: first, that the projection $\|_\mathsf{q} \mathsf{proj}(\mathsf{q}, C, \iota)$ of C can make the same transition; second, that if the projection makes a transition, it must be corresponding to that of the choreography above.

We now observe that the state of a generated CTMC is uniquely identified by the counter ι. The uniqueness of the label a makes sure that all and only those modules involved in this interaction synchronise with this action (this shows from the rules in Fig. 1). As a consequence of this and since choreographies are strongly connected, the commands generated by this step of the translation are such that any state S_+ is exclusively going to enable these commands (because of the guard $s_q = \iota$) which obviously implies that it must be done with rate λ_j applying the rules in Fig. 1. The same argument can be applied for the opposite direction. The other cases are similar. The case for DTMC is also similar. $\square$

5   Implementation

We implemented our language in 1246 lines of Java, by defining its grammar and using ANTLR [1] to generate both parser and visitor components. Each syntax node within the abstract syntax tree (AST) was encapsulated in a corresponding Node class, with methods within these classes used for PRISM code generation.

```
String generateCode(ArrayList<Node> mods, int index, int maxIndex, boolean isCtmc, ArrayList<String>
    ↪ labels, String prot);
```

Listing 1.1. The generateCode function

The generateCode function generates the projection from our language to PRISM. The input parameters for the projection function include:

- mods: a list of the modules. New commands are appended to the set of commands for each respective module as they are generated.
- index and maxIndex: indices for tracking the current module being analyzed.
- isCtmc: a boolean flag indicating if a CTMC is being generated, crucial for projection generation logic.
- labels: existing labels; essential for checking label uniqueness.
- prot: the name of the protocol currently under analysis.

The projection function operates recursively on each command in the choreographic language, systematically generating PRISM code based on the type of command being analyzed. While most code generations are straightforward, the focal point lies in how new states are created. Each module maintains its set of states, and when a new state needs to be generated, the function examines the last available state for the corresponding module and increments it by one. Recursion follows a similar pattern: every module has as a field that accumulates recursion protocols, along with the first and last states associated with each recursion. This recursive approach ensures a systematic and coherent generation of states within the modules, enhancing the efficiency of the projection.

One of the differences between formal syntax and implementation is the presence of module parameterizations in the latter. Specifically, to avoid repeating the same commands for each duplicated module, we utilize the notation "[i]" for each module with the same behaviour. This enables us to perform module renaming, a principle that also extends to variables and their updates. We report in Listing 1.2 the choreography presented in Example 2, but we suppose that the process P performs the same branch for each process Q[i]. For every module in the system, where the index i ranges from 1 to n, there exists a corresponding PRISM module. For instance, for the example in Listing 1.2, if i ranges from 1 to 2, we will generate the respective PRISM code as depicted in Listing 1.3.

```
C := P → Q[i] : (+["mu1*gamma[i]"] "(x'=1)" "(y[i]'=2)" ; C
               +["mu2*gamma[i]"] "(x'=3)" "(y[i]'=1)" ; C )
```

Listing 1.2. Example of an use of parameterization in the choreographic language

```
1    ctmc
2    module Q1
3       Q1_STATE : [0..1] init 0;
4       y1 : [0..N] init 0;
5       [RLICV] (Q1_STATE=0) → gamma1 : (y1'=2)&(Q1_STATE'=0);
6       [OKAMT] (Q1_STATE=0) → gamma1 : (y1'=1)&(Q1_STATE'=0);
7    endmodule
8
9    module Q2
10      Q2_STATE : [0..1] init 0;
11      y2 : [0..N] init 0;
12      [OMPXG] (Q2_STATE=0) → gamma2 : (y2'=2)&(Q2_STATE'=0);
13      [AQNZR] (Q2_STATE=0) → gamma2 : (y2'=1)&(Q2_STATE'=0);
14   endmodule
15
16   module P
17      P_STATE : [0..2] init 0;
18      x : [0..N] init 0;
19      [RLICV] (P_STATE=0) → mu1 : (x'=1)&(P_STATE'=0);
20      [OKAMT] (P_STATE=0) → mu2 : (x'=3)&(P_STATE'=0);
21      [OMPXG] (P_STATE=0) → mu1 : (x'=1)&(P_STATE'=0);
22      [AQNZR] (P_STATE=0) → mu2 : (x'=3)&(P_STATE'=0);
23   endmodule
```

Listing 1.3. PRISM code generated for the choreography in Listing 1.2

This modular approach systematically represents and integrates each system component within the PRISM framework, enabling comprehensive analysis and synthesis of the system's behavior. Importantly, these internal optimizations do not impact the projection process, as they focus on efficiency and code management rather than altering the overall structure or behavior of the projection.

The other differences are primarily syntactic. Updates of the same process are delineated by quotation marks, such as "(x'=1)". Additionally, rates and probabilities are represented differently. In our choreographic language the rate/probability of interaction is represented as the product of rates/probabilities of each process. For example, in Listing 1.2, we use mu1*gamma[i] to indicate that the rate of the first process (P) is mu1, while the rate of the second process (Q[i]) is represented by gamma[i]. If multiple processes are interacting, the rate/probability is the product of all corresponding rates/probabilities (lambda_1...*lambda_n).

In our implementation, we ensure a single enabled action per state by enforcing label uniqueness and unique state-associated variables. This clarity aids in accurately determining enabled actions and enhances system reliability, facilitating analysis and comprehension of system dynamics.

6   Benchmarking

In this section, we present an experimental evaluation of our language. The examples provided highlight two main points: firstly, the representation using choreographic language is significantly more concise; secondly, we demonstrate that PRISM behaves similarly on both the projection and the original model in PRISM also in our implementation. In particular, we focus on three benchmarks: a modified version of the example reported in Sect. 1; the Bitcoin Proof of Work protocol [7] and the Hybrid Casper protocol [12]. The generated PRISM files can be found in our online repository [3].

A Modified thinkteam Protocol. In this modified version of the thinkteam protocol introduced in the earlier sections, we extend the protocol to involve generalised interactions with possible many receivers. Specifically, the CheckOut process now communicates with two users simultaneously, User1 and User2 each tasked with performing distinct actions upon access to the file.

In the first branch, User1 increments the variable x by 1, while User2 decrements the variable y by 1. Conversely, in the second branch, the roles are reversed, with User1 decrementing x and User2 incrementing y.

```
C0 := CheckOut ⟶ User1, User2 : (+["1*lambda"] " " "(x=x+1)" "(y=y-1)"; C1
                                 +["1*lambda"] " " "(x=x-1)" "(y=y+1)"; C2)
C1 := CheckOut ⟶ User1, User2 : (+["1*theta"] ; C0)
C2 := CheckOut ⟶ User1, User2 : (+["1*mu "] ; C1 +["1*mu "] ; C2)
```

Listing 1.4. Choreography for the Modified thinkteam Protocol

Part of the generated PRISM model is reported in Listing 1.5.

```
1     module CheckOut
2         CheckOut_STATE : [0..2] init 0;
3         [MMHOL] (CheckOut_STATE=0) -> 1 : (CheckOut_STATE'=1);
4         [FFSFW] (CheckOut_STATE=0) -> 1 : (CheckOut_STATE'=2);
5         [ULCFN] (CheckOut_STATE=1) -> 1 : (CheckOut_STATE'=0);
6         [YHHWG] (CheckOut_STATE=2) -> 1 : (CheckOut_STATE'=1);
7         [XWSAO] (CheckOut_STATE=2) -> 1 : (CheckOut_STATE'=2);
8     endmodule
9     ...
10    module User2
11        User2_STATE : [0..2] init 0;
12        [MMHOL] (User2_STATE=0) -> lambda : (y'=y-1)&(User2_STATE'=1);
13        [FFSFW] (User2_STATE=0) -> lambda : (y'=y+1)&(User2_STATE'=2);
14        [ULCFN] (User2_STATE=1) -> mu : (User2_STATE'=0);
15        [YHHWG] (User2_STATE=2) -> theta : (User2_STATE'=1);
16        [XWSAO] (User2_STATE=2) -> theta : (User2_STATE'=2);
17    endmodule
```

Listing 1.5. Generated PRISM program

The generated PRISM model appears less clear compared to its choreographic representation, primarily due to its lack of sequential structure and lower readability. In the PRISM model, the absence of a clear sequential structure makes it harder to follow the flow of interactions between components, since module definitions and transition labels can be more challenging to read and comprehend compared to the concise and structured nature of the choreographic language.

Proof of Work Bitcoin Protocol. In [7], the authors extended the PRISM model checker syntax to incorporate dynamic data types, enhancing its capabilities to model the Proof of Work protocol used in the Bitcoin blockchain [21].

In summary, the code depicts miners engaging in solving PoW, updating their ledgers, and communicating with the network. The indices i represent the module renaming feature of the choreographic language. Thus, each interaction will be repeated for each miner and hasher of the protocol that we are considering. The protocol works as follows.

```
{PoW := Hasher[i] → Miner[i] :
(+["mR*hR[i]"] " " "(b[i]'=createB(b[i],B[i],c[i]))&(c[i]'=c[i]+1)" ;
   Miner[i] → Network : (["rB*1"] "(B[i]'=addBlock(B[i],b[i]))" foreach(k!=i) "(set[k]'=
      ↪ addBlockSet(set[k],b[i]))"@Network;PoW)
 +["lR*hR[i]"] ;
         if "!isEmpty(set[i])"@Miner[i] then {
           ["r"] "(b[i]'=extractBlock(set[i]))"@Miner[i] ;
              Miner[i] → Network :
                 (["1*1"] "(setMiner[i]'=addBlockSet(setMiner[i],b[i]))" "(set[i]' =
                     ↪ removeBlock(set[i],b[i]))";PoW)
         }
         else{
           if "canBeInserted(B[i],b[i])"@Miner[i] then {
             ["1"] "(B[i]'=addBlock(B[i],b[i]))&(setMiner[i]'=removeBlock(setMiner[i],b[i
                 ↪ ]))"@Miner[i];PoW
           }
           else{PoW}})}
```

Listing 1.6. Choreography for the Proof of Work Bitcoin Protocol

When synchronising with the hasher, a miner tries to solve a cryptographic puzzle. Successful attempts add a new block to its ledger and update other miners' block sets. Unsuccessful attempts involve extracting a block, updating its ledger and block sets, and continuing the PoW process.

The PRISM model we created is more verbose than the one in [7], mainly because we consistently generate the else branch for if-then-else expressions, resulting in a higher number of instructions. Despite this, the experimental results for block creation probability within a bound time T (Fig. 2) remain unaffected. Any discrepancies between the original and generated models are due to inherent variations in the simulation-based calculation of probability.

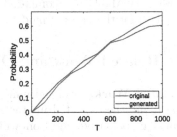

Fig. 2. Block creation probability over time

Hybrid Casper Protocol. We now present the Hybrid Casper Protocol [12]. The Hybrid Casper protocol represents a hybrid consensus protocol for blockchains, merging features from both Proof of Work and Proof of Stake protocols.

```
{PoS := Hasher[i] -> Validator[i] :
(+["mR*1"] "(b[i]'=createB(b[i],L[i],c[i]))&(c[i]'=c[i]+1)";
  if "!(mod(getHeight(b[i]),EpochSize)=0)"@Validator[i] then{...}
  else{
     Validator[i] -> Vote_Manager :(["1*1"] "(Votes'=addVote(Votes,b[i],stake[i]))"; PoS)
  }
 +["hR*1"] ; if "!isEmpty(set[i])"@Validator[i] then { ... }
           else{ PoS }
 +["rC*1"] "(lastCheck[i]'=extractCheckpoint(listCheckpoints[i],lastCheck[i]))"...}
```

Listing 1.7. Excerpt of the Hybrid Casper Protocol as a choreography

The modeling approach is very similar to the one used for the Proof of Work Bitcoin protocol. Specifically, the Hybrid Casper protocol is represented in PRISM as the parallel composition of n *Validator* modules, along with the modules

Vote_Manager and *Network*. Each *Validator* module closely resembles the *Miner* module from the previous protocol. The module *Vote_Manager* is responsible for storing maps containing votes for each block and computing associated rewards/penalties. The choreographic model for this example is reported in Listing 1.7. The code resembles that of the Proof of Work protocol, but each validator can either create a new block, receive blocks from the network module, or determine if it's eligible to vote for specific blocks. For lack of space, we detailed only part of the code, the complete model can be found in [3].

The generated code is very similar the one outlined in [12], with the main distinction being the greater number of lines in our generated model. This difference is due to the fact that certain commands could be combined, but our generation lacks the automatic capability to perform this check. While the results obtained for the probability of creating a block within the time T reported in Fig. 3 exhibit similarity, running simulations for the generated model takes PRISM 39.016 s, compared to the 22.051 s required for the original model.

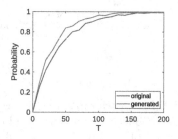

Fig. 3. Block creation probability over time

7   Related Work and Discussion

Related Work. Choreographic programming [20] is a language paradigm for specifying the expected interactions (communications) of a distributed system from a global viewpoint, from which decentralised implementations can be generated via projection. The notion of choreography has been substantially explored in the last decade, both from a theoretical perspective, e.g., [9,10], to full integration into fully-fledged programming languages, such as WS-CDL [15] and Choral [13]. Nevertheless, there is a scarcity of research on probabilistic aspects of choreographic programming. To the best of our knowledge, Aman and Ciobanu [4,5] are the only ones who studied the concept of choreography and probabilities. Their work augments multiparty session types (type abstractions for communicating systems that use the concept of choreography) with a probabilistic internal choice similar to the one used by our choreographic branching. However, they do not provide any semantics with state in terms of Markov chains, and, most importantly, they do not project into a probabilistic declarative language model such as PRISM. Carbone et al. [8] define a logic for expressing properties of a session-typed choreography language. However, the logic is undecidable and has no model-checking algorithm. As far as our knowledge extends, there is currently no work that generates probabilistic models from choreographic languages that can be then model-checked.

Discussion and Future Work. The ultimate goal of the proposed framework is to use the concept of choreographic programming to improve several aspects, including usability, correctness, and efficiency in modeling and analysing systems. In this paper, we address usability and efficiency of modelling systems by proposing a probabilistic choreography language. Our language improves the intuitive modeling of concurrent probabilistic systems. Traditional modeling languages often lack the expressive clarity needed to effectively capture the intricacies of such systems. By designing a language specific for choreographing system behaviors, we provide an intuitive means of specifying system dynamics. This approach enables a more natural and straightforward modeling process, essential for accurately representing real-world systems and ensuring the efficacy of subsequent analysis.

Although choreograhies and the projection function aim to abstract away low-level details, providing instead a higher-level representation of system behaviors, the choreographic approach can have some limitations in expressivity. Some of the case studies presented in the PRISM documentation [2] cannot be modeled by using our current language. Specifically, there are two main cases where our approach encounters limitations: *(i)* in the asynchronous leader election case study, our language prohibits the use of an 'if-then' statement without an accompanying 'else' to prevent deadlocked states; *(ii)* in probabilistic broadcast protocols or cyclic server polling system models, the system requires probabilistic branching to synchronise different modules based on the selected branch. These issues could be fixed by extending our choreographic language further and are therefore left as future work.

Additionally to these extensions, we conjecture that our semantics for choreographies may be used for improving performance by directly generating a CTMC or a DTMC from a choreography, bypassing the projection into the PRISM language. In fact, the Markov chain construction from a choreography seems to be faster than the construction from a corresponding projection in the PRISM language, since it is not necessary to take into account all the possible synchronisations in the rules from Fig. 1. A formal complexity analysis, an implementation, and performance benchmarking are left as future work.

In conclusion, this paper has introduced a framework for addressing the challenges of modelling and analysing concurrent probabilistic systems. The development of a choreographic language with tailored syntax and semantics offers an intuitive modeling approach. We have established the correctness of a projection function that translates choreographic models to PRISM-compatible formats. Additionally, our compiler enables seamless translation of choreographic models to PRISM, facilitating powerful analysis while maintaining expressive clarity. These contributions bridge the gap between high-level modeling and robust analysis in probabilistic systems, paving the way for advancements in the field.

Acknowledgments. The work is partially funded by H2020-MSCA-RISE Project 778233 (BEHAPI), by the ATHENE project "Model-centric Deductive Verification of Smart Contracts", and by the Carlsberg Foundation.

References

1. ANTLR - another tool for language recognition. https://www.antlr.org/
2. Prism documentation. https://www.prismmodelchecker.org/. Accessed 05 Sep 2023
3. Repository. https://github.com/adeleveschetti/ChoreoPRISM, Accessed 31 Jan 2024
4. Aman, B., Ciobanu, G.: Probabilities in session types. In: Marin, M., Craciun, A. (eds.) Proceedings Third Symposium on Working Formal Methods, FROM 2019, Timişoara, Romania, 3–5 September 2019. EPTCS, vol. 303, pp. 92–106 (2019). https://doi.org/10.4204/EPTCS.303.7
5. Aman, B., Ciobanu, G.: Interval probability for sessions types. In: Ciabattoni, A., Pimentel, E., de Queiroz, R.J.G.B. (eds.) Logic, Language, Information, and Computation - 28th International Workshop, WoLLIC 2022, Iaşi, Romania, September 20-23, 2022, Proceedings. LNCS, vol. 13468, pp. 123–140. Springer, Cham (2022).https://doi.org/10.1007/978-3-031-15298-6_8
6. ter Beek, M.H., Massink, M., Latella, D., Gnesi, S., Forghieri, A., Sebastianis, M.: Model checking publish/subscribe notification for thinkteam®. In: FMICS. Electronic Notes in Theoretical Computer Science, vol. 133, pp. 275–294. Elsevier (2004)
7. Bistarelli, S., Nicola, R.D., Galletta, L., Laneve, C., Mercanti, I., Veschetti, A.: Stochastic modeling and analysis of the bitcoin protocol in the presence of block communication delays. Concurr. Comput. Pract. Exp. **35**(16) (2023). https://doi.org/10.1002/cpe.6749
8. Carbone, M., Grohmann, D., Hildebrandt, T.T., López, H.A.: A logic for choreographies. In: Honda, K., Mycroft, A. (eds.) Proceedings Third Workshop on Programming Language Approaches to Concurrency and communication-cEntric Software, PLACES 2010, Paphos, Cyprus, 21st March 2010. EPTCS, vol. 69, pp. 29–43 (2010).https://doi.org/10.4204/EPTCS.69.3
9. Carbone, M., Honda, K., Yoshida, N.: Structured communication-centered programming for web services. ACM Trans. Program. Lang. Syst. **34**(2), 8:1–8:78 (2012). https://doi.org/10.1145/2220365.2220367
10. Carbone, M., Montesi, F.: Deadlock-freedom-by-design: multiparty asynchronous global programming. In: Giacobazzi, R., Cousot, R. (eds.) The 40th Annual ACM SIGPLAN-SIGACT Symposium on Principles of Programming Languages, POPL 2013, Rome, Italy - January 23–25, 2013, pp. 263–274. ACM (2013). https://doi.org/10.1145/2429069.2429101
11. Dannenberg, F., Kwiatkowska, M., Thachuk, C., Turberfield, A.J.: DNA walker circuits: computational potential, design, and verification. In: Soloveichik, D., Yurke, B. (eds.) DNA 2013. LNCS, vol. 8141, pp. 31–45. Springer, Cham (2013). https://doi.org/10.1007/978-3-319-01928-4_3
12. Galletta, L., Laneve, C., Mercanti, I., Veschetti, A.: Resilience of hybrid casper under varying values of parameters. Distributed Ledger Technol. Res. Pract. **2**(1), 5:1–5:25 (2023).https://doi.org/10.1145/3571587
13. Giallorenzo, S., Montesi, F., Peressotti, M.: Choral: Object-oriented choreographic programming. ACM Trans. Program. Lang. Syst. **46**(1), 1:1–1:59 (2024). https://doi.org/10.1145/3632398
14. Heath, J., Kwiatkowska, M., Norman, G., Parker, D., Tymchyshyn, O.: Probabilistic model checking of complex biological pathways. In: Priami, C. (ed.) CMSB 2006. LNCS, vol. 4210, pp. 32–47. Springer, Heidelberg (2006). https://doi.org/10.1007/11885191_3

15. Honda, K., Yoshida, N., Carbone, M.: Web services, mobile processes and types. Bull. EATCS **91**, 160–185 (2007)
16. Kwiatkowska, M., Norman, G., Parker, D.: Probabilistic verification of hermans self-stabilisation algorithm. Formal Aspects Comput. **24**(4), 661–670 (2012)
17. Kwiatkowska, M., Norman, G., Parker, D., Vigliotti, M.: Probabilistic mobile ambients. Theoret. Comput. Sci. **410**(12–13), 1272–1303 (2009)
18. Kwiatkowska, M., Norman, G., Segala, R.: Automated verification of a randomized distributed consensus protocol using cadence SMV and PRISM? In: Berry, G., Comon, H., Finkel, A. (eds.) CAV 2001. LNCS, vol. 2102, pp. 194–206. Springer, Heidelberg (2001). https://doi.org/10.1007/3-540-44585-4_17
19. Kwiatkowska, M., Norman, G., Sproston, J.: Probabilistic model checking of deadline properties in the IEEE 1394 FireWire root contention protocol. Formal Aspects Comput. **14**(3), 295–318 (2003)
20. Montesi, F.: Introduction to Choreographies. Cambridge University Press, Cambridge (2023)
21. Nakamoto, S.: Bitcoin: a peer-to-peer electronic cash system (2008). https://bitcoin.org/bitcoin.pdf
22. Norman, G., Shmatikov, V.: Analysis of probabilistic contract signing. J. Comput. Secur. **14**(6), 561–589 (2006)

Encoding Petri Nets into CCS

Benjamin Bogø$^{(\boxtimes)}$ ⓘ, Andrea Burattin ⓘ, and Alceste Scalas ⓘ

Technical University of Denmark, Kongens Lyngby, Denmark
`{bbog,andbur,alcsc}@dtu.dk`

Abstract. This paper explores the problem of determining which classes of Petri nets can be encoded into behaviourally-equivalent CCS processes. Most of the existing related literature focuses on the inverse problem (i.e., encoding process calculi belonging to the CCS family into Petri nets), or extends CCS with Petri net-like multi-synchronisation (Multi-CCS). In this work, our main focus are *free-choice* and *workflow* nets (which are widely used in process mining to describe system interactions) and our target is *plain* CCS. We present several novel encodings, including one from free-choice workflow nets (produced by process mining algorithms like the α-miner) into CCS processes, and we prove that our encodings produce CCS processes that are weakly bisimilar to the original net. Besides contributing new expressiveness results, our encodings open a door towards bringing analysis and verification techniques from the realm of process calculi into the realm of process mining.

Keywords: Petri nets · CCS · Encoding · Bisimulation · Free-choice workflow nets

1 Introduction

Process calculi and Petri nets are among the most successful tools for the modelling and verification of concurrent systems. The two models have significantly different designs: Petri nets have a more *semantic* flavour, whereas process calculi have a more *syntactic* flavour. This has resulted in significantly different approaches and application fields. In particular, Petri nets have found considerable success in the area of *Workflow Management*, as the theoretical foundation for several *Business Process Management* languages, and in *process mining*, whereas the syntactic nature of process calculi has fostered a rich literature on the static verification of behavioural properties (e.g. via type checking or the axiomatisation of bisimulation relations), often connected to programming languages.

This different focus on semantics-vs.-syntax has naturally encouraged the study of Petri nets as a possible semantic model for process calculi, through the development of various encodings and results of the form: *Petri nets (of the class X) are at least as expressive as the encoded calculus Y.* (For more details, see Sect. 2.) In this paper we investigate the opposite problem: *Which flavour of Petri nets can be encoded in Milner's Calculus of Communicating Systems*

ⓒ IFIP International Federation for Information Processing 2024
Published by Springer Nature Switzerland AG 2024
I. Castellani and F. Tiezzi (Eds.): COORDINATION 2024, LNCS 14676, pp. 38–55, 2024.
https://doi.org/10.1007/978-3-031-62697-5_3

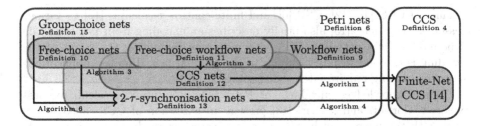

Fig. 1. Overview of the relation between Petri net classes and CCS considered in this paper. The arrows show algorithms for converting one class into another class.

(CCS)? A reason for this investigation is the observation that applications of Petri nets in process mining (e.g. via the α-miner algorithm [3]) often result in rather structured nets (in particular, *free-choice workflow nets* [3,10]) which are reminiscent of what is expressible in CCS. Therefore, we aim at proving whether this intuition is correct. Moreover, besides producing novel expressiveness results, developing an encoding from (selected classes of) Petri nets into CCS could also open new doors towards directly using process calculi in process mining, or applying analysis and verification techniques and tools originally developed for process calculi (e.g. model checkers) to the realm of process mining.

Contributions and Structure. Figure 1 gives an overview of the relation and conversion between Petri nets classes and CCS considered in this paper. We start by presenting related work in Sect. 2 and preliminaries in Sect. 3. Then, we present an encoding of *free-choice workflow nets* into weakly bismilar CCS processes (Theorem 4) in Sect. 4. Here, we also introduce a new class of Petri nets called *group-choice nets* (which include free-choice nets) and show how to encode them into weakly bismilar CCS processes (Theorem 7). We conclude and outline future work in Sect. 5. A software tool [7] has been created based on the results of this paper: a web application to import/draw Petri nets, classify them (according to Fig. 1) and encode them into CCS. Due to space limits, proofs and additional materials are available in a separate technical report [8].

2   Related Work

Many process mining algorithms (like the α-miner [3]) take a log of traces of *visible* actions and turn it into a *workflow net* [2]. Workflow nets are Petri nets used to describe how systems interact during a process. These kinds of interactions can also be described by process calculi like CCS with labeled semantics to capture the visible actions. There has been some debate about whether graphs like Petri nets or process calculi like the π-calculus are best for process mining [1]. Most of the existing work builds on Petri nets [11], but there is also work on how to represent patterns in process calculi [16].

Most existing work about encodings between process calculi and Petri nets focus on encoding the former into the latter: e.g., there are encodings from variants of CCS [4,5,12], CSP [6], and finite-control π-calculus [15] to various classes of Petri nets. [15] also briefly describes an encoding from *unlabeled* safe (1-bounded) Petri nets into CCS with reduction semantics; the result of the encoding is claimed weakly bisimilar to the original net. However, applications in process mining require *labelled* semantics.

To our knowledge, encodings of Petri nets into process calculi are less explored. Gorrieri and Versari [13] present an extension of CCS called *Multi-CCS*, with the purpose of having a one-to-one correspondence between unsafe P/T Petri nets and Multi-CCS; crucially, Multi-CCS can synchronize multiple processes at a time (like Petri nets) whereas CCS is limited to two synchronizing processes at a time. [13] also presents an encoding from Petri nets into strongly bisimilar Multi-CCS processes; they also show that encoding a restricted class of Petri nets (called *CCS nets*) yields strongly bisimilar *plain* CCS process. In this paper we start from this last result, and explore encodability beyond CCS nets — targeting *plain* CCS only (to enable reusing its well-established techniques e.g. for model checking and axiomatic reasoning), and with an eye toward classes of Petri nets relevant for process mining.

3   Preliminaries: LTSs, Bisimulations, CCS, Petri Nets

This section contains the basic standard definitions used in the rest of the paper.

LTSs and Bisimulations. We adopt standard definitions of strong and weak bisimulation between LTS states (Definitions 1, 2, and 3, based on [14]).

Definition 1 (Labeled Transition System). *A labeled transition system* (LTS) *is a triple* $(Q, A, \rightarrow)$ *where* Q *is a set of* states, A *is a set of* actions, *and* $\rightarrow \subseteq Q \times A \times Q$ *is a* labelled transition relation. *The set* A *may contain a distinguished* internal action τ, *and we dub any other action as* visible. *We write:*

- $q \xrightarrow{\mu} q'$ *iff* $(q, \mu, q') \in \rightarrow$
- $q \xrightarrow{a} q'$ *iff* $a \neq \tau$ *and* $(q, a, q') \in \rightarrow$ *(note that the action a is not silent)*
- $q \stackrel{\epsilon}{\Rightarrow} q'$ *iff* $q = q'$ *or* $q \xrightarrow{\tau} \cdots \xrightarrow{\tau} q'$ *(i.e.,* q *can reach* q' *in 0 or more τ-steps)*
- $q \stackrel{a}{\Rightarrow} q'$ *iff* $q \stackrel{\epsilon}{\Rightarrow}\xrightarrow{a}\stackrel{\epsilon}{\Rightarrow} q'$ *(* q *can reach* q' *via one a-step + 0 or more τ-steps)*

We say that q *is a* deadlock *if there are no transitions from* q. *A divergent path is an infinite sequence of LTS states* $q_1, q_2, \ldots$ *such that* $q_i \xrightarrow{\tau} q_{i+1}$.

Definition 2 (Strong Bisimulation). *A* strong bisimulation *between two LTSs* $(Q_1, A_1, \rightarrow_1)$ *and* $(Q_2, A_2, \rightarrow_2)$ *is a relation* $\mathcal{R} \subseteq Q_1 \times Q_2$ *where, if* $(q_1, q_2) \in \mathcal{R}$:

$$\forall q_1' : q_1 \xrightarrow{\mu}_1 q_1' \text{ implies } \exists q_2' : q_2 \xrightarrow{\mu}_2 q_2' \text{ and } (q_1', q_2') \in \mathcal{R}$$
$$\forall q_2' : q_2 \xrightarrow{\mu}_2 q_2' \text{ implies } \exists q_1' : q_1 \xrightarrow{\mu}_1 q_1' \text{ and } (q_1', q_2') \in \mathcal{R}$$

We say that q *and* q' *are* strongly bisimilar *or simply* bisimilar *(written* $q \sim q'$) *if there exists a bisimulation* $\mathcal{R}$ *with* $(q, q') \in \mathcal{R}$.

Definition 3 (Weak Bisimulation). *A* weak bisimulation *between two LTSs* $(Q_1, A_1, \rightarrow_1)$ *and* $(Q_2, A_2, \rightarrow_2)$ *is a relation* $\mathcal{R} \subseteq Q_1 \times Q_2$ *where, if* $(q_1, q_2) \in \mathcal{R}$*:*

$$\forall q_1' : q_1 \xrightarrow{a}_1 q_1' \text{ implies } \exists q_2' : q_2 \xRightarrow{a}_2 q_2' \text{ and } (q_1', q_2') \in \mathcal{R}$$
$$\forall q_1' : q_1 \xrightarrow{\tau}_1 q_1' \text{ implies } \exists q_2' : q_2 \xRightarrow{\epsilon}_2 q_2' \text{ and } (q_1', q_2') \in \mathcal{R}$$
$$\forall q_2' : q_2 \xrightarrow{a}_2 q_2' \text{ implies } \exists q_1' : q_1 \xRightarrow{a}_1 q_1' \text{ and } (q_1', q_2') \in \mathcal{R}$$
$$\forall q_2' : q_2 \xrightarrow{\tau}_2 q_2' \text{ implies } \exists q_1' : q_1 \xRightarrow{\epsilon}_1 q_1' \text{ and } (q_1', q_2') \in \mathcal{R}$$

We say that q *and* q' *are* weakly bisimilar *(written* $q \approx q'$*) if there is a weak bisimulation* $\mathcal{R}$ *with* $(q, q') \in \mathcal{R}$*.*

CCS. We adopt a standard version of CCS with LTS semantics, including restrictions and defining equations (Definitions 4 and 5, based on [14]).

Definition 4 (CCS Syntax). *The syntax of CCS is:*

$$\mu ::= \tau \mid a \mid \bar{a} \qquad P ::= \mathbf{0} \mid \mu.Q \mid P + P' \qquad Q ::= P \mid Q \mid Q' \mid (\nu a)Q \mid X$$

By Definition 4, an *action* μ can be the silent action τ, a visible action a, or its *co-action* $\bar{a}$. A *sequential CCS process* P can do nothing (**0**), perform an *action prefix* μ followed by Q ($\mu.Q$), or perform a *choice* ($P + P'$). A *process* Q can be a sequential process P, a *parallel composition* of two processes ($Q \mid Q'$), a *restriction* of action a to scope Q (($\nu a)Q$), or a *process name* X.

The LTS semantics of CCS is formalised in Definition 5 below, where it is assumed that there is a partial map of *defining equations* $\mathcal{D}$ from process names to processes, i.e., $\mathcal{D}(X) = Q$ means that $\mathcal{D}$ defines the name X as process Q.

Definition 5 (LTS Semantics of CCS). *The LTS of a CCS process* Q *with defining equations* $\mathcal{D}$*, written* $LTS(Q, \mathcal{D})$*, has the least transition relation* $\rightarrow$ *induced by the rules below:*

$$\text{PREF}\frac{}{\mu.Q \xrightarrow{\mu} Q} \qquad \text{SUM1}\frac{Q_1 \xrightarrow{\mu} Q_1'}{Q_1 + Q_2 \xrightarrow{\mu} Q_1'} \qquad \text{PAR1}\frac{Q_1 \xrightarrow{\mu} Q_1'}{Q_1 \mid Q_2 \xrightarrow{\mu} Q_1' \mid Q_2}$$

$$\text{CONS}\frac{Q \xrightarrow{\mu} Q'}{X \xrightarrow{\mu} Q'}\mathcal{D}(X) = Q \qquad \text{SUM2}\frac{Q_2 \xrightarrow{\mu} Q_2'}{Q_1 + Q_2 \xrightarrow{\mu} Q_2'} \qquad \text{PAR2}\frac{Q_2 \xrightarrow{\mu} Q_2'}{Q_1 \mid Q_2 \xrightarrow{\mu} Q_1 \mid Q_2'}$$

$$\text{COM}\frac{Q_1 \xrightarrow{a} Q_1' \quad Q_2 \xrightarrow{\bar{a}} Q_2'}{Q_1 \mid Q_2 \xrightarrow{\tau} Q_1' \mid Q_2'} \qquad \text{RES}\frac{Q \xrightarrow{\mu} Q'}{(\nu a)Q \xrightarrow{\mu} (\nu a)Q'}\mu \neq a, \bar{a}$$

By rule PREF in Definition 5, actions (a), co-actions ($\bar{a}$), and internal actions (τ) can be executed by consuming the prefix of a sequential process: for example, we have $a.\mathbf{0} \xrightarrow{a} \mathbf{0}$. The rules SUM1 and SUM2 allow for executing either the left or right branch of a choice: for example, we have $Q \xleftarrow{a} a.Q + b.Q' \xrightarrow{b} Q'$. By rule RES, actions and co-actions cannot be executed when restricted; for example, we have $(\nu b)(a.\mathbf{0}) \xrightarrow{a} (\nu b)\mathbf{0}$, whereas b cannot be executed in $(\nu b)(b.\mathbf{0})$. By rule COM, an action can *synchronize* with its co-action, producing an internal τ-action; for example, b can synchronize with $\bar{b}$, so we have $b.\mathbf{0} \mid \bar{b}.\mathbf{0} \xrightarrow{\tau} \mathbf{0} \mid \mathbf{0}$; this also works under restriction (by rule RES), so we have $(\nu b)(b.\mathbf{0} \mid \bar{b}.\mathbf{0}) \xrightarrow{\tau} (\nu b)(\mathbf{0} \mid \mathbf{0})$.

Petri Nets. We adopt standard definitions of labelled Petri nets (that we simply call *Petri nets*), marking, and firing rules (Definitions 6, 7, and 8, based on [3]). We also highlight two classes of Petri nets commonly used in process mining literature: *workflow nets* (Definition 9) and *free-choice nets* (Definition 10).

Definition 6 (Labelled Petri Net). *A* labelled Petri net *is a tuple* (P, T, F, A, σ) *where P is a finite set of* places, *T is a finite set of* transitions *such that $P \cap T = \emptyset$, and $F \subseteq (P \times T) \cup (T \times P)$ is a set of directed edges from places to transitions or vice versa; moreover, A is a set of* actions *and $\sigma : T \to A$ assigns an action to each transition.*

Notably, Definition 6 only allows for at most one (unweighted) edge between each pair of places and transitions, and does *not* allow co-actions in A: we keep co-actions exclusive to CCS (Definition 4) to avoid renaming in our encodings.

Definition 7 (Marking). *A* marking *of a Petri net (P, T, F, A, σ) is a mapping $M : P \to \mathbb{N}$ from each place $p \in P$ to the number of tokens in p (may be 0).*

Definition 8 (Firing Rule). *Given a Petri net (P, T, F, A, σ) and a marking $M : P \to \mathbb{N}$, a transition $t \in T$ is* enabled *if all places with an edge to t have tokens in M. Transition t can* fire *if enabled, and this firing consumes one token from all places with an edge to t, emits a label $\sigma(t)$, and produces one token for all places with an edge from t. This results in an updated marking M'.*

A Petri net $N = (P, T, F, A, \sigma)$ and an initial marking M_0 yields $LTS(N, M_0) = (Q, A, \to)$ where the states (Q) and the transition relation $(\to)$ are derived using the firing rule (Definition 8) until all enabled transitions t in all reachable markings are added to $\to$, with $\sigma(t)$ as transition label.

Process mining algorithms like the α-miner typically produce *workflow nets* (Definition 9) that are used to describe end-to-end processes with a clear start and completion. In practical applications, such workflow nets are often *free-choice*[1] (Definitions 10 and 11) where all choices are made by a single place—meaning that transitions can at most fight for one token in order to fire. Figures 2, 3, 4, and 5 show examples of Petri nets with small differences resulting in different classes.

Definition 9 (Workflow Net [3, Definition 2.8]). *A Petri net (P, T, F, A, σ) is a* workflow net *iff it satisfies the following three properties:*

- **Object Creation:** *P has an* input place *i with no ingoing edges.*
- **Object Completion:** *P has an* output place *o with no outgoing edges.*
- **Connectedness:** *For every $v \in P \cup T$, there exists a directed path of edges from i to o that goes through v.*

---

[1] The α-miner actually returns a further subclass of free-choice workflow nets called *structured workflow nets* [3].

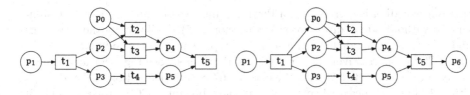

Fig. 2. Neither free-choice or workflow net.

Fig. 3. Workflow but not free-choice net.

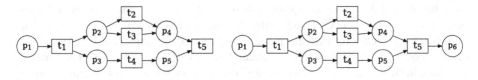

Fig. 4. Free-choice but not workflow net.

Fig. 5. Free-choice net and workflow net.

Definition 10 (Free-Choice Net [10]). *A Petri net (P, T, F, A, σ) is a* free-choice net *iff it satisfies the following two properties:*

- **Unique Choice**: *All places $p \in P$ with more than one outgoing edge only have edges to transitions with exactly one ingoing edge (edge from p).*
- **Unique Synchronisation**: *All transitions $t \in T$ with more than one ingoing edge only have edges from places with exactly one outgoing edge (edge to t).*

Definition 11 (Free-Choice Workflow Net). *If a Petri net is both a workflow net and free-choice, we call it a* free-choice workflow net.

The *connectedness* property in Definition 9 implies that all transitions in free-choice workflow nets have at least one ingoing edge and at least one outgoing edge. The same applies to all places except the special places i and o that respectively has no ingoing edges (i) and no outgoing edges (o). The *unique choice and synchronisation* properties in Definition 10 ensure that every choice is separated from all synchronisations and *vice versa*. This does *not* rule out cycles but *unique choice* restricts all outgoing edges *leaving* a cycle to lead to transitions with exactly one ingoing edge (because there is always one edge *continuing* the cycle). For instance, adding a new transition t_7 in Fig. 5 to form the cycle $(p_3, t_4, p_5, t_7, p_3)$ would violate *unique choice* (and *unique synchronisation*) because the edge (p_5, t_5) leaves the cycle but t_5 has two ingoing edges. Adding the cycle (p_3, t_7, p_3) is allowed because t_4 only has one ingoing edge.

4   Encoding Petri Nets into CCS, Step-by-Step

This section introduces our main contribution: an encoding into CCS of a super-class of free-choice nets, that we call *group-choice nets* (Definition 15); we prove that our encoding is correct, i.e., a Petri net and its encoding are weakly bisimilar and without added divergent states (Theorem 7). To illustrate the encodings and result, we proceed through a series of steps: a series of encoding algorithms into CCS for progressively larger classes of Petri nets. (See Fig. 1 for an outline.)

We begin (in Sect. 4.1) with the class of *CCS nets* (Definition 12), and Algorithm 1 that encodes such nets into strongly bisimilar CCS processes (Theorem 1).[2] Then (in Sect. 4.2) we develop a novel transformation from *free-choice workflow nets* (Definition 11) to weakly bismilar CCS nets using Algorithm 3 (Theorem 3). The composition of Algorithm 3 and Algorithm 1 then encodes free-choice workflow nets into weakly bismilar CCS processes (Theorem 4). In Sect. 4.3, we generalise CCS nets into *2-τ-synchronisation nets* (Definition 13, allowing for transitions with no ingoing edges) and we present Algorithm 4 to encode such nets into strongly bisimilar CCS processes (Theorem 6). Finally (cf. Sect. 4.4), we generalize free-choice nets to a new class called *group-choice nets* (Definition 15) and present Algorithm 6 that, composed with Algorithm 4, encodes group-choice nets into weakly bisimilar CCS processes (Theorem 7).

4.1   Encoding CCS Nets into CCS Processes

A challenge in encoding Petri nets into CCS processes is that a transition in a Petri net can consume tokens from any number of places in a single step — whereas the semantics of CCS (Definition 5) only allow for executing a single action or a synchronisation between two processes in each step. In other words, Petri nets are able to perform n-ary synchronisation, while CCS can only perform 2-ary synchronisation. Therefore, as a stepping stone towards our main result, we adopt *CCS nets* from [13], whose synchronisation capabilities match CCS.

Definition 12 (CCS Net [13]). *A Petri net (P, T, F, A, σ) is a CCS net iff each transition $t \in T$ has one or two ingoing edges — and in the latter case, $\sigma(t) = \tau$.*

The key insight behind Definition 12 is that transitions with two ingoing edges must be labeled with τ to have a 1-to-1 correspondence to synchronisation in CCS (that also emits a τ). Figure 12 shows a CCS net that later will be encoded.

Algorithm 1 encodes a CCS net (P, T, F, A, σ) and marking M_0 into a CCS process Q and its defining equations $\mathcal{D}$, where $\mathcal{D}$ defines a process named X_p for each place $p \in P$. The idea is that each token at place p is encoded as a parallel replica of the process X_p. We illustrate the algorithm in the next paragraphs.

On line 2–4, each place $p \in P$ is encoded as a *choice process* named X_p in $\mathcal{D}$: The choice is among placeholder processes named Y_t, for each transition t with an edge from p. (Notice that the placeholders Y_t are not in the domain of $\mathcal{D}$, but are substituted with sequential CCS processes in the next steps of

---

[2] The results in Sect. 4.1 can be also derived from [13], but here we provide a direct encoding algorithm, statements, and proofs for plain CCS, without using Multi-CCS.

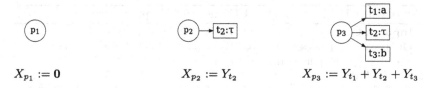

$$X_{p_1} := \mathbf{0}$$

$$X_{p_2} := Y_{t_2}$$

$$X_{p_3} := Y_{t_1} + Y_{t_2} + Y_{t_3}$$

Fig. 6. Place with 0 outgoing edges and its encoding.

Fig. 7. Place with 1 outgoing edge and its encoding.

Fig. 8. Place with 3 outgoing edges and its encoding.

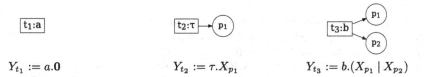

$$Y_{t_1} := a.\mathbf{0}$$

$$Y_{t_2} := \tau.X_{p_1}$$

$$Y_{t_3} := b.(X_{p_1} \mid X_{p_2})$$

Fig. 9. Encoding of transition with 0 outgoing edges.

Fig. 10. Encoding of transition with 1 outgoing edge.

Fig. 11. Encoding of transition with 2 outgoing edges.

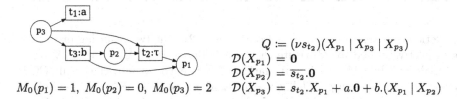

$M_0(p_1) = 1,\ M_0(p_2) = 0,\ M_0(p_3) = 2$

$$Q := (\nu s_{t_2})(X_{p_1} \mid X_{p_3} \mid X_{p_3})$$
$$\mathcal{D}(X_{p_1}) = \mathbf{0}$$
$$\mathcal{D}(X_{p_2}) = \overline{s_{t_2}}.\mathbf{0}$$
$$\mathcal{D}(X_{p_3}) = s_{t_2}.X_{p_1} + a.\mathbf{0} + b.(X_{p_1} \mid X_{p_2})$$

Fig. 12. CCS net N and initial marking M_0 with three tokens.

Fig. 13. Encoding of N and M_0 in Fig. 12 into Q and $\mathcal{D}$ produced by Algorithm 1.

the algorithm.) The choice process X_p models a token at p that *chooses* which transition it is used for. Figures 6, 7 and 8 show examples.

On line 5–7, each transition $t \in T$ with one ingoing edge from a place p^* is encoded as a process with an action prefix (obtained via the labelling function $\sigma(t)$) followed by the *parallel composition* of all processes named X_{p_i}, where place p_i has an ingoing edge from t. Figures 9, 10, and 11 show examples. The resulting process $\sigma(t).(X_{p_1} \mid \ldots \mid X_{p_k})$ (line 6) models the execution of the action $\sigma(t)$ followed by the production of tokens for places $p_1, \ldots, p_k$, and such a process is used to substitute the placeholder Y_t in $\mathcal{D}(X_{p^*})$.

On line 8–13, each transition $t \in T$ with two ingoing edges from p^* and p^{**} (where t has label $\sigma(t) = \tau$, by Definition 12) is encoded as a synchronisation between a fresh action s_t (which prefixes $(X_{p_1} \mid \ldots \mid X_{p_k})$ on line 11 to model

---

Algorithm 1: Encoding from CCS net to CCS process

Input : CCS net (P, T, F, A, σ) and marking $M_0 : P \to \mathbb{N}$

Output: CCS process Q and partial mapping of defining equations $\mathcal{D}$

1   $\mathcal{D} \leftarrow$ Empty mapping of defining equations

2   **for** $p \in P$ **do**

3 | $\mathcal{D}(X_p) \leftarrow (Y_{t_1} + Y_{t_2} + \cdots + Y_{t_k})$ **where** $\{t_1, t_2, \ldots, t_k\} = \{t \mid (p, t) \in F\}$

4   **end**

5   **for** $t \in \{t \mid t \in T \text{ and } t \text{ has 1 ingoing edge}\}$ **do**

6 | **substitute** Y_t in $\mathcal{D}(X_{p^*})$ **with** $\sigma(t).(X_{p_1} \mid X_{p_2} \mid \ldots \mid X_{p_k})$ **where**
        $(p^*, t) \in F$ and $\{p_1, p_2, \ldots, p_k\} = \{p \mid (t, p) \in F\}$

7   **end**

8   $A' \leftarrow \emptyset$

9   **for** $t \in \{t \mid t \in T \text{ and } t \text{ has 2 ingoing edges}\}$ **do**

10 | $A' \leftarrow A' \cup \{s_t\}$ **where** s_t is a fresh action

11 | **substitute** Y_t in $\mathcal{D}(X_{p^*})$ **with** $s_t.(X_{p_1} \mid X_{p_2} \mid \ldots \mid X_{p_k})$

12 | **substitute** Y_t in $\mathcal{D}(X_{p^{**}})$ **with** $\overline{s_t}.0$ **where**
        $(p^*, t), (p^{**}, t) \in F$ and $p^* \neq p^{**}$ and $\{p_1, p_2, \ldots, p_k\} = \{p \mid (t, p) \in F\}$

13   **end**

14   $\{s_1, s_2, \ldots, s_n\} \leftarrow A'$

15   $Q \leftarrow (\nu s_1)(\nu s_2) \ldots (\nu s_n) \left(X_{p_1}^{M_0(p_1)} \mid X_{p_2}^{M_0(p_2)} \mid \ldots \mid X_{p_{|P|}}^{M_0(p_{|P|})} \right)$

16   **return** $(Q, \mathcal{D})$

---

production of tokens), and its co-action $\overline{s_t}$ (line 12). The two resulting processes are respectively used to substitute the placeholder Y_t in $\mathcal{D}(X_{p^*})$ and $\mathcal{D}(X_{p^{**}})$.

Finally, on line 15, the initial marking M_0 is encoded into the result CCS process Q, which is the *parallel composition* of one place process X_{p_i} per token at place p_i, under a restriction of each fresh action s_i produced on line 10. Note that we write Q^n for the parallel composition of n replicas of Q, so $Q^3 = Q|Q|Q$, and $Q^1 = Q$, and $Q^0 = \mathbf{0}$. The algorithm also returns the partial mapping $\mathcal{D}$ with the definition of each process name X_p (for each $p \in P$) occurring in Q.

Figure 13 shows the encoding of the CCS net in Fig. 12. Observe that in X_{p_3}, the transitions t_1 and t_3 (which have one ingoing edge) yield respectively the sub-processes $a.\mathbf{0}$ and $b.(X_{p_1} \mid X_{p_2})$ (produced by line 5–7 in Algorithm 1); instead, t_2 (which has two ingoing edges and label τ) yields both sub-processes $s_{t_2}.X_{p_1}$ in X_{p_3} and $\overline{s_{t_2}}.\mathbf{0}$ in X_{p_2} (produced by line 9–13 in Algorithm 1).

Theorem 1 (Correctness of Algorithm 1). *Given a CCS net* $N = (P, T, F, A, \sigma)$ *and an initial marking* M_0, *let the result of applying Algorithm 1 to* N *and* M_0 *be the CCS process* Q *and defining equations* $\mathcal{D}$. *Then,* $LTS(N, M_0) \sim LTS(Q, \mathcal{D})$. *The translation time and the size of* $(Q, \mathcal{D})$ *are bound by* $O(|N| + \sum_{p \in P} M_0(p))$.

Proof. (Sketch, detailed proof in [8].) We define the following relation between markings and processes, and we prove it is a bisimulation:

$$\mathcal{R} := \left\{ \left(M, (\nu s_1) \ldots (\nu s_n) \left(X_{p_1}^{M(p_1)} \mid \ldots \mid X_{p_{|P|}}^{M(p_{|P|})} \right) \right) \mid M \in LTS(N, M_0) \right\}$$

where M is a reachable marking from the initial marking M_0 in N (i.e. M is a state in $LTS(N, M_0)$), and $s_1, \ldots, s_n$ are the restricted names in Q. The intuition is as that for every place p containing $M(p)$ tokens, the CCS process contains $M(p)$ replicas of the process named X_p (written $X_p^{M(p)}$). □

The strong bisimulation result in Theorem 1 ensures that there are no observable differences between the original Petri net and its encoding, so Algorithm 1 does not introduce new deadlocks nor divergent paths. The encoding is also linear in the size of the CCS net N and the size of the initial marking M_0.

4.2   Encoding Free-Choice Workflow Nets into CCS Processes

We now build upon the result in Sect. 4.1 to prove that *free-choice workflow nets* (Definition 11) are encodable into weakly bisimilar CCS processes. Specifically, we present a stepwise transformation procedure (Algorithm 2 and 3) from a free-choice workflow net into weakly bisimilar CCS net (Theorem 3), and then apply Algorithm 1 to get a weakly bisimilar CCS process (Theorem 4).

It should be noted (as illustrated in Fig. 1) that free-choice (workflow) nets does *not* contain the class of CCS nets: Fig. 12 is not a free-choice net since p_3 has multiple outgoing edges of which one leads to a transition with multiple ingoing edges. However, as will be shown in this section, a free-choice workflow net can be transformed into a CCS net by (non-deterministically) making a binary synchronisation order for each n-ary synchronisation.

An application of Algorithm 2 transforms an input Petri net by reducing the number of ingoing edges of the selected transition t^* (which must have two or more ingoing edges): it selects two distinct ingoing edges (line 1), creates a new τ-transition t^+ with an edge to a new place p^+, and connects the new place p^+ to the selected transition t^* (line 2–5). The cost of the transformation is that a new τ-transition t^+ with two ingoing edges is created. Figures 14 and 15 show an example application on a free-choice net, where t_1 is selected for transformation with the edges (p_2, t_1) and (p_3, t_1). Algorithm 2 can be iterated until all the original transitions only have one ingoing edge left; transitions with no ingoing edges are left untouched. Hence, transformed free-choice workflow nets will have no transitions with zero ingoing edges, hence Algorithm 1 could be applied.

Algorithm 2: Petri net transition preset reduction

Input : Petri net (P, T, F, A, σ), marking $M_0 : P \to \mathbb{N}$ and chosen transition $t^* \in T$ with at least two ingoing edges

Output: Petri net $(P', T', F', A', \sigma')$ and marking $M_0' : P' \to \mathbb{N}$

1 **select** $(p^*, t^*), (p^{**}, t^*) \in F$ **where** $p^* \neq p^{**}$

2 $P' \leftarrow P \cup \{p^+\}$ **where** $p^+ \notin P \cup T$

3 $T' \leftarrow T \cup \{t^+\}$ **where** $t^+ \notin P' \cup T$

4 $F' \leftarrow (F \setminus \{(p^*, t^*), (p^{**}, t^*)\}) \cup \{(p^*, t^+), (p^{**}, t^+), (t^+, p^+), (p^+, t^*)\}$

5 $N' \leftarrow (P', T', F', A \cup \{\tau\}, \sigma[t^+ \mapsto \tau])$

6 **return** $(N', M_0[p^+ \mapsto 0])$

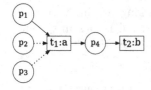

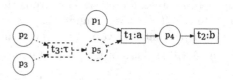

Fig. 14. Free-choice net where t_1 and the dotted edges (p_2, t_1) and (p_3, t_1) are chosen for transformation.

Fig. 15. Free-choice net obtained from Fig. 14 where the dotted edges have been moved and the dashed elements t_3 and p_5 have been added.

Figures 14 and 15 show that Algorithm 2 does *not* produce a Petri net that is strongly bisimilar to its input: if we only have one token in both p_2 and p_3, then Fig. 15 can fire the τ-transition while Fig. 14 is in a deadlock. However, Theorem 2 below proves that, when applied to free-choice nets (and thereby also free-choice workflow nets), Algorithm 2 produces a weakly bisimilar Petri net. Moreover, by Lemma 1, the returned net remains a free-choice net.

Theorem 2 (Correctness of Algorithm 2). *Given a free-choice net $N = (P, T, F, A, \sigma)$, a marking $M_0 : P \to \mathbb{N}$, and a transition $t^* \in T$ (with at least two ingoing edges), the result of applying Algorithm 2 on N, M_0, and t^* is a Petri net N' and marking M_0' such that $LTS(N, M_0) \approx LTS(N', M_0')$ and $LTS(N', M_0')$ contains a divergent path iff $LTS(N, M_0)$ contains a divergent path. The transformation time and the increase in size are amortized $O(1)$.*

Proof. (Sketch, detailed proof in [8].) We define the following relation between pair of markings, and we prove it is a bisimulation:

$$\mathcal{R} := \left\{ \left(M, \; M[p^* \mapsto M(p^*) - i][p^{**} \mapsto M(p^{**}) - i][p^+ \mapsto i] \right) \middle| \begin{array}{l} M \in LTS(N, M_0) \\ k = \min(M(p^*), M(p^{**})) \\ 0 \leq i \leq k \end{array} \right\}$$

where M is a reachable marking from the initial marking M_0 in the free-choice net N (M is a state in $LTS(N, M_0)$). The intuition behind the relation is: when $i = 0$, it covers the direct extension of a marking in N to one in N' where the new place p^+ has no tokens; when $i > 0$, it covers the cases where the new transition t^+ has been fired i times without firing t^* afterwards.

For instance, consider Figs. 14 and 15 where $t^* = t_1$, $p^* = p_2$, $p^{**} = p_3$, $t^+ = t_3$ and $p^+ = p_5$. Clearly, the initial markings (M_0, M_0') are in $\mathcal{R}$ since Algorithm 2 just extends M_0 to M_0' where p^+ has zero tokens. Now consider any pair $(M, M') \in \mathcal{R}$. The transition t_2 is not part of the transformed part, so t_2 can be fired in N iff it can be fired in N'. Firing t_1 in N can be replied in N' by firing t_1 when there is a token in p_5 ($i > 0$) and otherwise by firing t_3 followed by t_1 ($i = 0$). Firing t_1 in N' can be replied in N by also firing t_1. If t_3 is fired in N' then N should do nothing as this simply merges the tokens from p_2 and p_3 into one token in p_5 by a τ-action (increases i by one). All these cases result in a new pair in $\mathcal{R}$ which completes the proof of $LTS(N, M_0) \approx LTS(N', M_0')$.

Algorithm 3: Iterative Petri net transition preset reduction

Input : Free-choice net $N = (P, T, F, A, \sigma)$ and marking $M_0 : P \to \mathbb{N}$
Output: Petri net $(P', T', F', A', \sigma')$ and marking $M'_0 : P' \to \mathbb{N}$
1 $(N', M'_0) \leftarrow (N, M_0)$
2 **while** $\exists t^* \in T'$ **where** $|\{p \,|\, (p, t^*) \in F\}| > ($**if** $\sigma(t^*) = \tau$ **then** 2 **else** 1$)$ **do**
3 $\quad|\quad (N', M'_0) \leftarrow$ Algorithm $2(N', M'_0, t^*)$
4 **end**
5 **return** (N', M'_0)

In general, weak bisimulation alone does not ensure the absence of new divergent paths [14]. However, Algorithm 2 only extends existing paths to t^* by one τ-transition such that no divergent paths are changed, so $LTS(N', M'_0)$ contains a divergent path iff $LTS(N, M_0)$ contains a divergent path. □

Lemma 1 (Invariant of Algorithm 2). *If Algorithm 2 is given a free-choice net N, it returns a free-choice net N' that has no additional or changed transitions with no ingoing edges compared to N.* (Proof available in [8].)

To achieve our encoding of free-choice workflow into CCS nets we use Algorithm 3, which applies Algorithm 2 (by non-deterministically picking a transition t^*) until all transitions have at most one ingoing edge (or two for τ-transitions). If Algorithm 3 is applied to a free-choice workflow net, it returns a CCS net (Lemma 2) that is weakly bisimilar and has no new divergent paths (Theorem 3).

Lemma 2 (Algorithm 3 Output). *If applied to a free-choice workflow net (P, T, F, A, σ), Algorithm 3 returns a CCS net.* (Proof: [8].)

Theorem 3 (Correctness of Algorithm 3). *Given a free-choice net $N = (P, T, F, A, \sigma)$ and a marking $M_0 : P \to \mathbb{N}$, the result of applying Algorithm 3 on N and M_0 is a Petri net N' and marking M'_0 such that $LTS(N, M_0) \approx LTS(N', M'_0)$ and $LTS(N, M_0)$ has a divergent path iff $LTS(N', M'_0)$ has. Both the transformation time and the size of (N', M') are $O(|N|)$.*

Proof. (Sketch, detailed proof in [8].) Follows from induction on the number of applications of Algorithm 2 and transitivity of bisimulation [14]. □

The full encoding from a free-choice workflow net into a weakly bisimilar CCS process is obtained by composing Algorithm 3 and Algorithm 1, leading to Theorem 4. Algorithm 2 can at most be applied $|F|$ times. It runs in constant time and increases the size by a constant amount such that Algorithm 3 produces a linear-sized CCS net. Hence, the resulting CCS process is also linear in size of the original Petri net and marking.

Theorem 4 (Correctness of Encoding from Free-Choice Workflow Net to CCS). *Let $N = (P, T, F, A, \sigma)$ be a free-choice workflow net and M_0 :*

Algorithm 4: Encoding from 2-τ-synchronisation net to CCS process

---

Input : 2-τ-synchronisation net $N = (P, T, F, A, \sigma)$ and marking $M_0 : P \to \mathbb{N}$

Output: CCS process Q and partial mapping of defining equations $\mathcal{D}$

1 $(\_, \mathcal{D}) \leftarrow$ Algorithm 1(N, M_0)

2 $T_0 \leftarrow t \in \{t \mid t \in T$ and t has 0 ingoing edges$\}$

3 **for** $t \in T_0$ **do**

4 $\quad \mid \quad \mathcal{D}(X_t) \leftarrow \sigma(t).(X_t \mid X_{p_1} \mid \ldots \mid X_{p_k})$ **where** $\{p_1, \ldots, p_k\} = \{p \mid (t, p) \in F\}$

5 **end**

6 $Q \leftarrow (\nu s_1) \ldots (\nu s_n) \left(X_{p_1}^{M_0(p_1)} \mid \ldots \mid X_{p_{|P|}}^{M_0(p_{|P|})} \mid \underbrace{X_{t_1} \mid \ldots \mid X_{t_k}}_{t_i \in \{t_1, \ldots, t_k\} = T_0} \right)$

7 **return** $(Q, \mathcal{D})$

$P \to \mathbb{N}$ be a marking. N and M_0 can be encoded into a weakly bisimilar CCS process Q with defining equations $\mathcal{D}$ such that $LTS(N, M_0)$ has a divergent path iff $LTS(Q, \mathcal{D})$ has. The encoding time and the size of $(Q, \mathcal{D})$ are $O(|N| + \sum_{p \in P} M_0(p))$.

Proof. By Lemma 1+2, Theorem 3+1 and transitivity of bisimulation [14]. $\square$

4.3 Encoding Any Free-Choice Net into CCS

Although the focus of Sect. 4.2 is encoding free-choice *workflow* nets into CCS, many definitions and results therein can be applied to *any* free-choice net (Algorithm 2, Theorem 2, Lemma 1, Algorithm 3, Theorem 3). In this section we build upon them to develop an encoding from *any* free-choice net into CCS.

To achieve this result, we define a superclass of CCS nets (Definition 12) called *2-τ-synchronisation nets* (Definition 13, below), which may have transitions with no ingoing edges. Such transitions can be seen as *token generators*: they can always fire and produce tokens; they do not occur in workflow nets, and they would be dropped if given to Algorithm 1 because they do not originate from any place. For this reason, token generator transitions are handled separately in Algorithm 4 (which extends Algorithm 1).

Definition 13 (2-τ-Synchronisation Net). *A Petri net* (P, T, F, A, σ) *is a 2-τ-synchronisation net iff each transition* $t \in T$ *has at most two ingoing edges — and in the latter case,* $\sigma(t) = \tau$.

Line 1 of Algorithm 4 retrieves the defining equations $\mathcal{D}$ returned by Algorithm 1 (the returned CCS process is not used). Line 2 defines T_0 as all transitions $t \in T$ with no ingoing edges. Each transition $t \in T_0$ is encoded as a sequential process named X_t in $\mathcal{D}$ (line 3–5). X_t is defined as $\sigma(t)$ followed by the *parallel composition* of X_t (itself) and all processes named X_{p_i}, where p_i has an ingoing edge from t. This ensures that whenever X_t is used, then it spawns a new copy of itself that can be used again. Finally on line 6, all X_{t_i}, where $t_i \in T_0$, are included once in the process Q to be available from the start. For instance, the simple 2-τ-synchronisation net $N = (\{p_1\}, \{t_1\}, \{(t_1, p_1)\}, \{b\}, [t_1 \mapsto b])$ and marking M_0

with $M_0(p_1) = 0$ are encoded into $(X_{t_1}, \mathcal{D})$ where $\mathcal{D}(X_{t_1}) = b.(X_{t_1} \mid X_{p_1})$ which gives a process where X_{t_1} is always present: $X_{t_1} \xrightarrow{b} (X_{p_1} \mid X_{t_1}) \xrightarrow{b} (X_{p_1}^2 \mid X_{t_1}) \xrightarrow{b} \ldots$ Algorithm 4 also produces strongly bisimilar CCS processes like Algorithm 1.

Theorem 5 (Correctness of Algorithm 4). *Given a 2-τ-synchronisation net $N = (P, T, F, A, \sigma)$ and an initial marking $M_0 : P \to \mathbb{N}$, the result of applying Algorithm 4 on N and M_0 is $(Q, \mathcal{D})$ such that $LTS(N, M_0) \sim LTS(Q, \mathcal{D})$. The translation time and the size of $(Q, \mathcal{D})$ are bound by $O(|N| + \sum_{p \in P} M_0(p))$.*

Proof. (Sketch, detailed proof in [8].) Extend the proof of Theorem 1 by extending the parallel composition in *all* CCS processes in the relation $\mathcal{R}$ with the parallel composition of all X_{t_i}, where $t_i \in T_0$. $\square$

The CCS process obtained from Algorithm 4 is linear in size of the encoded 2-τ-synchronisation net and marking. Theorem 5 allows us to extend the encoding of free-choice workflow nets to free-choice nets.

Lemma 3 (Algorithm 3 Output). *If applied to a free-choice net (P, T, F, A, σ), Algorithm 3 returns a 2-τ-synchronisation net.* (Proof: [8].)

Theorem 6 (Correctness of Free-Choice Net to CCS Encoding). *Let $N = (P, T, F, A, \sigma)$ be a free-choice net and $M_0 : P \to \mathbb{N}$ be an initial marking. N and M_0 can be encoded into a weakly bisimilar CCS process Q with defining equations $\mathcal{D}$ such that $LTS(N, M_0)$ has a divergent path iff $LTS(Q, \mathcal{D})$ has. The encoding time and the size of $(Q, \mathcal{D})$ are $O(|N| + \sum_{p \in P} M_0(p))$.*

Proof. By Lemma 1+3, Theorem 3+5 and transitivity of bisimulation [14]. $\square$

4.4 Group-Choice Nets

We now further extend our CCS encodability results. Free-choice nets (Definition 10) only allow for choices taken by a *single* place; we relax this requirement by defining a larger class of nets called *group-choice nets* (Definition 15, below), where choices can be taken by a *group* of places which synchronise before making the choice. This requires that all places in the group *agree* on their options — which corresponds to all places in the group having the same postset (i.e., edges to the same transitions). No other places outside the group may have edges to those transitions (as that would affect the choice).

Definition 14 (Postset of a Place). *Let (P, T, F, A, σ) be a Petri net. The postset of a place $p \in P$ (written $p\bullet$) is the set of all transitions with an ingoing edge from p, i.e.: $p\bullet :- \{t \mid p \in P, (p, t) \in F\}$.*

Definition 15 (Group-Choice Net). *A Petri net N is a group-choice net iff all pairs of places either have a same postset, or disjoint postsets.*

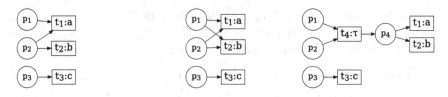

Fig. 16. Petri net with $p_1\bullet = \{t_1\}$, $p_2\bullet = \{t_1, t_2\}$ and $p_3\bullet = \{t_3\}$.

Fig. 17. Group-choice net with $p_1\bullet = p_2\bullet = \{t_1, t_2\}$ and $p_3\bullet = \{t_3\}$.

Fig. 18. Result of Algorithm 5 on Fig. 17. $p_1\bullet = p_2\bullet = \{t_4\}$, $p_3\bullet = \{t_3\}$ and $p_4\bullet = \{t_1, t_2\}$.

Algorithm 5: Group-choice net transition preset reduction

Input : Petri net $N = (P, T, F, A, \sigma)$, marking $M_0 : P \to \mathbb{N}$ and two selected places $p^*, p^{**} \in P$ where $p^*\bullet = p^{**}\bullet \neq \emptyset$

Output: Petri net $(P', T', F', A', \sigma')$ and marking $M_0' : P' \to \mathbb{N}$

1 $P' \leftarrow P \cup \{p^+\}$ **where** $p^+ \notin P \cup T$

2 $T' \leftarrow T \cup \{t^+\}$ **where** $t^+ \notin P' \cup T$

3 $F' \leftarrow \left(\begin{array}{l} \left(F \setminus (\{(p^*, t) \mid t \in p^*\bullet\} \cup \{(p^{**}, t) \mid t \in p^{**}\bullet\}) \right) \\ \cup \; \{(p^*, t^+), (p^{**}, t^+), (t^+, p^+)\} \cup \{(p^+, t) \mid t \in p^*\bullet\} \end{array} \right)$

4 $N' \leftarrow (P', T', F', A \cup \{\tau\}, \sigma[t^+ \mapsto \tau])$

5 **return** $(N', M_0[p^+ \mapsto 0])$

A group-choice net does not have partially overlapping place postsets. Therefore, its places can be split into *disjoint groups* where all places in a group have the same postset. Figures 16, 17, and 18 show examples of Petri nets and postsets for each place. Figure 16 is not a group-choice net because $p_1\bullet$ and $p_2\bullet$ are only partially overlapping (since p_2 has an edge to t_2 while p_1 does not). Figure 17 is a group-choice net, hence its places can be split into two disjoint groups $\{p_1, p_2\}$ and $\{p_3\}$. Figure 18 is a group-choice net with three groups of places.

A place postset of size at least two (like $p_4\bullet$ in Fig. 18) corresponds to a choice because the place can choose between at least two transitions. When at least two places have the same postset (like $p_1\bullet$ and $p_2\bullet$ in Fig. 18), it corresponds to synchronisation because the transitions in the postset have at least two ingoing edges. The definition of group-choice nets ensures that choice and synchronisation can only happen at the same time if the group of places can safely synchronise before making a choice together. A free-choice net further require that every place postset must not correspond to both choice and synchronisation.

The transformation of group-choice nets into 2-τ-synchronisation nets is intuitively similar to the transformation of free-choice nets (in Sect. 4.2). The key difference is that, since places in group-choice nets can have more than one outgoing edge when they synchronise on a transition, we consider whole place postsets instead of a single transition. Algorithm 5 does this by selecting two places p^*

and p^{**} with the same (non-empty) postset: It removes all their outgoing edges (line 3) and connects them to a new τ-transition t^+ (defined on line 2) with an edge to a new place p^+ (defined on line 1) that has outgoing edges to the same postset p^* and p^{**} originally had (lines 3–5). This reduces the number of ingoing edges (i.e., the *preset*) of *all* transitions in $p^* \bullet$ by one. Figure 18 shows the result of one application of Algorithm 5 on Fig. 17 with $p^* = p_1$ and $p^{**} = p_2$.

Algorithm 6: Iterative group-choice net transition preset reduction

Input : Group-choice net $N = (P, T, F, A, \sigma)$ and marking $M_0 : P \to \mathbb{N}$
Output: Petri net $(P', T', F', A', \sigma')$ and marking $M_0' : P' \to \mathbb{N}$
1 $(N', M_0') \leftarrow (N, M_0)$
2 **while** $\exists t^* \in T'$ where $|\{p \mid (p, t^*) \in F\}| >$ (**if** $\sigma(t^*) = \tau$ **then** 2 **else** 1) **do**
3   **select** $(p_1, t^*), (p_2, t^*) \in F$ **where** $p_1 \neq p_2$
4      $(N', M_0') \leftarrow$ Algorithm 5(N', M_0', p_1, p_2)
5 **end**
6 **return** (N', M_0')

Algorithm 6 keeps applying Algorithm 5 on the input group-choice net (in the same fashion as Algorithm 3) by non-deterministically picking p_1 and p_2, until a 2-τ-synchronisation net is obtained. All the proofs for the encoding of group-choice nets are similar to the ones for free-choice nets: The only difference is that the proofs for group-choice nets consider *sets* of impacted transitions instead of single transitions. Therefore, we only present the main result below.

Theorem 7 (Correctness of Group-Choice Net to CCS Encoding). *A group-choice net $N = (P, T, F, A, \sigma)$ and an initial marking $M_0 : P \to \mathbb{N}$ can be encoded into a weakly bisimilar CCS process Q with defining equations $\mathcal{D}$ s.t. $LTS(N, M_0)$ has a divergent path iff $LTS(Q, \mathcal{D})$ has. The encoding time and the size of $(Q, \mathcal{D})$ are $O(|N| + \sum_{p \in P} M_0(p))$. (Proofs in [8].)*

5   Conclusion and Future Work

In this paper we have formalised a direct encoding of CCS nets into strongly bisimilar CCS processes (akin to [13]), and on this foundation we have developed novel Petri net-to-CCS encodings and results, through a series of generalizations. We have introduced an encoding of *free-choice workflow nets* into weakly bisimilar CCS processes. We have generalized this result as an encoding from *any* free-choice net into a weakly bisimilar CCS processes, via a new superclass of CCS nets called *2-τ-synchronisation nets* (which may have token-generating transitions). Finally, we have presented a superclass of free-choice nets called *group-choice nets*, and its encoding into weakly bisimilar CCS processes.

On the practical side, we are now exploring the practical application of these results—e.g. using model checkers oriented towards process calculi (such as mCRL2 [9]) to analyse the properties of α-mined Petri nets encoded into CCS. On the theoretical side, we are studying how to encode even larger classes of Petri nets into weakly bisimilar CCS processes. One of the problems is how to handle partially-overlapping place postsets: in this paper, we focused on classes of Petri nets without such overlaps, and 2-τ synchronisation nets. Another avenue we are exploring is to develop further encodings after dividing a Petri net into groups of places/transitions, as we did for group-choice nets.

Acknowledgements. We wish to thank to the anonymous reviewers for their comments and suggestions, and Ekkart Kindler for the fruitful discussions.

References

1. van der Aalst, W.M.P.: Pi calculus versus petri nets: let us eat "humble pie" rather than further inflate the "pi hype". BPTrends **3** (2005)
2. van der Aalst, W.M.P.: Process Mining - Data Science in Action, 2nd edn. Springer (2016). https://doi.org/10.1007/978-3-662-49851-4
3. van der Aalst, W.M.P., Weijters, T., Maruster, L.: Workflow mining: Discovering process models from event logs. IEEE Trans. Knowl. Data Eng. **16**(9), 1128–1142 (2004). https://doi.org/10.1109/TKDE.2004.47
4. Aranda, J., Valencia, F.D., Versari, C.: On the expressive power of restriction and priorities in CCS with replication. In: de Alfaro, L. (ed.) Foundations of Software Science and Computational Structures, FOSSACS 2009. LNCS, vol. 5504, pp. 242–256. Springer (2009). https://doi.org/10.1007/978-3-642-00596-1_18
5. Baldan, P., Bonchi, F., Gadducci, F.: Encoding asynchronous interactions using open petri nets. In: Bravetti, M., Zavattaro, G. (eds.) CONCUR 2009 - Concurrency Theory, 20th International Conference, CONCUR 2009, Bologna, Italy, September 1-4, 2009. Proceedings. Lecture Notes in Computer Science, vol. 5710, pp. 99–114. Springer, Heidelberg (2009). https://doi.org/10.1007/978-3-642-04081-8_8
6. Baldan, P., Bonchi, F., Gadducci, F., Monreale, G.V.: Encoding synchronous interactions using labelled petri nets. In: Kühn, E., Pugliese, R. (eds.) Coordination Models and Languages, COORDINATION 2014. LNCS, vol. 8459, pp. 1–16. Springer, Heidelberg (2014). https://doi.org/10.1007/978-3-662-43376-8_1
7. Bogø, B.: Encoding petri nets into CCS (2024). https://doi.org/10.5281/zenodo.10855866. https://dtu.bogoe.eu/tools/pn2ccs/
8. Bogø, B., Burattin, A., Scalas, A.: Encoding petri nets into ccs (technical report) (2024). https://doi.org/10.48550/arXiv.2404.14385
9. Bunte, O., et al.: The mcrl2 toolset for analysing concurrent systems - improvements in expressivity and usability. In: Vojnar, T., Zhang, L. (eds.) Tools and Algorithms for the Construction and Analysis of Systems, TACAS 2019. LNCS, vol. 11428, pp. 21–39. Springer, Heidelberg (2019). https://doi.org/10.1007/978-3-030-17465-1_2
10. Desel, J., Esparza, J.: Free Choice Petri Nets, no. 40. Cambridge University Press (1995)
11. van Dongen, B.F., de Medeiros, A.K.A., Wen, L.: Process mining: overview and outlook of petri net discovery algorithms. Trans. Petri Nets Other Model. Concurr. **2**, 225–242 (2009). https://doi.org/10.1007/978-3-642-00899-3_13

12. Goltz, U.: CCS and petri nets. In: Guessarian, I. (ed.) Semantics of Systems of Concurrent Processes, LITP Spring School on Theoretical Computer Science. LNCS, vol. 469, pp. 334–357. Springer, Heidelberg (1990). https://doi.org/10.1007/3-540-53479-2_14

13. Gorrieri, R., Versari, C.: A process calculus for expressing finite place/transition petri nets. In: Fröschle, S.B., Valencia, F.D. (eds.) Proceedings 17th International Workshop on Expressiveness in Concurrency, EXPRESS 2010, Paris. EPTCS, vol. 41, pp. 76–90 (2010). https://doi.org/10.4204/EPTCS.41.6

14. Gorrieri, R., Versari, C.: Introduction to Concurrency Theory - Transition Systems and CCS. Texts in Theoretical Computer Science. An EATCS Series. Springer, Cham (2015). https://doi.org/10.1007/978-3-319-21491-7

15. Meyer, R., Khomenko, V., Hüchting, R.: A polynomial translation of π-calculus (FCP) to safe petri nets. In: Koutny, M., Ulidowski, I. (eds.) CONCUR 2012. LNCS, vol. 7454, pp. 440–455. Springer, Heidelberg (2012). https://doi.org/10.1007/978-3-642-32940-1_31

16. Stefansen, C.: SMAWL: a small workflow language based on CCS. In: Belo, O., Eder, J., e Cunha, J.F., Pastor, O. (eds.) The 17th Conference on Advanced Information Systems Engineering (CAiSE 2005), Porto, 13–17 June 2005, CAiSE Forum, Short Paper Proceedings. CEUR Workshop Proceedings, vol. 161. CEUR-WS.org (2005)

Field-Based Coordination for Federated Learning

Davide Domini[1] , Gianluca Aguzzi[1(✉)] , Lukas Esterle[2] ,
and Mirko Viroli[1]

[1] Alma Mater Studiorum – Università di Bologna, Cesena, Italy
{davide.domini,gianluca.aguzzi,mirko.viroli}@unibo.it
[2] Aarhus University, Aarhus, Denmark
lukas.esterle@ece.au.dk

Abstract. Federated Learning has gained increasing interest in the last years, as it allows the training of machine learning models with a large number of devices by exchanging only the weights of the trained neural networks. Without the need to upload the training data to a central server, privacy concerns and potential bottlenecks can be removed as fewer data is transmitted. However, the current state-of-the-art solutions are typically centralized, and do not provide for suitable coordination mechanisms to take into account *spatial* distribution of devices and local communications, which can sometimes play a crucial role. Therefore, we propose a field-based coordination approach for federated learning, where the devices coordinate with each other through the use of *computational fields*. We show that this approach can be used to train models in a completely peer-to-peer fashion. Additionally, our approach also allows for emergently create zones of interests, and produce specialized models for each zone enabling each agent to refine their models for the tasks at hand.

We evaluate our approach in a simulated environment leveraging aggregate computing—the reference global-to-local field-based coordination programming paradigm. The results show that our approach is comparable to the state-of-the-art centralized solutions, while enabling a more flexible and scalable approach to federated learning.

Keywords: Aggregate computing · Federated learning · Field-based coordination

1 Introduction

In recent years, the ubiquity of machine learning (ML) applications in daily life has necessitated the training of models (e.g., a neural network) across an increasingly vast array of devices. This surge has underscored the importance of decentralized learning methodologies, particularly as centralized data aggregation becomes impractical due to scalability constraints and privacy concerns. To

I. Castellani and F. Tiezzi (Eds.): COORDINATION 2024, LNCS 14676, pp. 56–74, 2024.
https://doi.org/10.1007/978-3-031-62697-5_4

mitigate these issues, federated learning (FL) has emerged as a promising approach, enabling devices to collaboratively learn a shared model while retaining data locally [23]. This paradigm not only alleviates the necessity for central data storage but also addresses privacy and efficiency concerns inherent in traditional systems with centralized learning.

Despite its advantages, in the current landscape of FL, training is distributed, but model construction is still predominantly centralized, posing challenges in scenarios characterized by geographical dispersion of devices, heightened risk of single points of failure, and naturally distributed datasets. Existing peer-to-peer solutions attempt to tackle these concerns; however, they often overlook the spatial distribution of devices and do not exploit the benefits of semantically similar knowledge among nearby devices. This builds on the assumption that devices in spatial proximity have similar experiences and make similar observations [17], as the phenomena to capture is intrinsically context dependent. Finally, there is a lack in flexibility to seamlessly transition between fully centralized and fully decentralized aggregation methods. This could be a role for coordination models and languages.

Therefore, in this paper, we introduce a novel field-based coordination mechanism for FL, utilizing computational fields (global maps from devices to values) as key abstraction to facilitate device coordination [21,35]. By field-based coordination, global-level system behaviour can be captured declaratively, with automatic translation into single-device local behaviour.

We find that this approach offers a versatile and scalable solution to FL, supporting both peer-to-peer interactions and the formation of specialized model zones. Most specifically, our approach actually relies on known field-based algorithms of information diffusion and aggregation developed in the context of aggregate computing [34], ultimately defining what we can define "fields of ML (sub)models". This method enables dynamic, efficient model aggregation without a centralized authority, thereby addressing the limitations of current FL frameworks. We evaluate our approach in a simulated environment, demonstrating its effectiveness in comparison to conventional centralized FL solutions. Our findings indicate that this field-based strategy not only matches the performance of existing methods but also provides enhanced scalability and flexibility in FL implementations.

The remainder of this paper is organized as follows: Sect. 2 provides a background and review of related work. Section 3 formalizes the problem statement. Section 4 details our field-based coordination strategy for FL. Section 5 presents an evaluation of our approach in a simulated setting. Finally, Sect. 6 concludes the paper and outlines avenues for future research.

2   Background and Related Work

2.1   Federated Learning

Federated learning [23] is a machine learning technique introduced to collaboratively train a joint model using multiple – potentially geographically *distributed*

– devices. Models kind can vary but in this paper, we focus on neural networks. The federation typically consists of multiple *client* devices and one *aggregation* server, which may be located in the cloud. The key idea behind FL is that the data always remains on the device to which it belongs: devices only share the weights of their models, thus making FL an excellent solution in contexts where *privacy* is a crucial aspect (e.g., in health-care applications [25,38]) or where data are *naturally distributed*, and their volume makes it infeasible to transfer them from each client device to a centralized server.

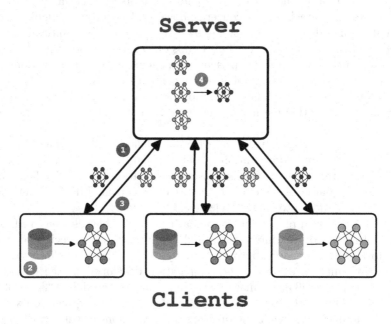

Fig. 1. Federated learning schema. In the first phase, the server shares the centralized model with the clients. In the second phase, the clients perform a local learning phase using data that is not accessible to the server. In the third phase, these models are communicated back to the central server, and finally, in the last phase, there is an aggregation algorithm.

Federated learning can be performed in three main ways [39]: *horizontal, vertical*, and *federated transfer learning*. Horizontal federated learning, also known as *sample-based federated learning*, occurs when different participants possess datasets with overlapping features but distinct samples. On the other hand, vertical federated learning, or *feature-based federated learning*, is applied when datasets share common samples but differ in the features they possess. Lastly, transfer learning federated learning bridges the gap between horizontal and vertical methods by leveraging the knowledge gained from one domain (source domain) to apply it to another (target domain) where data may be sparse, or privacy concerns limit the direct application of traditional machine learning techniques. Among the different types of FL, they share the same main four steps, namely (see Fig. 1):

1. *model distribution*, the server sends to each device its model;
2. *local training*, each device performs one, or more, training steps on its local data;
3. *local models sharing*, each device sends its own local model to the aggregation server;
4. *local models aggregation*, the server aggregates all the received local models using an aggregation algorithm.

The last two steps may be implemented in several ways, depending on the specific FL types of the problem. In this paper, we focus on horizontal FL. One of the most common algorithms for horizontal FL is *FedAVG* [24], where the server aggregates the models by averaging the weights of the models received from the client devices. Over the years, a myriad of strategies has been developed to enhance FL efficiency. One major challenge in FL is the impracticality of sharing large model weights due to significant *communication overhead*. To mitigate this, researchers have proposed selective sharing techniques, such as employing *Adapters* for model personalization [30] – a notable example being the approach by *Elvebakken et al.* [16] – or adopting model segmentation strategies [40]. Concurrently, there have been efforts to incorporate FL with sophisticated model aggregation mechanisms, including *knowledge distillation* methodologies [20,26].

Exploring the network topology presents another avenue for improvement, as the configuration of device communication can significantly influence FL performance. Various structures, such as *peer-to-peer* (P2P), *hierarchical*, and *centralized* networks, offer diverse benefits and challenges. Traditionally, FL systems have relied on a centralized server for model aggregation. However, this setup poses scalability challenges and risks introducing a single point of failure. In response, recent advancements have embraced P2P networks to address these limitations, going towards what is called decentralized federated learning. P2P architectures, devoid of a central authority, enhance scalability and robustness through the utilization of gossip [33] or consensus algorithms [31] for model aggregation.

2.2   Aggregate Computing

Coordination based on fields [10] (or *field-based coordination*) employs a methodology where computations are facilitated through the concept of *computational fields* (*fields* in brief), defined as distributed data structures that evolve over time and map locations with specific values. This method draws inspiration from foundational works such as Warren's *artificial potential fields* [36] and the concept of *co-fields* by Zambonelli et al. [22]. Specifically, in the context of co-fields, these computational fields encapsulate contextual data, which is sensed locally by agents and disseminated by either the agents themselves or the infrastructure following a specific distribution rule.

In our discussion, *coordination based on fields* refers to a distinct programming and computation framework, often referred to as *aggregate computing* [11]. This framework enables the programming of collective, self-organizing behaviours through the integration of functions that operate on fields, assigning computational values to a collection of individual agents (as opposed to locations within an environment). Thus, fields facilitate the association of a particular domain of agents with their sensory data, processed information, and instructions for action within their environment. Computed locally by agents yet under a unified perspective, fields enable the representation of collective instructions, such as a velocity vector field directing swarm movement or a field of numerical values reflecting the swarm's environmental perception. To comprehend field-based computing fully, we highlight the system model and the programming model in the following sections.

System Model. We envisage a network of *agents* that compute and interact within a specific *environment*. In the following, we better describe the structure, interaction, and behaviour of the agents in the system model, as well as the nature of the environment they inhabit.

Structure. An *agent* represents an autonomous unit furnished with *sensors* and *actuators* to interface with either a logical or physical *environment*. From a conceptual standpoint, an agent possesses *state*, capabilities for *communication* with fellow agents, and the ability to *execute* simple programs. An agent's *neighbourhood* is composed of other *neighbour* agents, forming a connected network that can be also represented as a graph—see Sect. 3 for more details. The composition of this network is determined by a *neighbouring relationship*, designed based on the specific application needs and constrained by the physical network's limitations. Commonly, neighbourhoods are defined by physical connectivity or spatial proximity, allowing for communication directly or via infrastructural support, based on certain proximity thresholds.

Interaction. Agents interact by asynchronously sending messages to neighbours, which can also occur stigmergically through environmental sensors and actuators. The nature and timing of these messages depend on the agent's programmed behaviour. Notably, our focus on modelling continuous, self-organizing systems suggest frequent interactions relative to the dynamics of the problem and environment.

Behaviour. Based on the interaction of agents, an agent's behaviour unfolds through iterative *execution rounds*, with each round encompassing the steps below, albeit with some flexibility in the actuation phase:

1. *Context acquisition:* agents accumulate context by considering both their prior state and the latest inputs from sensors and neighbouring messages.
2. *Computation:* agents process the gathered context, resulting in (i) an *output* for potential actions, and (ii) a *coordination message* for neighbourly collective coordination.

3. *Actuation and communication:* agents execute the actions as specified by the output and distribute the coordination message across the neighbourhood.

By cyclically executing these sense-compute-act rounds, the system exhibits a self-organizing mechanism that integrates and processes fresh data from both the environment and the agents, typically achieving self-stabilization

Programming Model. This system model establishes a foundation for collective adaptive behaviour, necessitating an in-depth elucidation of the "local computation step", facilitated by a *field-based programming model*. This model orchestrates the collective behaviour through a *field-based program*, executed by each agent in adherence to the prescribed model. Field calculus defines the computation as a composition of *function operations* on fields, and any variants of it allow the developers to express at least i) the temporal evolution of fields, ii) the data interchange among agents, and iii) the spatial partitioning of computation. Various incarnations of this model employ distinct constructs (e.g., share [8] xc [9] calculus). Among them, FScaFi [15] is a conceptual framework within the ScaFi [14] programming model. In this variant, the three main operator constructs are rep, nbr, and foldhood. For instance, to model the temporal evolution of a field, one can employ the rep construct as follows:

```
rep(0)(x => x + 1)
```

Hence, rep is the incremental evolution of a field with each cycle, representing a non-uniform field. Particularly, the above described code express a field of local counters, where each agent increments its own counter at each cycle.

To facilitate data exchange between agents, ScaFi leverages the nbr construct in conjunction with a folding operator:

```
foldhood(0)(_ + _)(nbr(1))
```

Here, nbr(1) signifies the neighbouring agent's field value, _ + _ denotes the folding operator, where 0 is the fold's initial value. This code snippet produces a field where each agent's value it is the number of its neighbours.

Lastly, to express spatio-temporal evaluation, a combination of the aforementioned constructs is utilized:

```
rep(mid) { minId => foldhood(0)(math.min)(nbr(minId)) }
```

This combination calculates the minimum value of ID in the entire network. This demonstrates the integration of spatial and temporal computation through a synergistic application of both constructs.

Coordination Building Blocks. Beyond these elementary operators, it is feasible to construct a suite of building blocks to foster coordinated collective behaviour. Notably, these blocks are designed to be *self-stabilizing*– converging to a stable state from any initial condition– and *self-organizing*—adapting dynamically to environmental changes and network topology variations. A cornerstone among these is the *self-healing gradient* computation, a distributed algorithm for calculating the distance from a source node to the rest of the network. Within ScaFi, this is described as follows:

```
def gradient(source: Boolean): Double
```

Building upon this foundation, more sophisticated coordination algorithms can be developed, such as:

- **Gradient cast:** a mechanism to disseminate information from a source node across the system using a gradient-based approach. In ScaFi, this is expressed as:

```
G[V](source: Boolean, value: V, accumulator: V => V)
```

   Here, `source` identifies the gradient's origin, `value` is the disseminated information, and `accumulator` is the function for aggregating the disseminated value.

- **Collect cast:** conceptually the inverse of gradient cast, it aggregates information from the system back to a specific zone. It is represented as:

```
C[V](potential: Double, accumulator: V, localValue: V, null: V)
```

   in this construct, potential indicates the collection's potential, `accumulator` is the function for aggregating values towards the source, `localValue` is the value being collected, and `null` signifies the absence of value.

- **Sparse choice:** a distributed mechanism for node subset selection and leader election, expressed as:

```
S(radius: Double): Boolean
```

   where `radius` specifies the selection radius of the area created by the leader.

By integrating these constructs, it becomes possible to execute complex collective behaviours, such as crowd management [11], distributed sensing and action [1,2], and swarm behaviours [6]. Furthermore, it is feasible to integrate the aforementioned programming model with deep learning techniques, advancing towards a paradigm known as *hybrid aggregate computing* [4]. AC can orchestrate or enhance the learning mechanisms [7], and conversely, learning methodologies can refine AC [3,5]. This paper adopts the initial perspective, delineating a field-based coordination strategy for FL. The objective is to create a distributed learning framework that is inherently self-stabilizing and self-organizing.

3   Problem Formulation

Consider a distributed network comprising a set of devices, denoted as N, where each device $d \in N$ possesses a dataset unique to it. The dataset on device d is used to train a local model, characterized by a weights vector $\mathbf{w}_d$. The objective

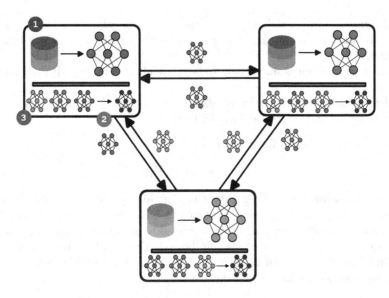

Fig. 2. Peer-to-peer federated learning schema. In the first phase, each node performs a local training process. In the second phase, the nodes share their models with their neighbours and finally in the third phase, the nodes aggregate the models received from their neighbours.

function local to device d, $f_d(\mathbf{w}_d)$, quantifies the performance of the model on this local dataset, with the aim being to minimize this function.

The general problem that FL seeks to solve it to construct a global model by optimizing a global objective function $f(\mathbf{w})$, formulated as the aggregate of all local objective functions, adjusted by the size of the local datasets. This is mathematically represented as:

$$f(\mathbf{w}) = \sum_{d \in N} \alpha_d f_d(\mathbf{w}_d), \tag{1}$$

where $\alpha_d = \frac{n_d}{|D|}$ signifies the weight of device d's data in the global objective, n_d is the count of samples in device d's dataset, and $|D| = \sum_{d \in N} n_d$ represents the total number of samples across all devices. In the peer-to-peer model of FL, even if the problem is conceptually the same, the clients, instead of taking a model from a central server, directly exchange information to collaboratively learn a global model without the intermediation of a central server. This network can be modelled as a graph $\mathcal{G} = (\mathcal{N}, \mathcal{E})$, with nodes representing devices and edges symbolizing direct communication links. A device d's neighbours, with whom it can exchange messages, are denoted by $\mathcal{N}_d = \{d' \in \mathcal{N} | (d, d') \in \mathcal{E}\}$ (Fig. 2).

The peer-to-peer federated learning process in this context unfolds over several rounds (see Algorithm 1), each encompassing:

1. *local training*: devices independently update their local models by training on their datasets for p epochs, aiming to minimize the local objective function $f_d(\mathbf{w}_d)$;
2. *model sharing*: devices share their updated weights vector $\mathbf{w}_d$ with their neighbours;
3. *model aggregation*: each device combines the received weights vectors from its neighbours to update its local model to $\mathbf{w}'_d$.

The model sharing step is formalized as follows:

$$\rightsquigarrow (\mathbf{w}_d, \{\mathbf{w}_{d'} | d' \in \mathcal{N}_d\}), \tag{2}$$

where $\rightsquigarrow$ represents the sharing algorithm, in this approach we directly share the model with all the neighbours, but potentially it is possible to incorporate strategies to minimize communication overhead by selectively sharing models or parts thereof (e.g., gradients or specific layers). Each node stores the received model in a buffer $\mathcal{B}_d$, and then the aggregation algorithm is executed.

The aggregation of models is defined by:

$$\mathbf{w}'_d = \mathcal{A}(\mathbf{w}_d, \{\mathbf{w}_{d'} | d' \in \mathcal{B}_d\}), \tag{3}$$

where $\mathcal{A}$ is the aggregation algorithm, which could range from simple averaging to more sophisticated methods.

Through the iterative execution of these steps, the system converges towards a unified model that approximates the outcome of a centrally coordinated federated learning process.

Algorithm 1. Peer-to-Peer Federated Learning Process

Require: devices $|N|$, Network graph $\mathcal{G}$, Epochs per round p, Maximum rounds $\mathcal{T}$
1: **procedure** P2PFEDERATEDLEARNING
2:    **for** round $= 1$ **to** $\mathcal{T}$ **do**
3:       **for all** $d \in N$ **do**
4:          **local training:** Minimize $f_d(\mathbf{w}_d)$ by training on d's dataset for p epochs
5:          **model sharing:** Share $\mathbf{w}_d$ with $\mathcal{N}_d$ following $\rightsquigarrow$
6:       **end for**
7:       **for all** $d \in N$ **do**
8:          **model aggregation:** Update $\mathbf{w}_d$ to $\mathbf{w}'_d$ using $\mathcal{A}(\mathbf{w}_d, \{\mathbf{w}_{d'} | d' \in \mathcal{B}_d\})$
9:       **end for**
10:    **end for**
11: **end procedure**

---

4 Field-Based Federated Learning

This section describes the contribution of this paper, namely the integration concepts of aggregate computing into the federated learning framework to improve adaptability and robustness in decentralized networks. Our approach enables the learning processes to *dynamically* conform to changes in network topology, effectively eliminating reliance on centralized coordination points. This adaptability ensures that the system autonomously reconfigures in case of failures to maintain operational stability and continue the learning process without significant interruptions.

4.1   Learning Process

At its core, FL can be conceptualized as an application of the Self-coordinated Region (SCR) pattern [13], where the coordination among nodes is pivotal. In our framework, nodes can be designated as *aggregators*—either through pre-assignment (e.g., edge servers) or dynamically selected based on the network's evolving topology, leveraging principles similar to those in *space-fluid* computing [12].

Initially, each participating node $d \in N$ initializes its model $\mathbf{w}_d^{(0)}$. Subsequently, at each iteration t, it undertakes a local learning step to update $\mathbf{w}_d^{(t)}$, after which the model updates are directed toward an aggregator node, guided by a dynamically formed potential field. Therefore, $\leadsto$ function is replaced by a field-based model sharing mechanism, where the potential field guides the model updates to the aggregators, using a collect cast operation to ensure that the model updates are directed to the appropriate nodes. Aggregator nodes play a crucial role in the system. They are responsible for collecting the model updates from participant nodes, computing a consensus model $\mathbf{w}^{(t+k)}$ (where k is the global epoch value) by averaging, and disseminating the updated model back to the nodes in their zone of influence. This process ensures a distributed yet coordinated approach to model learning and sharing across the network. To accommodate communication delays and ensure timely model updates, nodes are capable of adjusting their models with local corrections. This mechanism, denoted as $\Delta\mathbf{w}_d^{(t)}$, accounts for potential discrepancies between the model's state when shared and when the aggregated update is received, enabling a more resilient and responsive learning process.

Note that the aggregation and sharing part can follow different strategies, depending on the specific application requirements and the network's characteristics. In this work, we follow a standard FedAvg approach, where the aggregation is performed by averaging the models received from the neighbours, formally expressed as:

$$\mathbf{w}^{(t+k)} = \frac{1}{|\mathcal{A}|} \sum_{d \in \mathcal{A}} \mathbf{w}_d' \tag{4}$$

where $\mathcal{A}$ denotes the set of models received by an aggregator at iteration t, and $|\mathcal{A}|$ is the number of models. This ensures that despite the dynamic and decentralized nature of the network, a coherent and unified model is learned and shared among the nodes.

4.2 Implementation Insights

The following ScaFi code snippet provides an overview of the decentralized learning loop, highlighting the dynamic selection of aggregators, local model evolution, and model aggregation based on potential fields:

```
val aggregators = S(area, nbrRange) // Dynamic aggregator selection
rep(init())(model => { // Local model initialization
    // 1. Local training step
    model.evolve()
    val pot = gradient(aggregators) // Potential field for model sharing
    // 2. Model sharing
    val info = C[Double, Set[Model]](pot, _ ++ _, Set(model), Set.empty)
    // 3. Model aggregation
    val aggregateModel = aggregation(info)
    // 4. Global model update
    sharedModel = broadcast(aggregators, aggregateModel)
    mux(impulsesEvery(epochs))
        { combineLocal(sharedModel, model) } { model }
})
```

Furthermore, we propose a fully decentralized variant (that mimics what is described in Algorithm 1), where every node functions simultaneously as both learner and aggregator, exemplifying the flexibility and scalability of our approach:

```
rep(init() )(model => { // Local model initialization
    // 1. Local training
    model.evolve(localEpochs)
    // 2. Model sharing
    val info = foldhood(Set(model))(_ ++ _)(nbr(model))
    // 3. Model aggregation
    aggregation(info)
})
```

Our field-based FL approach shares benefits of distributed systems such as *adaptability*, *scalability* and *failure tolerance* while also allowing subsets of systems to *specialize*: by facilitating the creation of specialized learning zones our model can generate more nuanced and contextually relevant models, catering to the unique characteristics of data distributions within specific network regions.

5 Evaluation

To evaluate our approach, we performed learning on two well-known datasets in computer vision, namely: *MNIST* [19] and *Fashion MNIST* [37]. We implemented a traditional centralized federated learning algorithm and compared it to our field-based federated learning approach. Furthermore, we conducted an experiment to evaluate the capability in creating specialized models using SCR pattern and PM10 data from some European countries (inspired from the experiment in [12]). In both scenarios, we used: *PyTorch* [27], a state-of-the-art framework to efficiently train deep neural networks; *Alchemist* [28], a simulator for large scale distributed systems; *ScaFi* [14], a Scala implementation of aggregate computing; and *ScalaPy* [18], a tool that offers interoperability between Python functionalities and Scala programs.

To promote the reproducibility of the results, all the source code of the experiments, the data, and instructions for running have been made available on GitHub[1] and Zenodo[2].

5.1 Learning Setup

MNIST and Fashion MNIST: the training was conducted for both algorithms using the same parameters. The main difference lies in the topology of the devices in the federated network. In the case of centralized FL, there are 8 client devices that perform local training and one aggregation server, while in the case of field-based FL, there is a peer-to-peer network of 8 devices in which each of them can communicate with its five nearest neighbours. Both datasets were synthetically split to create sub-datasets, ensuring that the data distribution among the various clients was the same (i.e., iid data). For this task, a simple *convolutional neural network (CNN)* was used, more specifically the LeNet architecture [32]. The network is composed of two convolutional layers, followed by two fully connected layers. A total of 11 rounds of global communication were conducted, with each device performing 2 epochs for every local training, using the *Negative Log-Likelihood (NLL)* loss. The *ADAM* optimizer was utilized with hyperparameters set to a learning rate of 0.001 and weight decay of 0.0001. The *FedAvg* algorithm was used to aggregate the models, without applying any sampling technique. Instead, the devices exchanged the entire model. This choice was made to conduct the comparison in the simplest setting possible. However, it is still possible to integrate more advanced techniques to improve performance across different metrics (e.g., efficiency in communications or prevent information leakage [29]).

Air Quality: the PM10 dataset[3] was used to evaluate the capability of our approach to create specialized models. The dataset contains hourly measurements of PM10 concentration in the air collected from hundreds of stations across Europe, in particular we used data from 250 stations in the following countries: Belgium, Croatia, Hungary, Ireland, Slovakia, Slovenia Switzerland and United Kingdom. The goal was to create a model that can forecast the PM10 concentration in the air based on the data collected by the sensors. For this purpose, we trained a *Recurrent Neural Network (RNN)* composed of one recurrent layer and one linear layer, using as input sequences of 10 time steps. The learning process was

---

[1] https://github.com/davidedomini/code-coordination-2024-field-based-FL.
[2] https://doi.org/10.5281/zenodo.10854384.
[3] Dataset available at: https://www.eea.europa.eu/data-and-maps/dashboards/air-quality-statistics.

conducted for 30 global rounds, with each device performing 1 epoch for each local training, using the *Mean Squared Error (MSE)* loss. Figure 3a shows the concentration of PM10 in the year 2013 (data used for training) in the countries of interest. From the heatmap, we can see how the phenomenon differs among the different areas. For example, in Croatia, we have a much higher concentration than in Ireland. These observations were used during the experiment development phase. It was assumed that nearby areas have a similar trend in the phenomenon. This way, it is possible to create regions containing stations within a certain radius that learn a specialized shared model.

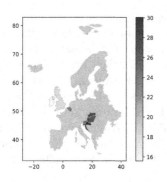

(a) PM10 concentration.

(b) PM10 sampling stations deployment using Alchemist.

Fig. 3. Experiment for Air Quality Prediction. On the left, a visualization of PM10 concentration in some European countries, while on the right, the deployment of the corresponding sampling stations through the Alchemist simulator.

Figure 3b shows the deployment of stations across Europe, which was done using the Alchemist simulator that allows managing geographic data based on the latitude and longitude of the various stations. Specifically, we can also see how the various stations are connected to each other. For this experiment, each station is connected to the closest other 10 stations within a radius of 200 km. Utilizing the ScaFi language within the Alchemist simulator, we executed an aggregate program delineated in Sect. 4.1, which: (i) delineates zones according to the network topology, (ii) appoints a zone leader to function as an aggregating edge server, and (iii) implements federated learning by training zone-specific models.

5.2   Discussion

MNIST and Fashion MNIST: the goal of this evaluation was to show how a peer-to-peer approach, based on field coordination, achieves comparable performance to that of a centralized FL while introducing all the advantages discussed in Sect. 4.2, such as: the absence of a single point of failure and the adaptability.

Figure 4 shows respectively results on the MNIST and Fashion MNIST datasets, more specifically: i) the average training loss, ii) the average validation loss, and iii) the average validation accuracy. It is worth noting that both the training and validation loss and accuracy exhibit similar trends. There are typical instabilities that can be observed across all federated learning experiments. However, they still achieve comparable performance after the same number of rounds of global communication, similar to the performance of traditional learning methods as observed in the literature.

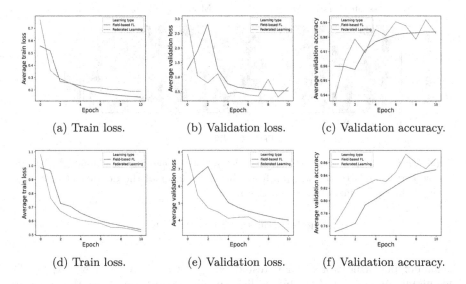

(a) Train loss.   (b) Validation loss.   (c) Validation accuracy.

(d) Train loss.   (e) Validation loss.   (f) Validation accuracy.

Fig. 4. Performance of centralized federated learning and field-based federated learning on MNIST (first line) and Fashion MNIST datasets (second line).

Air Quality: During this evaluation phase, we aimed to understand two main aspects of the system: i) whether learning had effectively occurred, evidenced by a collective decrease in loss, and ii) whether each zone had indeed learned a model with characteristics distinct from those of other zones. Regarding the first point, it is observable that, in the whole system, the loss decreases over various iterations (see Fig. 5a). This is significant as instabilities due to multi-hop communication in contrast to a central server might have impacted the system's performance.

As for the creation of zones, after an initial unstable phase, the system identified 16 zones. Consequently, some countries have more aggregators due to their larger size (e.g., London). By examining the weights of the last extracted layer (see Fig. 5c), we can see that these learn *similar* policies but with *variations* among different zones. Moreover, we select a model specialized in a specific zone (Belgium) and test it on another zone (Hungary). As we can observe in Fig. 5b,

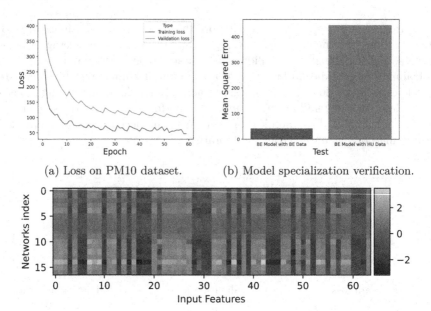

(a) Loss on PM10 dataset.   (b) Model specialization verification.

(c) Visualization of network weights across distinct geographical zones. Each row corresponds to the weights from the linear layer of the neural network, highlighting the model's specialization.

Fig. 5. Results on PM10 dataset.

the model performs worse when tested on a different zone, as we expected. This highlights the fact that, due to different pheromone dynamics, the network adapted to those specific zones, capturing the evolution in relation to a particular geographical area more effectively.

6   Conclusion

In this work, we introduced a novel field-based coordination approach for federated learning, enhancing the scalability, flexibility, and efficiency of distributed machine learning across spatially distributed devices. Our approach leverages computational fields to enable devices to dynamically coordinate, share, and aggregate models in a peer-to-peer fashion, thus circumventing the limitations of centralized coordination mechanisms but still achieving comparable performance as shown in the MNIST and Fashion MNIST datasets. Moreover, it features the ability to adaptively form zones of interest for specialized model training, thereby catering to the unique characteristics of data distributions within specific network regions as shown in the PM10 dataset experiment.

Future work will explore the extension of this framework to incorporate advanced machine learning algorithms and optimization techniques. Additionally, we aim to investigate the application of our field-based coordination approach in space-fluid scenario, to automatically segment learning zones based on evolving trends of the phenomenon we want to predict, rather than relying on predefined assumptions. The potential for this approach to facilitate specialized machine learning models in decentralized environments holds promise for a wide range of applications, from edge computing to IoT ecosystems.

Acknowledgments. Lukas Esterle was supported by the Independent Research Fund Denmark through the FLOCKD project under the grant number 1032-00179B.

Gianluca Aguzzi was supported by the Italian PRIN project "CommonWears" (2020 HCWWLP) and the EU/MUR FSE PON-R &I 2014–2020.

References

1. Aguzzi, G.: Research directions for aggregate computing with machine learning. In: El-Araby, E., et al. (eds.) IEEE International Conference on Autonomic Computing and Self-organizing Systems, ACSOS 2021, Companion Volume, Washington, DC, USA, 27 September–1 Octoter 2021, pp. 310–312. IEEE (2021). https://doi.org/10.1109/ACSOS-C52956.2021.00078
2. Aguzzi, G., Casadei, R., Pianini, D., Viroli, M.: Dynamic decentralization domains for the internet of things. IEEE Internet Comput. **26**(6), 16–23 (2022). https://doi.org/10.1109/MIC.2022.3216753
3. Aguzzi, G., Casadei, R., Viroli, M.: Addressing collective computations efficiency: towards a platform-level reinforcement learning approach. In: Casadei, R., et al. (eds.) IEEE International Conference on Autonomic Computing and Self-Organizing Systems, ACSOS 2022, Virtual, CA, USA, 19–23 September 2022, pp. 11–20. IEEE (2022). https://doi.org/10.1109/ACSOS55765.2022.00019
4. Aguzzi, G., Casadei, R., Viroli, M.: Machine learning for aggregate computing: a research roadmap. In: 42nd IEEE International Conference on Distributed Computing Systems, ICDCS Workshops, Bologna, Italy, 10 July 2022, pp. 119–124. IEEE (2022). https://doi.org/10.1109/ICDCSW56584.2022.00032
5. Aguzzi, G., Casadei, R., Viroli, M.: Towards reinforcement learning-based aggregate computing. In: ter Beek, M.H., Sirjani, M. (eds.) COORDINATION 2022. IFIP Advances in Information and Communication Technology, vol. 13271, pp. 72–91. Springer, Cham (2022). https://doi.org/10.1007/978-3-031-08143-9_5
6. Aguzzi, G., Casadei, R., Viroli, M.: MACROSWARM: a field-based compositional framework for swarm programming. In: Jongmans, S., Lopes, A. (eds.) COORDINATION 2023. LNCS, vol. 13908, pp. 31–51. Springer, Cham (2023). https://doi.org/10.1007/978-3-031-35361-1_2
7. Aguzzi, G., Viroli, M., Esterle, L.: Field-informed reinforcement learning of collective tasks with graph neural networks. In: IEEE International Conference on Autonomic Computing and Self-organizing Systems, ACSOS 2023, Toronto, ON, Canada, 25–29 September 2023, pp. 37–46. IEEE (2023).https://doi.org/10.1109/ACSOS58161.2023.00021
8. Audrito, G., Beal, J., Damiani, F., Pianini, D., Viroli, M.: Field-based coordination with the share operator. Log. Methods Comput. Sci. **16**(4) (2020). https://lmcs.episciences.org/6816
9. Audrito, G., Casadei, R., Damiani, F., Salvaneschi, G., Viroli, M.: The exchange calculus (XC): a functional programming language design for distributed collective systems. J. Syst. Softw. **210**, 111976 (2024). https://doi.org/10.1016/J.JSS.2024.111976

10. Audrito, G., Viroli, M., Damiani, F., Pianini, D., Beal, J.: On a higher-order cal-culus of computational fields. In: Pérez, J.A., Yoshida, N. (eds.) FORTE 2019. LNCS, vol. 11535, pp. 289–292. Springer, Cham (2019). https://doi.org/10.1007/978-3-030-21759-4_17

11. Beal, J., Pianini, D., Viroli, M.: Aggregate programming for the internet of things. Computer **48**(9), 22–30 (2015). https://doi.org/10.1109/MC.2015.261

12. Casadei, R., Mariani, S., Pianini, D., Viroli, M., Zambonelli, F.: Space-fluid adaptive sampling by self-organisation. Log. Methods Comput. Sci. **19**(4) (2023) https://doi.org/10.46298/LMCS-19(4:29)2023

13. Casadei, R., Pianini, D., Viroli, M., Natali, A.: Self-organising coordination regions: a pattern for edge computing. In: Riis Nielson, H., Tuosto, E. (eds.) COORDINA-TION 2019. LNCS, vol. 11533, pp. 182–199. Springer, Cham (2019). https://doi.org/10.1007/978-3-030-22397-7_11

14. Casadei, R., Viroli, M., Aguzzi, G., Pianini, D.: ScaFI: a scala DSL and toolkit for aggregate programming. SoftwareX **20**, 101248 (2022). https://doi.org/10.1016/J.SOFTX.2022.101248

15. Casadei, R., Viroli, M., Audrito, G., Damiani, F.: FScaFi: a core calculus for collective adaptive systems programming. In: Margaria, T., Steffen, B. (eds.) ISoLA 2020, Part II. LNCS, vol. 12477, pp. 344–360. Springer, Cham (2020). https://doi.org/10.1007/978-3-030-61470-6_21

16. Elvebakken, M.F., Iosifidis, A., Esterle, L.: Adaptive parameterization of deep learning models for federated learning. CoRR abs/2302.02949 (2023). https://doi.org/10.48550/ARXIV.2302.02949

17. Esterle, L.: Deep learning in multiagent systems. In: Deep Learning for Robot Perception and Cognition, pp. 435–460. Elsevier (2022)

18. Laddad, S., Sen, K.: ScalaPy: seamless python interoperability for cross-platform scala programs. In: Salvaneschi, G., Amin, N. (eds.) SPLASH 2020: Conference on Systems, Programming, Languages, and Applications, Software for Humanity, Virtual Event, USA, November 2020, pp. 2–13. ACM (2020) https://doi.org/10.1145/3426426.3428485

19. LeCun, Y., Cortes, C., Burges, C., et al.: MNIST handwritten digit database (2010)

20. Li, C., Li, G., Varshney, P.K.: Decentralized federated learning via mutual knowl-edge transfer. IEEE Internet Things J. **9**(2), 1136–1147 (2022). https://doi.org/10.1109/JIOT.2021.3078543

21. Lluch-Lafuente, A., Loreti, M., Montanari, U.: Asynchronous distributed execution of fixpoint-based computational fields. Log. Methods Comput. Sci. **13**(1) (2017). https://doi.org/10.23638/LMCS-13(1:13)2017

22. Mamei, M., Zambonelli, F., Leonardi, L.: Co-fields: a physically inspired approach to motion coordination. IEEE Pervasive Comput. **3**(2), 52–61 (2004). https://doi.org/10.1109/MPRV.2004.1316820

23. McMahan, B., Moore, E., Ramage, D., Hampson, S., y Arcas, B.A.: Communication-efficient learning of deep networks from decentralized data. In: Singh, A., Zhu, X.J. (eds.) Proceedings of the 20th International Conference on Artificial Intelligence and Statistics, AISTATS 2017, 20–22 April 2017, Fort Laud-erdale, FL, USA. Proceedings of Machine Learning Research, vol. 54, pp. 1273–1282. PMLR (2017). http://proceedings.mlr.press/v54/mcmahan17a.html

24. McMahan, H.B., Moore, E., Ramage, D., y Arcas, B.A.: Federated learning of deep networks using model averaging. CoRR abs/1602.05629 (2016). http://arxiv.org/abs/1602.05629

25. Nguyen, D.C., et al.: Federated learning for smart healthcare: a survey. ACM Comput. Surv. (CSUR) **55**(3), 1–37 (2022)

26. Papernot, N., Abadi, M., Erlingsson, Ú., Goodfellow, I.J., Talwar, K.: Semi-supervised knowledge transfer for deep learning from private training data. In: 5th International Conference on Learning Representations, ICLR 2017, Toulon, France, 24–26 April 2017, Conference Track Proceedings. OpenReview.net (2017). https://openreview.net/forum?id=HkwoSDPgg

27. Paszke, A., et al.: PyTorch: an imperative style, high-performance deep learning library. In: Wallach, H.M., Larochelle, H., Beygelzimer, A., d'Alché-Buc, F., Fox, E.B., Garnett, R. (eds.) Advances in Neural Information Processing Systems 32: Annual Conference on Neural Information Processing Systems 2019, NeurIPS 2019, 8–14 December 2019, Vancouver, BC, Canada, pp. 8024–8035 (2019). https://proceedings.neurips.cc/paper/2019/hash/bdbca288fee7f92f2bfa9f7012727740-Abstract.html

28. Pianini, D., Montagna, S., Viroli, M.: Chemical-oriented simulation of computational systems with ALCHEMIST. J. Simul. 7(3), 202–215 (2013). https://doi.org/10.1057/JOS.2012.27

29. Rajkumar, K., Goswami, A., Lakshmanan, K., Gupta, R.: Comment on "federated learning with differential privacy: Algorithms and performance analysis". IEEE Trans. Inf. Forensics Secur. 17, 3922–3924 (2022)

30. Rebuffi, S., Bilen, H., Vedaldi, A.: Efficient parametrization of multi-domain deep neural networks. In: 2018 IEEE Conference on Computer Vision and Pattern Recognition, CVPR 2018, Salt Lake City, UT, USA, 18–22 June 2018, pp. 8119–8127. Computer Vision Foundation/IEEE Computer Society (2018). https://doi.org/10.1109/CVPR.2018.00847, http://openaccess.thecvf.com/content_cvpr_2018/html/Rebuffi_Efficient_Parametrization_of_CVPR_2018_paper.html

31. Savazzi, S., Nicoli, M., Rampa, V.: Federated learning with cooperating devices: a consensus approach for massive IoT networks. IEEE Internet Things J. 7(5), 4641–4654 (2020). https://doi.org/10.1109/JIOT.2020.2964162

32. Szegedy, C., et al.: Going deeper with convolutions. CoRR abs/1409.4842 (2014). http://arxiv.org/abs/1409.4842

33. Vanhaesebrouck, P., Bellet, A., Tommasi, M.: Decentralized collaborative learning of personalized models over networks. In: Singh, A., Zhu, X.J. (eds.) Proceedings of the 20th International Conference on Artificial Intelligence and Statistics, AISTATS 2017, 20–22 April 2017, Fort Lauderdale, FL, USA. Proceedings of Machine Learning Research, vol. 54, pp. 509–517. PMLR (2017). http://proceedings.mlr.press/v54/vanhaesebrouck17a.html

34. Viroli, M., Audrito, G., Beal, J., Damiani, F., Pianini, D.: Engineering resilient collective adaptive systems by self-stabilisation. ACM Trans. Model. Comput. Simul. 28(2), 16:1–16:28 (2018). https://doi.org/10.1145/3177774, http://doi.acm.org/10.1145/3177774

35. Viroli, M., Beal, J., Damiani, F., Audrito, G., Casadei, R., Pianini, D.: From field-based coordination to aggregate computing. In: Di Marzo Serugendo, G., Loreti, M. (eds.) COORDINATION 2018. LNCS, vol. 10852, pp. 252–279. Springer, Cham (2018). https://doi.org/10.1007/978-3-319-92408-3_12

36. Warren, C.W.: Global path planning using artificial potential fields. In: Proceedings of the 1989 IEEE International Conference on Robotics and Automation, Scottsdale, Arizona, USA, 14–19 May 1989, pp. 316–321. IEEE Computer Society (1989). https://doi.org/10.1109/ROBOT.1989.100007

37. Xiao, H., Rasul, K., Vollgraf, R.: Fashion-MNIST: a novel image dataset for benchmarking machine learning algorithms. CoRR abs/1708.07747 (2017). http://arxiv.org/abs/1708.07747

38. Xu, J., Glicksberg, B.S., Su, C., Walker, P., Bian, J., Wang, F.: Federated learning for healthcare informatics. J. Healthc. Inform. Res. **5**, 1–19 (2021)

39. Yang, Q., Liu, Y., Chen, T., Tong, Y.: Federated machine learning: concept and applications. ACM Trans. Intell. Syst. Technol. **10**(2), 12:1–12:19 (2019) https://doi.org/10.1145/3298981

40. Zhang, Y., Xiang, T., Hospedales, T.M., Lu, H.: Deep mutual learning. In: 2018 IEEE Conference on Computer Vision and Pattern Recognition, CVPR 2018, Salt Lake City, UT, USA, 18–22 June 2018, pp. 4320–4328. Computer Vision Foundation/IEEE Computer Society (2018). https://doi.org/10.1109/CVPR.2018.00454, http://openaccess.thecvf.com/content_cvpr_2018/html/Zhang_Deep_Mutual_Learning_CVPR_2018_paper.html

COTS: Connected OpenAPI Test Synthesis for RESTful Applications

Christian Bartolo Burlò[1]([✉])(iD), Adrian Francalanza[2](iD), Alceste Scalas[3](iD),
and Emilio Tuosto[1](iD)

[1] Gran Sasso Science Institute, L'Aquila, Italy
`christian.bartolo@gssi.it`
[2] Department of Computer Science, University of Malta, Msida, Malta
[3] DTU Compute, Technical University of Denmark, Kongens Lyngby, Denmark

Abstract. We present a novel model-driven approach for testing REST-ful applications. We introduce a (*i*) domain-specific language for OpenAPI specifications and (*ii*) a tool to support our methodology. Our DSL, called COPENAPI, is inspired by session types and enables the modelling of communication protocols between a REST client and server. Our tool, dubbed COTS, generates (randomised) model-based test executions and reports software defects. We evaluate the effectiveness of our approach by applying it to test several open source applications. Our findings indicate that our methodology can identify nuanced defects in REST APIs and achieve comparable or superior code coverage when compared to much larger handcrafted test suites.

1 Introduction

Modern software is increasingly composed of concurrent and distributed components that are independently developed, and function by exchanging data across a communication network. The interaction of such components may be based on classic client-server Internet protocols (such as SMTP, IMAP, and POP3), various forms of remote procedure calls (RPCs), web-based standards—such as the REpresentational State Transfer (REST) architectural design.

Ensuring the correctness and reliability of these applications is notoriously hard. Software developers typically create handcrafted test suites, which must address many (and ever-growing) application usage scenarios: It is often the case that such manually-written test suites are developed intermittently, over long periods of time, by a variety of testers. This makes the software development and testing process error-prone and susceptible to inconsistencies [23,33]. A number of efforts have emerged with the aim of simplifying the testing process of component based-software by streamlining the amount of manual work through automatic test generation. Most of these efforts focus on automatic test generation for applications exposing an API over a network, where there is a considerable interest in addressing the popular REST API style [4,5,7,13,15,21,30–33,37,43].

© IFIP International Federation for Information Processing 2024
Published by Springer Nature Switzerland AG 2024
I. Castellani and F. Tiezzi (Eds.): COORDINATION 2024, LNCS 14676, pp. 75–92, 2024.
https://doi.org/10.1007/978-3-031-62697-5_5

```
1   paths:
2     /customer:
3       POST:
4         operationId: addCust
5         responses: '201' ...
6     /customer/id:
7       GET:
8         operationId: getCust
9         responses: '200' ...
10      DELETE:
11        operationId: deleteCust
12        responses: '204' ...
13    /card:
14      POST:
15        operationId: addCard
16        responses: '201' ...
17    /address:
18      POST:
19        operationId: addAddr
20        responses: '201' ...
```

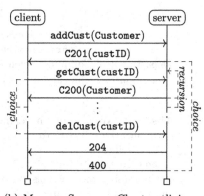

(a) OpenAPI spec. for an online store.

(b) Message Sequence Chart outlining the invocation dependencies in Fig. 1a.

Fig. 1. Typical documentation provided for REST APIs.

Example 1. Figure 1a shows a fragment of a REST API of the *SockShop* web application [38] written as an OpenAPI specification [28]. A new customer can be created by passing the necessary credentials as payload to the operation with ID addCust (lines 3–4); this operation returns a unique reference identifier for the customer, meant to be used in subsequent operations to create a payment card (addCard) and an address (addAddr) to associate with (previously created) customers. The customer information including any cards and addresses linked to it can be retrieved with getCust and deleted with deleteCust.   □

The OpenAPI in Fig. 1a is a typical instance of a REST API description. OpenAPI is used pervasively for such specifications: it provides information on the available URIs, the corresponding HTTP methods and respective responses with the associated data formats (omitted from Fig. 1a). However, OpenAPI does not specify the relationships and dependencies between different API invocations. For instance, Fig. 1a does *not* express that:

– Customer information can be added (addCard, addAddr), retrieved (getCust), or deleted (deleteCust) only after the customer is created (addCust).
– Operations addCard, addAddr or getCust cannot be executed after the customer has been deleted (deleteCust).
– Operations addCard, addAddr and getCust may be interleaved without effecting the successful outcome of the other invocations.

– The variable `custId`, an ID given to the customer upon creation is to be used to perform any operation on the customer (such as retrieval or deletion).

These dependencies induce an ordering in the API invocations, depicted in the message sequence chart in Fig. 1b. Unfortunately, this information is often omitted (cf. [8,19,38]) or only informally stated (as e.g., in [14]). In development contexts, this is often sufficient as developers are typically able to deduce the intended order of invocation by examining the descriptions of requests and the data types exchanged by each operation. However, this omission becomes problematic when testing. Deviations from the dependencies identified earlier in Fig. 1b can be categorized as *logic-based faults*, that is, errors stemming from incorrect or unintended actions within the business logic of the application. Such violations are often intricate and context-specific, arising from the unique interactions and workflows within the application. These faults are not easily detectable through basic system responses or standard error codes and typically necessitate comprehensive, scenario-based testing for identification. Furthermore, these faults are intrinsically linked to the essential operations and branching mechanisms of the application, impacting its ability to perform as intended.

Previous work on REST API testing proposes various *fully-automated* test generation strategies [5,21,33,42]. These *push-button* tools excel at detecting *systemic errors* that are related to the system's general functioning such as server crashes, malformed requests, unauthorized access attempts, or resource not found errors. However, it is unlikely that logic-based errors are uncovered by invoking the API without an explicit pre-defined model of the intended interaction with the API. *E.g.,* in the *SockShop* application from Example 1, such tools are able to detect if the SUT crashes when creating a new customer, but it is unlikely that they are able to detect whether the SUT allows the retrieval of a previously deleted customer. A test to detect such errors should create a customer and then try to retrieve the same customer after having deleted it. It has been empirically shown that the quality of tests substantially improves when conducted in a *stateful* manner, i.e., by exploring states of the system under test (SUT) that are reachable via sequences of invocations [5]. A recent work concludes that: *"existing tools fail to achieve high code coverage due to limitations of the approaches they use for generating parameter values and detecting operation dependencies"* [22].

The state-of-the-art of testing REST APIs can be seen on a spectrum. At one end, manual tests, though labor-intensive, excel at uncovering complex, logic-based errors. At the opposite end are fully-automated testing tools, which, while requiring minimal effort, fall short in detecting eloaborate errors. This work seeks a middle ground, leveraging a *model-based* approach. Our goal is to automate the identification of more logic-based faults, thus bridging the gap between labor-intensive manual testing and the scope of fully-automated tools.

Contributions. We present a model-based, tool-supported methodology for the automatic testing of web applications exposing REST APIs. Our approach allows the specification of API dependencies and constraints. Our contributions are:

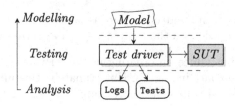

Fig. 2. Methodology overview

1. COPENAPI: a domain-specific language designed to specify dependencies between requests in an OpenAPI specification that capture the state of the interaction with the SUT and the sequencing of message exchanges;
2. COTS: an automated tool leveraging COPENAPI models to generate tests that interact with the SUT and assess the correctness of its responses.
3. Experimental results demonstrating the effectiveness of COPENAPI and COTS using case studies from various application domains. We compare our results against RESTful API testing tools and manually-written tests.

The key benefits of our approach are in terms of (*i*) a high degree of expressiveness due to the possibility of specifying data dependencies, (*ii*) effectiveness of the approach that can identify logic-based faults, and (*iii*) high level of coverage.

2   A Model-Driven, DSL-Based Methodology

2.1   Background

Based on the REST architectural style [16] and HTTP protocol, REST APIs facilitate software services on the web by exposing *resources* through HTTP URIs, which are manipulated using standard HTTP *request methods* like GET, POST, PUT, and DELETE. Responses are represented by standard HTTP codes (e.g., 200 for success, 404 for missing resources, 500 for server errors). While OpenAPI and GraphQL [18] are prominent for documenting REST APIs, our emphasis on OpenAPI stems from its broad adoption and tool support for generating client libraries across various programming languages. Though our methodology primarily targets OpenAPI, it's flexible for other web API standards like GraphQL.

The technical nature of REST APIs, their complex state-dependent interactions, and their evolving nature introduces challenges for which existing model-based testing methods and tools are ill-suited (see related work in Sect. 5). To bridge this gap, we introduce the COPENAPI DSL (Sect. 3), designed to articulate the intricate sequences and state dependencies characteristic of RESTful interactions, enabling precise testing beyond the capabilities of existing models and tools.

2.2 Methodology

Our methodology consists of the three phases depicted in Fig. 2:

(P1) *modelling phase:* construct a model that describes how a client application might interact with the SUT, and how the SUT is expected to respond to the client's inputs;

(P2) *testing phase:* automatically generate a *test driver* that tests the SUT by interacting with it according to the model, and reports whether the SUT responses violate the model;

(P3) *analysis phase:* inspect the outputs produced by test driver to identify faults in the SUT.

The phases **(P1)**, **(P2)** and **(P3)** are iterated when the model has to be refined according to the findings of the analysis or it has to be evolved according to the life cycle of the SUT. The main goal of our approach is to automate the testing phase, and let testers shift their efforts to the modelling phase, reducing the need to develop (and maintain) a large suite of handcrafted test.

The first step towards the methodology entails determining a suitable model for phase **(P1)**, allowing for the automatic derivation of tests for RESTful applications. To write such model, we design COPENAPI (see Sect. 3) taking inspiration from *(binary) session types* [20].

The next step in our methodology is **(P2)**, i.e., the testing phase. In this phase, the test driver interacts with the SUT by sending and receiving messages according to the COPENAPI model. The test driver needs to perform two types of interactions with the SUT:

– the test driver must send requests to the SUT of the correct format and payload type; and
– the test driver needs to check that the responses received from the SUT do not violate the COPENAPI model. These violations may be of three forms:
  • the response code received is not valid, or
  • the payload data does not have the expected format, or
  • the response code and payload data format are valid, but the payload data causes an assertion violation in the model (e.g., by violating a constraint involving data from a previous request/response).

The last phase of the methodology Item **(P3)** is devoted to the identification of faults in the SUT, by inspecting the outputs of the test driver. The test driver produces a successful test when it manages to complete a full traversal of the COPENAPI model without finding any of the aforementioned errors. To help with the analysis, the test driver produces two outputs:

1. a log file with information about every performed test: the random seed used to generate it, the sequence of messages sent and received and their respective payloads, and the test outcome (pass/fail); and
2. an offline representation of failed tests, usable for manually reproducing faults of the SUT without re-executing the test driver, useful for, e.g., bug reporting.

3   A DSL for OpenAPI

We introduce a DSL based on an augmented form of *session types* [12,20,36]. Intuitively, a session type specifies the valid sequences of message exchanges (i.e., the *protocol*) that regulate the interaction between communication programs; here we focus on *binary session types*, which model how a program is expected to interact with just one other program (in our case, a client with a RESTful server).

The formal syntax of our augmented session types S is:

$$
\begin{aligned}
\mathsf{S} \ ::=\ & +\{!operationId_i(\mathsf{gen}_i).\mathsf{S}_i\}_{i\in I} && (internal\ choice) \\
& |\ \ \&\{?responseCode_i(\mathsf{dec}_i)\langle A_i\rangle.\mathsf{S}_i\}_{i\in I} && (external\ choice) \\
& |\ \ \mathsf{rec}\ X.\mathsf{S} && (recursion) \\
& |\ \ X && (recursion\ variable) \\
& |\ \ \mathsf{end} && (termination) \\
\mathsf{T} \ ::=\ & \mathtt{Int}\ |\ \mathtt{String}\ |\ \ldots && (data\ types) \\
\mathsf{G} \ ::=\ & \mathtt{Int}(g)\ |\ \mathtt{String}(g)\ |\ \ \ldots && (data\ types\ with\ generators)
\end{aligned}
$$

where I is a finite non-empty set of indexes and for $i \in I$, gen_i is a *generator* assignment $x_{i,1} : \mathsf{G}_{i,1}, \ldots, x_{i,n_i} : \mathsf{G}_{i,n_i}$ (cf. Example 2) and dec is a type assignment $x_{i,1} : \mathsf{T}_{i,1}, \ldots, x_{i,n_i} : \mathsf{T}_{i,n_i}$) with $x_{i,1}, \ldots, x_{i,n_i}$ pairwise distinct. We use standard data types, including standard types (e.g., Int, String, ...) and user-defined types. Generators are also user-defined, tailored to the particular request being sent. This enables crafting input scenarios that are specifically aimed at exploring under-tested paths or complex behaviour of the API, enhancing both the depth and breadth of the testing coverage.

The communication units of our syntax are the *output* and *input* prefixes, respectively !*operationId* and ?*responseCode* where *operationId* is the corresponding identifier referring to the specific request in the OpenAPI specification and *responseCode* is the HTTP response code that is returned from the service after the request is made (see Sect. 5). Assertions A are boolean expressions that may refer to the variables occurring in preceding payload descriptions.

We illustrate the usage of COPENAPI with the following example which elaborates on the protocol in Fig. 1b.

Example 2. Figure 3 shows a testing model written in COPENAPI. The model corresponds to the message-sequence diagram from Fig. 1b. The model specifies that the interaction protocol should first create a customer by invoking addCust together with two payload generators:

1. genApiKey which retrieves a key to authenticate with the API; and
2. genCustInfo to generate the customer information.

The server is then expected to reply with the response code 201 indicating that the customer creation was successful, while also including an identification code of type String which is bound with the variable custId. Next, the driver

```
1  S_shop = !addCust(apiKey: String(genApiKey), c1: Customer(genCustInfo)).
2            ?C201(custId: String).
3            rec X.(
4              +{ !addCard(apiKey, custId, card: Card(getCardInfo)) .
5                   ?C201(CardId: String) . X,
6                 !addAddr(apiKey, custId, addr: Address(getAddrInfo)) .
7                   ?C201(addressId: String) . X,
8                 !getCust(apiKey, custId) .
9                   ?C200(c2: Customer)<checkCustomer(c1,c2)> . X,
10                !deleteCust(apiKey, custId).?C204() . end
11             }
12           )
```

Fig. 3. Example of a COPENAPI model using the OpenAPI specification in Fig. 1a, formalising the message-sequence diagram in Fig. 1b.

chooses between sending `addCard`, `addAddr`, `getCust` or `deleteCust`, including the data required in the respective payloads by either invoking the specified generators, or use previously-bound variables. For instance, in the case where `addCard` is selected, the payload must include: *(1)* the API key stored in the variable `apiKey`, *(2)* the specific customer ID stored in the variable `custId`, and *(3)* the card information, by invoking the generator `getCardInfo`.

The model also specifies the use of a user-provided assertion `checkCustomer` (line 9) to check the response sent by the SUT for the response `getCust`. The assertion checks whether the retrieved customer information (stored in $c2$) matches with the information provided when the customer was created when `addCust` was invoked (stored in $c1$). If the assertion succeeds, the test driver loops and performs the choice (line 3) once again. Otherwise, the test run terminates and the test is marked as failed. The recursion repeats until the test driver selects `delCust`, after which the protocol would terminate successfully.   □

3.1 Semantics of COPENAPI

We give a denotational semantics of COPENAPI by mapping its model to sets of finite sequences of input/output *events*. Given a output prefix π, $[\![\pi@i]\!]$ denotes the set of values in the codomain of the generator of the i-th parameter of π while for an input prefix π, $[\![\pi@i]\!]$ is the set of values inhabiting the type of the i-th parameter of π. We define

$$E = \{\pi(v_1, \ldots, v_n) \mid \pi \text{ is a prefix and } \forall 1 \leq i \leq n : v_i \in [\![\pi@i]\!]\}$$

Let M a COPENAPI model and ρ be a map assigning subsets of E^* to free recursion variables of M. The semantics of M in ρ, is the set $[\![M, \rho]\!]$ defined according to the equations in Fig. 4. The semantics is defined by induction on the structure of the COPENAPI models and returns a set of finite traces; the idea is that this set represents all the executions allowed by a COPENAPI specification. Basically, $[\![M, \rho]\!]$ yields the possible tests that the test driver might use. For

for all $i \in I, \pi_i$ output prefix, $\boldsymbol{x}_i = x_{i,1}, \ldots, x_{i,n_i}$ and $\boldsymbol{v}_i = v_{i,1}, \ldots, v_{i,n_i}$

$$\left[\!\!\left[+ \left\{ \pi_i(x_{i,1} : G_{i,1}, \ldots, x_{i,n_i} : G_{i,n_i}).S_i \right\}_{i \in I} \right]\!\!\right] \triangleq$$

$$\bigcup_{i \in I} \left\{ !\pi_i(\boldsymbol{v}_i).r_i \;\middle|\; \forall 1 \le j \le n_i : v_{i,j} \in \left[\!\!\left[\pi_i @ j \right]\!\!\right] \;:\; r_i \in \left[\!\!\left[S_i[\boldsymbol{v}_i/\boldsymbol{x}_i], \rho \right]\!\!\right] \right\}$$

for all $i \in I, \pi_i$ input prefix, $\boldsymbol{x}_i = x_{i,1}, \ldots, x_{i,n_i}$ and $\boldsymbol{v}_i = v_{i,1}, \ldots, v_{i,n_i}$

$$\left[\!\!\left[\& \left\{ \pi_i(x_{i,1} : G_{i,1}, \ldots, x_{i,n_i} : G_{i,n_i}).S_i \right\}_{i \in I} \right]\!\!\right] \triangleq$$

$$\bigcup_{i \in I} \left\{ \pi_i(\boldsymbol{v}_i).r_i \;\middle|\; \forall 1 \le j \le n_i : \; v_{i,j} \in \left[\!\!\left[\pi_i @ j \right]\!\!\right], A_i[\boldsymbol{v}_i/\boldsymbol{x}_i] \Downarrow \mathsf{tt}, r_i \in \left[\!\!\left[S_i[\boldsymbol{v}_i/\boldsymbol{x}_i], \rho \right]\!\!\right] \right\}$$

$$\left[\!\!\left[\mathsf{rec}\ X.S, \rho \right]\!\!\right] \triangleq \bigcap \left\{ R \;\middle|\; \left[\!\!\left[S, \rho[X \mapsto R] \right]\!\!\right] \subseteq R \right\} \qquad \left[\!\!\left[X, \rho \right]\!\!\right] \triangleq \rho(X) \qquad \left[\!\!\left[\mathsf{end}, \rho \right]\!\!\right] \triangleq \{\epsilon\}$$

Fig. 4. Semantics for the COPENAPI language.

example, the internal choice is defined as the set of all possible output prefixes in the choice with the different variations of the values that can be generated from the generators. The case for the external choice is similar, with the only exception that once the values are replaced in assertions of branches should hold. The semantics of end is standard. The map ρ keeps track of the recursive variables in S; initially we assume that M is *closed*, i.e., it has no free occurrences of recursion variables. This makes the semantics of recursion standard.

3.2 Implementation

We implement the COPENAPI language as part of a tool called COTS. Implemented in the Scala programming language, takes as input the COPENAPI model and the optional preamble, and generates the Scala source code of an executable *test driver* that interacts with the SUT according to the model. The test driver, in turn, interacts with the REST API exposed by the SUT by using a Scala API which is autogenerated from the provided OpenAPI specification, using OpenAPI Generator.[1] When the test driver runs, it invokes such Scala API methods to send HTTP requests to the SUT, and to receive and parse its responses; the model determines which requests are sent (and in what order) by the test driver, and which responses are expected. After completing the test runs, the test driver produces the following output:

(1) the level of model coverage achieved by the test runs;
(2) a log file with information about every performed test: the random seed used to generate the test, the sequence of requests/responses and their payloads, and the test outcome (pass/fail);
(3) an offline representation of failed tests as sequences of curl[2] commands, which can be executed from a shell to reproduce faults of the SUT without re-executing the test driver.

---

[1] https://openapi-generator.tech.
[2] https://curl.se.

Table 1. Case studies.

Application	Notes
FeaturesService [14]	Used in empirical evaluation of [4,24,33,41]
RESTCountries [27]	Used in the empirical evaluation of [41]
GestaoHospital [35]	Used in the empirical evaluation of [41]
LanguageTool [29]	Used in the empirical evaluation of [24,41]
PetClinic [8]	Used in the empirical evaluation of [10]
UsersRegistry [19]	Uses non-trivial API authentication
PetStore [9]	Used in the empirical evaluation of [24]
SockShop [38]	Used in the empirical evaluation of [1,6]
Openverse [39]	Industry app, part of WordPress project

4   Evaluation

In this section, we conduct a comprehensive evaluation of our methodology and its practical application in COTS. This assessment is twofold:

1. **Qualitative Analysis:** We aim to determine if the test-models defined by COpenAPI and the test drivers generated by COTS are effective in identifying logic-based faults.
2. **Quantitative Analysis:** We assess the effectiveness of our methodology in terms of code coverage, which is a standard metric for evaluating testing tools.

Given the novelty of our approach in user-written, model-based testing for REST-APIs, we establish our baseline comparison with: *i)* fully-automated REST testing approaches; and *ii)* manually crafted REST API tests.

4.1   Experiment Setup

To conduct such evaluation, and obtain the results presented in Sect. 4.2, we follow the preparatory steps illustrated in the rest of this section: we first select the artefacts, build their COpenAPI model, and we determine an adequate number of test runs per application.

Artefact selection. To conduct such an evaluation, we consider a sample of third-party applications listed in Table 1, satisfying the following criteria:

1. they must be open source, to facilitate reproducibility of our results;
2. they must have OpenAPI specifications, needed by COTS;
3. they should be non-trivial and thus representative of real-world RESTful applications;
4. ideally, they should include manually-written tests of their REST APIs, should be amenable to code coverage measurements, and should have been already used for evaluation in previous literature on testing.

All applications in Table 1 are open source, provide OpenAPI specifications, and are non-trivial; moreover, all of them (except *UsersRegistry* and *Openverse*) have been used in previous testing literature. The first 5 applications also satisfy the rest of our "ideal" criteria (item 4 above): they include handcrafted test suites for their REST APIs, and their architecture (consisting of a single Java-based executable) allow us to easily collect and analyse code coverage information using standard tools. Two other applications (*LanguageTool* and *PetStore*) also have similar architecture (allowing us to analyse code coverage), but do not include a test suite for their REST APIs.

Building the COpenAPI *Models.* As we are not the authors of the SUTs in Table 1, we were required to infer the usage of the SUTs as intended by their developers—in particular, what sequences of operations (request/responses) are valid, and how some requests may depend on others. As mentioned earlier, this information is typically only given informally in the application documentation, it may not be up-to-date, and is often omitted. Therefore, we often inferred this information by examining the pre-existing handcrafted tests, or by studying existing REST API clients. We also enriched our test models with application usage scenarios that, although possible, might have been overlooked in the existing handwritten tests. This way, our models may leverage SUT functionalities beyond those covered by the existing tests, and potentially reveal new faults in the SUTs.

Example 3. FeaturesService was the only application with documentation about some of its operations. For instance, the documentation says:

> *"The application should allow one to add a constraint such that when a feature requires another feature to be active, the latter feature cannot be deactivated without first deactivating the former."*

To test whether *FeaturesService* respects such a description, we formalise the COpenAPI model shown in Fig. 5 (abridged). This model specifies that the test driver should first add two features by invoking `addFeature`; their names are created by random generators and bound in variables *feat1* and *feat2*. Then, the test driver should invoke `addConstraint` specifying that *feat2* requires *feat1*. Finally, the test driver should attempt to delete *feat1* via `delFeature`, expecting the SUT to answer with a 400 "bad request" response. If the SUT was to answer with anything other than a 400, (such as 200, indicating that the operation was successful) it would indicate a fault in the logic of the SUT.   □

Determining an Adequate Number of Test Runs. After writing the COpenAPI model of each SUT and generating its test driver using COTS, we established an adequate number of test runs for each SUT. The optimal number of test runs is the smallest number that maximises *(1)* the number of discovered faults, *(2)* the level of code coverage, and *(3)* the level of model coverage. This number depends on the complexity of the SUT and the COpenAPI model in use. To determine the optimal number, we adopted an incremental approach: gradually

```
1  S_featuresService = rec X.(
2      +{ !addFeature(feat1: String(genFeatName)).?C201().
3            !addFeature(feat2: String(genFeatName)).?C201().
4              !addConstraint(feat1, feat2).?C201().
5                !delFeature(feat1).?C400().X,
6          ...
7      } )
```

Fig. 5. COPENAPI model for testing *FeaturesServices* (abridged), discussed in Example 3.

increase the number of test runs until the rate of bug discovery and code coverage plateau. This was determined by analysing the logs generated by COTS for each application and verifying that the model was being fully traversed.

4.2 Results

We now present our results, in terms of discovered faults (Sect. 4.2) and code coverage (Sect. 4.2).

Discovered Faults. Table 2 reports the number of faults discovered by our test models and the COTS-generated test drivers, categorised by the test oracle that detected the fault. We found 25 faults across the 9 selected applications and reported some of the most representative faults to the application maintainers; when we received a reply, in almost all cases the developers acknowledged that the faults were real bugs.[3]

Table 2 classifies the faults detected by COTS into logic-based and systematic categories. Logic-based faults, embedded in the SUT's logic, are discerned through testing specific operational sequences, while systematic faults, inherent in the SUT's overall function, can be identified by testing the requests in isolation of other requests. COTS successfully uncovered 10 logic-based and 15 systematic faults. Detecting the logic-based faults is attributed to COPENAPI models, which incorporate the SUT's domain knowledge, enabling COTS to navigate complex, interdependent request-response sequences. Such intricate sequences are unlikely to be deduced by fully-automated tools (e.g., Example 3), that, as mentioned earlier focus more on systematic faults. Furthermore, as Table 2 demonstrates, COTS effectively detects both fault types.

Some examples of logic-based faults follow:

- In the *PetClinic* model, we included an assertion to verify that a newly created resource can be subsequently retrieved from the SUT. However, COTS

---

[3] For *LanguageTool*, we reported 3 cases of *"500 Internal Server Error"* uncovered by our test model; such errors are considered faults in REST testing literature, but *LanguageTool* produces such errors to signal an unsupported functionality.

Table 2. Faults discovered by COTS test drivers and oracles, using our COPENAPI models.

ïź£

Application	Bad status code	Bad response body	Assertion fail	Total	Logical errors	Systematic errors
FeaturesService	6	0	0	6 (1, 0)	2	4
RESTCountries	0	2	0	2 (2, 0)	2	0
GestaoHospital	1	0	0	1 (1, 0)	0	1
LanguageTool	3	0	0	3 (3, 3)	0	3
PetClinic	5	0	2	7 (3, 3)	4	3
UsersRegistry	1	0	0	1 (1, 1)	0	1
PetStore	1	0	0	1 (1, 0)	0	1
SockShop	1	1	0	2 (2, 0)	1	1
Openverse	1	1	0	2 (2, 2)	1	1
Total	19	4	2	25 (16, 6)	10	15

discovered a fault: if a resource is updated, subsequent retrieval attempts fail, indicating an issue in the SUT's retrieval operation.

– Another fault in the *PetClinic* application involved inconsistent identification numbers. The SUT issues an ID number when a resource is created, but the list of resources returned shows different IDs than those originally assigned.

– The *FeaturesService* application did not adhere to the model shown in Example 3. It incorrectly permitted the deactivation of *feat1*, which should have been disallowed, and erroneously returned a successful HTTP status code of 204 instead of indicating failure.

– In the *SockShop* application, a significant fault was identified: the application fails to retrieve resources immediately after their creation. This fault was detected by first creating the resource and then attempting to retrieve it via the API sequence modelled via COPENAPI.

Code Coverage. Table 3 reports the size of the case studies,[4] and compares COTS model-based testing coverage results against handcrafted REST API test suites (when available as part of the selected case studies), and against fully-automated REST API testing.

The table shows the sizes (in lines of code) of our COPENAPI models against the handwritten REST API test suites. The COTS model sizes include the preambles, whereas the handwritten test sizes exclude their comments. Table 3

---

[4] The *LanguageTool* application has 5 API endpoints but only 2 are testable.

Table 3. Size information about the case studies, and comparison between COTS-based testing results (with COPENAPI models developed by us, executed for up to 1 min with default initial randomness seed), handwritten tests (part of the SUT source code), and Morest (average across 5 repetitions, each requiring 8 h of execution). The coverage is measured using JaCoCo 0.8.8 (https://www.eclemma.org/jacoco) with standard configuration; JaCoCo is also used in the Morest evaluation [24].

Application	Application LOC	#endpoints	COPENAPI model size (LOC)	Manual tests size (LOC)	Number of COTS test runs	COTS tests line coverage	Manual tests line coverage	Morest avg. line coverage [24]
RESTCountries	2409	22	247	300	100	**1722**	896	
GestaoHospital	4427	20	138	463	50	**2857**	2532	
PetClinic	10,416	35	225	1321	100	3099	**3127**	
UsersRegistry	5452	11	68	246	50	**2035**	1906	
FeaturesService	2026	18	98	377	150	**1626**	1576	360
LanguageTool	18,053	2	75		20	**4999**		935
PetStore	3693	20	111		100	**1987**		763.20
SockShop	3392	15	99		50			
OpenVerse	7117	16	124		1			

also shows the number of test runs performed using COTS and the number of lines covered by 1. COTS; 2. the applications' handwritten REST API tests; and 3. the fully-automated tool Morest [24,25]. We focus on Morest because a recent study [24] shows Morest to be superior to the other fully-automatic REST API testing tools in literature. Therefore, we selected Morest as representing the state-of-the-art, and included some of its case studies (*FeaturesService, LanguageTool* and *Petstore*) in our experiments.

In Table 3 we can observe that COPENAPI models are smaller than the handwritten tests provided by the SUTs—and yet, their code coverage is comparable, and higher for COTS in most cases. In the case of *RestCountries*, the COPENAPI model size is quite close to the handwritten tests size, but the COTS coverage is significantly higher. This suggests that a concise COPENAPI model can replace (part of) a larger handwritten test suite, allowing testers to "*concentrate on a (data) model and generation infrastructure instead of hand-crafting individual test*" [11].

With respect to the fully-automatic testing tool Morest, the benefits of developing a COPENAPI model are evident in the significantly higher line coverage achieved by COTS. In the three common applications we examined, COTS achieved 3 times as much coverage in *PetStore*, 4 times as much in *FeaturesService*, and 5 times as much in *LanguageTool*. Our results were obtained in a few seconds (once the COPENAPI model was developed), whereas the Morest coverage is averaged over 5 executions taking 8 h each. This suggests that, after the initial investment of time needed to write a COPENAPI model, our model-based approach pays off in terms of coverage achieved and time saved over repeated executions.

4.3 Threats to Validity and Limitations

The time taken to develop COPENAPI models for these case studies varied from one application to another, depending on the complexity of the requests of the applications. On average, we estimate that it took us 30 h to complete each model—including the time we used to infer the intended usage of the application in question. We believe that a developer or tester more familiar with the application domain and requirements would write equivalent (or better) test models in less time.

Internal Threats to Validity. The method for determining optimal test runs could lead to imprecisions due to local maxima. Our lack of precise knowledge about expected request/response sequences necessitated designing COPENAPI models based on application tests and source code, potentially introducing bias (Table 3). Additionally, the comparison does not account for the qualitative distinction between creating concrete test cases and developing more abstract COPENAPI models, with the latter possibly being viewed as more challenging.

External Threats to Validity. Our case studies, though diverse, may not universally represent all application types, limiting generalizability (Sect. 4.1). We aligned our study with REST API testing discourse, selecting artefacts common in literature to minimize bias and ensure relevance. Despite these efforts, the specific selection could limit applicability, though it was necessary for comparability with existing research.

5 Related Work

In contrast to existing methodologies, our COPENAPI DSL allows for a more nuanced and comprehensive modelling of REST API behaviour. It enables the description of complex sequences and dependencies that are essential for thoroughly testing RESTful services. This approach is a significant departure from traditional models, which typically address simpler scenarios or focus on individual API operations in isolation.

We classify studies on testing of REST APIs into two broad categories: *model-based* and *fully automatic*.

Model-Based Testing of REST APIs. Our work enriches model-based testing of REST APIs by introducing a sophisticated DSL, COPENAPI, for detailed modeling and testing, diverging from existing approaches by supporting complex test sequences and state dependencies within a single model (§3). Unlike Chakrabarti et al. [7] and Fertig et al. [15], who focus on isolated sequences or operations, our DSL enables multiple test paths and value assertions, surpassing the limitations of singular test sequence models and isolated API testing. Furthermore, while Seijas *et al.* [32] and Pinheiro *et al.* [30] contribute valuable perspectives on property-based and state machine-based modeling, they lack in addressing dynamic data generation and comprehensive evaluation. Francisco *et al.*'s [17] constraints-driven approach and Aichernig *et al.*'s [2] business rule modeling offer insights into precondition and postcondition specification, yet neither adequately tackles the RESTful API stateful interaction complexity our COPEN-NAPI DSL is designed for. In contrast, TorXakis, another model-based testing tool, applied in [34] to the Dropbox synchronization protocol, does not support RESTful APIs and extending it would entail significant development, including the creation of an adapter for translating REST API requests and responses and aligning OpenAPI data types with those of TorXakis [34]. Our approach uniquely facilitates capturing intricate dependencies across REST API requests and responses, a critical aspect for thorough testing of sophisticated web services.

Fully Automatic Testing of REST APIs. This category includes a variety of testing approaches [13,31,33,43] and tools such as RestTestGen [37], RESTler [5], EvoMaster [4], QuickREST [21], RestCT [40] and Morest [24,25]. Starting from an API specification like OpenAPI [28], these tools automatically generate tests primarily to check the correctness of individual API responses. They mostly rely on random data generators or generators automatically derived from the specifications, which might not fully capture the intricacies of the API's behaviour. In contrast, in our work, the sequencing of valid requests and responses is explicitly specified in the model, enabling complex interactions with the SUT. This is complemented by our use of non-random, tester-assigned data generators in the COPENAPI model, which allows for a more targeted and effective testing approach. This method provides a stark contrast to AGORA's invariant detection-based approach [3] and the approach in [26] focussing on the specification of inter-parameter dependencies. While these methodologies offer robust solutions in their respective areas, they do not offer the same level of specificity in interaction sequencing and tailored data generation as our COPEN-NAPI model-driven approach does.

6   Conclusion

We introduced COTS, a tool implementing a model-based testing approach for RESTful applications using COPENAPI DSL and OpenAPI specifications, which generates executable test drivers for model-based testing of web services. Our evaluation against third-party open source applications and comparison with existing automated REST API testing tools and manual test suites demonstrates the efficacy of COTS. It achieved comparable or better code coverage and fault detection with smaller, more manageable models, highlighting the potential for reduced effort in test creation and maintenance. Future work includes extending COTS to support other API specifications like GraphQL and gRPC, and enhancing COPENAPI's expressiveness by incorporating additional test oracles and timing constraints.

Acknowledgements. We thank the anonymous reviewers for their comments. This work was partially supported by: the Horizon Europe grant 101093006 (TaRDIS); the BehAPI project funded by the EU H2020 RISE under the Marie Skłodowska-Curie action (No: 778233); the PRIN 2022 PNRR project DeLiCE (F53D23009130001); the MUR project PON REACT EU; the PRO3 MUR project Software Quality; "the MUR dipartimento di eccellenza"; the PNRR MUR project VITALITY (ECS00000041); Spoke 2 ASTRA - Advanced Space Technologies and Research Alliance.

References

1. Aderaldo, C.M., Mendonça, N.C., Pahl, C., Jamshidi, P.: Benchmark requirements for microservices architecture research. In: ECASE@ICSE, pp. 8–13. IEEE (2017)
2. Aichernig, B.K., Schumi, R.: Property-based testing of web services by deriving properties from business-rule models. Softw. Syst. Model. **18**(2), 889–911 (2019)
3. Alonso, J.C., Segura, S., Ruiz-Cortés, A.: AGORA: automated generation of test oracles for REST APIs. In: ISSTA, pp. 1018–1030. ACM (2023)
4. Arcuri, A.: Restful API automated test case generation. In: QRS, pp. 9–20. IEEE (2017). https://doi.org/10.1109/QRS.2017.11
5. Atlidakis, V., Godefroid, P., Polishchuk, M.: RESTler: stateful REST API fuzzing. In: ICSE, pp. 748–758. IEEE/ACM (2019)
6. Avritzer, A., Ferme, V., Janes, A., Russo, B., Schulz, H., van Hoorn, A.: A quantitative approach for the assessment of microservice architecture deployment alternatives by automated performance testing. In: Cuesta, C.E., Garlan, D., Pérez, J. (eds.) ECSA 2018. LNCS, vol. 11048, pp. 159–174. Springer, Cham (2018). https://doi.org/10.1007/978-3-030-00761-4_11
7. Chakrabarti, S.K., Kumar, P.: Test-the-rest: an approach to testing restful web-services. In: 2009 Computation World: Future Computing, Service Computation, Cognitive, Adaptive, Content, Patterns, pp. 302–308 (2009). https://doi.org/10.1109/ComputationWorld.2009.116
8. Community, S.P.: Pet clinic application (2022). https://github.com/spring-petclinic/spring-petclinic-rest
9. Community, S.A.: Pet store application (2023). https://github.com/swagger-api/swagger-petstore
10. Corradini, D., Zampieri, A., Pasqua, M., Ceccato, M.: Empirical comparison of black-box test case generation tools for restful APIs. CoRR abs/2108.08196 (2021)
11. Dalal, S.R., et al.: Model-based testing in practice. In: ICSE, pp. 285–294. ACM (1999)
12. Dezani-Ciancaglini, M., de'Liguoro, U.: Sessions and session types: an overview. In: Laneve, C., Su, J. (eds.) WS-FM 2009. LNCS, vol. 6194, pp. 1–28. Springer, Heidelberg (2010). https://doi.org/10.1007/978-3-642-14458-5_1
13. Ed-Douibi, H., Izquierdo, J.L.C., Cabot, J.: Automatic generation of test cases for REST APIs: a specification-based approach. In: EDOC, pp. 181–190. IEEE Computer Society (2018)
14. noz Ferrara, J.M.: Features model microservice (2016). https://github.com/JavierMF/features-service

15. Fertig, T., Braun, P.: Model-driven testing of restful APIs. In: WWW (Companion Volume), pp. 1497–1502. ACM (2015)
16. Fielding, R.T., Taylor, R.N.: Architectural styles and the design of network-based software architectures. Ph.D. thesis, University of California, Irvine (2000)
17. Francisco, M.A., López, M., Ferreiro, H., Castro, L.M.: Turning web services descriptions into quickcheck models for automatic testing. In: Erlang Workshop, pp. 79–86. ACM (2013)
18. GraphQL (2023). https://graphql.org
19. Henrique, R.: Users registry application (2022). https://github.com/Throyer/springboot-api-rest-example
20. Hüttel, H., et al.: Foundations of session types and behavioural contracts. ACM Comput. Surv. **49**(1), 3:1–3:36 (2016). https://doi.org/10.1145/2873052
21. Karlsson, S., Causevic, A., Sundmark, D.: QuickREST: property-based test generation of OpenAPI-described restful APIs. In: ICST, pp. 131–141. IEEE (2020)
22. Kim, M., Xin, Q., Sinha, S., Orso, A.: Automated test generation for rest APIs: no time to rest yet. In: Proceedings of the 31st ACM SIGSOFT International Symposium on Software Testing and Analysis, pp. 289–301 (2022)
23. Lenarduzzi, V., Daly, J., Martini, A., Panichella, S., Tamburri, D.A.: Toward a technical debt conceptualization for serverless computing. IEEE Softw. **38**(1), 40–47 (2021)
24. Liu, Y., et al.: Morest: model-based RESTful API testing with execution feedback. In: ICSE, pp. 1406–1417. ACM (2022)
25. Liu, Y., Li, Y., Liu, Y., Wan, R., Wu, R., Liu, Q.: Morest: industry practice of automatic restful API testing. In: ASE, pp. 138:1–138:5. ACM (2022)
26. Martin-Lopez, A., Segura, S., Müller, C., Ruiz-Cortés, A.: Specification and automated analysis of inter-parameter dependencies in web APIs. IEEE Trans. Serv. Comput. **15**(4), 2342–2355 (2022)
27. Matos, A.: REST Countries. https://restcountries.com
28. OpenAPI (2023). https://www.openapis.org
29. Language Tool Organisation: Language tool. https://github.com/languagetool-org/languagetool
30. Pinheiro, P., Endo, A.T., da Silva Simão, A.: Model-based testing of RESTful web services using UML protocol state machines (2013)
31. Segura, S., Parejo, J.A., Troya, J., Cortés, A.R.: Metamorphic testing of restful web APIs. IEEE Trans. Softw. Eng. **44**(11), 1083–1099 (2018)
32. Seijas, P.L., Li, H., Thompson, S.J.: Towards property-based testing of restful web services. In: Erlang Workshop, pp. 77–78. ACM (2013)
33. Stallenberg, D.M., Olsthoorn, M., Panichella, A.: Improving test case generation for REST APIs through hierarchical clustering. In: ASE, pp. 117–128. IEEE (2021)
34. Tretmans, G.J., Laar, M.: Model-based testing with TorXakis: the mysteries of dropbox revisited (2019)
35. de Vargas, V.P.: Gestao hospital system. https://github.com/ValchanOficial/GestaoHospital
36. Vasconcelos, V.T.: Fundamentals of session types. Inf. Comput. **217**, 52–70 (2012). https://doi.org/10.1016/j.ic.2012.05.002
37. Viglianisi, E., Dallago, M., Ceccato, M.: RESTTESTGEN: automated black-box testing of restful APIs. In: ICST, pp. 142–152. IEEE (2020)
38. Weaveworks: Sock shop (2021). https://github.com/microservices-demo/microservices-demo
39. WordPress Foundation: Openverse. https://wordpress.org/openverse

40. Wu, H., Xu, L., Niu, X., Nie, C.: Combinatorial testing of restful APIs. In: ICSE, pp. 426–437. ACM (2022)
41. Zhang, M., Arcuri, A.: Open problems in fuzzing RESTful APIs: a comparison of tools. CoRR abs/2205.05325v2 (2022). https://arxiv.org/abs/2205.05325v2. Version 2
42. Zhang, M., Marculescu, B., Arcuri, A.: Resource-based test case generation for restful web services. In: GECCO, pp. 1426–1434. ACM (2019)
43. Zhang, M., Marculescu, B., Arcuri, A.: Resource and dependency based test case generation for restful web services. Empir. Softw. Eng. **26**(4), 76 (2021)

Modelling, Verifying and Testing the Contract Automata Runtime Environment with UPPAAL

Davide Basile[(⊠)] [iD]

Formal Methods and Tools Lab, CNR–ISTI, Pisa, Italy
`davide.basile@isti.cnr.it`

Abstract. The contract automata runtime environment (`CARE`) is a distributed middleware application recently introduced to realise service applications specified using a dialect of finite-state automata. In this paper, we detail the formal modelling and verification of `CARE`. We provide a formalisation as a network of stochastic timed automata. The model is verified against the desired properties with the tool UPPAAL, utilizing exhaustive and statistical model checking techniques. This research emphasises the advantages of employing formal modelling, verification and testing processes to enhance the dependability of an open-source distributed application. We discuss the methodology used for modelling the application and address the issues that have been identified and fixed.

1 Introduction

Behavioural contracts [1] have been introduced to formally describe the interactions among services, to enable to reason formally about well-behaving properties of their composition. Examples of properties are agreement among the parties or reachability of target states.

Contract automata are a dialect of finite state automata used to specify behavioural contracts formally in terms of offers and requests [7]. A composition of contracts is in *agreement* when all requests are matched by corresponding offers of other contracts. A composition can be refined to one in agreement using the orchestration synthesis algorithm [4,6], a variation of the synthesis algorithm from supervisory control theory [22]. The Contract Automata Runtime Environment (`CARE`) [3] provides a middleware to coordinate the services implementing contracts. In `CARE`, each transition of the orchestration automaton is executed by a series of interactions among the orchestrator and the `CARE` services, implemented using Java TCP/IP sockets. These interactions may vary according to the specific configuration chosen among those provided by `CARE`. In [3] the algorithms implemented in `CARE` are proved to enforce the adherence of each contract specification to its `CARE` implementation (basically, the control flow of the application follows the synthesised orchestration automaton).

In this paper, we describe the modelling and verification of the low-level interactions among `CARE` services and the orchestrator. This aspect is no less

© IFIP International Federation for Information Processing 2024
Published by Springer Nature Switzerland AG 2024
I. Castellani and F. Tiezzi (Eds.): COORDINATION 2024, LNCS 14676, pp. 93–110, 2024.
https://doi.org/10.1007/978-3-031-62697-5_6

important, as witnessed by known cases of algorithms proved to be correct (e.g., the Byzantine distributed consensus [16]) and whose low-level communication implementations were found to have issues, e.g. deadlocks [23]. We verify several properties, including the absence of deadlocks, absence of undelivered messages, and reachability of target states. The formal model is a network of stochastic timed automata as accepted by the UPPAAL toolbox. This work extends a preliminary verification summarised in [3] as follows. Different variants of the formal model are proposed. The model undergoes verification against the desired properties using UPPAAL, employing both exhaustive model checking, statistical model checking and model-based testing. All models, formulas, and logs are publicly available in [2], together with traceability and model-based testing information connecting the model to the source code. Finally, this paper tackles the challenge of providing a full-fledged model-based development and formal methods approach [12]. The final application has been graphically modelled at an abstract level, formally verified and tested using the formal model. The criteria followed for abstracting away irrelevant details are discussed together with the issues that have been found and fixed thanks to the formal modelling, verification and testing.

Related Work. Several applications of UPPAAL to various case studies are available in the literature, including land transport [5], maritime transport [24], medical systems [18], and autonomous agents path planning [14]. These case studies, along with the present paper, adopt a model-based approach, wherein partial representations of the applications are created using models.

In contrast to the previously mentioned literature, in this paper we present a bottom-up formal analysis of an established open-source system that has already been developed [3]. The availability of the source code further enables us to establish a connection between the abstract formal model and the actual source code. This capability facilitates the precise identification of specific aspects of the real system that have been abstracted in the formal model. Additionally, it allows us to validate the appropriateness of the chosen level of abstraction. To the best of our knowledge, there are no other non-trivial open-source applications for which their UPPAAL formal model is openly accessible and directly connected to the source code through traceability and model-based testing. This contribution assists in linking formal methods, particularly UPPAAL, to the software development process. As reported in [10], the question of qualification and validation of formal methods tools is "absolutely crucial". Other tools for behavioural contracts are present in the literature [13,20], but differently from CARE, many of these implementations have not undergone a process of formal verification.

Outline. Section 2 provides background. The modelling phase is described in Sect. 3, whilst the verification is described in Sect. 4. Finally, the conclusion and future work are presented in Sect. 5.

2   Background

In this section, we will provide background on contract automata, their software support, and the UPPAAL statistical model checker. The focus of this paper is on the formal analysis of the runtime environment of contract automata. While we offer a concise overview of contract automata to enhance comprehension of their runtime environment, they are not the focus of our formal analysis.

Contract Automata. Contract automata are a dialect of finite-state automata modelling services that exchange offers and requests. A contract automaton models either a single service or a composition of interacting services. Labels of transitions of contract automata are vectors of atomic elements called *actions*. Similarly, states of contract automata are vectors of atomic elements called basic states. The length of the vectors is equal to the number of services in the automaton (this number is called *rank*). A request (resp., offer) action is prefixed by ? (resp., !). The idle action is denoted by -. Labels are constrained to be one out of three types. In a *request* (resp., *offer*) label a service performs a request (resp., offer) action and all other services are idle. In a *match* label one service performs a request action, another service performs a matching offer action, and all other services are idle. For example, the contract automaton in Fig. 3 right has rank 2 and the label [?quit, !quit] is a match where the request action ?quit is matched by the offer action !quit. Note the difference between a request label, e.g. [?coffee, -], and a request action, e.g. ?coffee.

In a composition of contracts various properties can be analysed [7]. For example, the property of *agreement* requires to match all request actions, whereas offer actions can remain unmatched. The synthesis of the orchestration in agreement produces a sub-automaton of the composition where all services can match their requests with corresponding offers to reach a final state. Thus, in the orchestration in agreement labels of transitions are only matches or offers [6]. The contract automaton in Fig. 3 right is an orchestration in agreement.

Uppaal. UPPAAL SMC [11] is a variant of UPPAAL [9], which is a well-known toolbox for the verification of real-time systems. UPPAAL models are stochastic timed automata, in which non-determinism is replaced with probabilistic choices and time delays with probability distributions (uniform for bounded time and exponential for unbounded time). These automata may communicate via broadcast channels and shared variables. In this paper, we will use both exhaustive and statistical model checking. Statistical Model Checking (SMC) [17] involves running a sufficient number of (probabilistic) simulations of a system model to obtain statistical evidence (with a predefined level of statistical confidence) of the quantitative properties to be checked. Monte Carlo estimation with Chernoff-Hoeffding bound executes $N = \lceil (ln(2) - ln(\alpha))/(2\varepsilon^2) \rceil$ simulations ρ_i, $i \in 1...N$, to provide the interval $[p' - \varepsilon, p' + \varepsilon]$ with confidence $1 - \alpha$, where $p' = (\#\{\rho_i \mid \rho_i \models \varphi\})/N$, i.e., $\text{Pr}(|p' - p| \leq \varepsilon) \geq 1 - \alpha$ where p is the unknown value of the formula φ being estimated statistically and ε and α are the user-defined precision and confidence, respectively. Crucially, the number of simulations used to estimate a formula is independent of the model's size and depends only on the parameters α and ε. In practice the number of simulations required by UPPAAL to reach a specific confidence level is optimized and is thus lower than the above theoretical bound. UPPAAL supports template automata used to instantiate different copies (in different experiments) of the same automaton, distinguishable by their parameters. The selection of UPPAAL as the chosen tool is influenced by several factors. These include its extensive adoption by the community, expertise of the author, usability, primitive support for real-time and stochastic modeling, probabilistic and non-deterministic choices, and capabilities for statistical model checking, simulation, and model-based testing.

CARE. The Contract Automata Runtime Environment (CARE) [3] provides facilities for pairing the contract automata specifications with actual implementations of service-based applications. Note that our purpose is not to formally analyse the applications created using CARE, but to formally analyse CARE itself. The formal verification of applications developed using CARE is a consequence of the reliance of CARE on the formal guarantees provided by contract automata [3], along with the formal verification of CARE as an application. This paper addresses the latter aspect. The two core abstract Java classes are the RunnableOrchestration and the RunnableOrchestratedContract. The first one is the implementation of the orchestrator who reads the synthesised orchestration automaton and communicates with the RunnableOrchestratedContract services to realise the prescribed behaviour. Each RunnableOrchestratedContract is responsible for pairing its contract automaton specification with an implementation provided as a Java class, where each action of the automaton is in correspondence with a method of the class. Each time a new orchestration involving the service is initiated, the RunnableOrchestratedContract creates a new service. This service remains in a waiting state to receive commands from the orchestrator, which then triggers the execution of the corresponding methods. In case the orchestrator requires to perform an action not prescribed by its service contract, then a ContractViolationException will be raised by the service.

In CARE, two main aspects to implement are the execution of *choices* and *actions*. For choices, the two currently available implementations are DictatorialChoice (the orchestrator decides autonomously) and MajoritarianChoice (each service involved votes and the majority wins). For actions, the two currently available implementations are CentralisedAction and DistributedAction. In a CentralisedAction, the orchestrator acts as a broker forwarding the offers and requests of the two services to realise the match. In a DistributedAction, the orchestrator makes the two services aware of each other by communicating their addresses and ports. The two services autonomously realise the match action, after which control returns to the orchestrator. Recall that in an orchestration in agreement, labels can be matches or offers and in case of offers the orchestrator interacts with only one service.

3   Methodology and Formal Model

We now describe the methodology used for modelling the communications, abstracting away irrelevant details and ascertain the adequacy of the model with respect to the implementation.

3.1 Methodology

Modelling TCP/IP Sockets Communication. Java TCP/IP sockets communications are asynchronous with FIFO buffers [19]. In UPPAAL, the interactions are via channel synchronisation and global variables. Thus, TCP/IP sockets are solely employed in the actual implementation and are not utilized by the automata of the model. Instead, in the model, global (FIFO) arrays are used to model the TCP/IP sockets buffers. These arrays are only modified by functions for enqueueing and dequeuing messages. Each party communicates with the partner using two global arrays (one for sending and one for receiving, respectively). The local declarations of the two automata contain methods for sending and receiving from the partners and checking their queues of messages. Both automata declare a method `enqueue` for sending to the partner a message (that is one of the global constants described above). Indeed, in this model the actual payload of each communication is abstracted away. The identifier of the service `id` is only needed on the orchestrator side to identify the partner (there is only one orchestrator thus no identifier is needed for it). Similarly, both automata have a method `dequeue` for consuming messages from their respective arrays.

The default mode for Java TCP/IP sockets is *blocking* [15], meaning that the sender blocks when the buffer of the receiver is full, and waits until there is enough space to proceed. Accordingly, a transition having a send in its effect will check in its guard whether there is enough space left in the array of the partner by calling either the method `available` (returning the space left) or `isFull`. Similarly, in Java TCP/IP sockets the read operation is *blocking*. Accordingly, before reading it is always checked whether the array is not empty with the method `!isEmpty`. When the array is empty the automaton blocks until a message is received.

Source locations of sending and receiving transitions are neither committed nor urgent. In fact, an enabled committed transition (i.e., whose source location is committed, denoted with C) must be executed before any other non-committed transition in the network. Instead, an urgent transition must be executed without any delay. If a send or receiving transition were to be either committed or urgent, it would introduce the possibility of false positive deadlocks. This scenario arises when, for example, the receiver has a full buffer (i.e., array) and is prepared to free it, but the sender transition is enabled and committed. Similarly, this false positive can occur when the buffer is full, the send transition is urgent but the receive operation is not urgent, or vice versa, when the buffer is empty, the read transition is urgent, and the send operation is not urgent.

Hence, the operations of writing to and reading from a buffer are represented using stochastic delays, specifically following an exponential distribution. Two rates are employed to capture the delay associated with reading and writing. These exponential delays are present in all non-committed and non-final locations of both automata in Fig. 1 and Fig. 2. However, the presence of unbounded delays introduces scenarios where the receiver (resp., sender) may wait indefinitely without executing its read (resp., write) transition, even when it is enabled.

These scenarios would invalidate the exhaustive model checking of reachability properties that are satisfied by the actual system, leading to false positives. In the real implementation, Java TCP/IP sockets offer a timeout mechanism wherein an exception is thrown if no message exchange occurs within a specified time frame. All sockets used by CARE have this timeout. Consequently, a dedicated automaton called SocketTimeout is replicated for each service to model the timeout operation (see Fig. 3 left). Each send or receive operation in every socket resets the SocketTimeout clock c. If no reset operation is received within a certain duration (variable timeout), SocketTimeout enters a location called Timeout and broadcasts the signal fail, indicating that an exception has been thrown. All automata have a transition from every location (except for Terminated) to a location Timeout that is reached upon receiving the signal fail. For readability, these Timeout locations and all their incoming transitions are not shown in Figs. 1 and 2.

Abstractions. We have discussed the modelling of Java TCP/IP socket communications. We now discuss other aspects that have been abstracted away in the model. We note that the abstracted aspects are irrelevant for the analysis discussed in Sect. 4. In the model, the underlying orchestration automaton is abstracted together with the contracts of the services. Thus, all conditionals that are dependent from the underlying orchestration are abstracted as probabilistic choices. We assume that the orchestration has been correctly synthesised from the services contracts. This allows us to verify the interactions for any possible valid orchestration. If a specific orchestration would be modelled, then we would lose such generality. In particular, the payloads of the communications (e.g., which specific action, which choices) are abstracted. The conditions used to decide whether to perform a choice, an action or to stop are also abstracted away. The only modelled condition is that no two consecutive choices are allowed (i.e., after choosing, the chosen step must be performed). When executing a transition, the conditions used to check whether the label of the transition is an offer or a match are abstracted away in the model. Moreover, the identifiers of the services involved in performing a choice or an action (which are concretely extracted from the labels of the transitions) are also chosen non-deterministically. Indeed, all services are distinguished replicas of the same automaton. Finally, we model a single orchestration. In fact, when multiple orchestrations are executed, they operate independently of each other and can be verified individually.

Adequacy. The adequacy of the adopted level of abstraction is ascertained as follows. Each transition in the model is traced back to the specific lines of source code in [2]. The model-based testing functionality of UPPAAL has been employed to generate tests that demonstrate the model's adherence to the actual implementation. Roughly, each transition that involves enqueuing or dequeuing messages produces test code for writing to or reading from a socket, respectively. Due to lack of space, we refer to [2] for more details. The generated tests cover all transitions of the model and all interactions between the orchestrator and the services. The code coverage indicates that the tests derived from the model cover a significant portion of the source code. This suggests that the model is not excessively abstract compared to the actual implementation. Furthermore, the modelling and verification allowed us to fix some issues (see Sect. 4). This would not have been possible in case the abstraction were too coarse.

Remark. We highlight the advantages of employing graphical diagrams. When it comes to the implementation phase, developers typically work with the source code, which currently consists of 770 lines of code in the case of CARE. On the other hand, during the modelling phase with UPPAAL, designers graphically edit automata. The automata depicted in Fig. 1 and Fig. 2 succinctly and accurately specify the interaction logic of CARE.

3.2   Formal Model

The formal model of CARE is described. All models used in this paper together with the evaluated formulas are available in [2]. The network of automata is composed of a RunnableOrchestration automaton modeling the orchestrator, and each service is modeled by two automata: RunnableOrchestratedContract and SocketTimeout.

Figure 1   displays   the   template   automaton   for   the RunnableOrchestration (i.e., the orchestrator), while the template automaton for the RunnableOrchestratedContract (i.e., the service) has as parameter the id of the service and is depicted in Fig. 2. The behaviour according to the given configuration of action and choice is modelled inside each automaton. We anticipate that we will use variants of these two automata in Sect. 4, in order to perform different analyses. In particular, in Figs. 1 and 2 the configurations of choice and action (for both the services and the orchestrator) are instantiated non-deterministically. Another version of the model is also available where the configuration options are also parameters of the templates. The repository [2] contains the model equipped with traceability information, i.e., each transition of the model has a comment describing the class and the lines of the source code that correspond to the specific behaviour of the transition. The models used for generating tests, together with the generated tests, are also available in [2].

The UPPAAL model is composed of a list of global declarations, the two automata (with their local declarations) and the system set-up (i.e., the instantiation of the automata). Global declarations include the number of services N, the size of the buffers, the timeout threshold, the rates of the exponential distributions, two variables action and choice storing the corresponding configuration for all automata, and the communication buffers. Constants are also defined globally and their identifiers are in capital letters. Some names of locations are displayed in the automata for readability. Labels of transitions contain guards and effects and in a few cases also probabilistic selections.

Description of the Automata. We now briefly describe Fig. 1 and Fig. 2. The initial state is depicted with a double circle. In the first transition of the orchestrator, one of four options encoding the combinations of choice and action is selected non-deterministically. The function initialize(conf) instantiates

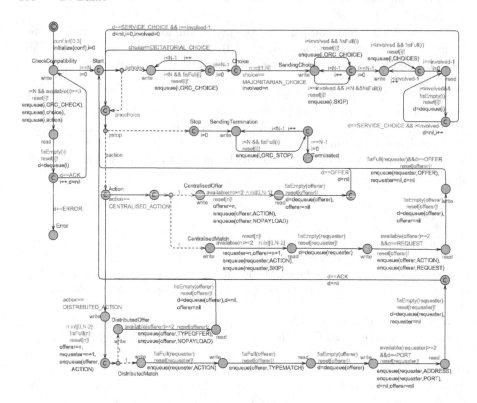

Fig. 1. The RunnableOrchestration UPPAAL template

accordingly the `choice` and `action` global variables such that all have the same configuration, and also initialises the communication buffers.

From the location `CheckCompatibility` of the orchestrator a loop is executed to communicate with all services to check if all have the same configuration. The orchestrator sends the message `ORC_CHECK` and its configuration (action and choice). If a service has the same configuration an `ACK` is sent, or an `ERROR` message otherwise. In case of no errors, the orchestration starts. From the location `Start` the orchestrator internally decides (based on the orchestration) whether to perform a choice or an action. The choice of termination is modelled as a third alternative. As stated previously, after a choice is completed the orchestrator moves to a state where only an action or termination can be chosen. After an action is completed, the orchestrator returns to the `Start` location.

In the case of termination, the orchestrator sends to all services an `ORC_STOP` message and the orchestration terminates. In the case of a choice, firstly all services receive the message `ORC_CHOICE`. If the choice is dictatorial, the orchestrator decides autonomously, and no further interactions are necessary. Otherwise, in the case of a majoritarian choice, the services involved in the choice are selected non-deterministically, and a message `ORC_CHOICE` is sent to them. Concretely,

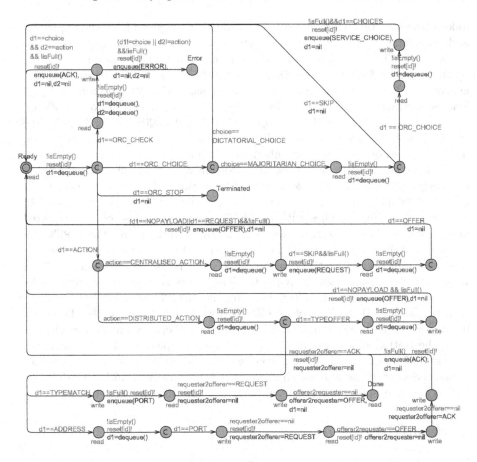

Fig. 2. The `RunnableOrchestratedContract` UPPAAL template

the involved services are those who perform an action in one of the outgoing transitions from the current state of the orchestration. The services that are not involved will receive a SKIP message. The involved services then receive from the orchestrator the available choices (i.e., the forward star of the current state). These concrete choices are abstracted by the constant CHOICES. Each involved service now replies with its choice, abstracted as a message SERVICE_CHOICE. After all involved services have voted, the orchestrator will decide accordingly.

In case of an action, the orchestration behaves differently depending on whether the configuration is centralised or distributed. In both cases, a probabilistic choice is made on whether the transition is an offer or a match. After that, the orchestrator picks non-deterministically an offerer and a requester (only in the case of a match transition) with consecutive identifiers (recall that their IDs are immaterial). In the case of a centralised offer action, the offerer receives from the orchestrator the invocation of the action, abstracted by the constant ACTION, followed by the NOPAYLOAD message (i.e., there is no payload from the requester) and the offerer replies with a payload abstracted by the constant OFFER.

In a centralised match the requester receives the action invocation, abstracted by the constant ACTION, and a SKIP command (i.e., the offer has not yet been generated). The requester replies with the message REQUEST (the concrete payload is abstracted away) that is forwarded by the orchestrator to the offerer, who receives in sequence the messages ACTION and REQUEST. Similarly to the previous case, the offerer sends to the orchestrator its offer payload (now based on the payload of the requester), abstracted again by the constant OFFER.

Concerning the distributed configuration, in case of an offer or match first the offerer receives the ACTION command from the orchestrator. In case of an offer, a TYPEOFFER message is received by the offerer followed by a NOPAYLOAD message. The offerer replies with an OFFER message. In case of a distributed match, the ACTION message is also sent to the requester and the TYPEMATCH message is sent to the offerer. The offerer opens a fresh port and communicates this port (abstracted by the constant PORT) to the orchestrator. The offerer waits for a connection from the requester. The orchestrator communicates to the requester (who was waiting after receiving the ACTION command) the address (constant ADDRESS) and PORT of the offerer. Now the requester and the offerer can interact without the orchestrator. The interactions between any two services in the orchestration all use two (one-position) buffers, implemented by the variables requester2offerer and offerer2requester. Indeed, it is never the case that some service interferes in a match in which it is not involved, and using different buffers for each pair of services would unnecessarily increase the state space.

4   Analysis

We now describe the analyses we performed on the model. The modelling activity led to some issues in both the implementation and the model, which were all fixed (we remark that an already existing application was modelled). Other formal checks on the model were performed to ensure the properties described in this section (e.g., absence of deadlocks, absence of orphan messages). We have used UPPAAL version 4.1.26-1, February 2022.

Validation Through Modelling. The first validation was performed during the modelling phase. Indeed, formal modelling requires an accurate analysis and review of the source code. Interactive simulation is used during modelling to animate and analyse the portion of the model designed so far, similarly to how the source code is debugged interactively (e.g., by choosing the next step). We note that in many model-based engineering tools, behavioural models (e.g., state charts) are validated by only relying on graphical interactive simulations [8]. Issues can be detected during this phase in particular if the source code has not been thoroughly tested, as was the case for CARE.

We report an issue detected in the source code during the modelling of the automaton in Fig. 1, and more specifically during the modelling of the loop in which the orchestrator is reading the SERVICE_CHOICE messages sent by the involved services. In the implementation, the orchestrator was waiting for a choice from all services, also comprehending those who received a SKIP message. This means that a deadlock could occur in case there was a service not involved in a choice. Initially, this issue was undetected because the tests had all services involved in all choices. It was fixed thanks to the activity described in this paper.

On a side note, thorough testing is generally more time-consuming than designing a formal model similar to the one in this paper, and UPPAAL has been used to automatically generate tests from the formal model.

Formal Verification. We discuss the formal verification performed on the model, encompassing both exhaustive and statistical model checking. In the initial phase, we employ a model variant that guarantees consistent configurations between the services and the orchestrator. In this variant, the selection of the choice and action configuration is performed non-deterministically by the first transition of RunnableOrchestration (variable conf, see Fig. 1), and it is always consistent. Subsequently, we move to another variant where the configuration of choice and action are treated as parameters. In this case, we formally prove that when configurations do not match, an error state is reached.

Performances. Statistical model checking has been used to scale to larger systems, and the verification has been performed in a few seconds on a standard laptop. Conversely, exhaustive model checking necessitated more resources and has been limited to smaller configurations generating hundreds of millions of states (see below). In this case, the verification has been performed on a machine with Intel(R) Core(TM) i9-9900K CPU @ 3.60 GHz equipped with 32 GB of RAM. UPPAAL has been configured for maximising the state space optimization and reusing the generated state space. Logs of the experiments are available in [2].

Parameters Tuning. The verification process involves employing specific parameter configurations within the model. This encompasses various aspects, such as setting the delays in reading and writing, setting socket timeout thresholds, adjusting buffer sizes, assigning probability weights, and determining the number of services involved (i.e., the instantiations of the RunnableOrchestratedContract template). For deriving the desired set-up of parameters, we employ statistical model checking. If not stated otherwise, the parameters α and ε of the statistical model checker are set to 0.05 and 0.005, respectively (see Sect. 2).

It is crucial to note that we do not employ statistical model checking to determine values (such as buffers size) for use in the concrete implementation. Instead, these quantified values are used solely within the model. For instance, in the actual implementation, the size of Java TCP/IP socket buffers is fixed (more below). Our objective is to employ parameter configurations that ensure realistic modelling and improve the performances of the exhaustive model checking. Realistic modeling entails accurately representing the behavior of the real system, by reducing the probability of filling the buffers, timeouts, or excessive communication delays. Failure to maintain these conditions could potentially

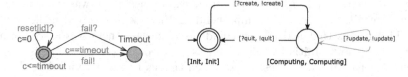

Fig. 3. On the left side, the SocketTimeout automaton. On the right side, the orchestration automaton taken from the composition service example in [3]

invalidate the results of the formal verification. Improving performances, on the other hand, entails reducing the state space of the model.

Firstly, the values of the *probabilities weights* pstop, pchoice, pnochoice, and paction (see Fig. 1) can be tuned based on average values extracted from the orchestrations subject of the analysis. Indeed, as stated in Sect. 3, the underlying orchestration automaton is abstracted away. Note that, e.g., in location Start the probability of performing a choice is $\frac{pchoice}{pchoice+pnochoice}$. For example, the orchestration in Fig. 3 (right) can be modelled by tuning the probabilities to pstop=25, pchoice=1, pnochoice=0, and paction=75.

Next, we address the *buffer size* (denoted as variable queueSize). It is important to note that the buffers in the model are represented by global arrays utilized by the automata for enqueuing and dequeuing values. These global arrays serve as models of the actual buffers found in Java TCP/IP sockets, where the default size is typically 8 KB. Our objective is to prevent unnecessary growth in the model's state space while ensuring a low probability of the buffers filling up, similar to the behavior observed in the real application. The formula:

```
E[<=500; 10000](max: sum(i:int[0,N-1]) (sum(j:int[0,queueSize-1])(orc2services[i][j]!=nil)))
```

computes, using 10000 simulations of 500 time units, the expected maximum number of non-empty positions of the buffers used by the orchestrator to send messages to the services (called orc2services). For all statistical evaluations, we set the number of services to 10. With buffer size set to 10, this formula evaluates to 4.5 ± 0.019. This indicates that, on average, the maximum number of utilized buffer positions is between 4 and 5. Consequently, in order to reduce the state space, it is safe to decrease the value of queueSize to less than 10 for the exhaustive model checking phase. This observation is further supported by the following formula: `Pr[<=500] (<>(exists (i:id_t) ror.isFull(i)))`, which measures the probability that, within 500 time units, one of the arrays orc2services[i] becomes full (ror is the orchestrator automaton). In three separate experiments where queueSize was varied between 3, 4, and 5, this formula yielded the respective evaluation intervals of $[0.990031, 1]$, $[0.00632077, 0.0163207]$ (with $\alpha = 0.005$), and $[0, 0.00996915]$. Based on these results, if not stated otherwise, queueSize is set to 5 for the subsequent experiments.

Next, we consider the real-time behavior of the model and focus on determining appropriate values for the *rates* write and read, which represent the delays in writing to and reading from a buffer, respectively. The average message delay in Java TCP/IP sockets is affected by multiple factors, such as network conditions and server load. Delays can be sampled using tools like `tcpdump`, and the rate can be estimated by calculating the inverse of the sample mean. Additionally, we consider the variable `timeout`, which represents the timeout threshold. Our aim is to achieve three objectives. First, we strive to maintain a low probability of encountering timeouts. Second, we seek to ensure a high probability of terminating within a specific timeframe, which we have set to be 500 time units, corresponding to the duration used in our experimental setup. Third, we aim to keep the timeout threshold at a lower value in order to decrease the state space and facilitate model checking. The formula `Pr[<=500] (<> ror.Timeout)` measures the likelihood of one or more service sockets experiencing a timeout (recall that in this case a failure signal is broadcasted and all automata enter their respective `Timeout` location). The probability of all services and the orchestrator successfully concluding their operations is evaluated with `Pr[<=500](<>ror.Terminated&&(forall (i:id_t) ROC(i).Terminated))` (ROC is used as an abbreviation of `RunnableOrchestratedContract`). In different experiments where we varied the values of the pair (rate,timeout), specifically in $(5, 14)$, $(4, 15)$, $(5, 15)$, respectively, the first formula (timeout probability) yielded the respective evaluation intervals $[3.06006e^{-06}, 0.00999494]$ (with $\alpha = 0.005$), $[0.0433422, 0.053341]$, and $[0, 0.00996915]$, while the second formula (probability of termination) yielded $[0.990005, 0.999997]$ (with $\alpha = 0.005$), $[0.948625, 0.958625]$ (with $\alpha = 0.005$), and $[0.990031, 1]$. Therefore, to fulfill the aforementioned three objectives, we have set the values of `write` and `read` to 5, while the value of `timeout` has been set to 15 for the subsequent experiments.

Concerning the *instances* of the templates, in all experiments there is one instance of the orchestrator template and either 4 or 5 instances of the service template. For the exhaustive model checking phase, we used two small configurations of (number of services, buffers size). The first is c1 $= (4, 5)$, the second is c2 $= (5, 3)$. In fact, the configuration $(5, 4)$ remained inconclusive in the experiments due to the need for generating billions of states and the inadequate memory capacity of the utilized machine. The verification of larger configurations necessitates either relying exclusively on statistical model checking or employing more powerful machines.

Verification. Once the model's parameter configuration is determined, our next step involves verifying additional formal properties.

Termination. We have already assessed the probability of non-termination and found it to be nearly zero (i.e., all runs do not satisfy the property, thus the probability lies within the interval $[0, 0 + \varepsilon]$ with probability $1 - \alpha$). However, it may be worthwhile to conduct an exhaustive verification specifically for this property. The property that in all executions eventually all services and the orchestrator terminate is not valid. Indeed, as described in Sect. 3, the orchestration contract automaton is abstracted away and at each iteration, a choice is performed to decide whether to terminate or not. Hence, there exists an execution in which the orchestration never terminates. A milder property does hold:

```
ror.Stop-->((ror.Terminated&&(forall(i:id_t)ROC(i).Terminated))
            ||(exists(i:id_t)SocketTimeout(i).Timeout))
```

i.e., if the orchestrator decides to terminate then eventually all services and the orchestrator terminate. The formula p-->q is a shortcut for A[](p imply A<>q). Thus, this formula states that for all executions and for all states either the orchestrator is not in the location ror.Stop or all executions passing through that location will eventually lead to a state where all services and the orchestrator have terminated or a timeout failure is experienced. The formula holds in both configurations c1 and c2. The first (resp. second) configuration required roughly 3 (resp. 30) minutes, 1.5 (resp. 12) Giga of memory, and explored 52 (resp. 426) million states.

Absence of Deadlocks. The likelihood of non-termination being very low also implies an almost negligible probability of encountering deadlocks. While it may be of interest to exhaustively prove the absence of deadlocks, the previous formula is insufficient for this purpose. Hence, to prove that there is no deadlock, we perform exhaustive model checking of the formula:

```
A[](not deadlock || (exists(i:id_t) SocketTimeout(i).Timeout) ||
    (ror.Terminated && (forall (i:id_t) ROC(i).Terminated)))
```

the formula states that for all executions and for all states of the composed system, either there is always at least one enabled transition or either a time-out failure has been experienced or all services and the orchestrator are in the Terminated location. In the formula, not deadlock is a special predicate provided by UPPAAL. As expected, this property is satisfied in both configurations. The first (resp. second) configuration required roughly 3 (resp. 40) minutes, 1.5 (resp. 13) Giga of memory, and explored 25 (resp. 189) million states. This also proves that in a correct configuration the Error location is never reached, because this would result in a deadlock and the above property would not be satisfied. This property is also satisfied when the size of the buffers is 3. However, if we further reduce the size, then a deadlock occurs. This is because from location CheckCompatibility the orchestrator requires to insert three messages in the buffer of the receiver in one step. By dividing these three send operations in three non-committed transitions it is possible to further reduce the buffer size.

We report a modelling issue detected during model checking the above formula. In an earlier version, it was assumed that the socket mode was non-blocking (i.e., sending to a recipient with a full buffer would cause an error). This was modelled by making committed (C) all source states of transitions with sending operations. In this way, if the buffer of the receiver would not have enough free space then an attempt to send to the receiver would cause a deadlock. In fact, in this earlier version of the model the above formula (absence of deadlocks) was not satisfied, for any possible size of the buffer. The counterexample trace of the model checker helped to understand and eventually fix this issue. Basically, in the model configured with a majoritarian choice there exists a loop in which the orchestrator alternates choices and actions, and enqueues a sequence of ORC_CHOICE and SKIP messages to a service that never consumes them and is never involved in neither choices nor actions, thus eventually filling its buffer and deadlocking. A similar issue also exists in the case of a dictatorial choice.

Note that this kind of problems are hard to detect without model checking. Indeed, the counterexample trace was generated automatically, and the counterexample trace is composed of hundreds of steps. Without model checking this would require to manually execute each step of this trace, and the longer the trace the less chance to discover it. After we detected this issue, we analysed the underlying Java TCP/IP socket semantics [15] and fixed the model as described in Sect. 3 (i.e., by modelling these sockets with default blocking mode). Another fix could be to include an ack after the reception of a SKIP message (this would however require to modify also the implementation).

Absence of Orphan Messages. We now prove that upon termination of an orchestration no messages are left in any buffer, i.e., all messages are consumed. To expedite the verification process, we begin by conducting statistical model checking of the following property:

```
Pr[<=500](<>!allEmpty()&&ror.Terminated&&(forall(i:id_t)ROC(i).Terminated))
```

this property quantifies the probability of termination with at least one message remaining in any buffer. To verify whether all buffers are empty, we utilize the predicate allEmpty(). As expected, the probability is found to be nearly zero. We proceed with an exhaustive verification by employing the property

```
A[]((ror.Terminated && (forall (i:id_t) ROC(i).Terminated)) imply allEmpty())
```

the above formula can be read as follows: in all states of all executions either all buffers are empty or someone has not terminated yet. The above property is valid in both configurations, as expected. The first (resp. second) configuration required roughly 2 (resp. 27) minutes, 1.5 (resp. 12.5) Giga of memory, and explored 25 (resp. 189) million states. It is also possible to verify that there is no dummy execution in which the services and the orchestrator never interact (and thus all buffers are trivially empty). This can be verified with the formula `E[] (allEmpty() && !ror.Timeout)` that, as stated above, checks if there exists an execution where all states have empty buffers (excluding the dummy execution scenario in which the timeout occurs at the beginning). As expected, this property is not valid in the model, for both configurations. The first (resp. second) configuration required roughly 3 (resp. 24) seconds, 1.4 (resp. 10) Giga of memory, and explored 24 (resp. 28) states.

No Interference. When discussing the distributed match action in Sect. 3, we stated that it is never the case that some service interferes in a match in which it is not involved. This guarantees that it is safe to use two one-position buffers for all communications between any two services involved in a match. To verify this, we perform statistical model checking of the following formula

```
Pr[<=500](<>exists(i:id_t)(i<N-1&&(ROC(i).d1==TYPEMATCH||ROC(i).d1==ADDRESS||ROC(i).d1==PORT))
        &&((ROC(i+1).d1==TYPEMATCH|| ROC(i+1).d1==ADDRESS||ROC(i+1).d1==PORT))&&
(exists(j:id_t)(j!=i&&j!=i+1&&(ROC(j).d1==TYPEMATCH||ROC(j).d1==ADDRESS||ROC(j).d1==PORT))))
```

the formula measures the probability of reaching a state where one service (index j) is interfering on a match between two other services (indexes i and i+1). We recall that in the model two matching services have consecutive indexes. We detect a service to be involved in a distributed match when its temporary variable d1 has one of the three values (TYPEMATCH, ADDRESS, PORT). The probability is found to be nearly zero.

We also include in the repository [2] a version of the model where each pair of services has its own buffers. All results in this section also hold in that model.

Compatibility Check. Next, we formally prove that if some service is not matching the configuration of the orchestrator, then the orchestration will not start and an Error location will always eventually be reached. Indeed, the possibility of mismatching configurations is allowed in the real system. However, in the model discussed in Sect. 3 this scenario is not possible because, by construction, all services and the orchestrator share the same configuration. The configuration is selected non-deterministically. In this way, for each formula being verified all possible configurations are checked automatically.

Only for this check the model has been slightly modified by adding two parameters action and choice to the templates and by updating accordingly the model. For this verification, the set-up of the system is of an orchestrator ror and three services alice, bob and carl and the size of each buffer is 4:

```
ror = RunnableOrchestration(MAJORITARIAN_CHOICE,DISTRIBUTED_ACTION);
alice = RunnableOrchestratedContract(0,MAJORITARIAN_CHOICE,DISTRIBUTED_ACTION);
bob = RunnableOrchestratedContract(1,MAJORITARIAN_CHOICE,DISTRIBUTED_ACTION);
carl = RunnableOrchestratedContract(2,DICTATORIAL_CHOICE,DISTRIBUTED_ACTION);
ast = SocketTimeout(0);bst = SocketTimeout(1);cst = SocketTimeout(2);
system ror,alice,bob,carl,ast,bst,cst;
```

Note that the configurations of choice and action are now parameters assigned to each automaton. This allows us to assign a mismatching configuration to verify that the Error location will be reached. Indeed, in the above set-up carl has a different configuration. We use the formula `A<>((ror.Error && carl.Error)||ror.Timeout)` stating that in all executions eventually the orchestrator and the service with a wrong configuration reach an Error location or a timeout is experienced. Alternatively, the formula `A[](!ror.Start)` states that in all executions the Start location of the orchestrator is never traversed (i.e., the orchestration never starts). Both properties are satisfied in this setup, thus verifying the correctness of the compatibility check. The first (resp. second) formula required visiting 19 (resp. 79) states. Both formulae used roughly 48 Megabytes of memory and a few milliseconds of CPU. We have proved that in case of mismatching configurations, the orchestration will not start.

5   Conclusion and Future Work

We have presented the formal modeling and verification of the Contract Automata Runtime Environment (CARE), an open-source platform. The adequacy of the abstract model has been described, and the transitions of the formal model have been linked to the corresponding lines of source code. The tests generated from the formal model have been employed to test the source code.

Both statistical and exhaustive model checking techniques have played a crucial role in formally verifying numerous desired properties of the modeled system, such as the absence of deadlocks, while also enhancing the accuracy of the formal model. Statistical model checking has been employed to fine-tune parameter settings within the formal model, such as the buffer size.

At present, the different artifacts such as the model, source code, tests, and tracing information are manually kept aligned. This process demands substantial effort whenever a new version of CARE is introduced, as each artifact needs to be updated accordingly. Future work involves studying techniques for automatic alignment of these artifacts. Furthermore, it would be interesting to exploit the facilities provided by the recently introduced tool Uppex [21] to factorize the different variants of the model discussed in the paper under a single, configurable Uppex model, and to automate the selection of a configuration.

Acknowledgment. Part of this study was carried out within the MUR PRIN 2022 PNRR P2022A492B project ADVENTURE (ADVancEd iNtegraTed evalUation of Railway systEms) funded by the European Union - NextGenerationEU, and the CNR project "Formal Methods in Software Engineering 2.0", CUP B53C24000720005.

References

1. Bartoletti, M., Cimoli, T., Zunino, R.: Compliance in behavioural contracts: a brief survey. In: Bodei, C., Ferrari, G.-L., Priami, C. (eds.) Programming Languages with Applications to Biology and Security. LNCS, vol. 9465, pp. 103–121. Springer, Cham (2015). https://doi.org/10.1007/978-3-319-25527-9_9

2. Basile, D.: Modelling and verifying the contract automata runtime environment, complementary materia. https://doi.org/10.5281/zenodo.8017613

3. Basile, D., ter Beek, M.H.: A runtime environment for contract automata. In: Chechik, M., Katoen, J., Leucker, M. (eds.) FM 2023. LNCS, vol. 14000, pp. 550–567. Springer, Cham (2023).https://doi.org/10.1007/978-3-031-27481-7_31, https://github.com/contractautomataproject/CARE

4. Basile, D., et al.: Controller synthesis of service contracts with variability. Sci. Comput. Program. **187** (2020).https://doi.org/10.1016/j.scico.2019.102344

5. Basile, D., ter Beek, M.H., Legay, A.: Strategy synthesis for autonomous driving in a moving block railway system with UPPAAL STRATEGO. In: Gotsman, A., Sokolova, A. (eds.) FORTE 2020. LNCS, vol. 12136, pp. 3–21. Springer, Cham (2020). https://doi.org/10.1007/978-3-030-50086-3_1

6. Basile, D., ter Beek, M.H., Pugliese, R.: Synthesis of orchestrations and choreographies: bridging the gap between supervisory control and coordination of services. Log. Methods Comput. Sci. **16**(2), 9:1–9:29 (2020). https://doi.org/10.23638/LMCS-16(2:9)2020

7. Basile, D., Degano, P., Ferrari, G.L.: Automata for specifying and orchestrating service contracts. Log. Methods Comput. Sci. **12**(4), 6:1–6:51 (2016). https://doi.org/10.2168/LMCS-12(4:6)2016

8. Basile, D., Mazzanti, F., Ferrari, A.: Experimenting with formal verification and model-based development in railways: the case of UMC and Sparx enterprise architect. In: Cimatti, A., Titolo, L. (eds.) FMICS 2023. LNCS, vol. 14290, pp. 1–21. Springer, Cham (2023). https://doi.org/10.1007/978-3-031-43681-9_1

9. Behrmann, G., et al.: UPPAAL 4.0. In: Proceedings 3rd International Conference on the Quantitative Evaluation of SysTems (QEST), pp. 125–126. IEEE (2006). https://doi.org/10.1109/QEST.2006.59

10. Boulanger, J.L.: Tool qualification. In: CENELEC 50128 and IEC 62279 Standards, chap. 9, pp. 287–308. Wiley (2015). https://doi.org/10.1002/9781119005056.ch9

11. David, A., Larsen, K.G., Legay, A., Mikučionis, M., Poulsen, D.B.: Uppaal SMC tutorial. Int. J. Softw. Tools Technol. Transf. **17**(4), 397–415 (2015). https://doi.org/10.1007/s10009-014-0361-y

12. Garavel, H., ter Beek, M.H., van de Pol, J.: The 2020 expert survey on formal methods. In: ter Beek, M.H., Ničković, D. (eds.) FMICS 2020. LNCS, vol. 12327, pp. 3–69. Springer, Cham (2020). https://doi.org/10.1007/978-3-030-58298-2_1

13. Gay, S., Ravara, A. (eds.): Behavioural Types: from Theory to Tools. River (2017). https://doi.org/10.13052/rp-9788793519817

14. Gu, R., Jensen, P.G., Poulsen, D.B., Seceleanu, C., Enoiu, E., Lundqvist, K.: Verifiable strategy synthesis for multiple autonomous agents: a scalable approach. Int. J. Softw. Tools Technol. Transf. **24**(3), 395–414 (2022). https://doi.org/10.1007/s10009-022-00657-z

15. https://docs.oracle.com/javase/7/docs/api/java/net/Socket.html

16. Lamport, L., Shostak, R.E., Pease, M.C.: The byzantine generals problem. ACM Trans. Program. Lang. Syst. **4**(3), 382–401 (1982). https://doi.org/10.1145/357172.357176

17. Legay, A., Lukina, A., Traonouez, L.M., Yang, J., Smolka, S.A., Grosu, R.: Statistical model checking. In: Steffen, B., Woeginger, G. (eds.) Computing and Software Science. LNCS, vol. 10000, pp. 478–504. Springer, Cham (2019). https://doi.org/10.1007/978-3-319-91908-9_23

18. Lehmann, S., Rogalla, A., Neidhardt, M., Reinecke, A., Schlaefer, A., Schupp, S.: Modeling $\mathbb{R}^3$ Needle Steering in Uppaal. In: Dubslaff, C., Luttik, B. (eds.) Proceedings of the 5th Workshop on Models for Formal Analysis of Real Systems (MARS). EPTCS, vol. 355, pp. 40–59 (2022). https://doi.org/10.4204/EPTCS.355.4

19. https://docs.oracle.com/javase/7/docs/api/java/io/ObjectOutputStream.html

20. Orlando, S., Pasquale, V.D., Barbanera, F., Lanese, I., Tuosto, E.: Corinne, a tool for choreography automata. In: Salaün, G., Wijs, A. (eds.) FACS 2021. LNCS, vol. 13077, pp. 82–92. Springer, Cham (2021). https://doi.org/10.1007/978-3-030-90636-8_5

21. Proença, J., Pereira, D., Nandi, G.S., Borrami, S., Melchert, J.: Spreadsheet-based configuration of families of real-time specifications. In: ter Beek, M.H., Dubslaff, C. (eds.) Proceedings of the First Workshop on Trends in Configurable Systems Analysis, TiCSA@ETAPS 2023. EPTCS, vol. 392, pp. 27–39 (2023). https://doi.org/10.4204/EPTCS.392.2

22. Ramadge, P.J., Wonham, W.M.: Supervisory control of a class of discrete event processes. SIAM J. Control. Optim. **25**(1), 206–230 (1987). https://doi.org/10.1137/0325013

23. Roggenbach, M., Cerone, A., Schlingloff, B., Schneider, G., Shaikh, S.A.: Formal Methods for Software Engineering: Languages, Methods, Application Domains. TTCS, Springer, Cham (2022). https://doi.org/10.1007/978-3-030-38800-3

24. Shokri-Manninen, F., Vain, J., Waldén, M.: Formal verification of COLREG-based navigation of maritime autonomous systems. In: de Boer, F., Cerone, A. (eds.) SEFM 2020. LNCS, vol. 12310, pp. 41–59. Springer, Cham (2020). https://doi.org/10.1007/978-3-030-58768-0_3

Simulation-Based Decision Support for Cross-Organisational Workflows
A Case Study of Emergency Handling

Muhammad Rizwan Ali[✉], Yngve Lamo, and Violet Ka I Pun

Western Norway University of Applied Sciences, Bergen, Norway
{Muhammad.Rizwan.Ali,Yngve.Lamo,Violet.Ka.I.Pun}@hvl.no

Abstract. Analysing and managing workflows across organisations can be a complex task. One of the main challenges is that planners often have a limited overview of shared resources and dependencies in collaborative workflows that extend beyond their local context. In this paper, we use an emergency handling workflow across multiple organisations as a case study to demonstrate how our recently developed formal language $\mathcal{R}$PL and its accompanying tool $\mathcal{R}$PLTool can be adopted to facilitate decision making on *resource allocation* in cross-organisational workflows. We formally model the workflow in $\mathcal{R}$PL, and simulate the model with multiple concurrency levels and resource configurations regarding their availability and efficiency using $\mathcal{R}$PLTool, allowing the decision-makers to observe how the changes in these scenarios impact the behaviour and the performance of the workflow.

Keywords: Formal modelling · Simulation-based decision support · Resource allocation · Cross-organisational workflows

1 Introduction

A cross-organisational workflow comprises concurrent, collaborative workflows that run in different departments or in multiple organisations. Tasks in such a workflow often rely on the completion of tasks in the other collaborative workflows, which may possibly share resources among them for task execution. Consider, for instance, a critical emergency handling workflow where teams like the police, firefighters and hospitals, each of which has its own workflows, need to collaborate effectively based on task dependencies and on the resources that they are sharing. Thus, designing cross-organisational workflows usually requires specific understanding of not only one but multiple specific domains, as well as an overview of the dependencies on the shared resources and task completion among the collaborative workflows.

The demand of such knowledge not only makes workflow optimisation challenging but also management error-prone: minor local changes may be non-trivially propagated to collaborative workflows and consequently disrupt the

© IFIP International Federation for Information Processing 2024
Published by Springer Nature Switzerland AG 2024
I. Castellani and F. Tiezzi (Eds.): COORDINATION 2024, LNCS 14676, pp. 111–128, 2024.
https://doi.org/10.1007/978-3-031-62697-5_7

entire system, which may lead to substantial financial loss and sometimes fatality in e.g., the domain of healthcare sector and aviation industry. Therefore, efficient coordination of tasks and shared resources are particularly important in these kinds of workflows, and there is a need not only to formally specify such dependencies, but also to properly observe the effect of changes in the shared resources on the behaviour of the workflows.

Our earlier work has presented a resource sensitive formal modelling language $\mathcal{R}$PL [5] to capture cross-organisational workflows with its dependencies on shared resources and task completion in the form of a concurrent program. The language uses an actor-based concurrency model [2] and has explicit notions of time advancement and task (modelled in terms of methods) completion deadlines, and allows specifying task dependencies. This formal modelling language enables increasing the reliability and ensuring correctness of workflow models by leveraging formal methods and program analysis, for example, a static cost analysis has been proposed to approximate the worst execution time of workflows modelled in $\mathcal{R}$PL [4]. The analysis is implemented as part of the prototype tool $\mathcal{R}$PLTool [6], which includes also the functionalities of modelling and simulation.

The goal of this case study paper is to showcase how the simulation function in the $\mathcal{R}$PLTool can be adopted to assist decision making on scheduling resources in cross-organisational workflows. In particular, we focus on accessing the potential impacts of changes in resource availability and efficiency on the metrics, namely deadline violations, execution time, and financial costs, within collaborative workflows. We adopt an emergency response procedure as a comprehensive case study to demonstrate, by leveraging simulation, how planners or analysts can observe the behaviour of the response procedure, modelled as a cross-organisational workflow, under various configurations with respect to resources and the number of concurrent emergency instances, as well as to identify potential bottlenecks to improve the resource allocation for the response procedure.

The rest of the paper is organised as follows: Sect. 2 presents the architecture of the proposed simulation-based decision support. Section 3 presents the description of the case study, the simulation model and discusses the simulation results. Section 4 discusses the related work. Finally, we summarise the paper and discuss possible future work in Sect. 5.

2 Simulation-Based Decision Support for Resource Allocation

In this section, we describe how $\mathcal{R}$PLTool can be used to provide simulation-based decision support for resource allocation in cross-organisational workflows to the planner. Figure 1 shows the decision support architecture. The simulation module of the tool takes as input a cross-organisational workflow modelled in $\mathcal{R}$PL and a simulation configuration specifying the concurrency level as well as the resource availability and efficiency. The module then outputs the simulation result that captures the performance metrics in terms of overall execution time,

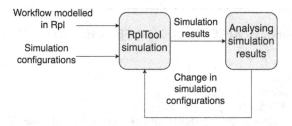

Fig. 1. Architecture of simulation-based decision support.

the number of deadline violations, and financial costs. Based on the result, the planner can analyse how the input simulation configuration affect the metrics, and then modify the simulation configuration to perform further simulation to observe the impact of the changes on the performance metrics.

2.1 Cross-Organisational Workflow Models in $\mathcal{R}$PL

One of the inputs of the simulation is a cross-organisational workflow modelled in $\mathcal{R}$PL [4], which is a formal modelling language designed for cross-organisational workflows. The language supports explicit notions of time advancement, task completion deadlines, and couples multiple workflows through shared resources and task dependencies. These features allow modelling and analysis of cross-organisational workflows, where time, deadlines, and resource constraints play critical roles.

Tasks in a workflow is modelled in $\mathcal{R}$PL as methods, and are executed through method invocations, which can be either synchronous or asynchronous. While synchronous method calls block the caller objects until the called methods return, asynchronous calls are non-blocking and allow the callers and callees running in parallel. An asynchronous method invocation is associated with a future, in which the invoked method stores the return value upon completion.

$$[\cdots,$$
$$r_1 \mapsto (\text{true}, \{30, \text{Boat}, 1000\}),$$
$$r_2 \mapsto (\text{true}, \{10, \text{Doctor}, 500\}),$$
$$r_3 \mapsto (\text{true}, \{12, \text{Policeman}, 500\}),$$
$$r_4 \mapsto (\text{false}, \{15, \text{FireFighter}, 500\}),$$
$$r_5 \mapsto (\text{false}, \{15, \text{Policeman}, 500\}),$$
$$\cdots]$$

Fig. 2. An example of resource map in $\mathcal{R}$PL shared between different departments.

Each task may have deadlines, indicated by the notion **dl**, and depend on the completion of other tasks, captured by the **after** keyword followed by the futures associated to the tasks (method calls). Time advances with the **cost** statement, and resources can be acquired and returned with statements **hold** and **release**.

Resources shared among the collaborative workflows are modelled by means of a map associating each resource r to a pair (b, Q), where b is a boolean value indicating the availability of the resource, and Q a set of resource qualities such as category, efficiency and financial usage cost. For example, Fig. 2 shows the map of the resources shared between the collaborating departments to handle

```
1   class Police {
2       Unit dealEmergency(ECC ecc, EOD eod, FB fb, Hospital h)
3       {
4           Fut<Int> f1; Fut<Int> f2;
5           Int x = 0;
6           f1 = !estEmgCtr(ecc) after dl 20;
7           x = rushToSite(this) after dl 50;
8           x = evalSituation(this,list[set[10,Policeman],set[10,Policeman]]) after dl 80;
9           f2 = !makeEmgPlan(ecc,eod,fb,h) after f1 dl 250;
10          await f2?;
11      }
12      Int evalSituation(List<Set<Quality>> res)
13      {
14          Int report = 0; Int financial_cost = 0;
15          Pair<List<Int>,Int> p = hold(res);
16          cost(t); // Time taken to evaluate the situation and update report
17          financial_cost = t*snd(p);
18          release(fst(p));
19          return report;
20      } }
```

Fig. 3. A simple example of collaborating workflows in $\mathcal{R}$PL.

an emergency situation. For instance, r_1 is a boat with a capacity of thirty passengers and a usage cost of 1000 per time unit while r_2 is a doctor with ten years of experience and a usage cost of 500 per time unit, and both of them are currently available. Note that the quality set Q each of the resource type can be extended with additional features. The rest of the language rather standard, and we refer the readers to [4] for the full syntax and semantics.

Figure 3 models in $\mathcal{R}$PL a simple emergency handling workflow in the Police, who needs to interact with the emergency command center (ECC), explosive ordnance disposal (EOD) team, fire brigade (FB), and Hospital. To handle an emergency situation, the police sends a request to ECC to establish an emergency command centre and at the same time hurries to the site, captured by the asynchronous method invocation in Line 6 and self-synchronous method call in Line 7, where the callee is indicated by first parameter of the method calls. Note that both method invocations in Lines 6 and 7 do not have any task dependency, indicated by having no future following the **after** keyword, but completion deadlines of twenty and fifty time units, respectively.

Two policemen with an efficiency of at least ten are required to evaluate the situation (Line 8) within eighty time units. They are first acquired from the resource pool in Line 15 and released in Line 18 after a report has been made, which is modelled as time advancement captured by the **cost** statement (the only statement that consumes time in $\mathcal{R}$PL). The **hold** statement returns a list of identifiers of the acquired resources and the sum of the usage cost per unit time, and Line 17 calculates the total financial costs of using the acquired resources over the time duration specified in the cost statement.

Once the report is received, the police can start making a plan for the emergency situation that involves EOD, FB, and the Hospital (Line 9), *after* ECC has successfully created an emergency command centre, indicated by the future f1 following the **after** keyword, where f1 is the future associated to the method call to ECC in Line 6.

2.2   Simulation with $\mathcal{R}$PLTool

The language described above is accompanied with a prototype tool, $\mathcal{R}$PLTool[1], consisting of two modules for simulating and analysing worst-case execution time (WCET) of cross-organisational workflows modelled in $\mathcal{R}$PL. In this paper, we focus on the discussion on how the simulation module can facilitate decision making on resource scheduling in a workflow under different configurations, and we refer interested readers to [6] for the full description of the $\mathcal{R}$PLTool. The simulation module allows users, e.g., workflow planners, to manipulate various parameters with respect to resources and levels of concurrency to assess the behaviour and resilience of a given workflow correspondingly.

In the following, we are going to discuss each of these parameters in the simulation configuration and briefly motivate the choices of such parameters.

Simulation Configurations

Another input of the simulation is a simulation configuration, which specifies the parameters and conditions that the simulation is based on. Our simulation tool allows the user to configure the parameters regarding the resources, concurrency levels in terms of number of instances that are running in parallel in the workflow, as well as how many times the simulation should run. These parameters capture the dynamics of cross-organisational workflows that share resources and enable the user to observe the workflow behaviour under different conditions.

Resource Availability and Efficiency. Ideally, all resources in a workflow should be available at all time and are always as efficient as they are expected. However, it is rarely the case in practice: personnel resources may be absent or cannot perform with full efficiency for various reasons, and equipment may not be available due to maintenance, or does not function with the efficiency as they should because of depreciation. These two parameters enable the user to specify different scenarios capturing different levels of availability and efficiency of a given pool of resources. Such kind of configuration allows for a comprehensive exploration of how these aspects affect system dynamics and performance, and enables the user to evaluate the sufficiency of the existing resource pool.

---

[1] https://github.com/razi236/Rpl-Tools.

Concurrent Instances. This parameter allows the user to specify the number of instances of same model running simultaneously in a given workflow. It enables the user to estimate the upper limit on the number of concurrent instances that can be handled by a given pool of resources, and obtain a comprehensive understanding of how the system behaves and performs under different degrees of stress and demand.

Number of Simulations. This parameter refers to the number of simulations to be performed under the scenario specified by means of the parameters mentioned above. Since it is important to run the simulation until it has stable performance as defined by the effect size of interest [25], and each workflow model is different, thus the number of simulations varies. This parameter enables the user to specify the required number of simulations for their particular model.

2.3   Simulation Result Analysis and Simulation Reconfiguration

The simulation results that captures different performance metrics will then be inspected and analysed by the user. The metrics include the overall execution time of the workflow model, the number of deadline violations, and the total financial cost. Based on these metrics, the user can evaluate how the specified resource availability and efficiency, as well as the concurrency level, affect the capacity, efficiency and resource utilisation patterns of a workflow. Furthermore, the user can revise the simulation configuration to assess the behaviour of the workflow in alternative scenarios. This iterative process of revising simulation configurations and evaluating simulation results not only facilitates decision making on the resource allocation for the workflow, but also helps identify potential bottlenecks in the workflow, which can eventually contribute to the decision support on resource pool expansion and workflow restructuring.

3   Case Study

In this section, we use a case study to illustrate how $\mathcal{R}$PLTool can be used to facilitate decision making on resource allocation. The case study is inspired by [29] and explores a hypothetical cross-organisational fire emergency response procedure on an isolated island in the sea, involving multiple organisations. The primary objectives of this response are the rescue of victims and the containment of the spreading fire.

3.1   Procedure Description

In Fig. 4 we graphically illustrate the partially modified cross-organisational fire emergency response procedure in BPMN. Due to space limitation, we omit the corresponding $\mathcal{R}$PL workflow model from the paper and refer the reader to the online repository[2].

---

[2] https://github.com/razi236/DSCOW/blob/master/examples/emergency.rpl.

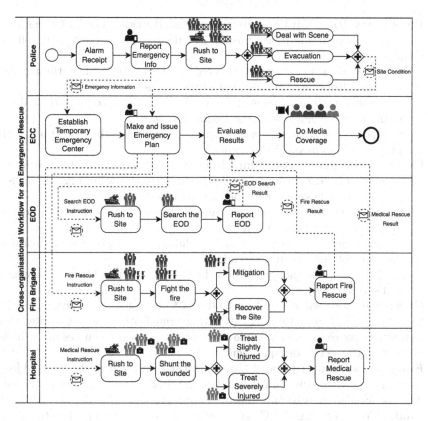

Fig. 4. Cross-organisational fire emergency response procedure.

Five organisations, namely, the police station, emergency command center (ECC), explosive ordnance disposal (EOD) team, fire brigade and hospital, collaborate with each other in this response procedure, which mainly consists of seven steps described as follows:

1. **Fire Emergency Alarm Reception.** The procedure begins with an activation of a fire emergency alarm that is received by the local police station, which serves as the first point of contact for the emergency.
2. **Police Response.** Upon receiving the alarm, the police immediately alert the ECC regarding the emergency, and then dispatch personnel and vehicles to the emergency site to gather information about the situation. Subsequently, they report their findings and the site conditions to the ECC.
3. **ECC Activation.** As soon as the ECC receives the emergency alert from the police, it establishes a temporary emergency command centre. Note that this task is executed *in parallel* with the tasks of going to the site and collecting information in the workflow of the police. Upon receiving the report from the police regarding the site, the ECC develops and disseminates emergency plans to the collaborating other organisations.

4. **Emergency Plans and Instructions Distribution.** The ECC constructs an emergency plan and issues specific instructions to three different collaborating organisations:
   - *search EOD instruction* is delivered to the EOD team, outlining their responsibilities for handling explosive ordnance,
   - *fire rescue instruction* is sent to the fire brigade, specifying their duties in fire containment and rescue operations, and
   - *medical rescue instruction* is communicated with the hospital for the preparation of medical emergencies.
5. **On-site Emergency Handling.** Upon receiving the instructions from the ECC, a support team from each of the three collaborating organisations is deployed to provide support at the emergency site as follows:
   - the *EOD team* carries out specialised disposal activities as required by the emergency situation, while
   - the *fire brigade* is responsible for firefighting, rescuing trapped individuals, and controlling the fire's spread, and
   - the *hospital* personnel perform medical triage and provide necessary medical care to victims.

   Each organisation will report back to the ECC as soon as they have completed their tasks. Note that these collaborating organisations are executing their own workflows *concurrently*, while they may be sharing resources like vehicles for getting to the site or equipment.
6. **Emergency Evaluation and Documentation.** Based on the received feedbacks, the ECC conducts an evaluation and produces a summary of the incident for further analysis and improvement.
7. **Media Coverage.** The ECC arranges media coverage to report to the public about the incident, together with the representatives from the collaborating organisations.

3.2   Simulation Model

In this section, we describe how a workflow planner can use the presented simulation tool to analyse the behaviour of the response procedure described in Sect. 3.1 under different simulation setups that can be configured using the parameters discussed in Sect. 2.2. The goal is to observe the impacts of these dynamic factors on the overall performance of the emergency response system in order to have a better understanding of the system's efficiency, effectiveness, and ability to adhere to time constraints, and consequently help make decision on refining cross-organisational workflows, particularly from the perspective of resource coordination.

Simulation Parameters. In this case study, we construct a comprehensive set of scenarios capturing relevant variations in resource efficiency and availability as well as different levels of concurrency for cross-organisational workflows.

We consider three levels of resource availability, namely, 100% (for optimal situation where resources are fully available for the workflow model), 80%

Table 1. Configurations of resource efficiency

C	Police	Clerks	EODTech	Firefighters	Doctors
C1	100	100	100	100	100
C2	100	80	50	100	80
C3	50	80	60	100	80
C4	80	100	80	50	50
C5	50	60	50	60	50
C6	50	50	50	50	50
C7	Rand	Rand	Rand	Rand	Rand

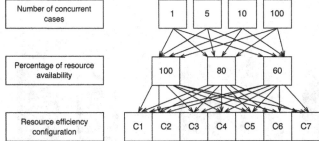

Fig. 5. Combinations of different simulation parameters.

(for occasional cases sick leave and maintenance) and 60% (for holiday seasons and maintenance periods). We further consider seven different configurations of resource efficiency presented in Table 1, where the first six configurations contain explicit values for each resource type, while the seventh randomly selects values between 50 and 100.

To approximate the performance of the workflow under varying degree of stress and demand for each combination of the variations of resource availability and efficiency, we configure the simulation with different number of emergency instances that may happen concurrently, specifically a single instance, as well as five, ten and 100 concurrent instances. Figure 5 illustrates the combinations of the simulation parameters described above, which result in 84 different scenarios.

Since it is crucial to run the simulation until it has stable performance, we follow a methodology similar to [15], and have conducted 400 simulations for scenarios with one, five, and ten concurrent instances. As for the scenarios with 100 concurrent instances, we have conducted ten simulations due to long simulation time (see the remark on this aspect in Sect. 3.4). Through averaging the outcomes across multiple simulations, our objective was to gain more precise insights into factors such as execution time, financial cost implications, and number of deadline violations. Employing this approach enhances the credibility of our findings and provides decision-makers with a deeper understanding of the effectiveness of emergency response systems under various resource scenarios. Remark that these parameters can be configured by the user as needed.

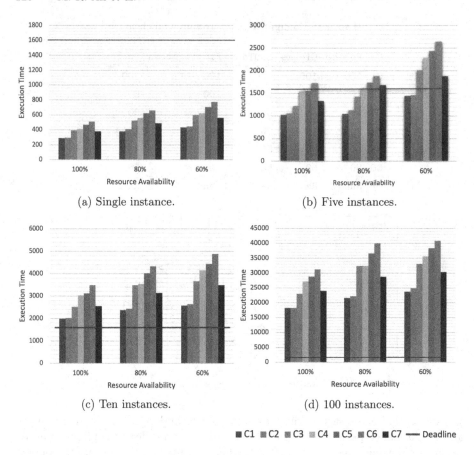

(a) Single instance.

(b) Five instances.

(c) Ten instances.

(d) 100 instances.

■ C1 ■ C2 ■ C3 ■ C4 ■ C5 ■ C6 ■ C7 —— Deadline

Fig. 6. Bar charts indicating average execution time and deadline violations for combinations of resource efficiency and resource availability with one, five, ten and 100 concurrent emergency instances.

Performance Metrics. The simulation module in $\mathcal{R}$PLTool allows the user to evaluate three performance metrics of the simulated model, namely, overall execution time, financial cost, and the number of deadline violations. The metric *overall execution time* measures the system's effectiveness in responding to emergencies, encompassing the duration from initiation to resolution. Variations in resource availability and efficiency directly affect the time taken and efficacy of the emergency response procedure. The number of *deadline violations* indicates the adherence to crucial time constraints of the workflow model, minimising delays and consequences. Analysing the *financial cost* for handling the emergencies provides insights into the financial implication of resource allocation, thus helps balance operational efficiency and fiscal responsibility. These metrics collectively gauge the performance of the model under different resource scenarios and concurrency levels, and help identify potential bottlenecks in the model, which consequently facilitates the optimisation of resource allocation.

Table 2. Simulation results wrt minimum, average and maximum execution time, standard daviation and percentage of deadline violations for combinations of resource efficiency and resource availability with one, five, ten and 100 concurrent emergency instances.

Avail	C	Execution Time Min	Avg	Max	Std	DV %
	C1	290	290	290	0	0
	C2	294	294	294	0	0
	C3	394	394	394	0	0
100%	C4	414	414	414	0	0
	C5	468	468	468	0	0
	C6	510	510	510	0	0
	C7	306	378	482	37	0
	C1	370	379	380	2.9	0
	C2	380	407	410	9.4	0
	C3	506	524	526	5.8	0
80%	C4	530	557	560	9.5	0
	C5	622	649	652	8.5	0
	C6	640	658	660	6.1	0
	C7	386	490	644	53.3	0
	C1	420	434	450	15	0
	C2	424	447	454	7	0
	C3	590	597	604	7.1	0
60%	C4	606	622	636	15	0
	C5	697	704	711	7.3	0
	C6	740	774	770	15	0
	C7	436	562	719	55	0

(a) Single instance.

Avail	C	Execution Time Min	Avg	Max	Std	DV %
	C1	996	1027	1092	22.8	0
	C2	1003	1058	1140	32,5	0
	C3	1134	1218	1289	36,8	0
100%	C4	1457	1543	1610	36.3	3,2
	C5	1478	1555	1633	36,8	11,7
	C6	1697	1724	1790	22	93
	C7	1046	1332	1670	148,2	12,7
	C1	1007	1051	1113	25,1	0
	C2	1047	1127	1174	30,1	0
	C3	1383	1427	1501	28	0
80%	C4	1537	1611	1680	33,9	81
	C5	1647	1736	1792	34,4	100
	C6	1770	1881	1923	36,3	100
	C7	1484	1678	1839	84.3	91.7
	C1	1378	1443	1504	29,9	0
	C2	1412	1460	1534	28,9	0
	C3	1932	2011	2097	39,2	100
60%	C4	2184	2280	2356	40,1	100
	C5	2259	2436	2636	89,5	100
	C6	2525	2643	2746	52,5	100
	C7	1640	1881	2074	103,1	100

(b) Five instances.

Avail	C	Execution Time Min	Avg	Max	Std	DV %
	C1	1770	1983	2330	133	100
	C2	1834	2023	2336	119,2	100
	C3	2192	2520	2880	163,4	100
100%	C4	2756	3033	3614	203,8	100
	C5	2666	3110	3588	219	100
	C6	3090	3483	4010	218,5	100
	C7	2177	2548	3041	205,2	100
	C1	2050	2369	2700	154,4	100
	C2	2079	2436	2742	157,5	100
	C3	3337	3483	3796	109	100
80%	C4	3026	3542	3954	220,4	100
	C5	3656	4023	4495	199,3	100
	C6	3720	4324	4880	275,5	100
	C7	2529	3137	3732	285,7	100
	C1	2250	2569	2990	175,7	100
	C2	2278	2641	3140	204,7	100
	C3	3414	3669	4013	142,3	100
60%	C4	3588	4146	4676	258,4	100
	C5	3935	4432	5053	265,5	100
	C6	4370	4875	5510	270,8	100
	C7	2765	3492	4034	301,4	100

(c) Ten instances.

Avail.	C	Execution Time Min	Avg	Max	Std	DV %
	C1	17440	18270	19070	465	100
	C2	16653	17934	18734	553	100
	C3	22342	23011	33790	493	100
100%	C4	26762	27176	27982	354	100
	C5	27857	28846	29666	545	100
	C6	30530	31270	32310	603	100
	C7	22119	23952	24169	685	100
	C1	21140	21593	22460	388	100
	C2	21510	22199	22815	444	100
	C3	31964	32425	32425	335	100
80%	C4	31766	32414	33480	505	100
	C5	35775	36606	37173	391	100
	C6	39070	39963	40770	514	100
	C7	27571	28734	30320	702	100
	C1	22310	23700	24576	538	100
	C2	23732	24876	25300	372	100
	C3	32591	33122	33904	312	100
60%	C4	34865	35645	36123	299	100
	C5	37945	38348	38864	219	100
	C6	39257	40810	41382	505	100
	C7	27337	30340	33942	1567	100

(d) 100 instances.

3.3 Observations About the Simulation Results

In this section, we discuss the simulation results in terms of the performance metrics of the various scenarios described in Sect. 3.2, and comment on how each parameter affects the metrics.

Execution Time and Deadline Violations. Figure 6 shows the impact of different resource configurations on the execution time and deadline violations, and compares the impacts under various concurrency levels, while Table 2 shows the detailed simulation results. In the table, Avail refers to the level of resource availability, C the different resource efficiency configurations specified in Table 1,

Min, Avg, Max correspond to the minimum, average and maximum of the execution time, respectively, of the 400 simulations (ten in the case of 100 concurrent instances), while Std refers to the standard deviation. The last column DV indicates the percentage of deadline violations.

As shown in Fig. 6a and Table 2a, the given pool of resources is more than sufficient to handle one single emergency instance, regardless of the levels of resource availability or the resource efficiency configurations. On the contrary, Figs. 6c and 6d (respectively Tables 2c and 2d) have shown that the provided resources obviously cannot handle ten or more emergency instances that happen simultaneously, even if in the ideal situation where the resources are fully available and efficient.

Nonetheless, Fig. 6b and Table 2b provide some interesting insights into the scenario of handling five concurrent emergency instances. For instance, the workflow model always meet the deadline with efficiency configurations C1 and C2 in Table 1, while it almost misses all the deadline with C6, despite the resource availability. If the resources have the efficiency specified in C3, the model can still meet the deadline with availability between 80% to 100%, but not 60%; with configurations C4 and C5, the model can meet the deadline most of the time with the resources that are fully available.

A similar observation can be made in the same figure and table for the *resource efficiency* configurations: an obvious increase in the overall execution time is evident as the configurations move away from fully efficient resources (C1) towards less efficient states (C6). Configurations C4, C5 and C6 clearly exhibit a significant spike in execution times. Based on Table 1, such effect is contributed by the decrement in the efficiency of Police, Doctors and Firefighters, whose impact is more substantial compared to a similar decrease in the efficiency of Clerks and EODTech in configurations C1 and C2, suggesting that the timely execution of tasks involving medical and emergency response personnel is crucial for maintaining efficient workflow performance.

As mentioned above, longer execution time leads to higher number of deadline violations. As a result, the reduced efficiency of Police, Doctors and Firefighters also contributes to an increased number of instances where deadlines are not met. Such insights are particularly important for time critical workflows, e.g., the emergency response procedure in this case study, as deadline violations can be disastrous.

Table 2 also provides insights into the variability in execution time by means of standard deviation. Variations can be observed when resources are not fully available for one or multiple instances. Note that in configuration C7, where resource efficiency is chosen randomly, there is notable variability in execution time across all levels of resource availability.

Financial Costs. Figure 7 illustrates how the financial cost, expressed in thousands, of the workflow varies under the various resource efficiency configurations and concurrency levels. Here we only show the scenarios where resources are fully (i.e., 100%) available due to page limit and because the other availability levels have the similar variation patterns for the financial costs.

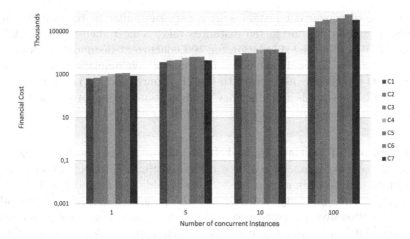

Fig. 7. Bar charts indicating an increase in financial cost (in thousands) of different resource efficiency configurations for different number of emergency instances.

From the figure, we can also see that on the one hand the difference of the cost between the resource efficiency configurations is relatively minor. On the other hand, there is a noticeable upward trend in financial expenditure with an increase in the number of concurrent instances. This pattern aligns with the common understanding that handling a higher volume of instances concurrently necessitates more resources, consequently driving up costs.

3.4 Discussions

In this section, we remark on the simulation time for this case study and discuss the potential other factors can be employed in the simulation configurations to observe workflows from other perspectives.

Simulation Time. Here, we would like to briefly comment on the simulation time with respect to the number of concurrent emergency instances in this case study. Figure 8 shows the time taken to run one simulation for the scenario where the resources are fully available and the efficiency configuration is randomly chosen for each resource type, i.e., configuration C7 in Table 1. Note that the simulation time for the other scenarios will increase in relation to

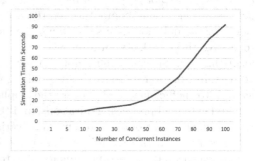

Fig. 8. Simulation time for 1 to 100 concurrent instances.

the number of concurrent instances in a pattern similar to the one shown in the figure. Simulating one to ten instances takes almost the same time, which is around 10 s, while the simulation for 100 concurrent instances takes around 100 s. Therefore, the total time taken for running 400 simulations for one, five, ten and 100 emergency instances with the 21 resource setups (i.e., the combination of availability levels and efficiency configurations) are approximately 23.3 h for the first three concurrency levels and 233 h for 100 instances.

Other Potential Factors. Beyond the fundamental parameters such as number of concurrent instances, resource availability and efficiency, other influential factors may also come into play. These include the rate at which tasks or jobs arrive, the complexity of tasks, and the policies governing resource allocation. Additionally, communication delays, resource sharing rules, and workload variability significantly impact the efficiency of workflows across different organisational units. The simulation should also account for resource prioritisation criteria, potential failure and recovery scenarios, and any technological constraints. The organisational structure, external influences such as market fluctuations, and the skill levels of personnel contribute to the overall complexity of the model. Cost models and sensitivity analysis further enhance the simulation, providing insights into the financial implications of resource usage and the system's responsiveness to parameter changes. By incorporating these parameters, the simulation study becomes a more realistic and robust representation of cross-organisational workflows and their intricate resource-sharing dynamics. We intend to extend our simulation tool to include a larger set of parameters in the future.

4   Related Work

In the investigation of resource allocation challenges, mathematical techniques like integer programming, dynamic programming, and branch-and-bound have been widely explored, for instance, [14,26,27]. However, these methods often necessitate significant computational resources and encounter difficulties in constructing models for diverse systems, particularly those featuring numerous repetitive tasks [31]. As an alternative, heuristic methods [7,8,23] and genetic algorithms [9,18] have been employed, yet these approaches often assess each activity in isolation, potentially overlooking concurrent resource fulfilment and leading to inefficiencies. Moreover, the application of Genetic Algorithms can demand extended processing durations, and these methods may not fully account for the involvement of other resources or variability in activity durations [31].

In contrast to these traditional and heuristic approaches, simulation based methodologies have gained prominence due to their capability to assess resource policies, evaluate performance, and address real-world system issues [3,19]. The work in [22] has proposed a method utilising Structural Causal Models (SCM) [24] to reason cause-effect assumptions leveraging the online BIMP [13] tool to simulate event logs based on selected Business Process Model and Notation (BPMN) [12] specifications. An approach has been implemented in [17] in Visual Miner [16] within ProM framework [11] for analysing causality in business processes. These studies, while valuable, often lack formal support for modelling cross-organisational workflows and may not provide the level of comprehensive insights required for decision-making in collaborative environments. The work in [10] has applied Dynamic Condition Response (DCR), a constraint-based modelling notation, to develop railway emergency response plans. DCR provides flexibility in modelling various emergency scenarios by representing essential rules or conditions; however, it lacks support for the concurrent execution of multiple independent events.

In the context of emergency response processes, previous formal studies have employed Petri nets [21, 28, 30]. Furthermore, variants of Petri nets like OTRM-nets, workflow nets, inter-organisational workflow nets, and resource allocation nets have been extensively used in the literature to model and analyse intra- and inter-organisational business processes and allocate resources to them [20]. However, Petri nets face limitations, particularly in advanced control flow representation for patterns involving multiple instances or advanced synchronisation patterns [1].

In comparison to traditional and alternative methodologies, the presented paper emphasises the contribution of a simulation-based decision support, using a modelling language $\mathcal{R}$PL [4] for modelling cross-organisational workflows within emergency response scenarios. The $\mathcal{R}$PLTool is employed to simulate workflows, providing a formalised representation that enables the integration of cross-organisational workflows through shared resources and task dependencies. This approach, distinct from other methodologies, not only allows decision-makers to anticipate consequences within individual workflows but also offers insights into the broader implications across all collaborating workflows. The holistic perspective and adaptability of $\mathcal{R}$PL for dynamic and collaborative environments position the proposed approach as a robust methodology for addressing the challenges posed by resource allocation, ultimately leading to improved efficiency and resilience in emergency response scenarios.

5   Conclusion

This paper has demonstrated the potential of employing a simulation based decision support for cross-organisational workflows, particularly using a formal modelling language, $\mathcal{R}$PL. Through the exploration of an emergency response scenario, the study has utilised $\mathcal{R}$PLTool to simulate workflows, emphasising the evaluation of the impact of changes in number of concurrent instances, resource availability and efficiency on deadline violations, execution time, and financial costs within collaborative workflows.

The selection of $\mathcal{R}$PL was driven by its capacity to provide a formalised representation of workflows, enabling the integration of cross-organisational workflows through shared resources and task dependencies. This formalised approach not only allows decision-makers to anticipate the consequences of changes within one workflow but also provides insights into the broader implications of all collaborating workflows. By doing so, it enhances the comprehension and management of cross-organisational workflows, ultimately leading to improved efficiency and resilience.

In addition to the insights from the current study, it is crucial to recognise various factors that impact cross-organisational workflows beyond resource availability and efficiency. These include task arrival rates, complexity, resource allocation policies, communication delays, workload variability, and technological constraints. Recognising the multifaceted nature of cross-organisational workflows, our future work aims to expand the scope of simulation by incorporating these influential factors. Apart from providing decision support on resource allocation, the bottlenecks in a workflow model identified by the simulation results can potentially be used in improving the structure of the model, for instance, sequentialise concurrent tasks that are competing for shared resources. Thus, a natural extension would be to provide support on restructuring workflow models.

Acknowledgements. This work is part of the CROFLOW project: Enabling Highly Automated Cross-Organisational Workflow Planning, funded by the Research Council of Norway (grant no. 326249).

References

1. van der Aalst, W.M., ter Hofstede, A.H.: YAWL: yet another workflow language. Inf. Syst. **30**(4), 245–275 (2005). https://doi.org/10.1016/j.is.2004.02.002
2. Agha, G.: Actors: A Model of Concurrent Computation in Distributed Systems. MIT Press (1986). https://doi.org/10.7551/mitpress/1086.001.0001
3. Ahuja, H.N., Nandakumar, V.: Simulation model to forecast project completion time. J. Constr. Eng. Manag. **111**(4), 325–342 (1985). https://doi.org/10.1061/(ASCE)0733-9364(1985)111:4(325)
4. Ali, M.R., Lamo, Y., Pun, V.K.I: Cost analysis for a resource sensitive workflow modelling language. Sci. Comput. Program. **225**, 102896 (2023). https://doi.org/10.1016/j.scico.2022.102896
5. Ali, M.R., Pun, V.K.I: Cost analysis for an actor-based workflow modelling language. In: Campos, S., Minea, M. (eds.) SBMF 2021. LNCS, vol. 13130, pp. 104–121. Springer, Cham (2021). https://doi.org/10.1007/978-3-030-92137-8_7
6. Ali, M.R., Pun, V.K.I: A static analyser for resource sensitive workflow models. In: David, C., Sun, M. (eds.) TASE 2023. LNCS, vol. 13931, pp. 305–312. Springer, Cham (2023). https://doi.org/10.1007/978-3-031-35257-7_18
7. Badiru, A.B.: A simulation approach to PERT network analysis. Simulation **57**(4), 245–255 (1991). https://doi.org/10.1177/003754979105700409
8. Boctor, F.F.: Heuristics for scheduling projects with resource restrictions and several resource-duration modes. Int. J. Prod. Res. **31**(11), 2547–2558 (1993). https://doi.org/10.1080/00207549308956882
9. Chan, W.T., Chua, D.K.H., Kannan, G.: Construction resource scheduling with genetic algorithms. J. Constr. Eng. Manag. **122**(2), 125–132 (1996). https://doi.org/10.1061/(ASCE)0733-9364(1996)122:2(125)

10. Debois, S., Hildebrandt, T., Sandberg, L.: Experience report: constraint-based modelling and simulation of railway emergency response plans. Procedia Comput. Sci. **83**, 1295–1300 (2016). https://doi.org/10.1016/j.procs.2016.04.269, the 7th International Conference on Ambient Systems, Networks and Technologies (ANT 2016)/The 6th International Conference on Sustainable Energy Information Technology (SEIT-2016)/Affiliated Workshops

11. van Dongen, B.F., de Medeiros, A.K.A., Verbeek, H.M.W., Weijters, A.J.M.M., van der Aalst, W.M.P.: The ProM framework: a new era in process mining tool support. In: Ciardo, G., Darondeau, P. (eds.) ICATPN 2005. LNCS, vol. 3536, pp. 444–454. Springer, Heidelberg (2005). https://doi.org/10.1007/11494744_25

12. Durán, F., Falcone, Y., Rocha, C., Salaün, G., Zuo, A.: From static to dynamic analysis and allocation of resources for BPMN processes. In: Bae, K. (ed.) WRLA 2022. LNCS, vol. 13252, pp. 3–21. Springer, Cham (2022). https://doi.org/10.1007/978-3-031-12441-9_1

13. Freitas, A.P., Pereira, J.L.: Process simulation support in bpm tools: the case of BPMN (2015). https://api.semanticscholar.org/CorpusID:61670021

14. Gavish, B., Pirkul, H.: Algorithms for the multi-resource generalized assignment problem. Manag. Sci. **37**(6), 695–713 (1991). https://doi.org/10.1287/mnsc.37.6.695

15. Gholamy, A., Kreinovich, V.: How many Monte-Carlo simulations are needed to adequately process interval uncertainty: an explanation of the smart electric grid-related simulation results. J. Innov. Technol. Educ. **5**(1), 1–5 (2018). https://scholarworks.utep.edu/cs_techrep/1214

16. Leemans, S.J.J., Fahland, D., van der Aalst, W.M.P.: Exploring processes and deviations. In: Fournier, F., Mendling, J. (eds.) BPM 2014. LNBIP, vol. 202, pp. 304–316. Springer, Cham (2015). https://doi.org/10.1007/978-3-319-15895-2_26

17. Leemans, S.J.J., Tax, N.: Causal reasoning over control-flow decisions in process models. In: Franch, X., Poels, G., Gailly, F., Snoeck, M. (eds.) CAiSE 2022. LNCS, vol. 13295, pp. 183–200. Springer, Cham (2022). https://doi.org/10.1007/978-3-031-07472-1_11

18. Leu, S.S., Yang, C.H.: A genetic-algorithm-based resource-constrained construction scheduling system. Constr. Manag. Econ. **17**(6), 767–776 (1999). https://doi.org/10.1080/014461999371105

19. Li, J., González, M., Zhu, Y.: A hybrid simulation optimization method for production planning of dedicated remanufacturing. Int. J. Prod. Econ. **117**(2), 286–301 (2009). https://doi.org/10.1016/j.ijpe.2008.11.005

20. Liu, G.: Petri nets modeling message passing and resource sharing. In: Liu, G. (ed.) Petri Nets, pp. 99–121. Springer, Singapore (2022). https://doi.org/10.1007/978-981-19-6309-4_4

21. Liu, G., Jiang, C., Zhou, M., Xiong, P.: Interactive Petri nets. IEEE Trans. Syst. Man Cybern. Syst. **43**(2), 291–302 (2013). https://doi.org/10.1109/TSMCA.2012.2204741

22. Narendra, T., Agarwal, P., Gupta, M., Dechu, S.: Counterfactual reasoning for process optimization using structural causal models. In: Hildebrandt, T., van Dongen, B.F., Röglinger, M., Mendling, J. (eds.) BPM 2019. LNBIP, vol. 360, pp. 91–106. Springer, Cham (2019). https://doi.org/10.1007/978-3-030-26643-1_6

23. Padilla, E.M., Carr, R.I.: Resource strategies for dynamic project management. J. Constr. Eng. Manag. **117**(2), 279–293 (1991). https://doi.org/10.1061/(ASCE)0733-9364(1991)117:2(279)

24. Pearl, J.: Causality. Cambridge University Press, Cambridge (2009). https://doi.org/10.1017/CBO9780511803161

25. Ritter, F.E., Schoelles, M.J., Quigley, K.S., Klein, L.C.: Determining the number of simulation runs: treating simulations as theories by not sampling their behavior. In: Rothrock, L., Narayanan, S. (eds.) Human-in-the-Loop Simulations, pp. 97–116. Springer, London (2011). https://doi.org/10.1007/978-0-85729-883-6_5

26. Stinson, J.P.: A branch and bound algorithm for a general class of resource-constrained scheduling problems. Unpublished Ph.D. Dissertation, University of North Carolina at Chapel Hill (1976). https://ci.nii.ac.jp/ncid/BB03308422

27. Talbot, F.B.: Resource-constrained project scheduling with time-resource tradeoffs: the nonpreemptive case. Manag. Sci. **28**(10), 1197–1210 (1982). https://doi.org/10.1287/mnsc.28.10.1197

28. Zeng, Q.T., Lu, F.M., Liu, C., Meng, D.C.: Modeling and analysis for cross-organizational emergency response systems using Petri nets. Chin. J. Comput **36**(11), 2290–2302 (2013). https://api.semanticscholar.org/CorpusID:63737243

29. Zeng, Q., Liu, C., Duan, H., Zhou, M.: Resource conflict checking and resolution controller design for cross-organization emergency response processes. IEEE Trans. Syst. Man Cybern. Syst. **50**(10), 3685–3700 (2020). https://doi.org/10.1109/TSMC.2019.2906335

30. Zeng, Q., Sun, S.X., Duan, H., Liu, C., Wang, H.: Cross-organizational collaborative workflow mining from a multi-source log. Decis. Support Syst. **54**(3), 1280–1301 (2013). https://doi.org/10.1016/j.dss.2012.12.001

31. Zhang, H., Li, H.: Simulation-based optimization for dynamic resource allocation. Autom. Constr. **13**(3), 409–420 (2004). https://doi.org/10.1016/j.autcon.2003.12.005

An Enhanced Exchange Operator for XC

Giorgio Audrito$^{(\boxtimes)}$, Daniele Bortoluzzi, Ferruccio Damiani,
Giordano Scarso, and Gianluca Torta

Università degli Studi di Torino, Via Verdi 8, 10124 Turin, Italy
{giorgio.audrito,daniele.bortoluzzi,ferruccio.damiani,
giordano.scarso,gianluca.torta}@unito.it

Abstract. Recent work in the area of coordination models and collective adaptive systems promotes a view of distributed computations
as functions manipulating computational fields (data structures spread
over space and evolving over time) and introduces the *eXchange Calculus
(XC)* as a novel formal foundation for field computations. In XC, evolution (time) and neighbor interaction (space) are handled by a single communication primitive called *exchange*, working on the *neighbouring value*
data structure to represent both received values and values to share.
However, the exchange primitive does not allow to directly retain information about neighbours across subsequent rounds of computation. This
hampers the convenient expression of useful algorithms in XC, such as the
computation of a *neighbour reliability score*. In this paper, we introduce
a new generalised version of the exchange primitive, also implementing
it into the FCPP DSL. This primitive allows for neighbour data retention across rounds, strictly expanding the expressiveness of the exchange
primitive in XC. The contribution is then evaluated through a case study
on distributed sensing in a wireless sensor network of battery-powered
devices, exploiting the reliability scores to improve robustness.

Keywords: Core calculus · Aggregate computing · C++ DSL

1 Introduction

The number and density of networked computing devices distributed throughout our environment is continuing to increase rapidly. In order to manage and
make effective use of such systems, there is likewise an increasing need for software engineering paradigms that simplify the engineering of resilient distributed
systems. Aggregate programming [10,19] is one such promising approach, providing a layered architecture in which programmers can describe computations
by combining resilient operations on "aggregate" data structures with values
spread over space and evolving in time.

The foundation of this approach is on field-based computations, originally
formalized by the field calculus (FC) [8], and later refined by the exchange calculus (XC) [4,5], a terse mathematical model of distributed computation that
simultaneously describes both collective system behavior and the independent,

© IFIP International Federation for Information Processing 2024
Published by Springer Nature Switzerland AG 2024
I. Castellani and F. Tiezzi (Eds.): COORDINATION 2024, LNCS 14676, pp. 129–145, 2024.
https://doi.org/10.1007/978-3-031-62697-5_8

unsynchronized actions of individual devices that will produce that collective behavior. In this approach, computation (executed in asynchronous rounds), communication (which is neighbour-based), and state over time, are all expressed by means of a single communication primitive, called `exchange`.

This primitive applies a given function to a single argument n (a view of the values produced by neighbours), obtaining as result a view s of the values to send back to neighbours. This mechanism provides a general communication pattern, but does not allow to directly retain information about neighbours across subsequent rounds of computation: the result s obtained on a device in a round is not available in that device on the following round. This prevents from conveniently expressing in XC useful algorithms, such as the computation of a *neighbour reliability score* based on statistics on messages received by neighbours. Since XC is Turing-complete, these algorithms could still be expressed, but only by breaking the neighbouring-value abstraction given by the language.

In this paper, we address this limitation by introducing a new generalised version of the exchange primitive that allows for neighbour data retention. The generalised exchange takes two arguments: both the same n as in XC, and a view o of the values produced for neighbours in the previous round of the same device. This strictly extends XC, retaining all previous expressiveness while opening the way for new possibilities. We illustrate the increase in expressiveness by means of examples, presenting two novel neighbour reliability metrics (uni-connection and mixed-connection), that can be used in the novel *stabilised single-path* collection algorithm. The proposal is then evaluated in a simulated case study on distributed sensing, set in an unreliable wireless sensor network of battery-powered devices. The evaluation is carried out through the FCPP simulator [1,7], that has been extended to support the generalised exchange primitive and a more advanced model of unreliable communication.

Following a background on field-based approaches (focusing on XC) in Sect. 2, we introduce the generalised exchange construct in Sect. 3, evaluate the effectiveness of the construct in a case study on reliable WSN sensing in Sect. 4, and conclude with a summary and discussion of future work in Sect. 5.

2   Background

In this section, we briefly present the class of field-based coordination approaches, and then dive into the system modeling, syntax and semantics of the *eXchange Calculus (XC)*. Please refer to [4,5] for more details.

2.1   Field-Based Coordination

Both XC [4,5] and its close predecessor FC [8] belong to the class of *field-based coordination* approaches to the design of distributed computing systems. Such approaches take an important natural source of inspiration from the concept of *field* in physics. A coordination field (or co-field) was initially introduced in [14] to facilitate the formation of self-organizing patterns in agent movement within complex environments. Building on this concept, the TOTA (Tuples On The Air) tuple-based middleware [13] was developed to enable field-based coordination for pervasive computing applications. In TOTA, each tuple inserted into a network node is endowed with content (the tuple data), a diffusion rule (determining how the tuple is to be replicated and spread), and a maintenance rule (dictating how the tuple should evolve over time or in response to events). One of the pioneering works linking field-based coordination with formalization tools, such as process algebras and transition systems, is the $\sigma\tau$-Linda model [20]. In this model, agents can inject *processes* into the space that propagate, gather, and decay tuples, thereby sustaining fields of tuples. In [12], the authors define the *SMuC* language as an extension of μ-calculus that is able to express global programs on fields that can be executed on a distributed system. Surveys reviewing approaches to abstract spatial collective adaptive systems can be found in [9,11,15,16].

2.2 System Model

The systems we aim to program can be conceptualized as sets of *nodes*, each capable of engaging with the environment via *sensors* and *actuators*, as well as communicating with neighboring nodes through message exchanges.

We operate under the assumption that each node executes in *asynchronous* cycles known as sense-compute-act rounds, where:

- **sense**: The node gathers current environmental data by querying sensors and collects recent messages from neighbors. This information constitutes the node's *context*.
- **compute**: The node processes a shared control program, which interprets the context (i.e., inputs from sensors and neighbors) to generate an output detailing the actions to be taken (e.g., actuations and communications).
- **act**: The node carries out the actions in output, potentially resulting in changes to the environment or the delivery of messages to neighbors.

This loop ensures continuous assessment of the context at discrete intervals, with reactions computed and executed continuously and asynchronously. An instance of system execution can be represented through an event structure (see Fig. 1). Here, events (denoted by ϵ) encapsulate entire sense-compute-act rounds, and the arrows linking events signify that certain source events have furnished inputs (i.e., messages) to target events. Specifically, if event ϵ' is linked by an arrow to ϵ, we designate ϵ' as a "neighbor" of ϵ, symbolized as $\epsilon' \rightsquigarrow \epsilon$. Therefore, programming the systems described in this section consists of establishing the control rules that dictate how the context at each event is translated into the messages intended for neighboring events.

2.3 Neighbouring Values

In XC, we categorize values into two types. The *Local* values, denoted by ℓ, encompass traditional atomic and structured types like integers, floats, strings,

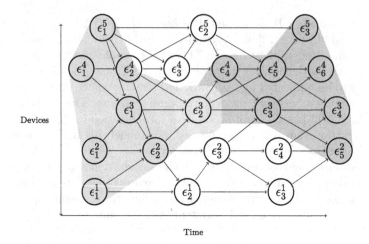

Fig. 1. An event structure modelling a distributed system execution. Node ϵ_k^δ denotes the k-th round of device δ. The yellow area contains a reference event, whose past (green) and future (blue) are identified from causal arrows between neighbour events. (Color figure online)

or lists. On the other hand, the neighboring values (referred to as nvalues) are mappings $\mathbf{w}$ from device identifiers δ_i to corresponding local values ℓ_i. Additionally, there's an extra local value ℓ acting as a default:

$$\mathbf{w} = \ell[\delta_1 \mapsto \ell_1, \dots, \delta_n \mapsto \ell_n]$$

An nvalue specifies the values received from or sent to neighbors: received values are gathered into nvalues, can then be processed locally, and the resulting nvalue can be interpreted as messages to be sent back to neighbors. Devices associated with an entry in the nvalue are typically a small subset of all devices, namely those close enough to the current device and working correctly.

The default value is used when a value isn't available for some neighbor δ'. For instance, if δ' has just been powered on and hasn't produced a value yet, or if it has just moved close enough to the current device δ to become one of its neighbors. Hence, the notation should be understood as follows: "the nvalue $\mathbf{w}$ is ℓ everywhere (i.e., for all devices) except for devices $\delta_1, \dots, \delta_n$, which have given values $\ell_1, \dots, \ell_n$, respectively."

To illustrate nvalues, consider Fig. 1. Upon waking up for computation ϵ_2^3, device δ_3 might process an nvalue $\mathbf{w} = 0[\delta_4 \mapsto 1, \delta_3 \mapsto 2, \delta_2 \mapsto 3]$, representing messages carrying scalar values 1, 2, and 3 received when asleep from δ_4, δ_3 (itself at the previous round), and δ_2. Entries for all other (neighbor) devices default to 0. After computation, δ_2 might send out messages represented by nvalue $\mathbf{w}' = 0[\delta_4 \mapsto 5, \delta_3 \mapsto 6]$, sending 5 to δ_4, 6 to δ_3, and 0 to every other (neighbor) device, such as a newly-connected device. For convenience, $\mathbf{w}(\delta')$ denotes the local value (specific or default) associated with δ' by $\mathbf{w}$.

Note that a local value ℓ can be naturally converted to an nvalue $\ell[]$, that holds the default value for every device. On the other hand, functions on local values are implicitly lifted to nvalues by applying them pointwise to the maps' content. For example, if w_1 assigns value 2 to δ_3 and w_2 assigns default value 1 to δ_3, then $w_3 = w_1 \cdot w_2$ assigns value $2 \cdot 1 = 2$ to δ_3. Local values and nvalues can thus be treated uniformly by the exchange calculus.

A fundamental operation on nvalues is provided by the built-in function $\texttt{nfold}(f : (A, B) \rightarrow A, \texttt{w} : B, \ell : A) : A$. This function folds over an nvalue $\texttt{w}$, starting from a base local value ℓ, repeatedly applying function f to neighbors' values in $\texttt{w}$, excluding the value for the current device. For instance, if δ_2 with a set of neighbors $\{\delta_1, \delta_3, \delta_4\}$ performs a $\texttt{nfold}$ operation $\texttt{nfold}(*, \texttt{w}, 1)$, the output will be $1 \cdot \texttt{w}(\delta_1) \cdot \texttt{w}(\delta_3) \cdot \texttt{w}(\delta_4)$. We usually assume that f is associative and commutative since nvalues are unordered maps. Other common built-in operator are:

- $\texttt{self}(\texttt{w} : A) : A$, that returns the local value $\texttt{w}(\delta)$ in $\texttt{w}$ for the self device δ.
- $\texttt{modOther}(\texttt{w} : A, \ell : A) : A$, that returns an nvalue where the default of $\texttt{w}$ is changed to ℓ, and all other values are the same as in $\texttt{w}$.
- $\texttt{mux}(\ell_1 : \texttt{bool}, \ell_2 : A, \ell_3 : A)$, that returns ℓ_2 if ℓ_1 is $\texttt{True}$, ℓ_3 otherwise (note that all arguments are evaluated).

Moreover, XC features a single communication primitive:

$$\texttt{exchange}(\texttt{e}_i, (\texttt{n}) \texttt{=>} (\texttt{e}_r, \texttt{e}_s))$$

evaluated as follows:

- The device computes the local value ℓ_i of $\texttt{e}_i$ (the *initial* value).
- To evaluate the function provided as the second argument, it substitutes variable $\texttt{n}$ with the nvalue $\texttt{w}$ of messages received from neighbors for this exchange, using ℓ_i as default.
- The expression returns the value $\texttt{w}_r$ from the evaluation of $\texttt{e}_r$.
- The second expression $\texttt{e}_s$ in the argument function's output evaluates to an nvalue $\texttt{w}_s$ consisting of local values to be sent to neighbor devices δ', which will use their corresponding $\texttt{w}_s(\delta')$ upon waking up and performing their next execution round.

In order to clarify the purpose of the two elements of the pair returned by an exchange, in the remainder of this paper we use the notation $\texttt{return } \texttt{e}_r \texttt{ send}$ $\texttt{e}_s$ as syntactic sugar for the pair $(\texttt{e}_r, \texttt{e}_s)$. When $\texttt{e}_r$ and $\texttt{e}_s$ coincide, we also use $\texttt{retsend } \texttt{e}$ as syntactic sugar for the pair $(\texttt{e}, \texttt{e})$. The *exchange* construct abstracts the general concept of message exchange and is expressive enough to allow common communication patterns to be expressed through it. If a program executes multiple exchange-expressions, XC ensures through *alignment* that the messages are dispatched across rounds to corresponding exchange-expressions (in the same position in the program AST, and with the same stack frames of function calls).

Syntax:	
e ::= x | fun x(x̄){e} | e(ē) | val x = e; e | ℓ | w	expression
w ::= ℓ[δ̄ ↦ ℓ̄]	nvalue
ℓ ::= b | fun x(x̄){e} | c(ℓ̄)	local literal
b ::= exchange | nfold | self | modOther | uid | mux | ...	built-in function

Free variables of an expression:
FV(x) = {x}   FV(ℓ) = FV(w) = ∅ FV(fun $x_0(x_1, ..., x_n)${e}) = FV(e) \ {$x_0, ..., x_n$}
FV($e_0(e_1, \_, e_n)$) = $\bigcup_{i=0..n}$ FV(e_i)   FV(val x = e; e′) = FV(e) ∪ FV(e′) \ {x}

Syntactic sugar:		
(x̄) => e	::= fun y(x̄){e}	*where* y *is a fresh variable*
def x(x̄){e}	::= val x = fun x(x̄){e};	
if(e){$e_\top$} else {$e_\perp$} ::= mux(e, () => $e_\top$, () => $e_\perp$)()		

Fig. 2. Syntax (top), free variables (middle) and syntactic sugar (bottom) in XC

2.4   Syntax and Semantics

Figure 2 (top) illustrates the syntax of XC. The overbar notation denotes a (possibly empty) sequence of elements, where $\bar{x}$ represents $x_1, ..., x_n$ $(n \geq 0)$. The syntax adheres to that of a standard functional language, without any distinct features for distribution, which become evident in the semantics.

An XC *expression* e can take various forms:

– a *variable* x;
– a (possibly recursive) *function* fun x(x̄){e}, which may contain free variables;
– a *function call* e(ē);
– a *let-style* expression val x = e; e;
– a *local literal* ℓ, such as a built-in function b, a defined function fun x(x̄){e} *without* free variables, or a data constructor c applied to local literals (possibly none);
– an *nvalue* w, as explained in Sect. 2.3.

XC can be typed with higher-order let-polymorphism, without differentiation between types for local and neighboring values. This is reflected in the semantics by having language constructs and built-in functions that accept nvalues as arguments, and by implicitly promoting local values ℓ to nvalues ℓ[]. Free variables are defined conventionally (Fig. 2, middle), and an expression e is considered *closed* if FV(e) = ∅. Programs, which are closed expressions, do not contain nvalues as sub-expressions, in order to not explicitly mention devices in them: nvalues only emerge during computations and are the sole values produced by evaluating programs. The basic syntax presented is then expanded through syntactic sugar to incorporate infix operators, omitted parentheses in 0-ary constructors, and other non-trivial encodings described in Fig. 2 (bottom).

The semantics of XC comprises *(i)* a big-step operational *device semantics*, delineating the computation of a device within a single round; and *(ii)*

a denotational *network semantics*, formalizing communication between different device rounds. The device semantics is expressed through the judgement $\delta; \sigma; \Theta \vdash e \Downarrow w; \theta$, interpreted as "expression e evaluates to nvalue w and value-tree θ on device δ with respect to sensor values σ and value-tree environment Θ". In this context:

- w is termed the *result* of e;
- values in σ may be accessed by built-in functions (sensors) called in e;
- θ is an ordered tree with nvalues on certain nodes, representing messages to be sent to neighbors by tracking the nvalues produced by exchange-expressions in e, and the stack frames of function calls; $v\langle\overline{\theta}\rangle$ denotes a value tree with root v and subtrees $\overline{\theta}$;
- Θ accumulates the (non-expired) value-trees received by the most recent rounds of δ's neighbors, stored as a map $\delta_1 \mapsto \theta_1, ..., \delta_n \mapsto \theta_n$ $(n \geq 0)$ from device identifiers to value-trees. Notation $\pi_1(\Theta)$ denotes the mapping of each device δ_i to the leftmost subtree of θ_i.

The big-step rules of the device semantics define the behaviour of this judgement in mostly standard terms, although taking care of correctly passing around the context Θ in order to ensure alignment, and referring to an auxiliary predicate $\Downarrow^*$ for the evaluation of built-in primitives. Of particular interest for the present work is the semantics of the *exchange* primitive, which is expressed by the following rule, capturing the behavior described in Sect. 2.3:

$$\text{[A-XC]} \quad \frac{\Theta = \overline{\delta} \mapsto \overline{w}\langle...\rangle \quad w^{nbr} = w^{init}[\overline{\delta} \mapsto \overline{w}(\delta)]}{\delta; \sigma; \pi_1(\Theta) \vdash w^{fun}(w^{nbr}) \Downarrow (w^{ret}, w^{send}); \theta}$$

$$\delta; \sigma; \Theta \vdash \textbf{exchange}(w^{init}, w^{fun}) \Downarrow^* w^{ret}; w^{send}\langle\theta\rangle$$

Let δ be the device where the *exchange* operator is executed, and $\overline{w}$ be the sequence of nvalues received from neighbours $\overline{\delta}$, stored in the environment Θ. The notation $w^{init}[\overline{\delta} \mapsto \overline{w}(\delta)]$ represents the nvalue w^{init} after replacing the value $w^{init}(\delta_k)$ for each neighbour device $\delta_k \in \overline{\delta}$ with the message $w_k(\delta)$ that δ_k sent to the local device δ. The resulting value w^{nbr} serves as an argument to function w^{fun}: the first element of the resulting pair is used as the overall expression result, while the second is used to label the root of the resulting value-tree (and is therefore exchanged with neighbours).

The denotational network semantics employs the device semantics to define the result of evaluating a program across an entire event structure. For detailed, formal descriptions of the XC semantics, please refer to [4,5].

3   Enhanced Exchange Operator

In this paper, we extend the exchange operator by allowing the use of a function w^{fun} that accepts two arguments: w^{old} and w^{nbr} (the changes w.r.t. the semantics of the previous exchange operator are colored in red).

$$[\text{A-XC'}] \quad \frac{\Theta = \overline{\delta} \mapsto \overline{\mathbf{w}}\langle\ldots\rangle \quad \mathbf{w}^{\text{nbr}} = \mathbf{w}^{\text{init}}[\overline{\delta} \mapsto \overline{\mathbf{w}}(\delta)] \quad \mathbf{w}^{\text{old}} = \begin{cases} \mathbf{w}_k\,|_{\overline{\delta}} & \text{if } \delta = \delta_k \text{ for a } k \\ \mathbf{w}^{\text{init}} & \delta \text{ not in } \overline{\delta} \end{cases}}{\delta; \sigma; \pi_1(\Theta) \vdash \mathbf{w}^{\text{fun}}(\mathbf{w}^{\text{old}}, \mathbf{w}^{\text{nbr}}) \Downarrow (\mathbf{w}^{\text{ret}}, \mathbf{w}^{\text{send}}); \theta}$$

$$\delta; \sigma; \Theta \vdash \text{exchange}(\mathbf{w}^{\text{init}}, \mathbf{w}^{\text{fun}}) \Downarrow^* \mathbf{w}^{\text{ret}}; \mathbf{w}^{\text{send}}\langle\theta\rangle$$

We define $\mathbf{w}^{\text{nbr}}$ as for the original *exchange* operator. If there is no value for the local device δ in the environment Θ (and thus, it is the first round that the current device is computing this exchange expression), we define $\mathbf{w}^{\text{old}}$ to equal the initialization value $\mathbf{w}^{\text{init}}$. If instead δ appears in the sequence of neighbours (and thus $\delta = \delta_k$ for some k), $\mathbf{w}^{\text{old}}$ is set to the nvalue $\mathbf{w}_k$ (extracted from $\overline{\mathbf{w}}$ in Θ) computed in the previous round by the local device as $\mathbf{w}^{\text{send}}$, with the domain restricted to the current neighbours $\overline{\delta}$. This is written with notation $\mathbf{w}\,|_D$, that corresponds to setting the value in $\mathbf{w}$ for any device δ' not in D to the default value of $\mathbf{w}$. Note that the extended *exchange* operator can exploit only the values sent by δ in the *previous* round. However, multi-step memory can be implemented in terms of single-step memory, e.g., by sending a history of previously sent values as an nvalue associating lists of values to devices. Note that an essentially analogous single-step approach is adopted for preserving state in other field-based languages, such as in the distributed implementation of the SMuC calculus [12], and in the FC *rep* operator [8]. In that case, multi-step memory can be built on top of *rep*, although for local values only.

In the following examples, we exploit the extended *exchange* operator to implement different connection counters between the current device and its neighbours. Such counters can be viewed as quantitative ranks of the connection reliability between nodes, an important piece of information that can be exploited in several contexts. In particular, in Sect. 4 we will present a single-path collection algorithm that uses such ranks to determine the best node to select as parent of the current node in order to find a path toward the source node.

Example 1 (Unidirectional Connection Counter). The following *uniconn-count* function produces an nvalue of inbound connection counters, associating every neighbour to the number of times a message has been received from it.

```
def uniconn-count() {
  exchange( 0, (o,n) => retsend o + modOther(1,0) )
}
```

We set the initial value of the exchange to 0. The update function increases the nvalue o by one unit for all neighbours, without changing its default value. This is achieved through the *modOther* function, which applied on 1 and 0 creates an nvalue with a default value of 0 and mapping all current neighbours to 1. Thus, this function counts the number of consecutive rounds in which neighbours remain neighbours, resetting to 0 each time a former neighbour stops being a neighbour. Since the neighbours are exactly those devices that successfully sent a message to the current device in recent times, this function measures the inbound connection's quality between the current device δ and its neighbours. On the other hand, it does not depend on the outbound connection's quality: even if the current device never sends messages successfully, the counters still increase. Notice that *uniconn-count* is based on argument o, and in fact it does not use argument n. Indeed, such function could not be expressed (without breaking the nvalue abstraction) with the classic one-argument exchange operator.

Example 2 (Bidirectional Connection Counter). The following *biconn-count* function produces an nvalue of bidirectional connection counters, associating every neighbour to the number of times a message has bounced back and forth between it and the current device.

```
def biconn-count() {
  exchange( 0, (o,n) => retsend n + modOther(1,0) )
}
```

This function is identical to *uniconn-count*, except that the update function passed to exchange uses argument n instead of o. Thus, in order for the counter to produce a value k larger than 1 for a current neighbour, such neighbour need to have sent a counter value of $k - 1$ to the local device. This can only happen if the neighbour had received a value of $k - 2$ from the local device, and so on.

In fact, if the local device δ is not able to send to a neighbour δ' but only to receive from it, the counter for δ' will never get larger than 1. Thus, this function allows to measure the combined inbound and outbound connection quality between the current device and its neighbours.

Notice that this function ignores the o parameter of the function passed to *exchange*, and thus essentially uses the original *exchange* described in Sect. 2.4. Indeed, this function was first introduced as an example of XC capabilities [4,5].

Example 3 (Mixed Connection Counter). Finally, the *mixedconn-count* function exploits the extended *exchange* operator with different *return* and *send* expressions, to enable a behavior which combines those of the two preceding examples, allowing to measure an outbound connection's counter.

```
1  def mixedconn-count() {
2    exchange( 0, (o,n) =>
3         return n
4         send mux(o == 0, n/2, o) + modOther(1, 0)
5    )
6  }
```

The value of the *send* expression (line 4) is the one that is sent to neighbours (contributing in forming their value of n in the following round), and will become parameter o in the next round of the same device. For each neighbour that has not a zero connection counter in o (i.e., is not a new neighbour), the *send* expression increases its connection counter by one, as in *uniconn-count*. Thus, this expression mostly computes a connection counter of received messages.

However, differently from *uniconn-count*, a new neighbour does not necessarily start from zero, but it starts instead from n/2, that is, half of the connection counter that the neighbour device has for the current device. In this way, occasionally losing a connection drops the counter without setting it drastically to zero: thus, the expression computes a counter of received messages "smoothed out" with a bidirectional connection pattern.

As a final difference from *uniconn-count*, the n value received from neighbours is the one returned by the function as the computed value (line 3). Since o is a smoothed counter of received messages, it follows that n will contain the smoothed counters of received messages that the neighbours have with me: in other words, it represents counters of sent messages. This allows to measure the outbound connection's quality between the current device and its neighbours in a more reliable way than both *uniconn-count* and *biconn-count*. As we will show in Sect. 4, this is the best computed information to use as rating for scenarios of data collection where information flows in just one direction from the peripheral nodes toward the source node.

4   Case Study: Reliable WSN Sensing

In order to illustrate the potential applications of the newly introduced *exchange* operator, we simulated a network of battery-powered IoT sensors recharging using solar panels, with varying battery charge level that influences their communication power. In such a network, we assumed the presence of a *gateway* device (the node with *uid* equal to 0) that is connected to the power supply, and thus is always at maximum battery charge and has the best connection parameters.

We assume that the network has to perform a distributed sensing task, where data perceived by individual sensors is aggregated towards the gateway. For simulation purposes, we consider the test scenario where the data to be collected is the sum of a sensed value of 1 for each device (that is, the task is counting the number of active nodes in the network). Even though this task may be too abstract as a distributed sensing application, from a coordination perspective it has the same complexity as any other data collection task, and thus it provides a useful test bed that is easy to evaluate and measure. The implementation of this simulated case study is publicly available online.[1]

4.1   The Aggregate Program

We implement the case study through the novel *stabilized* single-path collection strategy, shown as function `ssp_collection` in Fig. 3, with arguments:

- `dist`: estimated distance of the current device from the collection source;

---

[1] https://github.com/fcpp-experiments/oldnbr-evaluation.

```
1   // type: (num) -> num
2   def nbr(v) {
3     exchange( v, (o,n) => return n send v )
4   }
5
6   // type: (num, num, num, (num, num) -> num, num, num) -> num
7   def ssp_collection(dist, value, null, accum, rating, stale_factor) {
8     fst(exchange((null, 0.0, uid()), (o,n) =>
9       val result = nfold(accum, mux(trd(n) == uid(), fst(n), null), value);
10
11      val best_neigh = nfold( min, (nbr(dist), -rating, nbr(uid())) );
12      val best_neigh_rating = -snd(best_neigh);
13      val best_neigh_uid = trd(best_neigh);
14
15      val parent_rating = snd(o) * stale_factor;
16      val parent = trd(o);
17
18      if (parent_rating > best_neigh_rating) {
19        retsend (result, parent_rating, parent)
20      } else {
21        retsend (result, best_neigh_rating, best_neigh_uid)
22      }))
23  }
```

Fig. 3. Stabilized Single-Path Collection in XC.

- value: the value to be aggregated;
- null: the neutral element of the aggregation;
- accum: the aggregation function;
- rating: an nvalue ranking neighbours by reliability;
- stale_factor: factor resisting to changes of the aggregation path.

This function uses the common XC routine nbr(v), which sends v to neighbours and returns the nvalue n composed of the values received by neighbours (that is, their value for v), implemented in lines 2–4. It also uses the common functions fst, snd, and trd which return the first, second and third element of a tuple respectively; and function uid which returns the local device identifier.

The function consists of a single exchange operation, evolving a triple that consists of:

- the partial aggregate computed in the current node;
- the current rating of the parent chosen;
- the id of the *parent* chosen.

Initially, the partial aggregate is equal to null, and the parent is the local device with zero rating. As in classic single-path collection [18], the aggregation happens following the chosen *parents* of each node. This is realised in line 9, where the partial aggregation result is computed by folding the partial aggregation results of neighbouring nodes that selected the current device as their parent,

```
val dist = abf_hops(uid() == 0);
val sum = (x, y) => x + y;
val uni-res = ssp_collection(dist, 1.0, 0, sum, uniconn-count(),   0.7);
val bi-res  = ssp_collection(dist, 1.0, 0, sum, biconn-count(),    0.7);
val mix-res = ssp_collection(dist, 1.0, 0, sum, mixedconn-count(), 0.7);
```

Fig. 4. ssp_collection calls using different connection counters as rating.

via the given accumulate function. Whenever parents are chosen closer to the collection source than the current node, the aggregation is guaranteed to converge each value towards the source, where the aggregation result will be equal to the aggregation of each value in the network (except for values that have been lost during communication).

What distinguishes this algorithm from classic single-path collection is the strategy for choosing the parent. First, the best candidate among neighbours is computed in line 11–13, as the one with minimal distance (to ensure that we are getting closer to the source), distinguishing nodes with the same distance by choosing the one with maximal rating. We save the identifier of the best candidate in *best_neigh_uid* and its rating in *best_neigh_rating*.

Such candidate is then compared with the previous parent, extracted from o in lines 15–16, while reducing its rating by the stale_factor. If the reduced rating of the previous parent exceeds that of the best candidate among neighbours (line 18), the previous parent is retained as parent for the current round (line 19), otherwise the best neighbour becomes the new parent (line 21).

The usage of ssp_collection in the case study is shown in Fig. 4. We calculate argument dist using the adaptive Bellman-Ford algorithm implemented in XC,[2] measuring distance in hops. The value parameter is set to 1.0 (i.e., each device contributes 1.0 to the collected value), while the null value is 0 (the neutral element of the sum). The accum parameter is set to a function summing its arguments. The rating parameter is an nvalue computed with one of the three connection counters defined in Sect. 3. Finally, we set the value of stale_factor by observing that values close to 0.0 result in a system with faster response to perturbation but increased instability, while values close to 1.0 led to a more stable system with slower reaction to changes. We thus empirically set the stale_factor to 0.7 to balance sensitivity to changes and stability.

4.2 Simulation Settings

We tested the proposed SSP collection algorithm in a simulated network of stationary nodes through the FCPP simulator [1, 7] and its new feature to emulate

---

[2] The Bellman-Ford algorithm lends itself very well to distributed implementations in Field Calculus and XC [6].

Table 1. Battery profiles and their parameters

PROFILE	sleep_ratio	send_power_ratio	recv_power_ratio
SOURCE	0.00	1.00	1.00
HIGH	0.00	0.90	1.00
MEDIUM	0.00	0.75	0.99
LOW	0.10	0.25	0.75

unreliable connectivity. Table 1 shows that there are three possible battery level-profiles for battery-powered devices, which are *HIGH*, *MEDIUM*, and *LOW*, which in turn determine the values of three node parameters influencing its connectivity, namely *sleep_ratio*, *send_power_ratio*, and *recv_power_ratio*. The gateway has a special *SOURCE* profile which grants higher send power, modeling the advantage of being connected to the power supply.

The results in this paper are obtained by running 1000 simulations using different random generation seeds. Each simulation lasted 250 s and comprised 100 devices randomly spread in a 150 m × 150 m square area. Each device performed asynchronous rounds every second on average, with a variance of 10%.

The maximum communication range between two nodes varies depending on their battery profile, and is calculated as:

$$\text{range}(\delta_s, \delta_r) = comm\_range \cdot \text{send\_power\_ratio}(\delta_s) \cdot \text{recv\_power\_ratio}(\delta_r)$$

where the reference *comm_range* is set to 50 m, δ_s is the sender device and δ_r is the receiving device. Note that depending on the battery profile of δ_s and δ_r, range(δ_s, δ_r) may be different from range(δ_r, δ_s).

In the simulation, 100% of the messages from δ_s to δ_r are lost if their distance is past range(δ_s, δ_r), and 0% of the messages are lost if their distance is zero. In order to accurately model unreliability of communication, the probability of failure at intermediate distances is calculated according to a continuous step-like function inferred from real-world measurements [17], that reaches 50% of communication failure at a distance of $0.7 \cdot$ range(δ_s, δ_r). Parameter *sleep_ratio* models a further message failure probability, due to the device being in a sleeping state during the time window when the message should be received. Note that *sleep_ratio* equal to zero does not entail that the device is never sleeping: in real-world networks, it is usually achieved by negotiating listening time-windows with neighbours, sleeping only outside of those. To better emulate battery preserving policies, we consider that in the *LOW* state a device might miss some of this time-windows allowing an increase in the sleeping time.

In order to model varying lighting conditions on the solar panels, all nodes have a 1% probability to improve or to worsen their battery profile in every round. A connection with a neighbour is dropped if the current device is unable to receive a message from it for 5 s.

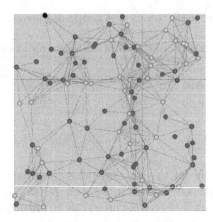

Fig. 5. Screenshot of a simulation of the case study in FCPP.

4.3   Experimental Results

Figure 5 shows the screenshot of a running simulation, with devices as nodes and existing connection as edges of a graph in the simulation area. The color of each node represents its current battery profile: red for LOW, yellow for MEDIUM, green for HIGH, and black for the gateway. Figure 6 shows the average (over 1000 simulations) of the number of nodes in the network the algorithm was able to count over time using different functions to compute the reliability rank.

We include a line with a count of the *working* nodes, i.e., with high or medium battery as reference. As expected the computed value is lower than the total number of nodes, due to communication failures, but it's closer to the number of working nodes. The classic (not stabilised) single-path collection strategy, in these scenarios with unreliable connectivity, performs poorly compared to SSP collection. This is due to always selecting as parent the node in the neighbourhood closest to the source with the lowest uid, which may not grant a high-quality connection and may change often. All three versions of SSP collection improve over it, as they make a more informed selection using rating information, and change parents less often thanks to the retention mechanism guided by the *stale factor*. Among the possible ratings, the *uniconn* rating performs the worst, as it computes its connection-counter from received messages only. That may cause the selection as parent of a node to which the current device is not able to reliably send messages, if connection links are sufficiently asymmetrical. The *biconn* rating improves over *uniconn* by deriving its connection counter from a two-way message exchange, which ensure that both the sender and the receiver of the communication are able to communicate.

The *mixedconn* rating further improves over *biconn*, by measuring the number of messages successfully sent to neighbours without the additional requirement to reliably receive data back. It also handles temporary disconnection of a node more gracefully, by retaining the rating decreased by a penalty, for nodes that exited the neighbourhood in the current round rather than resetting their rating

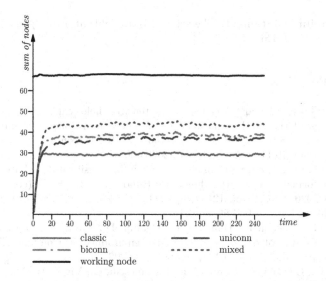

Fig. 6. Average number of nodes in the network counted by the source node using different connection counter functions over 1000 simulations. Time is in seconds.

back to the default value. This allows to further stabilise the parent selection, improving the collection performance.

5   Conclusions and Outlook

In this paper, we introduced a new generalised version of the exchange primitive in XC [4,5], also implementing it into the FCPP DSL [1,7]. This primitive allows for neighbour data retention across rounds, strictly expanding the expressiveness of the exchange primitive in XC. We illustrate the increased expressiveness by means of examples, introducing new connection metrics. We then evaluated the contribution by simulation of a case study on distributed sensing in a wireless sensor network of battery-powered devices. In the future, we plan to further investigate on which neighbour reliability score function can work best in different scenarios. Further, we will try to apply the reliability scoring technique, and in general the possibilities opened by the enhanced exchange primitive, to more advanced algorithms that have been shown to be more effective than classical single-path collection, such as the LIST and BLIST algorithms [2,3]. Finally, further investigations could be performed on the expressiveness of the enhanced exchange primitive possibly expanding the self-stabilising patterns in [18].

Acknowledgment. This paper is part of the project NODES which has received funding from the MUR – M4C2 1.5 of PNRR with grant agreement no. ECS00000036. It has also been carried out within the Agritech National Research Center, funded by the European Union Next-GenerationEU of PNRR, MISSIONE 4 COMPONENTE 2, INVESTIMENTO 1.4 - D.D. 1032 17/06/2022, CN00000022. The work was also partially supported by the Italian PRIN project "CommonWears" (2020HCWWLP).

Data Availability Statement. The artefact is available at https://zenodo.org/doi/10.5281/zenodo.10797596.

References

1. Audrito, G.: FCPP: an efficient and extensible field calculus framework. In: Proceedings of the 1st International Conference on Autonomic Computing and Self-Organizing Systems, ACSOS, pp. 153–159. IEEE Computer Society (2020). https://doi.org/10.1109/ACSOS49614.2020.00037

2. Audrito, G., Bergamini, S., Damiani, F., Viroli, M.: Resilient distributed collection through information speed thresholds. In: Bliudze, S., Bocchi, L. (eds.) COORDI-NATION 2020. LNCS, vol. 12134, pp. 211–229. Springer, Cham (2020). https://doi.org/10.1007/978-3-030-50029-0_14

3. Audrito, G., Casadei, R., Damiani, F., Pianini, D., Viroli, M.: Optimal resilient distributed data collection in mobile edge environments. Comput. Electr. Eng. (2021). https://doi.org/10.1016/j.compeleceng.2021.107580

4. Audrito, G., Casadei, R., Damiani, F., Salvaneschi, G., Viroli, M.: Functional programming for distributed systems with XC. In: 36th European Conference on Object-Oriented Programming, ECOOP 2022. LIPIcs, vol. 222, pp. 20:1–20:28. Schloss Dagstuhl (2022). https://doi.org/10.4230/LIPIcs.ECOOP.2022.20

5. Audrito, G., Casadei, R., Damiani, F., Salvaneschi, G., Viroli, M.: The exchange calculus (XC): a functional programming language design for distributed collective systems. J. Syst. Softw. **210**, 111976 (2024). https://doi.org/10.1016/J.JSS.2024.111976

6. Audrito, G., Casadei, R., Torta, G.: On the dynamic evolution of distributed computational aggregates. In: 2022 IEEE International Conference on Autonomic Computing and Self-Organizing Systems Companion (ACSOS-C), pp. 37–42 (2022). https://doi.org/10.1109/ACSOSC56246.2022.00024

7. Audrito, G., Rapetta, L., Torta, G.: Extensible 3D simulation of aggregated systems with FCPP. In: ter Beek, M.H., Sirjani, M. (eds.) COORDINATION 2022, vol. 13271, pp. 55–71. Springer, Cham (2022). https://doi.org/10.1007/978-3-031-08143-9_4

8. Audrito, G., Viroli, M., Damiani, F., Pianini, D., Beal, J.: A higher-order calculus of computational fields. ACM Trans. Comput. Logic **20**(1), 5:1–5:55 (2019). https://doi.org/10.1145/3285956

9. Beal, J., Dulman, S., Usbeck, K., Viroli, M., Correll, N.: Organizing the aggregate: languages for spatial computing. In: Formal and Practical Aspects of Domain-Specific Languages: Recent Developments, chap. 16, pp. 436–501. IGI Global (2013). https://doi.org/10.4018/978-1-4666-2092-6.ch016

10. Beal, J., Pianini, D., Viroli, M.: Aggregate programming for the Internet of Things. IEEE Comput. **48**(9) (2015). https://doi.org/10.1109/MC.2015.261

11. Dobson, S., et al.: A survey of autonomic communications. TAAS **1**(2), 223–259 (2006)

12. Lluch-Lafuente, A., Loreti, M., Montanari, U.: Asynchronous distributed execution of fixpoint-based computational fields. Log. Methods Comput. Sci. **13**(1) (2017). https://doi.org/10.23638/LMCS-13(1:13)2017

13. Mamei, M., Zambonelli, F.: Programming pervasive and mobile computing applications: the TOTA approach. ACM Trans. Softw. Eng. Methodol. **18**(4), 1–56 (2009). https://doi.org/10.1145/1538942.1538945

14. Mamei, M., Zambonelli, F., Leonardi, L.: Co-fields: towards a unifying approach to the engineering of swarm intelligent systems. In: Petta, P., Tolksdorf, R., Zambonelli, F. (eds.) ESAW 2002. LNCS (LNAI), vol. 2577, pp. 68–81. Springer, Heidelberg (2003). https://doi.org/10.1007/3-540-39173-8_6

15. Menezes, R., Tolksdorf, R.: Adaptiveness in Linda-based coordination models. In: Di Marzo Serugendo, G., Karageorgos, A., Rana, O.F., Zambonelli, F. (eds.) ESOA 2003. LNCS (LNAI), vol. 2977, pp. 212–232. Springer, Heidelberg (2004). https://doi.org/10.1007/978-3-540-24701-2_15

16. Omicini, A., Viroli, M.: Coordination models and languages: from parallel computing to self-organisation. Knowl. Eng. Rev. **26**(1), 53–59 (2011)

17. Torrent-Moreno, M., Corroy, S., Schmidt-Eisenlohr, F., Hartenstein, H.: IEEE 802.11-based one-hop broadcast communications: understanding transmission success and failure under different radio propagation environments. In: Alba, E., Chiasserini, C., Abu-Ghazaleh, N.B., Cigno, R.L. (eds.) Proceedings of the 9th International Symposium on Modeling Analysis and Simulation of Wireless and Mobile Systems, MSWiM 2006, Terromolinos, Spain, 2–6 October 2006, pp. 68–77. ACM (2006). https://doi.org/10.1145/1164717.1164731

18. Viroli, M., Audrito, G., Beal, J., Damiani, F., Pianini, D.: Engineering resilient collective adaptive systems by self-stabilisation. ACM Trans. Model. Comput. Simul. **28**(2), 16:1–16:28 (2018). https://doi.org/10.1145/3177774

19. Viroli, M., Beal, J., Damiani, F., Audrito, G., Casadei, R., Pianini, D.: From distributed coordination to field calculus and aggregate computing. J. Log. Algebraic Methods Program. **109** (2019). https://doi.org/10.1016/j.jlamp.2019.100486

20. Viroli, M., Pianini, D., Beal, J.: Linda in space-time: an adaptive coordination model for mobile ad-hoc environments. In: Sirjani, M. (ed.) COORDINATION 2012. LNCS, vol. 7274, pp. 212–229. Springer, Heidelberg (2012). https://doi.org/10.1007/978-3-642-30829-1_15

Short Paper

The Concurrent Calculi Formalisation Benchmark

Marco Carbone[1] [iD], David Castro-Perez[2] [iD], Francisco Ferreira[3] [iD],
Lorenzo Gheri[4] [iD], Frederik Krogsdal Jacobsen[5] (✉) [iD], Alberto Momigliano[6] [iD],
Luca Padovani[7] [iD], Alceste Scalas[5] [iD], Dawit Tirore[1] [iD], Martin Vassor[8] [iD],
Nobuko Yoshida[8] [iD], and Daniel Zackon[9] [iD]

[1] IT University of Copenhagen, Copenhagen, Denmark
{maca,dati}@itu.dk
[2] University of Kent, Canterbury, UK
d.castro-perez@kent.ac.uk
[3] Royal Holloway, University of London, Egham, UK
francisco.ferreiraruiz@rhul.ac.uk
[4] University of Liverpool, Liverpool, UK
lorenzo.gheri@liverpool.ac.uk
[5] Technical University of Denmark, Kgs. Lyngby, Denmark
{fkjac,alcsc}@dtu.dk
[6] Università degli Studi di Milano, Milan, Italy
momigliano@di.unimi.it
[7] Università di Camerino, Camerino, Italy
luca.padovani@unicam.it
[8] University of Oxford, Oxford, UK
{martin.vassor,nobuko.yoshida}@cs.ox.ac.uk
[9] McGill University, Montreal, Canada
daniel.zackon@mail.mcgill.ca

Abstract. POPLMark and POPLMark Reloaded sparked a flurry of
work on machine-checked proofs, and fostered the adoption of proof
mechanisation in programming language research. Both challenges were
purposely limited in scope, and they do not address concurrency-related
issues. We propose a new collection of benchmark challenges focused on
the difficulties that typically arise when mechanising formal models of
concurrent and distributed programming languages, such as process calculi. Our benchmark challenges address three key topics: linearity, scope
extrusion, and coinductive reasoning. The goal of this new benchmark
is to clarify, compare, and advance the state of the art, fostering the
adoption of proof mechanisation in future research on concurrency.

Keywords: Mechanisation · Process calculi · Benchmark · Linearity ·
Scope extrusion · Coinduction

1 Introduction

The POPLMark challenge [4] played a pivotal role in advancing the field of proof
assistants, libraries, and best practices for the mechanisation of programming

© IFIP International Federation for Information Processing 2024
Published by Springer Nature Switzerland AG 2024
I. Castellani and F. Tiezzi (Eds.): COORDINATION 2024, LNCS 14676, pp. 149–158, 2024.
https://doi.org/10.1007/978-3-031-62697-5_9

language research. By providing a shared framework for systematically evaluating mechanisation techniques, it catalysed a significant shift towards publications that include mechanised proofs within the programming language research community. POPLMark Reloaded [1] introduced a similar programme for proofs using logical relations. These initiatives had a narrow focus, and their authors recognised the importance of addressing topics such as coinduction and linearity in the future.

In this spirit, we introduce a new collection of benchmarks crafted to tackle common challenges encountered during the mechanisation of formal models of concurrent and distributed programming languages. We focus on process calculi, as they provide a simple but realistic showcase of these challenges. Concurrent calculi are notably subtle: for instance, it took some years before an incorrect subject reduction proof in the original paper on session subtyping [25] was discovered and then rectified in the extended journal version [26] with the use of polarities. Similarly, other key results in papers on session types have subsequently been proven incorrect [27,45], demonstrating the need for machine-checked proofs.

While results about concurrent formalisms have already been mechanised (as we will discuss further below), our experience is that choosing appropriate mechanisation techniques and tools remains a significant challenge and that their trade-offs are not well understood. This often leads researchers toward a trial-and-error approach, resulting in sub-optimal solutions, wasted mechanisation efforts, and techniques and results that are hard to reuse. For example, Cruz-Filipe et al. [17] note that the high-level parts of mechanised proofs closely resemble the informal ones, while the main challenge lies in getting the infrastructure right.

Our benchmark challenges (detailed on our website linked below) consider *in isolation* three key aspects that frequently pose difficulties when mechanising concurrency theory: *linearity, scope extrusion,* and *coinductive reasoning,* as we will discuss in more detail in the next section. Mechanisations must often address several of these aspects at the same time; however, we see the combination of techniques as a next step, as argued in Sect. 3.

We have begun collecting solutions to our challenges on our website:

https://concurrentbenchmark.github.io/

We intend to use the website to promote best practices and tutorials derived from solutions to our challenges. We encourage readers to try the challenges using their favourite techniques, and to send us their solutions and experience reports.

2   Overview and Design Considerations

In this section, we outline the factors considered when designing the benchmark challenges. We begin with some general remarks, then describe the individual design considerations for each challenge, and the criteria for evaluating solutions.

Similarly to the authors of POPLMark, we seek to answer several questions about the mechanisation of the meta-theory of process calculi:

(Q1) What is the current state of the art?

(Q2) Which techniques and best practices can be recommended?

(Q3) What improvements are needed to make mechanisation tools more user-friendly?

To provide a framework in which to answer these questions, our benchmark is designed to satisfy three main design goals:

(G1) To enable the comparison of proof mechanisation approaches by making the challenges accessible to mechanisation experts who may be unfamiliar with concurrency theory;

(G2) To encourage the development of guidelines and tutorials demonstrating and comparing existing proof mechanisation techniques, libraries, and proof assistant features; and

(G3) To prioritise the exploration of reusable mechanisation techniques.

We also aim at strengthening the culture of mechanisation, by rallying the community to collaborate on exploring and developing new tools and techniques.

To achieve design goal (G1), our challenges explore the three aspects (linearity, scope extrusion, coinduction) independently, so that they may be solved individually and in any order; each challenge is small and easily understandable with basic knowledge of textbook concurrency theory, process calculi, and type theory. For mechanisation experts, our challenges should thus be accessible even without any prior understanding of process calculi. The process calculi used in the challenges focus on the features that we want to emphasise, and omit all constructs that would complicate the mechanisation without bringing tangible insights. For concurrency experts venturing into mechanisation, our challenges thus serve as good first steps. The minimality and uniformity of the calculi also allows us to target design goal (G2). For experts in both mechanisation and concurrency, our challenges serve as a framework in which to consider and share best practices and tutorials. Aligned with design goal (G3), our challenges concern the fundamental meta-theory of process calculi. Our challenges centre around well-established results, showcasing proof techniques that can be leveraged in many applications (as we will further discuss in Sect. 3).

2.1 Linearity

Linear typing systems enable the tracking of resource usage in a program. In the case of typed (in particular, session-typed) process calculi, linearity is widely used for checking if and how a channel is used to send or receive values. This substructurality [39, Ch. 1] gives rise to mechanisation difficulties: *e.g.* deciding how to *split the typing context* in a parallel composition.

The goal of our challenge on linear reasoning is to prove a type safety theorem for a process calculus with session types, by combining subject reduction with the absence of errors. For simplicity we model only linear (as opposed to shared) channels. Inspired by Vasconcelos [49], we define a syntax where a restriction (νab) binds two dual names a and b as opposite endpoints of the same channel;

their duality is reflected in the type system. We model a simple notion of error: well-typed processes must never use dual channel endpoints in a non-dual way (*e.g.* by performing concurrent send/receive operations on the same endpoint, or two concurrent send operations on dual endpoints). The operational semantics is a standard reduction relation. Proving subject reduction thus requires proving type preservation for structural congruence.

We designed this challenge to focus on linear reasoning while minimising definitions and other concerns. We therefore forgo name passing: send/receive operations only support values that do not include channel names, so the topology of the communication network described by a process cannot change. We do not allow recursion or replication, hence infinite behaviours cannot be expressed. We also forgo more sophisticated notions of error-freedom (*e.g.* deadlock freedom) as proving them would distract from the core linear aspects of the challenge.

In mechanised meta-theory, addressing linearity means choosing an appropriate representation of a linear context. While the latter is perhaps best seen as a multiset, most proof assistants have better support for lists. This representation is intuitive, but may require establishing a large number of technical lemmata that are orthogonal to the problem under study (in our case, proving type safety for session types). Several designs are possible: one can label occurrences of resources to constrain their usage (*e.g.* [16]), or impose a multiset structure over lists (*e.g.* [15,19]). Alternatively, contexts can be implemented as finite maps (as in [12]), whose operations are sensitive to a linear discipline. In all these cases, the effort required to develop the infrastructure is significant. One alternative strategy is to bypass the problem of context splitting by adopting ideas from algorithmic linear type checking. One such approach, known as "typing with leftovers," is exemplified in [51]. Similarly, context splitting can be eliminated by delegating linearity checks to a *linear predicate* defined on the process structure (*e.g.* [44]). These checks serve as additional conditions within the typing rules. Whatever the choice, list-based encodings can be refined to be intrinsically-typed if the proof assistant supports dependent types (see [16,42,47]).

A radically different approach is to adopt a *substructural* meta-logical framework, which handles resource distribution implicitly, including splitting and substitution: users need only map their linear operations to the ones offered by the framework. The only such framework is *Celf* [46] (see the encoding of session types in [8]); unfortunately, *Celf* does not yet fully support the verification of meta-theoretic properties. A compromise is the *two-level* approach, *i.e.* encoding a substructural specification logic in a mainstream proof assistant and then using that logic to state and prove linear properties (for a recent example, see [23]).

2.2 Scope Extrusion

This challenge revolves around the mechanisation of scope extrusion, by which a process can send restricted names to another process, as long as the restriction can safely be extruded to include the receiving process. The setting for this challenge is a "classic" untyped π-calculus, where (unlike the calculi in the other challenges) names can be sent and received, and bound by input constructs. We define two different semantics for our system:

1. A reduction system: this avoids explicit reasoning about scope extrusion by using structural congruence, allowing implementers to explore different ways to encode the latter (*e.g.* via process contexts or compatible refinement);
2. An (early) labelled transition system.

The goal of our challenge on scope extrusion is to prove that the two semantics are equivalent up to structural congruence.

This is the challenge most closely related to POPLMark, as it concerns the properties of binders, whose encoding has been extensively studied with respect to λ-calculi. Process calculi present additional challenges, typically including several different binding constructs: inputs bind a received name or value, recursive processes bind recursion variables, and restrictions bind names. The first two act similarly to the binders in λ-calculi, but restrictions may be more challenging due to scope extrusion. Scope extrusion requires reasoning about free variables, so approaches that identify α-equivalent processes cannot be directly applied.

Given those peculiarities, the syntax and semantics of π-calculi have been mechanised from an early age (see [37]) with many proof assistants and in many encoding styles. Despite this, almost all of these mechanisations rely on ad-hoc solutions to encode scope extrusion. They range from concrete encodings based on named syntax [37] to basic de Bruijn [30,38] and locally-nameless representation [12]. Nominal approaches are also common (see [6]), but they may be problematic in proof assistants based on constructive type theories. An overall comparison is still lacking, but the case study [3] explores four approaches to encoding binders in Coq in the context of higher-order process calculi. The authors report that working directly with de Bruijn indices was easiest since the approaches developed for λ-calculus binders worked poorly with scope extrusion.

Higher-order abstract syntax (HOAS) has seen extensive use in formal reasoning in this area [13,14,22,32,48]. Its weak form aligns reasonably well with mainstream inductive proof assistants, significantly simplifying the encoding of typing systems and operational semantics. However, when addressing more intricate concepts like bisimulation, extensions to HOAS are needed. These extensions may take the form of additional axioms [32] or require niche proof assistants such as Abella, which features a special quantifier for handling properties related to names [24].

2.3   Coinduction

Process calculi typically include constructs that allow processes to adopt infinite behaviours. Coinduction serves as a fundamental method for the definition and analysis of infinite objects, enabling the examination of their behaviours.

The goal of our challenge on coinductive reasoning is to prove that *strong barbed bisimilarity* can be turned into a congruence by making it sensitive to substitution and parallel composition. The crux of our challenge is the effective use of coinductive up-to techniques. The intention is that the result should be relatively easy to achieve once the main properties of bisimilarity are established.

The setting for our challenge is an untyped π-calculus augmented with process replication in order to enable infinite behaviours. We do not include name passing since it is orthogonal to our aim of exploring coinductive proof techniques. We base our definition of bisimilarity on a labelled transition system semantics and an observability predicate describing the communication steps available to a process. The description of strong barbed bisimulation is one of the first steps when studying the behaviour of process calculi, both in textbooks (e.g. [43]) and in existing mechanisations. Though weak barbed congruence is a more common behavioural equivalence, we prefer strong equivalences to simplify the theory by avoiding the need to abstract over the number of internal transitions in a trace.

While many proof assistants support coinductive techniques, they do so through different formalisms. Some systems even offer multiple abstractions for utilising coinduction. For instance, Agda offers musical notation, co-patterns and productivity checking via sized types [2]; Coq features guarded recursion and refined fixed point approaches via libraries for e.g. parameterised coinduction [34], coinduction up-to [41] and interaction trees [50].

When reasoning over bisimilarity many authors rely on the native coinduction offered by the chosen proof assistant [7,27,35,47], while others prefer a more "set-theoretic" approach [6,30,36,40]. Some use both and establish an internal adequacy [32]. Few extend the proof assistant foundations to allow, e.g., reasoning about bisimilarity up-to [14].

2.4   Evaluation Criteria

The motivation behind our benchmark is to obtain evidence towards answering questions (Q1) to (Q3). We are therefore interested not only in the solutions, but also in the experience of solving the challenges with the chosen approach. Solutions to our challenges should be compared on three axes:

1. Mechanisation overhead: the amount of manually-written infrastructure and setup needed to express the definitions in the mechanisation;
2. Adequacy of the formal statements in the mechanisation: whether the proven theorems are easily recognisable as the theorems from the challenge; and
3. Cost of entry for the tools and techniques employed: the difficulty of learning to use the techniques.

Solutions to our challenges need not strictly follow the definitions and lemmata set out in the challenge text, but solutions which deviate from the original challenges should present more elaborate argumentation for their adequacy.

3   Future Work and Conclusions

Our benchmark challenges do not cover all issues in the field, but focus on the fundamental aspects of linearity, scope extrusion, and coinduction. Many mechanisations need to combine techniques to handle several of these aspects, and some may also need to handle aspects that are not covered by our benchmark.

Combining techniques for mechanising the fundamental aspects covered in our benchmark is non-trivial. While we focus on the aspects individually to simplify the challenges, we are also interested in exploring how techniques interact.

Much current research on concurrent calculi includes aspects that are not covered by our benchmark challenges, for example constructs such as choice and recursion. Some interesting research topics that build on the fundamental aspects in our benchmark include multiparty session types [31], choreographies [11], higher-order calculi [29], conversation types [10], psi-calculi [5], and encodings between different calculi [20,28]. The meta-theory of these topics includes aspects—*e.g.* well-formedness conditions on global types, partiality of end-point projection functions, *etc.*—that we do not address.

Our coinduction challenge only treats two notions of process equivalence, but many more exist in the literature. Coinduction may also play a role in recursive processes and session types: recursive session types can be expressed in *infinitary form* by interpreting their typing rules coinductively [21,33].

Unlike POPLMark, we consider *animation* of calculi (as in [13]) out of scope for our benchmark. Finally, our challenges encourage, but do not require, exploring proof automation, as offered by *e.g.* the *Hammer* protocol [9,18].

Ultimately, the fundamental aspects covered by our benchmark serve as the building blocks for most current research on concurrent calculi. It is our hope and aim that exploring and comparing solutions to our challenges will move the community closer to a future where the key basic proof techniques for concurrent calculi are as easy to mechanise as they are to write on paper.

Acknowledgments. The work is partially supported by the UK Engineering and Physical Sciences Research Council (EPSRC) grants EP/T006544/2, EP/V000462/1 and EP/X015955/1; Independent Research Fund Denmark RP-1 grant "Hyben"; and Independent Research Fund Denmark RP-1 grant "MECHANIST".

Disclosure of Interests. Alberto Momigliano is a member of the Gruppo Nazionale Calcolo Scientifico-Istituto Nazionale di Alta Matematica (GNCS-INdAM).

References

1. Abel, A., et al.: POPLMark reloaded: mechanizing proofs by logical relations. J. Funct. Program. **29**, 19 (2019). https://doi.org/10.1017/S0956796819000170
2. Abel, A., Pientka, B., Thibodeau, D., Setzer, A.: Copatterns: programming infinite structures by observations. In: POPL 2013: Proceedings of the 40th Annual ACM SIGPLAN-SIGACT Symposium on Principles of Programming Languages, pp. 27–38. ACM, New York (2013). https://doi.org/10.1145/2429069.2429075
3. Ambal, G., Lenglet, S., Schmitt, A.: HOπ in Coq. J. Autom. Reason. **65**(1), 75–124 (2021). https://doi.org/10.1007/S10817-020-09553-0
4. Aydemir, B.E., et al.: Mechanized metatheory for the masses: the POPLMARK challenge. In: Hurd, J., Melham, T. (eds.) TPHOLs 2005. LNCS, vol. 3603, pp. 50–65. Springer, Heidelberg (2005). https://doi.org/10.1007/11541868_4

5. Bengtson, J., Johansson, M., Parrow, J., Victor, B.: Psi-calculi: a framework for mobile processes with nominal data and logic. Log. Methods Comput. Sci. **7** (2011). https://doi.org/10.2168/LMCS-7(1:11)2011

6. Bengtson, J., Parrow, J.: Formalising the pi-calculus using nominal logic. Log. Methods Comput. Sci. **5** (2009). https://doi.org/10.2168/LMCS-5(2:16)2009

7. Bengtson, J., Parrow, J., Weber, T.: Psi-calculi in Isabelle. J. Autom. Reason. **56**, 1–47 (2016). https://doi.org/10.1007/s10817-015-9336-2

8. Bock, P., Murawska, A., Bruni, A., Schürmann, C.: Representing session types (2016). https://pure.itu.dk/en/publications/representing-session-types, in Dale Miller's Festschrift

9. Böhme, S., Nipkow, T.: Sledgehammer: judgement day. In: Giesl, J., Hähnle, R. (eds.) IJCAR 2010. LNCS (LNAI), vol. 6173, pp. 107–121. Springer, Heidelberg (2010). https://doi.org/10.1007/978-3-642-14203-1_9

10. Caires, L., Vieira, H.T.: Conversation types. Theor. Comput. Sci. **411**(51–52), 4399–4440 (2010). https://doi.org/10.1016/j.tcs.2010.09.010

11. Carbone, M., Montesi, F.: Deadlock-freedom-by-design: multiparty asynchronous global programming. In: POPL 2013: Proceedings of the 40th Annual ACM SIGPLAN-SIGACT Symposium on Principles of Programming Languages, pp. 263–274. ACM, New York (2013). https://doi.org/10.1145/2429069.2429101

12. Castro, D., Ferreira, F., Yoshida, N.: EMTST: engineering the meta-theory of session types. In: Biere, A., Parker, D. (eds.) TACAS 2020. LNCS, vol. 12079, pp. 278–285. Springer, Cham (2020). https://doi.org/10.1007/978-3-030-45237-7_17

13. Castro-Perez, D., Ferreira, F., Gheri, L., Yoshida, N.: Zooid: a DSL for certified multiparty computation: from mechanised metatheory to certified multiparty processes. In: PLDI 2021: Proceedings of the 42nd ACM SIGPLAN International Conference on Programming Language Design and Implementation, pp. 237–251. ACM, New York (2021). https://doi.org/10.1145/3453483.3454041

14. Chaudhuri, K., Cimini, M., Miller, D.: A lightweight formalization of the metatheory of bisimulation-up-to. In: Leroy, X., Tiu, A. (eds.) CPP 2015: Proceedings of the 4th ACM SIGPLAN Conference on Certified Programs and Proofs, pp. 157–166. ACM (2015). https://doi.org/10.1145/2676724.2693170

15. Chaudhuri, K., Lima, L., Reis, G.: Formalized meta-theory of sequent calculi for linear logics. Theor. Comput. Sci. **781**, 24–38 (2019). https://doi.org/10.1016/j.tcs.2019.02.023

16. Ciccone, L., Padovani, L.: A dependently typed linear π-calculus in Agda. In: PPDP 2020: 22nd International Symposium on Principles and Practice of Declarative Programming, pp. 8:1–8:14. ACM (2020). https://doi.org/10.1145/3414080.3414109

17. Cruz-Filipe, L., Montesi, F., Peressotti, M.: Formalising a turing-complete choreographic language in Coq. In: Cohen, L., Kaliszyk, C. (eds.) ITP 2021: Proceedings of the 12th International Conference on Interactive Theorem Proving. Leibniz International Proceedings in Informatics, Dagstuhl, Germany, vol. 193, pp. 15:1–15:18. Schloss Dagstuhl – Leibniz-Zentrum für Informatik (2021). https://doi.org/10.4230/LIPIcs.ITP.2021.15

18. Czajka, L., Kaliszyk, C.: Hammer for Coq: automation for dependent type theory. J. Autom. Reason. **61**(1–4), 423–453 (2018). https://doi.org/10.1007/S10817-018-9458-4

19. Danielsson, N.A.: Bag equivalence via a proof-relevant membership relation. In: Beringer, L., Felty, A. (eds.) ITP 2012. LNCS, vol. 7406, pp. 149–165. Springer, Heidelberg (2012). https://doi.org/10.1007/978-3-642-32347-8_11

20. Dardha, O., Giachino, E., Sangiorgi, D.: Session types revisited. Inf. Comput. **256**, 253–286 (2017). https://doi.org/10.1016/j.ic.2017.06.002
21. Derakhshan, F., Pfenning, F.: Circular proofs as session-typed processes: a local validity condition. Log. Methods Comput. Sci. **18**(2) (2022). https://doi.org/10.46298/LMCS-18(2:8)2022
22. Despeyroux, J.: A higher-order specification of the π-calculus. In: van Leeuwen, J., Watanabe, O., Hagiya, M., Mosses, P.D., Ito, T. (eds.) TCS 2000. LNCS, vol. 1872, pp. 425–439. Springer, Heidelberg (2000). https://doi.org/10.1007/3-540-44929-9_30
23. Felty, A.P., Olarte, C., Xavier, B.: A focused linear logical framework and its application to metatheory of object logics. Math. Struct. Comput. Sci. **31**(3), 312–340 (2021). https://doi.org/10.1017/S0960129521000323
24. Gacek, A., Miller, D., Nadathur, G.: Nominal abstraction. Inf. Comput. **209**(1), 48–73 (2011). https://doi.org/10.1016/J.IC.2010.09.004
25. Gay, S., Hole, M.: Types and subtypes for client-server interactions. In: Swierstra, S.D. (ed.) ESOP 1999. LNCS, vol. 1576, pp. 74–90. Springer, Heidelberg (1999). https://doi.org/10.1007/3-540-49099-X_6
26. Gay, S.J., Hole, M.: Subtyping for session types in the pi calculus. Acta Informatica **42**(2–3), 191–225 (2005). https://doi.org/10.1007/S00236-005-0177-Z
27. Gay, S.J., Thiemann, P., Vasconcelos, V.T.: Duality of session types: the final cut. In: Proceedings of the PLACES 2020. Electronic Proceedings in Theoretical Computer Science, vol. 314, pp. 23–33. Open Publishing Association (2020). https://doi.org/10.4204/eptcs.314.3
28. Gorla, D.: Towards a unified approach to encodability and separation results for process calculi. Inf. Comput. **208**(9), 1031–1053 (2010). https://doi.org/10.1016/j.ic.2010.05.002
29. Hirsch, A.K., Garg, D.: Pirouette: Higher-order typed functional choreographies. Proc. ACM Program. Lang. **6** (2022). https://doi.org/10.1145/3498684
30. Hirschkoff, D.: A full formalisation of π-calculus theory in the calculus of constructions. In: Gunter, E.L., Felty, A. (eds.) TPHOLs 1997. LNCS, vol. 1275, pp. 153–169. Springer, Heidelberg (1997). https://doi.org/10.1007/BFb0028392
31. Honda, K., Yoshida, N., Carbone, M.: Multiparty asynchronous session types. J. ACM **63**(1) (2016). https://doi.org/10.1145/2827695
32. Honsell, F., Miculan, M., Scagnetto, I.: π-calculus in (co)inductive-type theory. Theor. Comput. Sci. **253**(2), 239–285 (2001). https://doi.org/10.1016/S0304-3975(00)00095-5
33. Horne, R., Padovani, L.: A logical account of subtyping for session types. In: Castellani, I., Scalas, A. (eds.) Proceedings of the 14th Workshop on Programming Language Approaches to Concurrency and Communication-Centric Software. EPTCS, vol. 378, pp. 26–37. Open Publishing Association (2023). https://doi.org/10.4204/EPTCS.378.3
34. Hur, C.K., Neis, G., Dreyer, D., Vafeiadis, V.: The power of parameterization in coinductive proof. In: POPL 2013: Proceedings of the 40th Annual ACM SIGPLAN-SIGACT Symposium on Principles of Programming Languages, pp. 193–206. ACM, New York (2013). https://doi.org/10.1145/2429069.2429093
35. Kahsai, T., Miculan, M.: Implementing Spi calculus using nominal techniques. In: Beckmann, A., Dimitracopoulos, C., Löwe, B. (eds.) CiE 2008. LNCS, vol. 5028, pp. 294–305. Springer, Heidelberg (2008). https://doi.org/10.1007/978-3-540-69407-6_33

36. Maksimović, P., Schmitt, A.: HOCore in Coq. In: Urban, C., Zhang, X. (eds.) ITP 2015. LNCS, vol. 9236, pp. 278–293. Springer, Cham (2015). https://doi.org/10.1007/978-3-319-22102-1_19

37. Melham, T.F.: A mechanized theory of the π-calculus in HOL. Nordic J. Comput. **1**(1), 50–76 (1994)

38. Perera, R., Cheney, J.: Proof-relevant π-calculus: a constructive account of concurrency and causality. Math. Struct. Comput. Sci. **28**(9), 1541–1577 (2018). https://doi.org/10.1017/S096012951700010X

39. Pierce, B.C. (ed.): Advanced Topics in Types and Programming Languages. MIT Press, London (2004)

40. Pohjola, J., Gómez-Londoño, A., Shaker, J., Norrish, M.: Kalas: a verified, end-to-end compiler for a choreographic language. In: Andronick, J., de Moura, L. (eds.) ITP 2022: Proceedings of the 13th International Conference on Interactive Theorem Proving. Leibniz International Proceedings in Informatics, Dagstuhl, Germany, vol. 237, pp. 27:1–27:18. Schloss Dagstuhl – Leibniz-Zentrum für Informatik (2022). https://doi.org/10.4230/LIPIcs.ITP.2022.27

41. Pous, D.: Coinduction all the way up. In: Grohe, M., Koskinen, E., Shankar, N. (eds.) Proceedings of the 31st Annual ACM/IEEE Symposium on Logic in Computer Science, LICS 2016, New York, NY, USA, 5–8 July 2016, pp. 307–316. ACM (2016). https://doi.org/10.1145/2933575.2934564

42. Rouvoet, A., Poulsen, C.B., Krebbers, R., Visser, E.: Intrinsically-typed definitional interpreters for linear, session-typed languages. In: Proceedings of the CPP 2020, pp. 284–298. ACM (2020). https://doi.org/10.1145/3372885.3373818

43. Sangiorgi, D., Walker, D.: The π-calculus: A Theory of Mobile Processes. Cambridge University Press, Cambridge (2001)

44. Sano, C., Kavanagh, R., Pientka, B.: Mechanizing session-types using a structural view: enforcing linearity without linearity. Proc. ACM Program. Lang. **7**(OOPSLA), 235:374–235:399 (2023). https://doi.org/10.1145/3622810

45. Scalas, A., Yoshida, N.: Less is more: Multiparty session types revisited. Proc. ACM Program. Lang. **3** (2019). https://doi.org/10.1145/3290343

46. Schack-Nielsen, A., Schürmann, C.: Celf – a logical framework for deductive and concurrent systems (system description). In: Armando, A., Baumgartner, P., Dowek, G. (eds.) IJCAR 2008. LNCS (LNAI), vol. 5195, pp. 320–326. Springer, Heidelberg (2008). https://doi.org/10.1007/978-3-540-71070-7_28

47. Thiemann, P.: Intrinsically-typed mechanized semantics for session types. In: Proceedings of the 21st International Symposium on Principles and Practice of Declarative Programming, PPDP 2019. ACM, New York (2019). https://doi.org/10.1145/3354166.3354184

48. Tiu, A., Miller, D.: Proof search specifications of bisimulation and modal logics for the π-calculus. ACM Trans. Comput. Logic **11**(2) (2010). https://doi.org/10.1145/1656242.1656248

49. Vasconcelos, V.T.: Fundamentals of session types. Inf. Comput. **217**, 52–70 (2012). https://doi.org/10.1016/j.ic.2012.05.002

50. Xia, L.Y., et al.: Interaction trees: representing recursive and impure programs in Coq. Proc. ACM Program. Lang. **4** (2019). https://doi.org/10.1145/3371119

51. Zalakain, U., Dardha, O.: π with leftovers: a mechanisation in Agda. In: Peters, K., Willemse, T.A.C. (eds.) FORTE 2021. LNCS, vol. 12719, pp. 157–174. Springer, Cham (2021). https://doi.org/10.1007/978-3-030-78089-0_9

Survey Paper

Team Automata: Overview and Roadmap

Maurice H. ter Beek[1]([✉]) [ID], Rolf Hennicker[2], and José Proença[3] [ID]

[1] CNR–ISTI, Pisa, Italy
maurice.terbeek@isti.cnr.it
[2] LMU Munich, Munich, Germany
hennicker@ifi.lmu.de
[3] CISTER, Faculty of Sciences, University of Porto, Porto, Portugal
jose.proenca@fc.up.pt

Abstract. Team Automata is a formalism for interacting component-based systems proposed in 1997, whereby multiple sending and receiving actions from concurrent automata can synchronise. During the past 25+ years, team automata have been studied and applied in many different contexts, involving 25+ researchers and resulting in 25+ publications. In this paper, we first revisit the specific notion of synchronisation and composition of team automata, relating it to other relevant *coordination models*, such as Reo, BIP, Contract Automata, Choreography Automata, and Multi-Party Session Types. We then identify several aspects that have recently been investigated for team automata and related models. These include *communication properties* (which are the properties of interest?), *realisability* (how to decompose a global model into local components?) and *tool support* (what has been automatised or implemented?). Our presentation of these aspects provides a snapshot of the most recent trends in research on team automata, and delineates a roadmap for future research, both for team automata and for related formalisms.

1 Introduction

Team automata (TA) were first proposed at the 1997 ACM SIGGROUP Conference on Supporting Group Work [82] for modelling components of groupware systems and their interconnections. They were inspired by Input/Output (I/O) automata [110] and in particular inherit their distinction between internal and external (i.e., input and output) actions used for communication with the environment (i.e., other I/O automata). Technically, team automata are an extension of I/O automata, since a number of the restrictions of I/O automata were dropped for more flexible modelling of several kinds of interactions in groupware systems. The underlying philosophy is that automata cooperate and collaborate by jointly executing (synchronising) transitions with the same action label (but possibly of different nature, i.e., input or output) as agreed upon upfront. They can be composed using a synchronous product construction that defines a unique composite automaton, the transitions of which are exactly those combinations of component transitions that represent a synchronisation on a common action by all the components that share that action. The effect of a synchronously executed action on the state of the composed automaton is described in terms of

I. Castellani and F. Tiezzi (Eds.): COORDINATION 2024, LNCS 14676, pp. 161–198, 2024.
https://doi.org/10.1007/978-3-031-62697-5_10

the local state changes of the automata that take part in the synchronisation. The automata not involved remain idle and their current states are unaffected.

Team automata were formally defined in Computer Supported Cooperative Work (CSCW)—The Journal of Collaborative Computing [41], in terms of component automata that synchronise on certain executions of actions. Unlike I/O automata, team automata impose hardly any restrictions on the role of actions in components and their composition is not limited to the synchronous product. Composing a team automaton requires defining its transitions by providing the actions and synchronisations that can take place from the combined states of the components. Each team automaton is thus a composite automaton defined over component automata. However, a given fixed set of component automata does not define a single unique team automaton, but rather a range of team automata, one for each choice of the team's transitions (individual or synchronising transitions from the component automata). This is in contrast with the usual synchronous product construction. The distinguishing feature of team automata is this very loose nature of synchronisation according to which specific synchronisation policies can be determined, defining how many component automata can participate in the synchronised execution of a shared external action, either as a sender (i.e., via an output action) or as a receiver (i.e., via an input action). This flexibility makes team automata capable of capturing in a precise manner a variety of notions related to coordination in distributed systems (of systems).

To illustrate this, consider the Race example in Fig. 1, borrowed from [31], which is meant to model a controller Ctrl that wants to *simultaneously* send to runners R1 and R2 a start message, after which it is able to receive from each runner *separately* a finish message once that runner *individually* has run. Here and in all subsequent examples and figures, components have exactly one initial state, indicated by a small incoming arrow head, and typically denoted by 0, and external actions may be prefixed by "!" (for output) or "?" (for input).

It is important to note that the synchronous product (as used in I/O automata and many other formalisms) of these three automata has a deadlock: after synchronisation of the three start transitions, Ctrl is blocked in state 1 until both R1 and R2 have executed their run action; at that point, full synchronisation of the finish transitions leads to a deadlock, with Ctrl in state 2 and R1 and R2 in their initial state. Team automata allow to exclude the latter synchronisation, yet at the same time enforcing the full synchronisation of start.

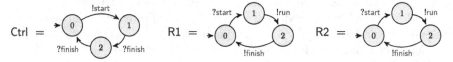

Fig. 1. Race example: a controller Ctrl and two runners R1 and R2

Contribution. We first revisit the specific notion of synchronisation and composition of team automata (Sect. 2). Next, we relate team automata to other coordination models frequently presented at the COORDINATION conferences, such as Reo, BIP, Contract Automata, Choreography Automata, and Multi-Party Session Types (cf., e.g., [10,11,20,22,31,46]), inspired by a preliminary comparison in [119] (Sect. 3). We compare them by giving for each formalism (1) the definition, means of (2) composition (via synchronisation), (3) a model of the Race example, (4) a brief relation with team automata, and (5) tool support.

Table 1. Coordination formalisms and aspects analysed in this paper

Coordination Formalism (Sects. 2 & 3)	Communication Properties (Sect. 4)	Realisability (Sect. 5)	Verification (Sects. 4 & 5)	Supporting Tools (Sects. 3, 4 & 5)	Variability (Sect. 6)	Data (Sect. 6)
Team Automata [41,82]	✓	✓	✓	✓	✓	
Reo via Port Automata [2,102]			✓	✓	✓	✓
BIP [26,64]			✓	✓	✓	✓
Contract Automata [18,24]	✓	✓	✓	✓	✓	
Choreography Automata [10,12]	✓	✓	✓	✓		
Multi-Party Session Types [126,127]		✓	✓		✓	✓

We then focus on two aspects of team automata that we investigated during the last five years: *communication properties* (Sect. 4) and *realisability* (Sect. 5).

§4 We report results on compliance with communication requirements in terms of receptiveness (no message loss) and responsiveness (no indefinite waiting), give a thorough comparison with other compatibility notions, incl. deadlock-freedom, and give a roadmap for future work on communication properties.

§5 We report results on the decomposition (realisability) of a global interaction model in terms of a (possibly distributed) system of component automata coordinated according to a given synchronisation type specification. In particular, we provide a revised and extended comparison of our approach with that of Castellani et al. [73] and a roadmap for future work on realisability.

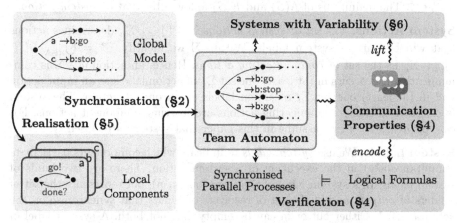

Fig. 2. Aspects of team automata addressed in this paper

Finally, we mention other aspects of team automata and of some of the related coordination models (Sect. 6) and conclude (Sect. 7). Table 1 shows the relations between the formalisms and aspects discussed in this paper. Figure 2 summarises this paper's contribution. Appendix A lists selected team automata publications.

2   Team Automata in a Nutshell

Team automata were originally introduced by Ellis [82] and formally defined in [41]. They form an automaton model for systems of reactive components that differentiate input (passive), output (active), and internal (privately active) actions. In this section, we recall the basic notions of (extended) team automata.

A *labelled transition system* (LTS) is a tuple $\mathcal{L} = (Q, q_0, \Sigma, E)$ such that Q is a finite set of states, $q_0 \in Q$ is the initial state, Σ is a finite set of action labels, and $E \subseteq Q \times \Sigma \times Q$ is a transition relation. Given an LTS $\mathcal{L}$, we write $q \xrightarrow{a}_{\mathcal{L}} q'$, or shortly $q \xrightarrow{a} q'$, to denote $(q, a, q') \in E$. Similarly, we write $q \xrightarrow{a}_{\mathcal{L}}$ to denote that a is *enabled* in $\mathcal{L}$ at state q, i.e., there exists $q' \in Q$ such that $q \xrightarrow{a} q'$. For $\Gamma \subseteq \Sigma$, we write $q \xrightarrow{\Gamma}{}^{*} q'$ if there exist $q \xrightarrow{a_1} q_1 \xrightarrow{a_2} \cdots \xrightarrow{a_n} q'$ for some $n \geq 0$ and $a_1, \ldots, a_n \in \Gamma$. A state $q \in Q$ is *reachable by* Γ if $q_0 \xrightarrow{\Gamma}{}^{*} q$, it is *reachable* if $q_0 \xrightarrow{\Sigma}{}^{*} q$. The set of reachable states of $\mathcal{L}$ is denoted by $\mathcal{R}(\mathcal{L})$.

CA. A *component automaton* (CA) is an LTS $\mathcal{A} = (Q, q_0, \Sigma, E)$ such that $\Sigma = \Sigma^? \uplus \Sigma^! \uplus \Sigma^\tau$ is a set of *action labels* with disjoint sets $\Sigma^?$ of *input actions*, $\Sigma^!$ of *output actions*, and Σ^τ of *internal actions*. Cf. Fig. 1 for examples of CA.

Systems. A *system* is a pair $\mathcal{S} = (\mathcal{N}, (\mathcal{A}_n)_{n \in \mathcal{N}})$, with $\mathcal{N}$ a finite, nonempty set of names and $(\mathcal{A}_n)_{n \in \mathcal{N}}$ an $\mathcal{N}$-indexed family of CA $\mathcal{A}_n = (Q_n, q_{0,n}, \Sigma_n, E_n)$. Any system $\mathcal{S}$ induces an LTS defined by $\mathsf{lts}(\mathcal{S}) = (Q, q_0, \Lambda(\mathcal{S}), E(\mathcal{S}))$, where $Q = \prod_{n \in \mathcal{N}} Q_n$ is the set of *system states*, $q_0 = (q_{0,n})_{n \in \mathcal{N}}$ is the *initial system state*, $\Lambda(\mathcal{S})$ is the set of *system labels*, and $E(\mathcal{S})$ is the set of *system transitions*. Each system state $q \in Q$ is an $\mathcal{N}$-indexed family $(q_n)_{n \in \mathcal{N}}$ of local CA states $q_n \in Q_n$. The definitions of $\Lambda(\mathcal{S})$ and $E(\mathcal{S})$ follow after that of *system action*.

System Actions. The set of *system actions* $\Sigma = \bigcup_{n \in \mathcal{N}} \Sigma_n$ determines actions that will be part of system labels. Within Σ we identify $\Sigma^\bullet = \bigcup_{n \in \mathcal{N}} \Sigma_n^? \cap \bigcup_{n \in \mathcal{N}} \Sigma_n^!$ as the set of *communicating actions*. Hence, an action $a \in \Sigma$ is communicating if it occurs in (at least) one set Σ_k of action labels as an input action and in (at least) one set Σ_ℓ of action labels as an output action. The system is *closed* if all non-communicating actions are internal component actions. For ease of presentation, we assume in this paper that systems are closed.

System Labels. We use *system labels* to indicate which components participate (simultaneously) in the execution of a system action. There are two kinds of system labels. In a system label of the form (out, a, in), out represents the set of senders of *outputs* and in the set of receivers of *inputs* that synchronise on the action $a \in \Sigma^\bullet$. Either out or in can be empty, but not both. A system label of the form (n, a) indicates that component n executes an internal action $a \in \Sigma_n^\tau$. Formally, the set $\Lambda(\mathcal{S})$ of system labels of $\mathcal{S}$ is defined as follows:

$$\Lambda(\mathcal{S}) = \{ (\mathsf{out}, a, \mathsf{in}) \mid \varnothing \neq (\mathsf{out} \cup \mathsf{in}) \subseteq \mathcal{N}, \forall_{n \in \mathsf{out}} \cdot a \in \Sigma_n^!, \forall_{n \in \mathsf{in}} \cdot a \in \Sigma_n^? \}$$
$$\cup \{ (n, a) \mid n \in \mathcal{N}, a \in \Sigma_n^\tau \}$$

Note that $\Lambda(\mathcal{S})$ depends only on $\mathcal{N}$ and on the sets Σ_n of action labels for each $n \in \mathcal{N}$. If $\mathsf{out} = \{n\}$ is a singleton, we write (n, a, in) instead of $(\{n\}, a, \mathsf{in})$, and similarly for singleton sets in. In all figures and examples, interactions $(\mathsf{out}, a, \mathsf{in})$ are presented by the notation $\mathsf{out} \to \mathsf{in} : \mathsf{a}$ and internal labels (n, a) by $\mathsf{n} : \mathsf{a}$. System labels provide an appropriate means to describe which components in a system execute, possibly together, a computation step, i.e., a system transition.

System Transitions. A *system transition* $t \in E(\mathcal{S})$ has the form $(q_n)_{n \in \mathcal{N}} \xrightarrow{\lambda}_{\mathsf{lts}(\mathcal{S})} (q_n')_{n \in \mathcal{N}}$ such that $\lambda \in \Lambda(\mathcal{S})$ and

- either $\lambda = (\mathsf{out}, a, \mathsf{in})$ and:
  - $q_n \xrightarrow{a}_{\mathcal{A}_n} q_n'$, for all $n \in \mathsf{out} \cup \mathsf{in}$, and $q_m = q_m'$, for all $m \in \mathcal{N} \backslash (\mathsf{out} \cup \mathsf{in})$;
- or $\lambda = (n, a)$, $a \in \Sigma_n^\tau$ is an internal action of some component $n \in \mathcal{N}$, and:
  - $q_n \xrightarrow{a}_{\mathcal{A}_n} q_n'$ and $q_m = q_m'$, for all $m \in \mathcal{N} \backslash \{n\}$.

We write Λ and E instead of $\Lambda(\mathcal{S})$ and $E(\mathcal{S})$, respectively, if $\mathcal{S}$ is clear from the context. Surely, at most the components that are in a local state where action a is locally enabled can participate in a system transition for a. Since, by definition of system labels, $(\mathsf{out} \cup \mathsf{in}) \neq \varnothing$, at least one component participates in any system transition. Given a system transition $t = q \xrightarrow{\lambda}_{\mathsf{lts}(\mathcal{S})} q'$, we write $t.\lambda$ for λ.

Example 1. The Race system in Fig. 1 has both, desired system transitions such as $(0, 0, 0) \xrightarrow{(\mathsf{Ctrl}, \mathsf{start}, \{\mathsf{R1}, \mathsf{R2}\})} (1, 1, 1)$ and $(1, 2, 2) \xrightarrow{(\mathsf{R1}, \mathsf{finish}, \mathsf{Ctrl})} (2, 0, 2)$, and undesired ones like $(0, 0, 0) \xrightarrow{(\mathsf{Ctrl}, \mathsf{start}, \varnothing)} (1, 0, 0)$, and $(1, 2, 2) \xrightarrow{(\{\mathsf{R1}, \mathsf{R2}\}, \mathsf{finish}, \mathsf{Ctrl})}$ $(2, 0, 0)$. The LTS of the Race system, denoted by $\mathsf{lts}(\mathsf{Race})$, contains all possible system transitions. As mentioned in the Introduction, the latter two are undesired since the controller is supposed to start both runners simultaneously, whereas they should finish individually. These and other system transitions will be discarded based on synchronisation restrictions for teams considered next.   ▷

Team Automata. Synchronisation types specify which synchronisations of components are admissible in a specific system $\mathcal{S}$. A *synchronisation type* $(O, I) \in \mathsf{Intv} \times \mathsf{Intv}$ is a pair of intervals O and I which determine the number of outputs and inputs that can participate in a communication. Each interval has the form $[min, max]$ with $min \in \mathbb{N}$ and $max \in \mathbb{N} \cup \{*\}$ where $*$ denotes 0 or more participants. We write $x \in [min, max]$ if $min \leq x \leq max$ and $x \in [min, *]$ if $x \geq min$.

A *synchronisation type specification* (STS) over $\mathcal{S}$ is a function $\mathsf{st} : \Sigma^\bullet \to \mathsf{Intv} \times \mathsf{Intv}$ that assigns to any communicating action a an individual synchronisation type $\mathsf{st}(a)$. A system label $\lambda = (\mathsf{out}, a, \mathsf{in})$ *satisfies* $\mathsf{st}(a) = (O, I)$, denoted by $\lambda \models \mathbf{st}(a)$, if $|\text{out}| \in O \wedge |\text{in}| \in I$. Each STS $\mathbf{st}$ generates the following subsets $\Lambda(\mathcal{S}, \mathbf{st})$ of system labels and $E(\mathcal{S}, \mathbf{st})$ of corresponding system transitions.

$$\Lambda(\mathcal{S}, \mathbf{st}) = \{\, \lambda \in \Lambda \mid \lambda = (\text{out}, a, \text{in}) \Rightarrow \lambda \models \mathbf{st}(a) \,\}$$
$$E(\mathcal{S}, \mathbf{st}) = \{\, t \in E \mid t.\lambda \in \Lambda(\mathcal{S}, \mathbf{st}) \,\}$$

Thus, for communicating actions, the set of system transitions is restricted to those transitions whose labels respect the synchronisation type of their communicating action. For internal actions no restriction is applied, since an internal action of a component can always be executed when it is locally enabled.

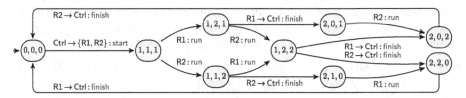

Fig. 3. Team automaton of the Race system example in Fig. 1

Components interacting in accordance with an STS $\mathbf{st}$ over a system $\mathcal{S}$ are seen as a team whose behaviour is represented by the (extended) *team automaton* (TA) $\mathbf{ta}(\mathcal{S}, \mathbf{st})$ generated over $\mathcal{S}$ by $\mathbf{st}$ and defined by the LTS

$$\mathbf{ta}(\mathcal{S}, \mathbf{st}) = (Q, q_0, \Lambda(\mathcal{S}, \mathbf{st}), E(\mathcal{S}, \mathbf{st})).^1$$

We write $\Lambda(\mathcal{S}, \mathbf{st})$ and $E(\mathcal{S}, \mathbf{st})$ instead of $\Lambda(\mathcal{S}, \mathbf{st})$ and $E(\mathcal{S}, \mathbf{st})$, respectively, if $\mathcal{S}$ is clear from the context, and assume that $\Lambda(\mathcal{S}, \mathbf{st}) \neq \varnothing$. Labels in $\Lambda(\mathcal{S}, \mathbf{st})$ are called *team labels* and transitions in $E(\mathcal{S}, \mathbf{st})$ are called *team transitions*.

Example 2. For the Race system $\mathcal{S}_{\mathsf{Race}}$ in Fig. 1. we define the runners to *start* simultaneously and *finish* individually by the STS $\mathbf{st}_{\mathsf{Race}} = \{\mathsf{start} \mapsto ([1,1],[2,2]), \mathsf{finish} \mapsto ([1,1],[1,1])\}$. The resulting TA $\mathbf{ta}(\mathbf{st}_{\mathsf{Race}}, \mathcal{S}_{\mathsf{Race}})$ is shown in Fig. 3, with interactions (n, a, m) written as $\mathsf{n} \to \mathsf{m} : \mathsf{a}$ and internal labels (n, a) as $\mathsf{n} : \mathsf{a}$.   ▷

3   Related Coordination Formalisms

In this section, we introduce a selection of formal coordination models and languages and compare them to team automata by providing, for each formalism, (1) the definition of the variant considered here, (2) the definition of composition (via synchronisation), (3) a possible model of our Race example in the formalism, (4) a brief relation with team automata, and (5) existing tool support.

---

[1] Starting with [44], we use the system labels $(\text{out}, a, \text{in})$ in $\Lambda(\mathcal{S}, \mathbf{st})$ as the actions in team transitions of what we coined extended team automata (ETA). This is the main difference with the 'classical' team automata from [41,82] and subsequent papers, where actions $a \in \Sigma$ have been used in team transitions. However, to study communication properties [36], compositionality [44] and realisability [47], explicit rendering of the CA that actually participate in a transition of the team turned out useful.

3.1 Reo via Port Automata

Reo [2,96] is a coordination language to specify and compose *connectors*, i.e., patterns of valid synchronous interactions of ports of components or other connectors. For example, a FIFO1 connector has two ports: a source port to receive data and a sink port to send data. It initially allows the source port to interact while blocking the sink port, after which it allows the sink port to interact while blocking the source port. The duplicator connector has a single source port and two sink ports, only allowing all ports to interact at the same time or none.

Constraint automata [7] is a reference model for Reo's semantics [96]. We use a simplified variant called *port automata* [102], which abstracts away from data constraints, focusing on *synchronisation* and *composition*.

Definition. A port automaton (PA) $P = (Q, \Sigma, \rightarrow, Q_0)$ consists of a set of states Q, a set of ports Σ, a transition relation $\rightarrow\ \subseteq Q \times 2^{\Sigma} \times Q$, and a set of initial states $Q_0 \subseteq Q$. We have $(q, \{a, b\}, q') \in\ \rightarrow$ when the PA can evolve from state q to q' by *simultaneously executing* ports a and b.

Composition. Two PA $(Q_1, \Sigma_1, \rightarrow_1, Q_{0,1})$ and $(Q_2, \Sigma_2, \rightarrow_2, Q_{0,2})$ with shared ports and disjoint states can be composed by forcing the shared ports to synchronise. Then the composition yields a new PA $(Q_1 \times Q_2, \Sigma_1 \cup \Sigma_2, \rightarrow, Q_{0,1} \times Q_{0,2})$ where $\rightarrow$ is defined by the following rules (and the symmetric of the second rule):

$$\frac{q_1 \xrightarrow{\sigma_1}_1 q_1' \quad q_2 \xrightarrow{\sigma_2}_2 q_2' \quad \sigma_1 \cap \Sigma_2 = \sigma_2 \cap \Sigma_1}{\langle q_1, q_2 \rangle \xrightarrow{\sigma_1 \cup \sigma_2} \langle q_1', q_2' \rangle} \qquad \frac{q_1 \xrightarrow{\sigma_1}_1 q_1' \quad \sigma_1 \cap \Sigma_2 = \varnothing}{\langle q_1, q_2 \rangle \xrightarrow{\sigma_1} \langle q_1', q_2 \rangle}$$

Note that the condition $\sigma_1 \cap \Sigma_2 = \sigma_2 \cap \Sigma_1$ intuitively means that any shared action of σ_1 must be available in σ_2 as well, and vice versa.

Race in Port Automata. Unlike TA, Reo's focus is on building connectors by composing simpler connectors, instead of composing components, to produce a system. Hence one could produce a Reo connector by composing a set of simpler primitive connectors that, once composed, would allow only the valid interaction patterns of our Race example. A possible connector is depicted in Fig. 4, borrowed from [119], which composes two FIFO1 connectors (⊢□↦), two synchronous barriers (>——◁), three replicators (→•◿ after start$_{Ctrl}$, finish$_{R1}$, and finish$_{R2}$), and one interleaving merger (⋟•↦ before finish$_{Ctrl}$). Each has a PA for its semantics, and their composition yields the PA depicted on the right of Fig. 4.

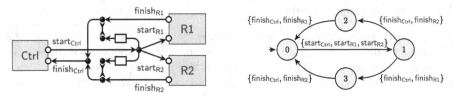

Fig. 4. Reo connector for the Race example (left) and its semantics as a PA (right), after hiding internal ports shared among sub-connectors

Brief Relation with TA. Many variants of constraint automata exist [96, Sect. 3.2.2], some distinguishing inputs from outputs as in TA. Synchronisation types in TA restrict the number of inputs and outputs of ports with shared names; synchronisation in PA force how. No variant uses a similar notion to TA's synchronisation types, although they can be expressed using intermediate ports.

Tool Support. There are tools to *analyse, edit, visualise,* and *execute* Reo connectors. Analyses include model checking, using either the dedicated model checker Vereofy [101] or encoding Reo into mCRL2 [103,118], and simulation of extensions with parameters [120] and with reactive programming notions [122], many accessible online at http://arcatools.org/reo. Editors and visualisation engines include an Eclipse-based implementation [4] and editors based on JavaScript that run in a browser [76,130]. Execution engines for Reo include a Java-based implementation [78] and a distributed engine using actors in Scala [121,123].

3.2 BIP Without Priorities

BIP [26,64] is formal language to specify architectures for interacting components. A program describes the **B**ehaviour of each component, the valid **I**nteractions between their ports, and the **P**riority among interactions. Multiple formal models for specifying interactions exist, such as an algebra of connectors [64]. We follow the formalisation of the operational semantics of Bliudze and Sifakis [64], disregarding the priority aspect for simplicity. In this paper, ports of BIP are called actions to facilitate the comparison with TA.

Definition. A *local behaviour B* is given by an LTS (Q, q_0, Σ, E), with set Q of states, initial state q_0, labels Σ for actions, and transition relation $E : Q \times \Sigma \times Q$.

Composition into a BIP Program. A BIP program without priorities is a pair consisting of (1) an $\mathcal{N}$-indexed family of local behaviours $(B_n)_{n \in \mathcal{N}} = (Q_n, q_{0,n}, \Sigma_n, E_n)$, with pairwise disjoint action sets Σ_n, one for each agent n, and (2) a set of valid interactions I where each interaction $a \in I$ is a family $(a_n)_{n \in N}$ such that $N \subseteq \mathcal{N}$ and $a_n \in \Sigma_n$, for all $n \in N$, and I is a set of such interactions. The semantics of a BIP program BP is given by an LTS $\mathsf{lts}(BP) = (\prod_{n \in \mathcal{N}} Q_n, (q_{0,n})_{n \in \mathcal{N}}, I, E)$, where E is defined by the following rule:

$$\frac{a = (a_n)_{n \in N} \in I \ \wedge \ \forall n \in N : \left(q_n \xrightarrow{a_n}_{B_n} q'_n \right) \ \wedge \ \forall n \in \mathcal{N} \setminus N : q_n = q'_n}{(q_n)_{n \in \mathcal{N}} \xrightarrow{a}_{\mathsf{lts}(BP)} (q'_n)_{n \in \mathcal{N}}}$$

Race in BIP. The encoding of our Race example in BIP without priorities is depicted in Fig. 5. It consists of the three components on the left, where we use a set notation for each interaction in I. This set I of valid interactions generalises the synchronisation policies of TA, imposing all start actions to synchronise and the finish actions to synchronise two at a time between the controller and one runner. The LTS of the BIP program is the same as the PA on the right side of Fig. 4, omitting the internal action run included in the TA model of the Race example.

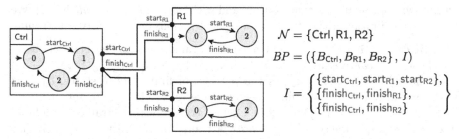

$$\mathcal{N} = \{\mathsf{Ctrl}, \mathsf{R1}, \mathsf{R2}\}$$

$$BP = (\{B_{\mathsf{Ctrl}}, B_{\mathsf{R1}}, B_{\mathsf{R2}}\}, I)$$

$$I = \left\{ \begin{array}{l} \{\mathsf{start}_{\mathsf{Ctrl}}, \mathsf{start}_{\mathsf{R1}}, \mathsf{start}_{\mathsf{R2}}\}, \\ \{\mathsf{finish}_{\mathsf{Ctrl}}, \mathsf{finish}_{\mathsf{R1}}\}, \\ \{\mathsf{finish}_{\mathsf{Ctrl}}, \mathsf{finish}_{\mathsf{R2}}\} \end{array} \right\}$$

Fig. 5. Race example in BIP: individual components are labelled by actions, restricted to the interactions allowed by I, imposed by the (stateless) connector

Brief Relation with TA. We have previously [31] compared TA with BIP [26], describing how some explicit patterns of interaction of BIP, such as broadcasts, are modelled in TA. In this paper, we used precise formalisations of TA and BIP without priorities [104], presented in a similar style to facilitate the comparison.

There are some technical core differences between these formalisations of BIP and TA. BIP's formalisation does not include explicit internal actions, although they do exist at implementation level (e.g., in JavaBIP [63]). BIP's synchronisation mechanism ignores inputs and outputs. However, the flow of data at each interaction is sometimes described orthogonally [63], where ports can either be *enforceable* by the environment (similar to input actions) or *spontaneous* by the components (similar to output actions). A more thorough comparison of the expressiveness of different BIP formalisations is given by Baranov and Bliudze [8]. These differences reflect a different focus: less emphasis on communication properties (Sect. 4), internal behaviour of local components, and realisability notions (Sect. 5); yet more focus on the exploration of different formalisms to compose interactions and programs, supported by tools to connect to running systems [63].

Similar to TA's synchronisation types, BIP has a formalisation parameterised on the number of components [111]. Ports can have multiple instances, and are enriched with a bound on the number of allowed agents they can synchronise with, and a bound on the number of interactions they can be involved in.

Tool Support. Several tools exist for BIP, including verification tools that traverse the state space of BIP programs [62] or use the VerCors model checker [61], and a toolset LALT-BIP for verifying freedom from global and local deadlocks [6]. BIP also has a C++ reference engine [27] and a Java engine called JavaBIP [63].

3.3 Contract Automata

Contract automata [18,24] are a finite state automata dialect proposed to model multi-party composition of contracts that can perform *request* or *offer* actions, which need to match to achieve *agreement* among a composition of contracts. Contract automata have been equipped with variability in [15,19] by *modalities* to specify when an action *must* be matched (necessary) and when it *may* be withdrawn (optional) in a composition, and with *real-time constraints* in [17]. We first give a definition without modalities, silent actions or variability constraints.

Definition. Let $\bar{v} = [e_1, \ldots, e_n]$ be a vector of rank $n \geq 1$ and let $v(i)$ denote its ith element. A *contract automaton* of rank $n \geq 1$ is a tuple $(Q, \bar{q}_0, \Sigma^r, \Sigma^o, \rightarrow, F)$ such that $Q = Q_1 \times \ldots \times Q_n$ is the product of finite sets of states, $\bar{q}_0 \in Q$ is the initial state, Σ^r is a finite set of requests, Σ^o is a finite set of offers, $\rightarrow \subseteq Q \times (\Sigma^r \cup \Sigma^o \cup \{-\})^n \times Q$ is a set of transitions constrained as follows next, and $F \subseteq Q$ a the set of final states. A transition $(\bar{q}, \bar{a}, \bar{q}') \in \rightarrow$ is such that $\bar{a}$ is either a single offer (i.e., $\exists i \,.\, \bar{a}(i) = !a \in \Sigma^o$ and $\forall j \neq i \,.\, \bar{a}(j) = -$), a single request (i.e., $\exists i \,.\, \bar{a}(i) = ?a \in \Sigma^r$ and $\forall j \neq i \,.\, \bar{a}(j) = -$) or a single pair of matching request and offer (i.e., $\exists i, j \,.\, \bar{a}(i) = !a \wedge \bar{a}(j) = ?a$ and $\forall k \neq i, j \,.\, \bar{a}(k) = -$), and $\forall i \,.\, \bar{a}(i) = - \implies \bar{q}(i) = \bar{q}'(i)$.

Next we define contract automata with committed states as introduced in [21]: whenever a state $\bar{q}$ has a committed element $\bar{q}(i)$, then all outgoing transitions of $\bar{q}$ have a label $\bar{a}$ such that $\bar{a}(i) \neq -$, i.e., whenever the intermediate state of two concatenated transitions is committed, the two transitions are executed atomically: after the first transition has been executed, the second transition is executed prior to any other transition of any other service in the composition.

Composition. Composition of contracts is rendered through the composition of their contract automaton models by means of the *composition operator* $\otimes$, a variant of the synchronous product, which interleaves or matches the transitions of the component (contract) automata such that whenever two components are enabled to execute their respective request/offer action, then the match must happen. A composition is in *agreement* if each request is matched with an offer.

Race in Contract Automata. We use contract automata with committed states to mimick multi-party synchronisation (cf. Fig. 6). In their composition in Fig. 7, states $[C, 1, 0]$ and $[C, 0, 1]$ have a committed state, meaning that only outgoing transitions in which Ctrl changes state are permitted. In [21], silent (τ) actions are introduced, but we choose to model internal run actions as offer actions !run (which do not interfere with agreement) rather than silent actions τ_{run}.

Brief Relation with TA. In [25], contract automata are compared with communicating machines [66]. To guarantee that a composition corresponds to a

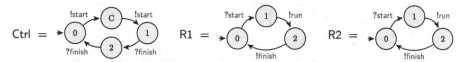

Fig. 6. Contract automata with committed states for the Race example

well-behaving (i.e., *realisable*) choreography, a *branching condition* is used. This condition requires contract automata to perform their offers independently of the other component automata in the composition. As noted in [15], this condition is related to the phenomenon of *state sharing* in team automata [83], meaning that system components influence potential synchronisations through their local (component) states even if not involved in the actual global (system) transition. While a synchronous product of (I/O) automata can directly be seen as a Petri net, for team automata this only holds for non-state-sharing vector team automata [52,68]. The relation between the branching condition of contract automata and (non-)state-sharing in (vector) team automata needs further study.

Tool Support. Contract automata are supported by a software API called Contract Automata Library (CATLib) [14], which a developer can exploit to specify contract automata and perform operations like composition and synthesis. The synthesis operation uses supervisory control theory [124], properly revisited in [23] for synthesising orchestrations and choreographies of contract automata. An application developed with CATLib is thus formally validated *by-construction* against well-behaving properties from the theory of contract automata [15,18,23]. CATLib was designed to be easily extendable to support related formalisms; it currently supports synchronous communicating machines [105].

3.4 Choreography Automata

Choreography Automata (ChorAut) [10] are automata with labels that describe interactions, including a sender, a receiver, and a message name. This section is less detailed than the previous ones due to the similarity with contract automata.

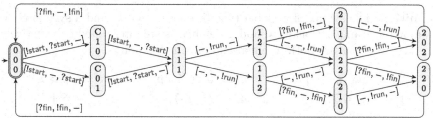

Fig. 7. Composition Ctrl ⊗ R1 ⊗ R2 of contract automata

Race in ChorAut. A ChorAut model of our Race example without the internal run actions is depicted in Fig. 8.

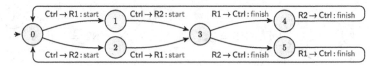

Fig. 8. ChorAut of the Race example (without internal run actions)

Brief Relation with TA. Internal actions are not captured by ChorAut (as in Reo and BIP's formalisations) and only binary synchronisations are supported (as in contract automata): each interaction has a single sender (the agent that *offers*) and a single receiver (the agent that *requests*). Desirable properties of ChorAut include deadlock-freedom, among others, focused on the language accepted by these automata [11]. Consequently, properties that rely on observational equivalence notions such as bisimilarity are not covered by these analyses.

Tool Support. Corinne [117] can be used to visualise ChorAut and to automatise operations like projection, composition, and checking for well-formedness.

3.5 Synchronous Multi-Party Session Types

Multi-Party Session Types (MPST) [126] are a family of formalisms based on calculi to describe communication protocols between multiple agents (*multiparty*). A *session* in these calculi represents a communication channel shared by a group of agents, to which they can read or write data. In MPST, each agent has a *behavioural type*, which describes the allowed patterns of reading-from and writing-to sessions, providing some compile-time guarantees for the concrete agents to follow the communication patterns. Most approaches distinguish (1) a *global type*, often a starting point, describing the composed system; and (2) the *local types*, often derived from the global type, describing the local view of each agent.

This paper uses the definitions of a simple synchronous MPST (SyncMPST) used by Seviri and Dezani-Ciancaglini [127] that only supports binary synchronisations. Other SyncMPST exist, some supporting multiple receivers [58] or multiple senders [95]. We opt to use a simpler model that can be compactly described and provides enough insights to relate SyncMPST with TA.

Definition. The syntax of a global type $\mathcal{G}$, a local type $\mathcal{L}$, and a system $\mathcal{S}$ are given by the grammars below. $\mathcal{G}$ and $\mathcal{L}$ definitions are interpreted coinductively, i.e., their solutions are both minimal and maximal fixpoints.

$$\mathcal{G} ::= \mathsf{end} \mid \mathsf{p} \to \mathsf{q} : \Gamma \qquad \mathcal{L} ::= 0 \mid \mathsf{p!}\Lambda \mid \mathsf{p?}\Lambda \qquad \mathcal{S} ::= \mathsf{p} \triangleright \mathcal{L}$$
$$\Gamma ::= \{a_i.\mathcal{G}_i\}_{1 \leq i \leq k} \qquad \Lambda ::= \{a_i.\mathcal{L}_i\}_{1 \leq i \leq k} \qquad \mid \mathcal{S} \| \mathcal{S}$$

The following conditions must hold: (1) branches Γ and Λ must have disjoint initial messages a_i; (2) agents p in $\mathcal{S}$ appearing in the left of $\mathsf{p} \triangleright \mathcal{L}$ must be different and each $\mathcal{L}$ must not include p; and (3) for every $\mathsf{p} \to \mathsf{q} : \Gamma$ and $\mathsf{r} \notin \{\mathsf{p}, \mathsf{q}\}$, r *should not distinguish* any choice in Γ. The third point captures *projectability* [127], which is not formalised here and is closely related to realisability (cf. Sect. 5). Whenever clear we omit curly brackets and trailing **end** and 0.

The semantics of a global type is given by the rules below. The semantics of a system is given by the composition of local types presented in the next paragraph. The system obtained by projecting a global type is guaranteed to accept the same language as the global type [127].

$$\frac{}{\mathsf{p} \to \mathsf{q} : \{a.\mathcal{G}, \dots\} \xrightarrow{\mathsf{p} \to \mathsf{q}:a} \mathcal{G}} \qquad \frac{\{\mathsf{p},\mathsf{q}\} \cap \{\mathsf{r},\mathsf{s}\} = \varnothing \qquad \forall_{1 \le i \le k} : \mathcal{G}_i \xrightarrow{\mathsf{p} \to \mathsf{q}:b} \mathcal{G}'_i}{\mathsf{r} \to \mathsf{s} : \{a_i.\mathcal{G}_i\}_{1 \le i \le k} \xrightarrow{\mathsf{p} \to \mathsf{q}:b} \mathsf{r} \to \mathsf{s} : \{a_i.\mathcal{G}'_i\}_{1 \le i \le k}}$$

Composition. A system $\mathcal{S}$ of agents, each with a given local type, evolves according to the following rule:

$$\frac{}{\mathsf{p} \rhd \mathsf{q}!\{a.\mathcal{L}_\mathsf{p}, \dots\} \parallel \mathsf{q} \rhd \mathsf{p}?\{a.\mathcal{L}_\mathsf{q}, \dots\} \parallel \mathcal{S} \xrightarrow{\mathsf{p} \to \mathsf{q}:a} \mathsf{p} \rhd \mathcal{L}_\mathsf{p} \parallel \mathsf{q} \rhd \mathcal{L}_\mathsf{q} \parallel \mathcal{S}}$$

Race in SyncMPST. The Race example cannot be directly modelled using this SyncMPST. We model a variant in Fig. 9, using only binary synchronisation and using distinct start_1 and start_2 to differentiate the choice in the branch. Some other SyncMPST approaches also consider non-binary synchronisations [58,95], which could support the synchronisation of **start** with all three participants. There is also a need to prefix every choice with a concrete message between participants, leading to the need for distinguishing start_1 from start_2. This requirement is common among most MPST, which lead to our variant of the Race where an early choice is taken with start_1 or start_2 about which runner finishes first. For simplicity our variation assumes that R1 receives the **start** earlier. Alternatively we could have allowed either runners to start, as done with contract automata (Fig. 6) and choreography automata (Fig. 8). This would lead to a duplication of the code (one for each option) and to the introduction of a new initial action that prefixes the choice of which runner starts.

$$\mathcal{G} = \mathsf{Ctrl} \to \mathsf{R1} : \mathsf{start}.\mathsf{Ctrl} \to \mathsf{R2} : \left\{ \begin{array}{l} \mathsf{start}_1.(\mathsf{R1} \to \mathsf{Ctrl} : \mathsf{finish}.\mathsf{R2} \to \mathsf{Ctrl} : \mathsf{finish}.\mathcal{G}), \\ \mathsf{start}_2.(\mathsf{R2} \to \mathsf{Ctrl} : \mathsf{finish}.\mathsf{R1} \to \mathsf{Ctrl} : \mathsf{finish}.\mathcal{G}) \end{array} \right\}$$

$\mathcal{S} = \mathsf{Ctrl} \rhd \mathcal{L}_\mathsf{Ctrl} \parallel \mathsf{R1} \rhd \mathcal{L}_\mathsf{R1} \parallel \mathsf{R2} \rhd \mathcal{L}_\mathsf{R2}$

$\mathcal{L}_\mathsf{Ctrl} = \mathsf{R1}!\mathsf{start}.\mathsf{R2}! \left\{ \mathsf{start}_1.(\mathsf{R1}?\mathsf{finish}.\mathsf{R2}?\mathsf{finish}.\mathcal{L}_\mathsf{Ctrl}), \mathsf{start}_2.(\mathsf{R2}?\mathsf{finish}.\mathsf{R1}?\mathsf{finish}.\mathcal{L}_\mathsf{Ctrl}) \right\}$

$\mathcal{L}_\mathsf{R1} = \mathsf{Ctrl}?\mathsf{start}.\mathsf{Ctrl}!\mathsf{finish}.\mathcal{L}_\mathsf{R1}$

$\mathcal{L}_\mathsf{R2} = \mathsf{Ctrl}? \left\{ \mathsf{start}_1.\mathsf{Ctrl}!\mathsf{finish}.\mathcal{L}_\mathsf{R2}, \mathsf{start}_2.\mathsf{Ctrl}!\mathsf{finish}.\mathcal{L}_\mathsf{R2} \right\}$

Fig. 9. Global type ($\mathcal{G}$) and system ($\mathcal{S}$) of a Race example variant in SyncMPST

Brief Relation with TA. SyncMPSTs support a relatively strict subset of interaction patterns. Consequently, many useful properties may be syntactically verified, like deadlock-freedom or the preservation of behaviour after projection, at the cost of expressivity.

Regarding internal behaviour, neither global nor local types support internal actions. As an alternative to internal actions in types, many MPST variations describe a separate syntax for processes with data and control structures, and define well-typedness w.r.t. local types (cf., e.g., Bejleri and Yoshida [58]).

A rich variety of tools are built over variants of MPST. A recent survey by Yoshida [134] of MPST implementations over different programming languages reflects the focus on producing trustworthy distributed implementations.

3.6   Other Coordination Formalisms

Many other coordination formalisms involve similar notions of composition and synchronisation of agent behaviour. These include the specification languages provided by model checkers such as Uppaal [57,107] and mCRL2 [5,85], as well as more generic formalisms like Petri nets [60,125], message sequence charts [89, 93], event structures [115,133] and I/O automata [99,110]. Without pretending completeness, we discuss some of these in this section.

Uppaal accepts systems modelled by (stochastic, timed) automata, with matching input-output actions that must synchronise (either 1-to-1 or 1-to-many). The latter requires a sender to synchronise with all, possibly zero, available receivers at that time, which differs from the synchronisation policies of TA. Contract automata's committed states stem from Uppaal's concept of committed states. Uppaal also provides partial support for priorities over actions, but not over interactions as in BIP.

mCRL2 accepts systems modelled as a parallel composition of algebraic processes, with special operators to allow the synchronous execution of groups of actions, and the restriction of given actions. This is powerful enough to enumerate all valid synchronisations between concurrent agents, yet quite verbose, which we exploited to verify communication properties of TA [36].

Petri nets come in many flavours, and provide a compact representation of a global model of interaction that avoids the explosion of states caused by the interleaving of independent actions. In [52], a subclass of TA—non-state-sharing vector team automata—has been encoded into *Individual Token Net Controllers*—a model of vector-labeled Petri nets—covering TA in which the synchronisation of a set of agents cannot be influenced by the remaining agents (cf. Sect. 3.3). *Zero-safe nets* are another extension of Petri nets with a transactional mechanism that distinguishes observable from hidden states, used to formalise Reo [74]. This extension could also be used to model TA's synchronisation mechanism, although the analysis of these nets is non-trivial.

MSC (Message Sequence Charts) are visual diagrams commonly used to describe scenarios with interacting agents which have historically been used to describe telecommunication protocols. They are not always precise, and can be enriched with constructs to denote loops, choices, and parallel threads. On the right, we include an informal MSC that captures our Race example, using a loop and a parallel block. Katoen and Lambert [98] have used *pomsets* to formalise MSC, where each possible trace is described as a (multi-)set of actions with a partial

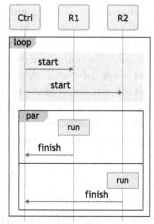

order. Guanciale and Tuosto used a pomset semantics for choreographies to reason over realisability [87], and we extended pomsets with a hierarchical structure [80], reasoned over realisability, and compared it to event structures [115] (often used to give semantics to Petri nets). How to use a pomset variation to represent global models for TA is currently being investigated.

I/O automata and related formalisms like I/O systems [97], interface automata [77], reactive transition systems [70], interacting state machines [116], and component-interaction (CI) automata [67] all distinguish input, output, and internal actions. However, I/O automata are *input-enabled*: in every state of the automaton every input action of the automaton is enabled (i.e., executable). In fact, team automata are a generalisation of I/O automata [50]. All formalisms define composition as the synchronous product of automata except for interface automata [77], which restrict product states to compatible states, and CI automata, which were specifically designed to have this distinguishing feature of team automata. CI automata however restrict communication to binary synchronisation between a pair of input and output actions. Contrary to 'classical' team automata, CI automata use system labels to preserve the information about their communication, a feature which inspired the introduction of extended team automata in [44] (cf. Footnote 1 on page 6).

4   Communication Properties

Compatibility of components is an important issue for systems to guarantee successful (*safe*) communication [13,31,32,46,65,69,71,79], i.e., free from message loss (output actions not accepted as input by some other component) and indefinite waiting (for input to be received in the form of an appropriate output action provided by another component). In [31], we identified representative *synchronisation types* to classify synchronisation policies that are realisable in team automata (e.g., binary, multicast and broadcast communication, synchronous product) in terms of ranges for the number of sending and receiving components participating in synchronisations. Moreover, we provided a generic procedure to derive, for each synchronisation type, requirements for *receptiveness* and for *responsiveness* of team automata that prevent outputs not being accepted and inputs not being provided, respectively, i.e., guaranteeing safe communication. This allowed us to define a notion of *compatibility* for team automata in terms of their compliance with communication requirements, i.e., receptiveness and responsiveness. A team automaton was said to be *compliant* with a given set of communication requirements if in each of its reachable states, the desired communications can immediately occur; it was said to be *weakly compliant* if the communication can eventually occur after some internal actions have been performed (akin to weak compatibility [28,90] or agreement of lazy request actions [15]). Since communication requirements are derived from synchronisation types, we get a family of compatibility notions indexed by synchronisation types.

We revisited the definition of *safe communication* in terms of receptive- and responsiveness requirements in [44,46], due to limitations of our earlier approach.

First, the assignment of a single synchronisation type to a team automata was deemed too restrictive, so we decided to fine tune the number of synchronising sending and receiving components *per action*. For this purpose we introduced, in [44], *synchronisation type specifications* which assign a synchronisation type individually to each communicating action. As we have seen in Sect. 2, such specifications uniquely determine a team automaton. Any synchronisation type specification generates communication requirements to be satisfied by the team.

Receptiveness. Here is the idea. If, in a reachable state q of $\mathbf{ta}(\mathcal{S}, \mathbf{st})$, a group $\{\mathcal{A}_n \mid n \in \mathsf{out}\}$ of CA with $\varnothing \neq \mathsf{out} \subseteq \mathcal{N}$ is (locally) enabled to perform an output action a, i.e., for all $n \in \mathsf{out}$ holds $a \in \Sigma_n^!$ and $q_n \xrightarrow{a} \mathcal{A}_n$, and if moreover both (1) the number of CA in out fits that of the senders allowed by the synchronisation type $\mathbf{st}(a) = (O, I)$, i.e., $|\mathsf{out}| \in O$, and (2) the CA need at least one receiver to join the communication, i.e., $0 \notin I$, then we get a *receptiveness requirement*, denoted by $\mathbf{rcp}(\mathsf{out}, a)@q$. If $\mathsf{out} = \{n\}$, we write $\mathbf{rcp}(n, a)@q$ for $\mathbf{rcp}(\{n\}, a)@q$.

Responsiveness. For input actions, one can formulate responsiveness requirements with the idea that enabled inputs should be served by appropriate outputs. The expression $\mathbf{rsp}(\mathsf{in}, a)@q$ is a *responsiveness requirement* if $q \in \mathcal{R}(\mathbf{ta}(\mathcal{S}, \mathbf{st}))$, for all $n \in \mathsf{in}$ we have $a \in \Sigma_n^?$ and $q_n \xrightarrow{a} \mathcal{A}_n$, and $|\mathsf{in}| \in I, 0 \notin O$ for $\mathbf{st}(a) = (O, I)$.

Second, we realised that even the weak compliance notion is too restrictive for practical applications. So, in [44], we introduced a much more liberal notion.

Compliance. The TA $\mathbf{ta}(\mathcal{S}, \mathbf{st})$ is compliant with a receptiveness requirement $\mathbf{rcp}(\mathsf{out}, a)@q$ if the group of components (with names in out) can find partners in the team which synchronise with the group by taking (receiving) a as input. If reception is immediate, then we speak of receptiveness; if the other components may still perform *arbitrary intermediate actions* (i.e., not limited to internal ones) before accepting a, then we speak of weak receptiveness. We now formally define (weak) compliance, (weak) receptiveness and (weak) responsiveness.

The TA $\mathbf{ta}(\mathcal{S}, \mathbf{st})$ is *compliant* with $\mathbf{rcp}(\mathsf{out}, a)@q$ if $\exists_{\mathsf{in}} . q \xrightarrow{(\mathsf{out}, a, \mathsf{in})}_{\mathbf{ta}(\mathcal{S}, \mathbf{st})}$ while it is *weakly compliant* with $\mathbf{rcp}(\mathsf{out}, a)@q$ if $\exists_{\mathsf{in}} . q \xrightarrow{(\Lambda(\mathbf{st})_{\setminus \mathsf{out}})^* ; (\mathsf{out}, a, \mathsf{in})}_{\mathbf{ta}(\mathcal{S}, \mathbf{st})}$, where $\Lambda(\mathsf{st})_{\backslash \mathsf{out}}$ denotes the set of team labels in which no component of out participates. Formally, $\Lambda(\mathcal{S}, \mathsf{st})_{\backslash \mathsf{out}} = \{\, (\mathsf{out}', a, \mathsf{in}) \in \Lambda(\mathcal{S}, \mathsf{st}) \mid (\mathsf{out}' \cup \mathsf{in}) \cap \mathsf{out} = \varnothing \,\} \cup \{\, (n, a) \in \Lambda(\mathcal{S}, \mathsf{st}) \mid n \notin \mathsf{out} \,\}$.

The TA $\mathsf{ta}(\mathcal{S}, \mathsf{st})$ is *compliant* with $\mathsf{rsp}(\mathsf{in}, a)@q$ if $\exists_{\mathsf{out}} \cdot q \xrightarrow{(\mathsf{out}, a, \mathsf{in})} \mathsf{ta}(\mathcal{S}, \mathsf{st})$, while it is *weakly compliant* with $\mathsf{rsp}(\mathsf{in}, a)@q$ if $\exists_{\mathsf{out}} \cdot q \xrightarrow{(\Lambda(\mathsf{st})_{\backslash \mathsf{in}})^* \,;\, (\mathsf{out}, a, \mathsf{in})} \mathsf{ta}(\mathcal{S}, \mathsf{st})$, where $\mathsf{st}(\Lambda)_{\backslash \mathsf{in}} = \{\, (\mathsf{out}, a, \mathsf{in}') \in \mathsf{st}(\Lambda) \mid (\mathsf{out} \cup \mathsf{in}') \cap \mathsf{in} = \varnothing \,\} \cup \{\, (n, a) \in \mathsf{st}(\Lambda) \mid n \notin \mathsf{in} \}$ denotes the set of team labels in which no component of in participates.

TA: (Weak) Receptiveness. The TA $\mathsf{ta}(\mathcal{S}, \mathsf{st})$ is *(weakly) receptive* if for all reachable states $q \in \mathcal{R}(\mathsf{ta}(\mathcal{S}, \mathsf{st}))$, the TA $\mathsf{ta}(\mathcal{S}, \mathsf{st})$ is (weakly) compliant with *all* receptiveness requirements $\mathsf{rcp}(\mathsf{out}, a)@q$ established for q.

Example 3 (Receptiveness and Compliance). In the initial state $(0, 0, 0)$ of the Race team (cf. Fig. 3), there is a receptiveness requirement of the controller who wants to start the competition, expressed by $\mathsf{rcp}(\mathsf{Ctrl}, \mathsf{start})@(0, 0, 0)$ The TA $\mathsf{ta}(\mathsf{Race}, \mathsf{st}_{\mathsf{Race}})$ is compliant with this requirement. When the first runner is in state 2, the desire to send finish leads to three receptiveness requirements: $\mathsf{rcp}(\mathsf{R1}, \mathsf{finish})@(1, 2, 1)$, $\mathsf{rcp}(\mathsf{R1}, \mathsf{finish})@(1, 2, 2)$, and $\mathsf{rcp}(\mathsf{R1}, \mathsf{finish})@(2, 2, 0)$. If the second runner is in state 2, we get three more receptiveness requirements: $\mathsf{rcp}(\mathsf{R2}, \mathsf{finish})@(1, 1, 2)$, $\mathsf{rcp}(\mathsf{R2}, \mathsf{finish})@(1, 2, 2)$, and $\mathsf{rcp}(\mathsf{R2}, \mathsf{finish})@(2, 0, 2)$. The TA $\mathsf{ta}(\mathsf{Race}, \mathsf{st}_{\mathsf{Race}})$ is compliant also with these. ▷

Unlike output actions, the selection of an input action of a component is not controlled by the component but by the environment, i.e., there is an external choice. If, for a choice of enabled inputs $\{a_1, \dots, a_n\}$, *only one of them* can be supplied with a corresponding output of the environment this suffices to guarantee progress of each component waiting for input.

TA: (Weak) Responsiveness. The TA $\mathsf{ta}(\mathcal{S}, \mathsf{st})$ is *(weakly) responsive* if for all reachable states $q \in \mathcal{R}(\mathsf{ta}(\mathcal{S}, \mathsf{st}))$ and for all $n \in \mathcal{N}$ the following holds: if there is a responsiveness requirement $\mathsf{rsp}(\mathsf{in}, a)@q$ established for q with $n \in \mathsf{in}$, then the TA $\mathsf{ta}(\mathcal{S}, \mathsf{st})$ is (weakly) compliant with at least one of these requirements.[2]

Example 4 (Responsiveness and Compliance). In the initial state $(0, 0, 0)$ of the Race team, there is a responsiveness requirement of the two runners who want the competition to start, expressed by $\mathsf{rsp}(\{\mathsf{R1}, \mathsf{R2}\}, \mathsf{start})@(0, 0, 0)$. The TA $\mathsf{ta}(\mathsf{Race}, \mathsf{st}_{\mathsf{Race}})$ is compliant with this requirement. When the controller is in state 1, there are responsiveness requirements $\mathsf{rsp}(\mathsf{Ctrl}, \mathsf{finish})@(1, q_1, q_2)$ for any $q_1, q_2 \in \{1, 2\}$. In state $(1, 1, 1)$, at least one run must happen before a finish is sent; in all other cases, this requirement is immediately fulfilled. Hence, the TA $\mathsf{ta}(\mathsf{Race}, \mathsf{st}_{\mathsf{Race}})$ is weakly compliant. There are four more responsiveness requirements when the controller is in state 2, two of which are only weakly fulfilled. ▷

---

[2] This version of (weak) responsiveness is slightly stronger than in our previous work, driven by the comparison with local deadlock-freedom below.

As far as we know, such powerful compliance notions for I/O-based, synchronous component systems were not studied before. In case of open systems the arbitrary immediate actions before a desired communication happens may be output or input actions open to the environment. Then local communication properties could be violated upon composition with other team automata. This led us to consider *composition* of open team automata and to investigate conditions ensuring *compositionality* of communication properties [33, 44, 45].

Roadmap. A third limitation has so far not been tackled. In [46], we argued that it may be the case that (local) enabledness of an action indicates only readiness for communication and not so much that communication is required. Therefore, to make this distinction between possible and required communication explicit, we proposed to add designated *final states* to components, where execution can stop but may also continue, in addition to states where progress is required. The addition of final states to component automata has significant consequences for the derivation of communication requirements and for our compliance notions, which would have to be adjusted accordingly.

Verification and Tool Support. Automatically verifying communication properties is non-trivial, as it may involve traversing networks of interacting automata with large state spaces. We pursued a different approach by providing a *logical* characterisation of receptiveness and responsiveness in terms of formulas of a (test-free) propositional dynamic logic [88] using (complex) interactions as modalities (cf. [35, 36]). Verification of communication properties then relies on model checking receptive- and responsiveness formulas against a system of component automata taking into account a given synchronisation type specification.

We developed an open-source prototypical tool [56] to support our theory. It implements a transformation of CA, systems, and TA into mCRL2 [5] processes and of the characterising dynamic logic formulas into μ-calculus formulas. The latter is straightforward, whereas the former uses mCRL2's allow operator to suitably restrict the number of multi-action synchronisations such that the semantics of systems of CA is preserved. Then we can automatically check communication properties with the model-checking facilities offered by mCRL2, which outputs the result of the formula as well as a witness or counterexample.

Related Work. The genericity of our approach w.r.t. synchronisation policies allows us to capture compatibility notions for various multi-component coordination strategies. In the literature, compatibility notions are mostly considered for systems relying on peer-to-peer communication, i.e., all synchronisation types are ([1,1],[1,1]). Our notion of receptiveness is inspired by the compatibility notion of interface automata [77] and indeed both notions coincide for closed systems and 1-to-1 communication. It also coincides with receptiveness in [70]. Weak receptiveness is inspired by the notion of weak compatibility in [28] and also corresponds to unspecified reception in the context of n-protocol compatibility in [79] and lazy request in contract automata [15]. We are not aware of compatibility notions concerning responsiveness. In [70], it is captured by deadlock-freedom and in [79] it is expressed by part of the definition of bidirectional complementary compatibility which, however, does not support choice of inputs as we do.

The relationship between deadlock-freedom, used in different variations in the literature, and our communication properties is subtle. Note that the distinction between input and output actions is not relevant for the deadlock notions and that two types of deadlocks are often distinguished: global and local deadlocks (cf., e.g., [6]). For the following discussion, we assume that the components of a system have no final state (i.e., for each local state there is an outgoing transition). We further assume that all local actions are external, i.e., input or output, and that the synchronisation types of all output actions are $([1,1],[1,*])$ and $([1,*],[1,1])$ for all input actions. Then weak receptiveness together with weak responsiveness of team automata implies (global) deadlock-freedom in the sense of BIP [84] and the equivalent notion of stuck-freeness in MPST [126]. The weaker notion of deadlock-freedom in ChorAut [10] is also implied by the combination of weak receptiveness with weak responsiveness.

Global deadlock-freedom does, however, not imply weak receptiveness. For instance, assume that there are two CA $\mathcal{A}_1$ and $\mathcal{A}_2$ such that in the initial state q_1 of $\mathcal{A}_1$ there is a choice of two outputs a and b, and in the initial state q_2 of $\mathcal{A}_2$ there is only one outgoing transition with input a. Then the system state (q_1, q_2) is not a deadlock state but the receptiveness requirement for b is violated at state (q_1, q_2) since the autonomous choice of output b by the first component would not be accepted by the second. Also weak responsiveness is not implied by global deadlock-freedom. For a counterexample we would need three components, two with a single input, say a for the first and b for the second, and one with a single output, say a. Assume that all components have loops around the initial state. Then the system, considered under 1-to-1 communication, would be (globally) deadlock-free but not (weakly) responsive, since the second component would never receive b.

This example points out the crucial difference between global and local deadlocks, covered by the notions of "individual deadlock" in BIP [84], "lock" in ChorAut [10], and "strong lock" in MPST [126]. The difference between the latter two is that [10] assumes fair runs. The notion of individual deadlock in [84] is defined differently, but seems equivalent to a "lock" in [10] for 1-to-1 communication. Weak receptiveness together with weak responsiveness is equivalent to individual deadlock-freedom in BIP if the interaction model fits to the synchronisation types assumed above. Hence, this is also equivalent to lock-freedom in [10]. Strong lock-freedom in MPST [126] is indeed a stronger requirement.

The compatibility notions above formalise general requirements for safe communication. Some approaches prefer to formulate individual compatibility requirements tailored to particular applications by formulas in a logic for dynamic systems using model-checking tools for verification (cf., e.g., [3,101, 103,118]).

5   Realisability

In this section, we consider a top-down method where first a global model $\mathcal{M}$ for the intended interaction behaviour of a system is provided on the basis of a given system signature and synchronisation type specification (STS) **st**. Then our goal is to construct a system $\mathcal{S}$ of component automata from which a team automaton $\mathbf{ta}(\mathcal{S}, \mathbf{st})$ can be generated that complies with the global model $\mathcal{M}$.

For this purpose, we instantiate the generic approach investigated in [47]. This instantiation applies the localisation style with so-called "poor" local actions of the form !a for outputs and ?a for inputs; localisations with "rich" local actions, which mention in the local context of a component n the name of a receiver m of a message (e.g., by $nm!a$) or the sender m of a message (e.g., by $mn?a$), are treated in [47] as well, but they are not relevant for team automata.

We assume the notions of component automaton (CA), system $\mathcal{S}$, synchronisation type specification **st**, and generated team automaton $\mathbf{ta}(\mathcal{S}, \mathbf{st})$, as provided in Sect. 2. Our realisation method is summarised in Fig. 10 and will be explained in more detail in the next sections.

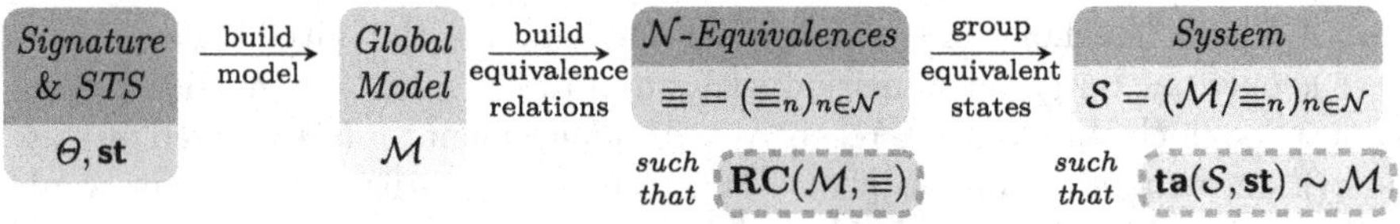

Fig. 10. Realisation method

5.1   Global Models of Interaction

Our method starts with a *system signature* $\Theta = (\mathcal{N}, (\Sigma_n)_{n \in \mathcal{N}})$, where $\mathcal{N}$ is a finite, nonempty set of component names and $(\Sigma_n)_{n \in \mathcal{N}}$ is an $\mathcal{N}$-indexed family of action sets $\Sigma_n = \Sigma_n^? \uplus \Sigma_n^!$ split into disjoint sets $\Sigma_n^?$ of *input actions* and $\Sigma_n^!$ of *output actions*. As in Sect. 2, let $\Sigma^\bullet = \bigcup_{n \in \mathcal{N}} \Sigma_n^? \cap \bigcup_{n \in \mathcal{N}} \Sigma_n^!$ be the set of *communicating actions*. We do not consider internal actions here and we assume that all system actions $a \in \bigcup_{n \in \mathcal{N}} \Sigma_n$ are communicating.

Together with the system signature a synchronisation type specification **st** must be provided assigning to each $a \in \Sigma^\bullet$ a pair of intervals $\mathbf{st}(a) = (O, I)$, as explained in Sect. 2. The system signature Θ together with the STS **st** determine the following set $\Lambda(\Theta, \mathbf{st})$ of *(multi-)interactions* respecting the constraints of the given synchronisation types:

$$\Lambda(\Theta, \mathbf{st}) = \{\, (\mathsf{out}, a, \mathsf{in}) \mid \varnothing \neq (\mathsf{out} \cup \mathsf{in}) \subseteq \mathcal{N}, \, \forall_{n \in \mathsf{out}} \cdot a \in \Sigma_n^!, \, \forall_{n \in \mathsf{in}} \cdot a \in \Sigma_n^?,$$
$$\mathbf{st}(a) = (O, I) \Rightarrow |\mathsf{out}| \in O \wedge |\mathsf{in}| \in I \,\}$$

We model the global interaction behaviour of the intended system by an LTS whose labels are (multi-)interactions in $\Lambda(\Theta, \mathsf{st})$. Hence, a *global interaction model* over Θ and st is an LTS of the form $\mathcal{M} = (Q, q_0, \Lambda(\Theta, \mathsf{st}), E)$.

Example 5. To develop the Race system we would start with system signature Θ_{Race} with component names Ctrl, R1, R2 and action sets $\Sigma_{\mathsf{Ctrl}}^? = \{\mathsf{finish}\} = \Sigma_{\mathsf{R1}}^! = \Sigma_{\mathsf{R2}}^!$ and $\Sigma_{\mathsf{Ctrl}}^! = \{\mathsf{start}\} = \Sigma_{\mathsf{R1}}^? = \Sigma_{\mathsf{R2}}^?$. We do not consider the internal run action. As in Example 2, we use the STS $\mathsf{st}_{\mathsf{Race}}$ with $\mathsf{st}_{\mathsf{Race}}(\mathsf{start}) = ([1,1],[2,2])$ and $\mathsf{st}_{\mathsf{Race}}(\mathsf{finish}) = ([1,1],[1,1])$. Figure 11 shows on the left the induced interaction set $\Lambda(\Theta_{\mathsf{Race}}, \mathsf{st}_{\mathsf{Race}})$ (abbreviated by Λ_{Race}) and on the right a global interaction model $\mathcal{M}_{\mathsf{Race}}$. It imposes the system to start in a (global) state, where the controller starts both runners at once. Each runner separately sends a finish signal to the controller (in arbitrary order). After that a new run can start. ▷

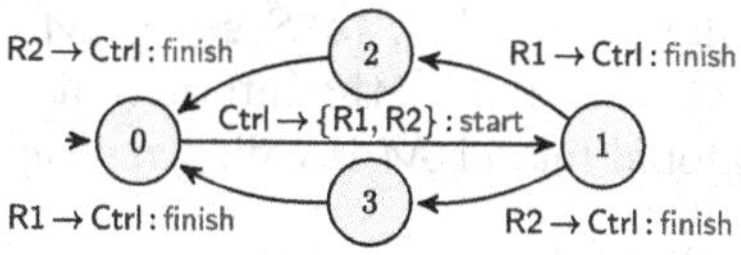

Fig. 11. Interaction set Λ_{Race} and global interaction model $\mathcal{M}_{\mathsf{Race}}$

Remark 1. Our development methodology can be extended by providing first an abstract specification of desired and forbidden interaction properties from a global perspective. In [47], we proposed a propositional dynamic logic for this purpose where interactions are used as atomic actions in modalities such that we can express safety and (a kind of) liveness properties. For instance, we could express the following requirements for the Race system by dynamic logic formulas, using the usual box modalities $[\cdot]$ and $\langle\cdot\rangle$, sequential composition (;), choice (+), and iteration ($\cdot^*$):

1. *"For any started runner, it should be possible to finish her/his run."*
$$\left[some^*; \mathsf{Ctrl} \to \{\mathsf{R1}, \mathsf{R2}\} : \mathsf{start}\right] \begin{pmatrix} \langle some^*; \mathsf{R1} \to \mathsf{Ctrl} : \mathsf{finish}\rangle \ true \ \wedge \\ \langle some^*; \mathsf{R2} \to \mathsf{Ctrl} : \mathsf{finish}\rangle \ true \end{pmatrix}$$
2. *"No runner should finish before she/he was started by the controller."*
$$\left[\left(- (\mathsf{Ctrl} \to \{\mathsf{R1}, \mathsf{R2}\} : \mathsf{start})\right)^* ; \begin{pmatrix} \mathsf{R1} \to \mathsf{Ctrl} : \mathsf{finish} \ + \\ \mathsf{R2} \to \mathsf{Ctrl} : \mathsf{finish} \end{pmatrix}\right] false$$

▷

To check that a global interaction model satisfies a specification, we propose to use the mCRL2 toolset [5,85]. For this purpose, as explained in [36], we can use the translation from LTS models into process expressions and the translation from our interaction-based dynamic logic into the syntax used by mCRL2.

5.2 Realisation of Global Models of Interaction

Our central task concerns the realisation (decomposition) of a global interaction model $\mathcal{M}$ in terms of a (possibly distributed) system $\mathcal{S}$ of component automata which are coordinated according to the given synchronisation type specification.

In order to formulate our realisation notion, we briefly recall the standard notion of bisimulation. Let $\mathcal{L}_n = (Q_n, q_{n,0}, \Sigma, E_n)$ be two LTS (for $n = 1, 2$) over the same action set Σ. A *bisimulation relation* between $\mathcal{L}_1$ and $\mathcal{L}_2$ is a relation $B \subseteq Q_1 \times Q_2$ such that for all $(q_1, q_2) \in B$ and for all $a \in \Sigma$ the following holds:

1. if $q_1 \xrightarrow{a}_{\mathcal{L}_1} q_1'$, then there exist $q_2' \in Q_2$ and $q_2 \xrightarrow{a}_{\mathcal{L}_2} q_2'$ such that $(q_1', q_2') \in B$;
2. if $q_2 \xrightarrow{a}_{\mathcal{L}_2} q_2'$, then there exist $q_1' \in Q_1$ and $q_1 \xrightarrow{a}_{\mathcal{L}_1} q_1'$ such that $(q_1', q_2') \in B$.

$\mathcal{L}_1$ and $\mathcal{L}_2$ are *bisimilar*, denoted by $\mathcal{L}_1 \sim \mathcal{L}_2$, if there exists a bisimulation relation B between $\mathcal{L}_1$ and $\mathcal{L}_2$ such that $(q_{1,0}, q_{2,0}) \in B$.

Now, we assume given a system signature $\Theta = (\mathcal{N}, (\Sigma_n)_{n \in \mathcal{N}})$, an STS **st** and a global interaction model $\mathcal{M}$ with labels $\Lambda(\Theta, \mathbf{st})$. A system $\mathcal{S} = (\mathcal{N}, (\mathcal{A}_n)_{n \in \mathcal{N}})$ of component automata $\mathcal{A}_n$ with actions Σ_n is a *realisation* of $\mathcal{M}$ w.r.t. **st** if the team automaton $\mathbf{ta}(\mathcal{S}, \mathbf{st})$ generated over $\mathcal{S}$ by **st** (as defined in Sect. 2) is bisimilar to $\mathcal{M}$, i.e., $\mathbf{ta}(\mathcal{S}, \mathbf{st}) \sim \mathcal{M}$. We note that the team labels $\Lambda(\mathcal{S}, \mathbf{st})$ of $\mathbf{ta}(\mathcal{S}, \mathbf{st})$ are exactly the interactions in $\Lambda(\Theta, \mathbf{st})$, i.e., the actions of the LTS $\mathcal{M}$. The global model $\mathcal{M}$ is called *realisable* if such a system $\mathcal{S}$ exists.

Remark 2. Technically, the definition of realisability in [47] uses a synchronous Γ-composition $\otimes_\Gamma (\mathcal{A}_n)_{n \in \mathcal{N}}$ [47, Def. 7] of the component automata. Transferred to the context of synchronisation types, Γ would be $\Lambda(\Theta, \mathbf{st})$. Moreover, $\otimes_\Gamma (\mathcal{A}_n)_{n \in \mathcal{N}}$ contains only reachable states, which need not to be the case for the team automaton $\mathbf{ta}(\mathcal{S}, \mathbf{st})$. However, we can restrict $\mathbf{ta}(\mathcal{S}, \mathbf{st})$ to its reachable sub-LTS which coincides with $\otimes_\Gamma (\mathcal{A}_n)_{n \in \mathcal{N}}$. Note also that any LTS is bisimilar to its reachable sub-LTS, such that this restriction does not harm.   ▷

Since our realisability notion relies on bisimulation, we are able to deal with non-deterministic behaviour. Note that, according to the invariance of propositional dynamic logic under bisimulation (cf. [59]), we obtain that global models and their realisations satisfy the same propositional dynamic logic formulas when (multi-)interactions are used as atomic actions as proposed in [36, 47].

Next, we consider the following two important questions:

1. How can we check whether a given global model $\mathcal{M}$ is realisable?
2. If it is, how can we build/synthesise a concrete realisation?

To tackle the first question, we propose to find a family $\equiv = (\equiv_n)_{n \in \mathcal{N}}$ of equivalence relations on the *global* state space Q of $\mathcal{M}$ such that, for each component name $n \in \mathcal{N}$ and states $q, q' \in Q$, $q \equiv_n q'$ expresses that q and q' are indistinguishable from the viewpoint of i. It is required that at least any two global states $q, q' \in Q$ which are related by a global transition $q \xrightarrow{(\mathrm{out}, a, \mathrm{in})}_\mathcal{M} q'$ should be indistinguishable for any $i \in \mathcal{N}$ which does not participate in the interaction, i.e., $q \equiv_n q'$ for all $n \notin \mathrm{out} \cup \mathrm{in}$. A family $\equiv = (\equiv_n)_{n \in \mathcal{N}}$ of equivalence relations $\equiv_n \subseteq Q \times Q$ with this property is called an $\mathcal{N}$-*equivalence*.

We can now formulate our realisability condition for the global model $\mathcal{M} = (Q, q_0, \Lambda(\Theta, \mathbf{st}), E)$. Our goal is to find an $\mathcal{N}$-equivalence $\equiv\, = (\equiv_n)_{n \in \mathcal{N}}$ over $\mathcal{M}$ such that the following *realisability condition* $\mathbf{RC}(\mathcal{M}, \equiv)$ holds.

$\mathbf{RC}(\mathcal{M}, \equiv)$: For each interaction $(\mathsf{out}, a, \mathsf{in}) \in \Lambda(\Theta, \mathbf{st})$, whenever there is (1) a map $\ell : \mathsf{out} \cup \mathsf{in} \to Q$ assigning a global state $q_n = \ell(n)$ to each $n \in \mathsf{out} \cup \mathsf{in}$ together with (2) a global *"glue"* state g, i.e., $q_n \equiv_n g$ for each $n \in \mathsf{out} \cup \mathsf{in}$, then we expect: for all $n \in \mathsf{out} \cup \mathsf{in}$ and global transitions $q_n \xrightarrow{(\mathsf{out}_n, a, \mathsf{in}_n)}_{\mathcal{M}} q_n'$ in which n participates (i.e., $n \in \mathsf{out}_n \cap \mathsf{in}_n$), there is be a global transition $g \xrightarrow{(\mathsf{out}, a, \mathsf{in})}_{\mathcal{M}} g'$ such that $q_n' \equiv_n g'$ for each $n \in \mathsf{out} \cup \mathsf{in}$.

The intuition for this requirement is that if component n can participate in executing an action a in state q_n, then n should also be able to participate in executing a in state g, since n cannot distinguish q_n and g. Because this should hold for all $n \in \mathsf{out} \cup \mathsf{in}$, the interaction $(\mathsf{out}, a, \mathsf{in})$ should be enabled in g and preserve indistinguishability of states for all $n \in \mathsf{out} \cup \mathsf{in}$.

As a consequence of our results in [47], in particular Thm. 3, we obtain that if there is an $\mathcal{N}$-equivalence $\equiv\, = (\equiv_n)_{n \in \mathcal{N}}$ such that the realisability condition $\mathbf{RC}(\mathcal{M}, \equiv)$ holds, then the global model $\mathcal{M} = (Q, q_0, \Lambda(\Theta, \mathbf{st}), E)$ can indeed be realised by the system $\mathcal{S}_{\equiv} = (\mathcal{M}/\equiv_n)_{n \in \mathcal{N}}$ of component automata constructed as local quotients of $\mathcal{M}$, i.e., $\mathbf{ta}(\mathcal{S}_{\equiv}, \mathbf{st}) \sim \mathcal{M}$. More precisely, the *local n-quotient* of $\mathcal{M}$ is the component automaton $\mathcal{M}/\equiv_n = (Q/\equiv_n, [q_0]_{\equiv_n}, \Sigma_n, (E/\equiv_n))$, where

- $Q/\equiv_n\, = \{\, [q]_{\equiv_n} \mid q \in Q \,\}$,
- $E/\equiv_n$ is the least set of transitions generated by the rule

$$\frac{q \xrightarrow{(\mathsf{out}, a, \mathsf{in})}_{\mathcal{M}} q' \qquad n \in \mathsf{out} \cup \mathsf{in}}{[q]_{\equiv_n} \xrightarrow{a}_{(\mathcal{M}/\equiv_n)} [q']_{\equiv_n}}$$

Example 6. Take the global LTS $\mathcal{M}_{\mathsf{Race}}$ in Fig. 11. We use the family of equivalences $\equiv\, = (\equiv_n)_{n \in \{\mathsf{Ctrl}, \mathsf{R1}, \mathsf{R2}\}}$ that obeys $\mathbf{RC}(\mathcal{M}_{\mathsf{Race}}, \equiv)$ (see below) and partitions the state space Q in $Q/\equiv_{\mathsf{Ctrl}} = \{\{0\}, \{1\}, \{2, 3\}\}$, $Q/\equiv_{\mathsf{R1}} = \{\{0, 2\}, \{1, 3\}\}$, and $Q/\equiv_{\mathsf{R2}} = \{\{0, 3\}, \{1, 2\}\}$. Using these equivalences, the local quotients are:

So we obtained a system that is a realisation of $\mathcal{M}_{\mathsf{Race}}$. This means the team automaton $\mathbf{ta}(\mathcal{S}_{\equiv}, \mathbf{st}_{\mathsf{Race}})$ generated by $\mathcal{S}_{\equiv}$ and $\mathbf{st}_{\mathsf{Race}}$ is bisimilar to $\mathcal{M}_{\mathsf{Race}}$. Indeed, both are the same LTS up to renaming of states: state $(\{0\}, \{0, 2\}, \{0, 3\})$ in $\mathbf{ta}(\mathcal{S}_{\equiv}, \mathbf{st}_{\mathsf{Race}})$ instead of state 0 in $\mathcal{M}_{\mathsf{Race}}$, $(\{1\}, \{1, 3\}, \{1, 2\})$ instead of 1, $(\{2, 3\}, \{0, 2\}, \{1, 2\})$ instead of 2, and $(\{2, 3\}, \{1, 3\}, \{0, 3\})$ instead of 3.

We now show how to check $\mathbf{RC}(\mathcal{M}_{\mathsf{Race}}, \equiv)$ using interaction $\mathsf{R1} \to \mathsf{Ctrl} : \mathsf{finish}$ as example. We have $1 \xrightarrow{\mathsf{R1} \to \mathsf{Ctrl} : \mathsf{finish}}_{\mathcal{M}_{\mathsf{Race}}} 2$ and $1 \xrightarrow{\mathsf{R2} \to \mathsf{Ctrl} : \mathsf{finish}}_{\mathcal{M}_{\mathsf{Race}}} 3$. Taking

1 as a (trivial) glue state, we thus have, as required, $1 \xrightarrow{\text{R1} \to \text{Ctrl}:\text{finish}}_{\mathcal{M}_{\text{Race}}} 2$, *but also* it is required that $2 \equiv_{\text{Ctrl}} 3$ must hold, which is the case. Note that we would not have succeeded here if we had taken the identity for $\equiv_{\text{Ctrl}}$. $\triangleright$

Tool Support. We implemented a prototypical tool, called Ceta, to perform realisability checks and system synthesis (cf. [47, 48]). It is open source, available at https://github.com/arcalab/choreo/tree/ceta, and executable by navigating to https://lmf.di.uminho.pt/ceta. It provides a web browser where one can input a global protocol described in a choreographic language, resembling regular expressions of interactions. It offers automatic visualisation of the protocol as a state machine representing a global model and it includes examples with descriptions.

Ceta implements a *constructive* approach to the *declarative* description of the realisability conditions. It builds a family of equivalence relations, starting with one that groups states connected by transitions in which the associate participant is not involved. This family of minimal equivalence relations is checked for satisfaction of the realisability condition w.r.t. the global model. If it fails, a new attempt is started after extending the equivalence relations appropriately. If no failure occurs, then the realisability condition is satisfied and the resulting equivalence classes are used to join equivalent states in the global model, yielding local quotients which can again be visualised. Thus a realisation of the global model is constructed. There are several widgets that provide further insights, such as the intermediate equivalence classes, the synchronous composition of local components, and bisimulations between global models and team automata. Readable error messages are given when a realisability condition does not hold.

5.3   Related Work

Our approach is driven by specified sets of multi-interactions supporting any kind of synchronous communication between multiple senders and multiple receivers. To the best of our knowledge, realisations of global models with arbitrary multi-interactions have not yet been studied in the literature. There are, however, specialised approaches that deal with realisations of global models or decomposition of transition systems. In this section, we first provide a revised and extended comparison of our approach with that of Castellani et al. [73], followed by a brief comparison with other approaches.

Relationship to [73]. Our realisability condition $\mathbf{RC}(\mathcal{M}, \equiv)$, based on the notion of $\mathcal{N}$-equivalence $\equiv$, is strongly related to a condition for implementability in [73, Theorem 3.1]. The main differences are:

1. In [73], there is no distinction between input and output actions.

2. In [73], interactions are always full synchronisations on an action a, while we deal with individual multi-interactions (out, a, in) specified by an STS. Of course, we can also use an STS $\mathbf{st}_{full}$ for full synchronisation. Then we define, for each action a, $\mathbf{st}_{full}(a) = ([\#out(a), \#out(a)], [\#in(a), \#in(a)])$, where $\#out(a) = |\{n \in \mathcal{N} \mid a \in \Sigma_n^!\}|$ is the number of components having a as an output action and $\#in(a) = |\{n \in \mathcal{N} \mid a \in \Sigma_n^?\}|$ is the number of components having a as an input action.

3. In [73], they provide a characterisation of implementability up to isomorphism, while we provide a criterion for realisability modulo bisimulation, thus supporting non-determinism. To achieve this, we basically omitted condition (ii) of [73, Theorem 3.1] which requires that whenever two global states q and q' are n-equivalent for all $n \in \mathcal{N}$, then $q = q'$. In [48, Example 8], we provide a simple example for a global interaction model which satisfies our realisability condition but for which there is no realisation up to isomorphism. Note that [73, Theorem 6.2] provides a proposal to deal with a characterisation of implementability modulo bisimulation under the assumption of deterministic product transition systems. The authors also report on a result to characterise implementability for non-deterministic product systems which uses infinite execution trees and is thus, unfortunately, not effective.

Relationship to Other Approaches

1. Our correctness notion for realisation of global models by systems of communicating local components is based on bisimulation, beyond language-based approaches like [11,72] with realisability expressed by language equivalence.

2. For realisable global models, we construct realisations in terms of systems of local quotients. This technique differs from projections used, e.g., in the field of MPST, where projections are partial operations depending on syntactic conditions (cf., e.g., [58]). In our approach, no restrictions on the form of global models are assumed. On the other hand, the syntactic restrictions used for global types guarantee some kind of communication properties of a resulting system which we consider separately (cf. Sect. 4).

3. There are other papers in the literature in the context of different formalisms dealing with decomposition of port automata [102], Petri nets, or algebraic processes into (indecomposable) components [109,112] used for the efficient verification and parallelisation of concurrent systems [75,86] or to obtain better (optimised) implementations [131,132].

Roadmap

1. Our current realisability approach does not deal with internal actions, which are however also an ingredient of the team automata framework and represented by system labels of the form (n, a) (cf. Sect. 2). They naturally appear when we build a team of CA which have internal actions. We believe, however, that internal actions should not be part of a global interaction model whose purpose is to present the *observable* interaction behaviour of an intended system. To bridge the gap, the idea is to relax the realisation notion by requiring only a weak bisimulation relation between a global model and the team automaton of a system realisation with internal actions.

2. Another aspect concerns the fact that, in general, it may happen that a global interaction model does not satisfy the realisability condition but is nevertheless realisable. Therefore, we want to look for a weaker version of our realisability condition making it necessary and sufficient for realisations based on bisimulation. The following example shows that our current realisability condition is only sufficient.

Example 7. Consider the system signature Θ with component names $\mathcal{N} = \{p, q, r\}$ and with the action sets $\Sigma_n^! = \{a\}, \Sigma_n^? = \varnothing$ for $n \in \mathcal{N}$ and We use the STS with $\mathbf{st}(a) = ([2, 2], [0, 0])$. Then the interaction set is $\Lambda(\Theta, \mathbf{st}) = \{\{p, q\} \to \varnothing : a, \{q, r\} \to \varnothing : a, \{p, r\} \to \varnothing : a\}$. The global model $\mathcal{M}$ in Table 2 (left) is realisable by the system $\mathcal{S} = \{\mathcal{M}_p, \mathcal{M}_q, \mathcal{M}_r\}$, whose CA are shown in Table 2 (middle). To see this, we compute the team automaton $\mathbf{ta}(\mathcal{S}, \mathbf{st})$ shown in Table 2 (right). Obviously, $\mathcal{M}$ and $\mathbf{ta}(\mathcal{S}, \mathbf{st})$ are bisimilar and hence $\mathcal{M}$ is realisable. However, there is no $\mathcal{N}$-equivalence $\equiv$ such that the realisability condition holds. We now prove this by contradiction.

Assume that $\equiv = \{\equiv_p, \equiv_q, \equiv_r\}$ is an $\mathcal{N}$-equivalence such that $\mathbf{RC}(\mathcal{M}, \equiv)$ holds. Now consider the interaction $\{p, q\} \to \varnothing : a$, the global state 0 of $\mathcal{M}$ and the transition $0 \xrightarrow{\{p,q\} \to \varnothing : a}_\mathcal{M} 1$. Obviously, $0 \equiv_p 1$ and $1 \equiv_q 0$ must hold because of the transition $0 \xrightarrow{\{q,r\} \to \varnothing : a}_\mathcal{M} 1$ in which p does not participate and the transition $0 \xrightarrow{\{p,r\} \to \varnothing : a}_\mathcal{M} 1$ in which q does not participate. So we can take 1 as a glue state between the global states $q_1 = 0$ and $q_2 = 0$. Then we consider the interaction $\{p, q\} \to \varnothing : a$ one time for q_1 and one time for q_2. Since we assumed $\mathbf{RC}(\mathcal{M}, \equiv)$, there must be a transition $1 \xrightarrow{\{p,q\} \to \varnothing : a}_\mathcal{M}$ leaving the glue state, which is not the case. Contradiction! $\triangleright$

3. We are interested in a compositional approach to construct larger realisations from smaller ones. Then compositionality of realisability is important.

4. We want to study under which conditions on global models and synchronisation types our communication properties can be guaranteed for realisations.

Table 2. Global $\mathcal{M}$ does not satisfy $\mathbf{RC}(\mathcal{M}, \equiv)$, but $\mathcal{S} = \{\mathcal{M}_p, \mathcal{M}_q, \mathcal{M}_r\}$ realises $\mathcal{M}$

global $\mathcal{M}$	local $\mathcal{M}_p$	local $\mathcal{M}_q$	Local $\mathcal{M}_r$	$\mathbf{ta}(\S, \mathbf{st})$

6 Further Aspects

Recently, we also proposed featured team automata [34] to support *variability* in the development and analysis of teams, capable of concisely capturing a family of concrete product (automaton) models for specific configurations determined by feature selection, as is common in software product line engineering [1]. Variability has also been studied for several related coordination models, such as BIP [104,111], Contract automata [15,16,19], Reo [120], Petri nets [113,114], and I/O automata [106,108]. We did not address *data*, for which Reo and BIP provide native support, since team automata cannot currently deal with that.

In the past, we studied in detail the computations and behaviour of team automata in relation to that of their constituting component automata [49,51], identifying several types of team automata that satisfy *compositionality* in terms of (synchronised) shuffles of their computations (i.e., formal languages). In [42, 43], a process calculus for modelling team automata was introduced, extending some classical results on I/O automata as well as the family of team automata that guarantee a degree of compositionality. Finally, team automata were used for the analysis of *security* aspects in communication protocols [29,54,55,81], in particular for spatial and spatio-temporal access control [40,94].

7 Conclusion

We provided an overview of team automata, a model for capturing a variety of notions related to coordination in distributed systems of systems with decades of history (cf. Appendix A) as witnessed by 25+ publications by 25+ researchers,[3] and compared them rather informally with related models for coordination (cf. Table 1). A single running example modelled in the various formalisms eases their comparison. We focused on differences in synchronisation and composition, but also addressed communication properties, realisability, verification, and tool support—all aspects we investigated during the last five years. Team automata support very flexible types of synchronous communication. They are

---

[3] http://fmt.isti.cnr.it/~mtbeek/TA.html.

not designed for asynchronous communication (yet), like asynchronous multiparty session types [92] or systems of communicating finite state machines [66], for which other kinds of compositions and communication properties are relevant [9].

Acknowledgements. We thank Davide Basile, Simon Bliudze and the three anonymous reviewers for their comments and suggestions that helped us to improve this paper.

Maurice ter Beek was funded by MUR PRIN 2020TL3X8X project T-LADIES (Typeful Language Adaptation for Dynamic, Interacting and Evolving Systems) and CNR project "Formal Methods in Software Engineering 2.0", CUP B53C24000720005.

José Proença was supported by the CISTER Research Unit (UIDP/UIDB/04234/2020), financed by National Funds through FCT/MCTES (Portuguese Foundation for Science and Technology), and by project IBEX (PTDC/CCI-COM/4280/2021) financed by national funds through FCT.

A   Selected Publications from 25+ Years of Team Automata

Year		Title	Venue
2023	[47]	Realisability of Global Models of Interaction	ICTAC'23
2023	[119]	Overview on Constrained Multiparty Synchronisation in Team Automata	FACS'23
2023	[36]	Can we Communicate? Using Dynamic Logic to Verify Team Automata	FM'23
2021	[34]	Featured Team Automata	FM'21
2020	[46]	Team Automata@Work: On Safe Communication	COORDINATION'20
2020	[44]	Compositionality of Safe Communication in Systems of Team Automata	ICTAC'20
2017	[31]	Communication Requirements for Team Automata	COORDINATION'17
2016	[32]	Conditions for Compatibility of Components: The Case of Masters and Slaves	ISoLA'16
2014	[53]	On Distributed Cooperation and Synchronised Collaboration	JALC
2013	[69]	Compatibility in a multi-component environment	TCS
2012	[52]	Vector Team Automata	TCS
2010	[94]	Team Automata Based Framework for Spatio-Temporal RBAC Model	BAIP'10
2009	[51]	Associativity of Infinite Synchronized Shuffles and Team Automata	Fundam. Inform.
2008	[128]	Extending Team Automata to Evaluate Software Architectural Design	COMPSAC'08

Year		Title	Venue
2008	[43]	A calculus for team automata	ENTCS
2007	[129]	A Review on Specifying Software Architectures Using Extended Automata-Based Models	FSEN'07
2006	[81]	Modelling a Secure Agent with Team Automata	ENTCS
2006	[55]	A Team Automaton Scenario for the Analysis of Security Properties in Communication Protocols	JALC
2005	[54]	Team Automata for Security – A Survey –	ENTCS
2005	[50]	Modularity for Teams of I/O Automata	IPL
2004	[37]	Teams of Pushdown Automata	IJCM
2004	[68]	Interactive Behaviour of Multi-Component Systems	Workshop
2003	[30]	Team Automata: A Formal Approach to the Modeling of Collaboration Between System Components	PhD thesis
2003	[49]	Team Automata Satisfying Compositionality	FME'03
2003	[29]	Team Automata for Security Analysis of Multicast/Broadcast Communication	Workshop
2003	[100]	Team Automata for CSCW – A Survey –	LNCS
2003	[41]	Synchronizations in Team Automata for Groupware Systems	CSCW
2002	[83]	Towards Team-Automata-Driven Object-Oriented Collaborative Work	LNCS
2001	[40]	Team Automata for Spatial Access Control	ECSCW'01
2001	[39]	Team Automata for CSCW	Workshop
2000	[91]	A Conflict-Free Strategy for Team-Based Model Development	Workshop
1999	[38]	Synchronizations in Team Automata for Groupware Systems	Tech. Rep.
1997	[82]	Team Automata for Groupware Systems	GROUP'97

References

1. Apel, S., Batory, D., Kästner, C., Saake, G.: Feature-Oriented Software Product Lines: Concepts and Implementation. Springer, Heidelberg (2013). https://doi.org/10.1007/978-3-642-37521-7

2. Arbab, F.: Reo: a channel-based coordination model for component composition. Math. Struct. Comput. Sci. **14**(3), 329–366 (2004). https://doi.org/10.1017/S0960129504004153

3. Arbab, F., Kokash, N., Meng, S.: Towards using Reo for compliance-aware business process modeling. In: Margaria, T., Steffen, B. (eds.) ISoLA 2008. CCIS, vol. 17, pp. 108–123. Springer, Heidelberg (2008). https://doi.org/10.1007/978-3-540-88479-8_9

4. Arbab, F., Krause, C., Maraikar, Z., Moon, Y.J., Proença, J.: Modeling, testing and executing Reo connectors with the Eclipse coordination tools. Tool demo session of FACS 2008 (2008)

5. Atif, M., Groote, J.F.: Understanding Behaviour of Distributed Systems Using mCRL2. Springer, Cham (2023). https://doi.org/10.1007/978-3-031-23008-0

6. Attie, P.C., Bensalem, S., Bozga, M., Jaber, M., Sifakis, J., Zaraket, F.A.: Global and local deadlock freedom in BIP. ACM Trans. Softw. Eng. Methodol. **26**(3), 9:1–9:48 (2018). https://doi.org/10.1145/3152910

7. Baier, C., Sirjani, M., Arbab, F., Rutten, J.J.M.M.: Modeling component connectors in Reo by constraint automata. Sci. Comput. Program. **61**(2), 75–113 (2006). https://doi.org/10.1016/J.SCICO.2005.10.008

8. Baranov, E., Bliudze, S.: Expressiveness of component-based frameworks: a study of the expressiveness of BIP. Acta Inform. **57**, 761–800 (2020). https://doi.org/10.1007/s00236-019-00337-7

9. Barbanera, F., de'Liguoro, U., Hennicker, R.: Connecting open systems of communicating finite state machines. J. Log. Algebr. Methods Program. **109** (2019). https://doi.org/10.1016/j.jlamp.2019.07.004

10. Barbanera, F., Lanese, I., Tuosto, E.: Choreography automata. In: Bliudze, S., Bocchi, L. (eds.) COORDINATION 2020. LNCS, vol. 12134, pp. 86–106. Springer, Cham (2020). https://doi.org/10.1007/978-3-030-50029-0_6

11. Barbanera, F., Lanese, I., Tuosto, E.: Formal choreographic languages. In: ter Beek, M.H., Sirjani, M. (eds.) COORDINATION 2022. LNCS, vol. 13271, pp. 121–139. Springer, Cham (2022). https://doi.org/10.1007/978-3-031-08143-9_8

12. Barbanera, F., Lanese, I., Tuosto, E.: A theory of formal choreographic languages. Log. Meth. Comp. Sci. **19**(3), 9:1–9:36 (2023). https://doi.org/10.46298/LMCS-19(3:9)2023

13. Bartoletti, M., Cimoli, T., Zunino, R.: Compliance in behavioural contracts: a brief survey. In: Bodei, C., Ferrari, G.-L., Priami, C. (eds.) Programming Languages with Applications to Biology and Security. LNCS, vol. 9465, pp. 103–121. Springer, Cham (2015). https://doi.org/10.1007/978-3-319-25527-9_9

14. Basile, D., ter Beek, M.H.: Contract automata library. Sci. Comput. Program. **221** (2022). https://doi.org/10.1016/j.scico.2022.102841

15. Basile, D., et al.: Controller synthesis of service contracts with variability. Sci. Comput. Program. **187** (2020). https://doi.org/10.1016/j.scico.2019.102344

16. Basile, D., ter Beek, M.H., Di Giandomenico, F., Gnesi, S.: Orchestration of dynamic service product lines with featured modal contract automata. In: Proceedings of the 21st International Systems and Software Product Line Conference (SPLC 2017), vol. 2, pp. 117–122. ACM (2017). https://doi.org/10.1145/3109729.3109741

17. Basile, D., ter Beek, M.H., Legay, A.: Timed service contract automata. Innov. Syst. Softw. Eng. **2**(16), 199–214 (2020). https://doi.org/10.1007/s11334-019-00353-3

18. Basile, D., Degano, P., Ferrari, G.L.: Automata for specifying and orchestrating service contracts. Log. Meth. Comp. Sci. **12**(4:6), 1–51 (2016). https://doi.org/10.2168/LMCS-12(4:6)2016

19. Basile, D., Di Giandomenico, F., Gnesi, S., Degano, P., Ferrari, G.L.: Specifying variability in service contracts. In: Proceedings of the 11th International Workshop on Variability Modelling of Software-intensive Systems (VaMoS 2017), pp. 20–27. ACM (2017). https://doi.org/10.1145/3023956.3023965

20. Basile, D., ter Beek, M.H.: A clean and efficient implementation of choreography synthesis for behavioural contracts. In: Damiani, F., Dardha, O. (eds.) COORDINATION 2021. LNCS, vol. 12717, pp. 225–238. Springer, Cham (2021). https://doi.org/10.1007/978-3-030-78142-2_14

21. Basile, D., ter Beek, M.H.: Advancing orchestration synthesis for contract automata. J. Log. Algebr. Methods Program. (2024)

22. Basile, D., ter Beek, M.H., Pugliese, R.: Bridging the gap between supervisory control and coordination of services: synthesis of orchestrations and choreographies. In: Riis Nielson, H., Tuosto, E. (eds.) COORDINATION 2019. LNCS, vol. 11533, pp. 129–147. Springer, Cham (2019). https://doi.org/10.1007/978-3-030-22397-7_8

23. Basile, D., ter Beek, M.H., Pugliese, R.: Synthesis of orchestrations and choreographies: bridging the gap between supervisory control and coordination of services. Log. Meth. Comp. Sci. **16**(2), 9:1–9:29 (2020). https://doi.org/10.23638/LMCS-16(2:9)2020

24. Basile, D., Degano, P., Ferrari, G., Tuosto, E.: From orchestration to choreography through contract automata. In: Lanese, I., Lluch Lafuente, A., Sokolova, A., Torres Vieira, H. (eds.) Proceedings of the 7th Interaction and Concurrency Experience (ICE 2014). EPTCS, vol. 166, pp. 67–85 (2014). https://doi.org/10.4204/EPTCS.166.8

25. Basile, D., Degano, P., Ferrari, G., Tuosto, E.: Relating two automata-based models of orchestration and choreography. J. Log. Algebr. Methods Program. **85**(3), 425–446 (2016). https://doi.org/10.1016/J.JLAMP.2015.09.011

26. Basu, A., Bozga, M., Sifakis, J.: Modeling heterogeneous real-time components in BIP. In: Proceedings of the 4th IEEE International Conference on Software Engineering and Formal Methods (SEFM 2006), pp. 3–12. IEEE (2006). https://doi.org/10.1109/SEFM.2006.27

27. Basu, A., et al.: Rigorous component-based system design using the BIP framework. IEEE Softw. **28**(3), 41–48 (2011). https://doi.org/10.1109/MS.2011.27

28. Bauer, S.S., Mayer, P., Schroeder, A., Hennicker, R.: On weak modal compatibility, refinement, and the MIO workbench. In: Esparza, J., Majumdar, R. (eds.) TACAS 2010. LNCS, vol. 6015, pp. 175–189. Springer, Heidelberg (2010). https://doi.org/10.1007/978-3-642-12002-2_15

29. ter Beek, M., Lenzini, G., Petrocchi, M.: Team Automata for Security Analysis of Multicast/Broadcast Communication. In: Proceedings of the ICATPN Workshop on Issues in Security and Petri Nets (WISP 2003). pp. 57–71. Eindhoven University of Technology (2003)

30. ter Beek, M.H.: Team automata—a formal approach to the modeling of collaboration between system components. Ph.D. thesis, Leiden University (2003). https://hdl.handle.net/1887/29570

31. ter Beek, M.H., Carmona, J., Hennicker, R., Kleijn, J.: Communication requirements for team automata. In: Jacquet, J.-M., Massink, M. (eds.) COORDINATION 2017. LNCS, vol. 10319, pp. 256–277. Springer, Cham (2017). https://doi.org/10.1007/978-3-319-59746-1_14

32. ter Beek, M.H., Carmona, J., Kleijn, J.: Conditions for compatibility of components. In: Margaria, T., Steffen, B. (eds.) ISoLA 2016. LNCS, vol. 9952, pp. 784–805. Springer, Cham (2016). https://doi.org/10.1007/978-3-319-47166-2_55

33. ter Beek, M.H., Cledou, G., Hennicker, R., Proença, J.: Featured team automata. Technical report, arXiv (2021). https://doi.org/10.48550/arXiv.2108.01784

34. ter Beek, M.H., Cledou, G., Hennicker, R., Proença, J.: Featured team automata. In: Huisman, M., Păsăreanu, C., Zhan, N. (eds.) FM 2021. LNCS, vol. 13047, pp. 483–502. Springer, Cham (2021). https://doi.org/10.1007/978-3-030-90870-6_26

35. ter Beek, M.H., Cledou, G., Hennicker, R., Proença, J.: Can we communicate? Using dynamic logic to verify team automata (extended version). Technical report, Zenodo (2022). https://doi.org/10.5281/zenodo.7418074

36. ter Beek, M.H., Cledou, G., Hennicker, R., Proença, J.: Can we communicate? Using dynamic logic to verify team automata. In: Chechik, M., Katoen, J.P., Leucker, M. (eds.) FM 2023. LNCS, vol. 14000, pp. 122–141. Springer, Cham (2023). https://doi.org/10.1007/978-3-031-27481-7_9

37. ter Beek, M.H., Csuhaj-Varjú, E., Mitrana, V.: Teams of pushdown automata. Int. J. Comput. Math. **81**(2), 141–156 (2004). https://doi.org/10.1080/00207160310001650099

38. ter Beek, M.H., Ellis, C.A., Kleijn, J., Rozenberg, G.: Synchronizations in team automata for groupware systems. Technical report, TR-99-12, Leiden Institute of Advanced Computer Science, Leiden University (1999)

39. ter Beek, M.H., Ellis, C.A., Kleijn, J., Rozenberg, G.: Team automata for CSCW. In: Proceedings of the 2nd International Colloquium on Petri Net Technologies for Modelling Communication Based Systems, pp. 1–20. Fraunhofer ISST (2001)

40. ter Beek, M.H., Ellis, C.A., Kleijn, J., Rozenberg, G.: Team automata for spatial access control. In: Prinz, W., Jarke, M., Rogers, Y., Schmidt, K., Wulf, V. (eds.) Proceedings of the 7th European Conference on Computer-Supported Cooperative Work (ECSCW 2001), pp. 59–77. Kluwer (2001). https://doi.org/10.1007/0-306-48019-0_4

41. ter Beek, M.H., Ellis, C.A., Kleijn, J., Rozenberg, G.: Synchronizations in team automata for groupware systems. Comput. Sup. Coop. Work 12(1), 21–69 (2003). https://doi.org/10.1023/A:1022407907596

42. ter Beek, M.H., Gadducci, F., Janssens, D.: A calculus for team automata. In: Ribeiro, L., Moreira, A.M. (eds.) Proceedings of the 9th Brazilian Symposium on Formal Methods (SBMF 2006), pp. 59–72. Istituto de Informatica da UFRGS, Porto Alegre (2006)

43. ter Beek, M.H., Gadducci, F., Janssens, D.: A calculus for team automata. Electron. Notes Theor. Comput. Sci. 195, 41–55 (2008). https://doi.org/10.1016/j.entcs.2007.08.022

44. ter Beek, M.H., Hennicker, R., Kleijn, J.: Compositionality of safe communication in systems of team automata. In: Pun, V.K.I., Stolz, V., Simao, A. (eds.) ICTAC 2020. LNCS, vol. 12545, pp. 200–220. Springer, Cham (2020). https://doi.org/10.1007/978-3-030-64276-1_11

45. ter Beek, M.H., Hennicker, R., Kleijn, J.: Compositionality of safe communication in systems of team automata. Technical report, Zenodo (2020). https://doi.org/10.5281/zenodo.4050293

46. ter Beek, M.H., Hennicker, R., Kleijn, J.: Team Automata@Work: on safe communication. In: Bliudze, S., Bocchi, L. (eds.) COORDINATION 2020. LNCS, vol. 12134, pp. 77–85. Springer, Cham (2020). https://doi.org/10.1007/978-3-030-50029-0_5

47. ter Beek, M.H., Hennicker, R., Proença, J.: Realisability of global models of interaction. In: Ábrahám, E., Dubslaff, C., Tapia Tarifa, S.L. (eds.) ICTAC 2023. LNCS, vol. 14446, pp. 236–255. Springer, Cham (2023). https://doi.org/10.1007/978-3-031-47963-2_15

48. ter Beek, M.H., Hennicker, R., Proença, J.: Realisability of global models of interaction (extended version). Technical report, Zenodo (2023). https://doi.org/10.5281/zenodo.8377188

49. ter Beek, M.H., Kleijn, J.: Team automata satisfying compositionality. In: Araki, K., Gnesi, S., Mandrioli, D. (eds.) FME 2003. LNCS, vol. 2805, pp. 381–400. Springer, Heidelberg (2003). https://doi.org/10.1007/978-3-540-45236-2_22

50. ter Beek, M.H., Kleijn, J.: Modularity for teams of I/O automata. Inf. Process. Lett. 95(5), 487–495 (2005). https://doi.org/10.1016/j.ipl.2005.05.012

51. ter Beek, M.H., Kleijn, J.: Associativity of infinite synchronized shuffles and team automata. Fundam. Inform. 91(3–4), 437–461 (2009). https://doi.org/10.3233/FI-2009-0051

52. ter Beek, M.H., Kleijn, J.: Vector team automata. Theor. Comput. Sci. 429, 21–29 (2012). https://doi.org/10.1016/j.tcs.2011.12.020

53. ter Beek, M.H., Kleijn, J.: On distributed cooperation and synchronised collaboration. J. Autom. Lang. Comb. **19**(1-4), 17–32 (2014). https://doi.org/10.25596/jalc-2014-017

54. ter Beek, M.H., Lenzini, G., Petrocchi, M.: Team automata for security – a survey. Electron. Notes Theor. Comput. Sci. **128**, 105–119 (2005). https://doi.org/10.1016/j.entcs.2004.11.044

55. ter Beek, M.H., Lenzini, G., Petrocchi, M.: A team automaton scenario for the analysis of security properties in communication protocols. J. Autom. Lang. Comb. **11**(4), 345–374 (2006). https://doi.org/10.25596/jalc-2006-345

56. ter Beek, M.H., Cledou, G., Hennicker, R., Proença, J.: Can we Communicate? Using Dynamic Logic to Verify Team Automata (Software Artefact) (2022). https://doi.org/10.5281/zenodo.7338440. http://arcatools.org/feta

57. Behrmann, G., David, A., Larsen, K.G.: A tutorial on UPPAAL. In: Bernardo, M., Corradini, F. (eds.) SFM-RT 2004. LNCS, vol. 3185, pp. 200–236. Springer, Heidelberg (2004). https://doi.org/10.1007/978-3-540-30080-9_7

58. Bejleri, A., Yoshida, N.: Synchronous multiparty session types. Electr. Notes Theor. Comput. Sci. **241**, 3–33 (2008). https://doi.org/10.1016/j.entcs.2009.06.002

59. van Benthem, J., van Eijck, J., Stebletsova, V.: Modal logic, transition systems and processes. J. Log. Comput. **4**(5), 811–855 (1994). https://doi.org/10.1093/logcom/4.5.811

60. Best, E., Devillers, R.: Petri Net Primer: A Compendium on the Core Model, Analysis, and Synthesis. Springer, Cham (2024). https://doi.org/10.1007/978-3-031-48278-6

61. Bliudze, S., van den Bos, P., Huisman, M., Rubbens, R., Safina, L.: JavaBIP meets VerCors: towards the safety of concurrent software systems in Java. In: Lambers, L., Uchitel, S. (eds.) FASE 2023. LNCS, vol. 13991, pp. 143–150. Springer, Cham (2023). https://doi.org/10.1007/978-3-031-30826-0_8

62. Bliudze, S., et al.: Formal verification of infinite-state BIP models. In: Finkbeiner, B., Pu, G., Zhang, L. (eds.) ATVA 2015. LNCS, vol. 9364, pp. 326–343. Springer, Cham (2015). https://doi.org/10.1007/978-3-319-24953-7_25

63. Bliudze, S., Mavridou, A., Szymanek, R., Zolotukhina, A.: Exogenous coordination of concurrent software components with JavaBIP. Softw. Pract. Exper. **47**(11), 1801–1836 (2017). https://doi.org/10.1002/spe.2495

64. Bliudze, S., Sifakis, J.: The algebra of connectors: structuring interaction in BIP. IEEE Trans. Comput. **57**(10), 1315–1330 (2008). https://doi.org/10.1109/TC.2008.26

65. Bordeaux, L., Salaün, G., Berardi, D., Mecella, M.: When are two web services compatible? In: Shan, M.-C., Dayal, U., Hsu, M. (eds.) TES 2004. LNCS, vol. 3324, pp. 15–28. Springer, Heidelberg (2005). https://doi.org/10.1007/978-3-540-31811-8_2

66. Brand, D., Zafiropulo, P.: On communicating finite-state machines. J. ACM **30**(2), 323–342 (1983). https://doi.org/10.1145/322374.322380

67. Brim, L., Cerná, I., Vareková, P., Zimmerova, B.: Component-interaction automata as a verification-oriented component-based system specification. ACM Softw. Eng. Notes **31**(2) (2006). https://doi.org/10.1145/1118537.1123063

68. Carmona, J., Kleijn, J.: Interactive behaviour of multi-component systems. In: Proceedings of the ICATPN Workshop on Token-Based Computing (ToBaCo 2004), pp. 27–31. Università di Bologna (2004)

69. Carmona, J., Kleijn, J.: Compatibility in a multi-component environment. Theor. Comput. Sci. **484**, 1–15 (2013). https://doi.org/10.1016/j.tcs.2013.03.006

70. Carmona, J., Cortadella, J.: Input/Output compatibility of reactive systems. In: Aagaard, M.D., O'Leary, J.W. (eds.) FMCAD 2002. LNCS, vol. 2517, pp. 360–377. Springer, Heidelberg (2002). https://doi.org/10.1007/3-540-36126-X_22

71. Castagna, G., Gesbert, N., Padovani, L.: A theory of contracts for web services. ACM Trans. Program. Lang. Syst. **31**(5), 19:1–19:61 (2009). https://doi.org/10.1145/1538917.1538920

72. Castagna, G., Dezani-Ciancaglini, M., Padovani, L.: On global types and multiparty sessions. Log. Meth. Comp. Sci. **8**(1), 24:1–24:45 (2012). https://doi.org/10.2168/LMCS-8(1:24)2012

73. Castellani, I., Mukund, M., Thiagarajan, P.S.: Synthesizing distributed transition systems from global specifications. In: Rangan, C.P., Raman, V., Ramanujam, R. (eds.) FSTTCS 1999. LNCS, vol. 1738, pp. 219–231. Springer, Heidelberg (1999). https://doi.org/10.1007/3-540-46691-6_17

74. Clarke, D.: Coordination: Reo, nets, and logic. In: de Boer, F.S., Bonsangue, M.M., Graf, S., de Roever, W.-P. (eds.) FMCO 2007. LNCS, vol. 5382, pp. 226–256. Springer, Heidelberg (2008). https://doi.org/10.1007/978-3-540-92188-2_10

75. Corradini, F., Gorrieri, R., Marchignoli, D.: Towards parallelization of concurrent systems. RAIRO Theor. Informatics Appl. **32**(4–6), 99–125 (1998). https://doi.org/10.1051/ita/1998324-600991

76. Cruz, R., Proença, J.: ReoLive: analysing connectors in your browser. In: Mazzara, M., Ober, I., Salaün, G. (eds.) STAF 2018. LNCS, vol. 11176, pp. 336–350. Springer, Cham (2018). https://doi.org/10.1007/978-3-030-04771-9_25

77. de Alfaro, L., Henzinger, T.A.: Interface automata. In: Proceedings of the 8th European Software Engineering Conference held jointly with 9th ACM SIGSOFT International Symposium on Foundations of Software Engineering (ESEC/FSE 2001), pp. 109–120. ACM (2001). https://doi.org/10.1145/503209.503226

78. Dokter, K., Arbab, F.: Treo: textual syntax for Reo connectors. In: Bliudze, S., Bensalem, S. (eds.) Proceedings of the 1st International Workshop on Methods and Tools for Rigorous System Design (MeTRiD 2018). EPTCS, vol. 272, pp. 121–135 (2018). https://doi.org/10.4204/EPTCS.272.10

79. Durán, F., Ouederni, M., Salaün, G.: A generic framework for n-protocol compatibility checking. Sci. Comput. Program. **77**(7–8), 870–886 (2012). https://doi.org/10.1016/j.scico.2011.03.009

80. Edixhoven, L., Jongmans, S.S., Proença, J., Castellani, I.: Branching pomsets: design, expressiveness and applications to choreographies. J. Log. Algebr. Methods Program. **136** (2024). https://doi.org/10.1016/j.jlamp.2023.100919

81. Egidi, L., Petrocchi, M.: Modelling a secure agent with team automata. Electron. Notes Theor. Comput. Sci. **142**, 111–127 (2006). https://doi.org/10.1016/j.entcs.2004.12.046

82. Ellis, C.A.: Team automata for groupware systems. In: Proceedings of the International ACM SIGGROUP Conference on Supporting Group Work: The Integration Challenge (GROUP 1997), pp. 415–424. ACM (1997). https://doi.org/10.1145/266838.267363

83. Engels, G., Groenewegen, L.: Towards team-automata-driven object-oriented collaborative work. In: Brauer, W., Ehrig, H., Karhumäki, J., Salomaa, A. (eds.) Formal and Natural Computing. LNCS, vol. 2300, pp. 257–276. Springer, Heidelberg (2002). https://doi.org/10.1007/3-540-45711-9_15

84. Gössler, G., Sifakis, J.: Composition for component-based modeling. Sci. Comput. Program. **55**, 161–183 (2005). https://doi.org/10.1016/j.scico.2004.05.014

85. Groote, J.F., Mousavi, M.R.: Modeling and Analysis of Communicating Systems. MIT Press, Cambridge (2014)

86. Groote, J.F., Moller, F.: Verification of parallel systems via decomposition. In: Cleaveland, R. (ed.) CONCUR 1992. LNCS, vol. 630, pp. 62–76. Springer, Heidelberg (1992). https://doi.org/10.1007/BFb0084783

87. Guanciale, R., Tuosto, E.: Realisability of pomsets. J. Log. Algebr. Methods Program. **108**, 69–89 (2019). https://doi.org/10.1016/J.JLAMP.2019.06.003

88. Harel, D., Kozen, D., Tiuryn, J.: Dynamic Logic. Foundations of Computing. MIT Press, Cambridge (2000). https://doi.org/10.7551/mitpress/2516.001.0001

89. Harel, D., Thiagarajan, P.S.: Message sequence charts. In: Lavagno, L., Martin, G., Selic, B. (eds.) UML for Real: Design of Embedded Real-Time Systems, pp. 77–105. Kluwer (2003). https://doi.org/10.1007/0-306-48738-1_4

90. Hennicker, R., Bidoit, M.: Compatibility properties of synchronously and asynchronously communicating components. Log. Meth. Comp. Sci. **14**(1), 1–31 (2018). https://doi.org/10.23638/LMCS-14(1:1)2018

91. 't Hoen, P.J., ter Beek, M.H.: A conflict-free strategy for team-based model development. In: Proceedings of the International Workshop on Process support for Distributed Team-based Software Development (PDTSD 2000), pp. 720–725. IIIS (2000)

92. Honda, K., Yoshida, N., Carbone, M.: Multiparty asynchronous session types. In: POPL 2008, pp. 273–284. ACM (2008). https://doi.org/10.1145/1328438.1328472

93. International Telecommunication Union (ITU): Message Sequence Chart (MSC). Recommendation ITU-T Z.120 (2011). http://www.itu.int/rec/T-REC-Z.120

94. Jaisankar, N., Veeramalai, S., Kannan, A.: Team automata based framework for spatio-temporal RBAC model. In: Das, V.V., et al. (eds.) BAIP 2010. CCIS, vol. 70, pp. 586–591. Springer, Heidelberg (2010). https://doi.org/10.1007/978-3-642-12214-9_106

95. Ji, Z., Wang, S., Xu, X.: Session types with multiple senders single receiver. In: Hermanns, H., Sun, J., Bu, L. (eds.) SETTA 2023. LNCS, vol. 14464, pp. 112–131. Springer, Cham (2023). https://doi.org/10.1007/978-981-99-8664-4_7

96. Jongmans, S.S.T.Q., Arbab, F.: Overview of thirty semantic formalisms for Reo. Sci. Ann. Comput. Sci. **22**(1), 201–251 (2012). https://doi.org/10.7561/SACS.2012.1.201

97. Jonsson, B.: Compositional verification of distributed systems. Ph.D. thesis, Uppsala University (1987)

98. Katoen, J.P., Lambert, L.: Pomsets for message sequence charts. In: Lahav, Y., Wolisz, A., Fischer, J., Holz, E. (eds.) Proceedings of the 1st Workshop of the SDL Forum Society on SDL and MSC (SAM 1998), pp. 197–207. Humboldt-Universität zu Berlin (1998)

99. Kaynar, D.K., Lynch, N., Segala, R., Vaandrager, F.: The Theory of Timed I/O Automata, 2 edn. Synthesis Lectures on Distributed Computing Theory. Springer, Cham (2010). https://doi.org/10.1007/978-3-031-02003-2

100. Kleijn, J.: Team automata for CSCW – a survey. In: Ehrig, H., Reisig, W., Rozenberg, G., Weber, H. (eds.) Petri Net Technology for Communication-Based Systems. LNCS, vol. 2472, pp. 295–320. Springer, Heidelberg (2003). https://doi.org/10.1007/978-3-540-40022-6_15

101. Klein, J., Klüppelholz, S., Stam, A., Baier, C.: Hierarchical modeling and formal verification. an industrial case study using Reo and Vereofy. In: Salaün, G., Schätz, B. (eds.) FMICS 2011. LNCS, vol. 6959, pp. 228–243. Springer, Heidelberg (2011). https://doi.org/10.1007/978-3-642-24431-5_17

102. Koehler, C., Clarke, D.: Decomposing port automata. In: Shin, S.Y., Ossowski, S. (eds.) Proceedings of the 24th ACM Symposium on Applied Computing (SAC 2009), pp. 1369–1373. ACM (2009). https://doi.org/10.1145/1529282.1529587

103. Kokash, N., Krause, C., de Vink, E.P.: Data-aware design and verification of service compositions with Reo and mCRL2. In: Proceedings of the 25th ACM Symposium on Applied Computing (SAC 2010), pp. 2406–2413. ACM (2010). https://doi.org/10.1145/1774088.1774590

104. Konnov, I.V., Kotek, T., Wang, Q., Veith, H., Bliudze, S., Sifakis, J.: Parameterized systems in BIP: design and model checking. In: Desharnais, J., Jagadeesan, R. (eds.) CONCUR 2016. LIPIcs, vol. 59, pp. 30:1–30:16. Schloss Dagstuhl - Leibniz-Zentrum für Informatik (2016). https://doi.org/10.4230/LIPICS.CONCUR.2016.30

105. Lange, J., Tuosto, E., Yoshida, N.: From communicating machines to graphical choreographies. In: Proceedings of the 42nd ACM SIGPLAN-SIGACT Symposium on Principles of Programming Languages (POPL 2015), pp. 221–232. ACM (2015). https://doi.org/10.1145/2676726.2676964

106. Larsen, K.G., Nyman, U., Wąsowski, A.: Modal I/O automata for interface and product line theories. In: De Nicola, R. (ed.) ESOP 2007. LNCS, vol. 4421, pp. 64–79. Springer, Heidelberg (2007). https://doi.org/10.1007/978-3-540-71316-6_6

107. Guldstrand Larsen, K., Lorber, F., Nielsen, B.: 20 years of *real* real time model validation. In: Havelund, K., Peleska, J., Roscoe, B., de Vink, E. (eds.) FM 2018. LNCS, vol. 10951, pp. 22–36. Springer, Cham (2018). https://doi.org/10.1007/978-3-319-95582-7_2

108. Lauenroth, K., Pohl, K., Töhning, S.: Model checking of domain artifacts in product line engineering. In: Proceedings of the 24th International Conference on Automated Software Engineering (ASE 2009), pp. 269–280. IEEE (2009). https://doi.org/10.1109/ASE.2009.16

109. Luttik, B.: Unique parallel decomposition in branching and weak bisimulation semantics. Theor. Comput. Sci. **612**, 29–44 (2016). https://doi.org/10.1016/j.tcs.2015.10.013

110. Lynch, N.A., Tuttle, M.R.: An introduction to Input/Output automata. CWI Q. **2**(3), 219–246 (1989). https://ir.cwi.nl/pub/18164

111. Mavridou, A., Baranov, E., Bliudze, S., Sifakis, J.: Architecture diagrams: a graphical language for architecture style specification. In: Proceedings of the 9th Interaction and Concurrency Experience (ICE 2016). EPTCS, vol. 223, pp. 83–97 (2016). https://doi.org/10.4204/EPTCS.223.6

112. Milner, R., Moller, F.: Unique decomposition of processes. Theor. Comput. Sci. **107**(2), 357–363 (1993). https://doi.org/10.1016/0304-3975(93)90176-T

113. Muschevici, R., Proença, J., Clarke, D.: Modular modelling of software product lines with feature nets. In: Barthe, G., Pardo, A., Schneider, G. (eds.) SEFM 2011. LNCS, vol. 7041, pp. 318–333. Springer, Heidelberg (2011). https://doi.org/10.1007/978-3-642-24690-6_22

114. Muschevici, R., Proença, J., Clarke, D.: Feature nets: behavioural modelling of software product lines. Softw. Sys. Model. **15**(4), 1181–1206 (2016). https://doi.org/10.1007/s10270-015-0475-z

115. Nielsen, M., Plotkin, G.D., Winskel, G.: Petri nets, event structures and domains. Part I. Theor. Comput. Sci. **13**, 85–108 (1981). https://doi.org/10.1016/0304-3975(81)90112-2

116. Oheimb, D.: Interacting state machines: a stateful approach to proving security. In: Abdallah, A.E., Ryan, P., Schneider, S. (eds.) FASec 2002. LNCS, vol. 2629, pp. 15–32. Springer, Heidelberg (2003). https://doi.org/10.1007/978-3-540-40981-6_4

117. Orlando, S., Pasquale, V.D., Barbanera, F., Lanese, I., Tuosto, E.: Corinne, a tool for choreography automata. In: Salaün, G., Wijs, A. (eds.) FACS 2021. LNCS, vol. 13077, pp. 82–92. Springer, Cham (2021). https://doi.org/10.1007/978-3-030-90636-8_5
118. Proença, J., Madeira, A.: Taming hierarchical connectors. In: Hojjat, H., Massink, M. (eds.) FSEN 2019. LNCS, vol. 11761, pp. 186–193. Springer, Cham (2019). https://doi.org/10.1007/978-3-030-31517-7_13
119. Proença, J.: Overview on constrained multiparty synchronisation in team automata. In: Cámara, J., Jongmans, S.S. (eds.) FACS 2023. LNCS, vol. 14485, pp. 194–205. Springer, Cham (2023). https://doi.org/10.1007/978-3-031-52183-6_10
120. Proença, J., Clarke, D.: Typed connector families and their semantics. Sci. Comput. Program. **146**, 28–49 (2017). https://doi.org/10.1016/j.scico.2017.03.002
121. Proença, J., Clarke, D., de Vink, E., Arbab, F.: Dreams: a framework for distributed synchronous coordination. In: Proceedings of the 27th ACM Symposium on Applied Computing (SAC 2012), pp. 1510–1515. ACM (2012). https://doi.org/10.1145/2245276.2232017
122. Proença, J., Cledou, G.: ARx: reactive programming for synchronous connectors. In: Bliudze, S., Bocchi, L. (eds.) COORDINATION 2020. LNCS, vol. 12134, pp. 39–56. Springer, Cham (2020). https://doi.org/10.1007/978-3-030-50029-0_3
123. Proença, J.: Synchronous coordination of distributed components. Ph.D. thesis, Leiden University (2011). https://hdl.handle.net/1887/17624
124. Ramadge, P.J., Wonham, W.M.: Supervisory control of a class of discrete event processes. SIAM J. Control. Optim. **25**(1), 206–230 (1987). https://doi.org/10.1137/0325013
125. Reisig, W.: Understanding Petri Nets: Modeling Techniques, Analysis Methods, Case Studies. Springer, Heidelberg (2013). https://doi.org/10.1007/978-3-642-33278-4
126. Scalas, A., Yoshida, N.: Less is more: multiparty session types revisited. Proc. ACM Program. Lang. **3**, 30:1–30:29 (2019). https://doi.org/10.1145/3290343
127. Severi, P., Dezani-Ciancaglini, M.: Observational equivalence for multiparty sessions. Fundam. Inform. **170**(1–3), 267–305 (2019). https://doi.org/10.3233/FI-2019-1863
128. Sharafi, M.: Extending team automata to evaluate software architectural design. In: Proceedings of the 32nd IEEE International Computer Software and Applications Conference (COMPSAC 2008), pp. 393–400. IEEE (2008). https://doi.org/10.1109/COMPSAC.2008.57
129. Sharafi, M., Shams Aliee, F., Movaghar, A.: A review on specifying software architectures using extended automata-based models. In: Arbab, F., Sirjani, M. (eds.) FSEN 2007. LNCS, vol. 4767, pp. 423–431. Springer, Heidelberg (2007). https://doi.org/10.1007/978-3-540-75698-9_30
130. Smeyers, M.: A browser-based graphical editor for Reo networks. Master's thesis, Leiden University (2018). https://theses.liacs.nl/1536
131. Teren, V., Cortadella, J., Villa, T.: Decomposition of transition systems into sets of synchronizing state machines. In: Proceedings of the 24th Euromicro Conference on Digital System Design (DSD 2021), pp. 77–81. IEEE (2021). https://doi.org/10.1109/DSD53832.2021.00021
132. Teren, V., Cortadella, J., Villa, T.: Decomposition of transition systems into sets of synchronizing Free-choice Petri Nets. In: Proceedings of the 25th Euromicro Conference on Digital System Design (DSD 2022), pp. 165–173. IEEE (2022). https://doi.org/10.1109/DSD57027.2022.00031

133. Winskel, G.: An introduction to event structures. In: de Bakker, J.W., de Roever, W.P., Rozenberg, G. (eds.) REX 1988. LNCS, vol. 354, pp. 364–397. Springer, Heidelberg (1988). https://doi.org/10.1007/BFB0013026

134. Yoshida, N.: Programming language implementations with multiparty session types. In: de Boer, F.S., Damiani, F., Hähnle, R., Johnsen, E.B., Kamburjan, E. (eds.) Active Object Languages: Current Research Trends. LNCS, vol. 14360, pp. 147–165. Springer, Cham (2024). https://doi.org/10.1007/978-3-031-51060-1_6

Tool Papers

An OpenWhisk Extension for Topology-Aware Allocation Priority Policies

Giuseppe De Palma[1,2]([✉]) [iD], Saverio Giallorenzo[1,2] [iD], Jacopo Mauro[3] [iD],
Matteo Trentin[1,2,3] [iD], and Gianluigi Zavattaro[1,2] [iD]

[1] Università di Bologna, Bologna, Italy
{giuseppe.depalma2,saverio.giallorenzo2,matteo.trentin2,
gianluigi.zavattaro}@unibo.it
[2] OLAS Research Team, INRIA, Sophia Antipolis, France
[3] University of Southern Denmark, Odense, Denmark
mauro@imada.sdu.dk

Abstract. The Topology-aware Allocation Priority Policies (tAPP) language allows users of serverless platforms to orient the scheduling of their functions w.r.t. the topological properties of the available computation nodes. A tAPP-based platform can support multiple scheduling policies, which one would usually enforce via (brittle) ad-hoc multi-instance platform deployments.

In this paper, we present an extension of the Apache OpenWhisk serverless platform that supports tAPP-based scripts. We show that our extension does not negatively impact the performance of generic, non-topology-bound serverless scenarios, while it increases the performance of topology-bound ones.

1 Introduction

Function-as-a-Service (FaaS) is a serverless cloud computing model where users deploy architectures of stateless functions and a platform handles all system operations [14].

While the FaaS model abstracts away infrastructural details, informing the scheduler on important infrastructural traits can improve the performance of serverless architectures. Indeed, function execution performance can depend on which computing resource, also called *worker*, the function runs. Effects like *data locality* [12]—related to data-access latencies—or *session locality* [12]—due to the overhead of establishing connections to other services—can negatively impact the run time of functions.

This work has been partially supported by the research project FREEDA (CUP: I53D23003550006) funded by the framework PRIN 2022 (MUR, Italy), RTM&R (CUP: J33C22001170001) funded by the MUR National Recovery and Resilience Plan (European Union - NextGenerationEU) and the French ANR project SmartCloud ANR-23-CE25-0012.

I. Castellani and F. Tiezzi (Eds.): COORDINATION 2024, LNCS 14676, pp. 201–218, 2024.
https://doi.org/10.1007/978-3-031-62697-5_11

The tAPP language [9] (briefly introduced in Sect. 3) allows users to declaratively express minimal infrastructural constraints to orient function scheduling.

In previous work [9] we presented a serverless platform that supports tAPP-specified scheduling policies. In this tool paper, we describe and evaluate the performance of our platform, which builds upon the widely adopted open-source serverless platform Apache OpenWhisk, extended to support tAPP—c.f. Section 4. In particular, the extension regarded the introduction of new components—e.g., a *watcher* service, which informs the gateway and the controllers on the current status of the nodes of the platform—and the extension of existing ones with new functionalities—e.g., to capture topological information at the level of workers and controllers, to enable live-reloading of tAPP policies, to let controllers and gateways follow tAPP policies depending on topological zones, etc.

The main contribution is in Sect. 5, where we validate our implementation through a set of benchmarks that include both generic and data-locality-bound serverless architectures, comparing the performance of vanilla OpenWhisk and our prototype. In particular, we collected a set of representative serverless test applications, divided into ad-hoc and real-world ones. Ad-hoc tests stress specific issues of serverless platforms. Real-world tests are functions taken from publicly available, open-source repositories of serverless applications used in production and selected from the Wonderless [10] serverless benchmark dataset. We show that our prototype does not exert a noticeable overhead over generic benchmarks while it substantially improves the performance of locality-bound ones (paired with dedicated tAPP scripts). A video that showcases our platform is available at https://vimeo.com/915098870.

2   Background

We dedicate this section to explaining background knowledge for readers unfamiliar with serverless and the OpenWhisk FaaS platform in particular.

Serverless Function Scheduling. The serverless development cycle is divided in two main parts: *a*) the writing of a function using a programming language supported by the platform (e.g., JavaScript, Python, C#) and *b*) the definition of an event that should trigger the execution of the function. For example, an event is a request to store some data, which triggers a process managing the selection, instantiation, scaling, deployment, fault tolerance, monitoring, and logging of the functions linked to that event. A Serverless provider schedules functions on its workers, controlling the scaling of the architecture by adjusting its available resources and billing its users on a per-execution basis. When instantiating a function, the provider has to create the appropriate execution environment for the function. Containers [8] and Virtual Machines (VM) [6] are the main technologies used to implement isolated execution environments for functions. If the provider allocates a new container/VM for every request, the initialisation overhead of the container would negatively affect both the performance of the single

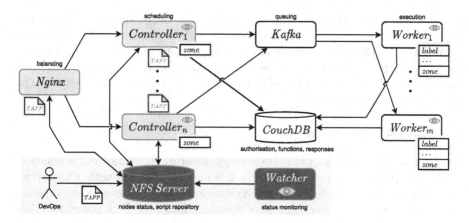

Fig. 1. Architectural view of our OpenWhisk extension. The existing OpenWhisk components we modified are in light blue while the new ones are in yellow (Color figure online).

function and heavily increase the load on the worker. A solution to tackle this problem is to maintain a "warm" pool of already-allocated containers. This matter is usually referred to as *code locality* [12]. Resource allocation also includes I/O operations that need to be properly considered and can avoid bad allocations over I/O-bound devices following the principle of *session locality* [12], i.e., taking advantage of already established user connections to workers. Another important aspect to consider to schedule functions is that of *data locality*, which comes into play when functions need to intensively access (connection- or payload-wise) some data storage (e.g., databases or message queues). Intuitively, a function that needs to access some data storage and that runs on a worker with high-latency access to that storage (e.g., due to physical distance or thin bandwidth) is more likely to undergo heavier latencies than if run on a worker "closer" to it.

Apache OpenWhisk. To build our tAPP prototype we concentrate on the widely-adopted open-source project Apache OpenWhisk. While we focus on the architecture of OpenWhisk, serverless platforms share common architectural patterns [11], making this contribution useful also as a guideline for alternative serverless platforms.

The upper part of Fig. 1 above the yellow box reports the architectural view of OpenWhisk.[1] From the left, *Nginx* is the entry point and load balancer of the system and distributes the incoming requests to the *Controllers*. Controllers then decide on which of the available computation nodes, called *Workers* (or "invokers" in OpenWhisk's parlance) to schedule the execution of a given function. *Controllers* allocate functions on Workers following a hard-coded policy that

---

[1] For space reason, Fig. 1 shows also the elements we modified and added to support tAPP—these will be detailed in Sect. 4.

allocates requests to the same function on the same list of *Workers*. The principle behind this policy is caching functions on workers to reduce cold starts—the downtime due to fetching the code and loading the runtime of functions. Finally, we have Apache *Kafka* [16] and *CouchDB* [5]; the first handles the routing and queueing of requests, while CouchDB manages authorisation and the storage of functions and their responses.

3   The tAPP Language

We can now introduce the tAPP language, presenting its syntax and semantics.

We report the syntax of tAPP in Fig. 2, which is compliant with YAML [18]. The basic entities of the language are *a*) scheduling policies, defined by a *policy tag* identifier to which users can associate their functions—the policy-function association is a one-to-many relation—and *b*) workers, identified by a *worker label*—where a label identifies a collection of computation nodes. All identifiers are strings. Given a tag, the corresponding policy includes a list of blocks, possibly closed with `strategy` and `followup` options. A block includes four parameters: an optional `controller` selector, a collection of `workers`, a possible scheduling `strategy`, and an `invalidate` condition. The outer `strategy` defines the policy we must follow to select among the blocks of the tag, while the inner `strategy` defines how to select workers from the items specified within a chosen `workers` block. The `controller` defines the identifier of a specific controller we want the gateway to redirect the invocation request to. When used, it is possible to define a `topology_tolerance` option to further refine how tAPP handles failures (of controllers). The collection of `workers` can be either a list of labels pointing to specific workers (`wrk`), or a worker `set`. In lists, the user can specify the `invalidate` condition of each single worker, while in sets, the `invalidate` condition applies to all the workers included in the set. When users specify an `invalidate` condition at block level, this is directly applied to all `workers` items (`wrk` and `set`) that do not define one. In `sets` the user can also specify a `strategy` followed to choose workers within the set. Finally, the `followup` value defines the behaviour to take in case no specified controller or worker in a tag is available to handle the invocation request.

We discuss the tAPP semantics, and the possible parameters, by commenting on the comprehensive script shown in Fig. 3. The tAPP script starts with the tag `default`, which is a special tag used to specify the policy for non-tagged functions, or to be adopted when a tagged policy has all its members invalidated, and the `followup` option is `default`. In Fig. 3, the `default` tag describes the default behaviour of the serverless platform running tAPP. In this case, we use a `workers` `set` to select workers, with no value specified for `set` which represents all worker labels. The `strategy` selected is the `platform` default. In our prototype in Sect. 4 the `platform` strategy corresponds to a selection algorithm that mediates load balancing and code locality by associating a function to a numeric hash and a step size—a number that is co-prime of and smaller than the number of workers. The `invalidate` strategy considers a worker non-usable when it is `overloaded`, i.e., it does not have enough resources to run the function.

```
app          ::= - tag
tag          ::= policy_tag : - controller?  workers  strategy?  invalidate?  strategy?  followup?
controller   ::= controller : label   ( topology_tolerance  : ( all  — same  — none ) )?
workers      ::= workers: - wrk : label  invalidate?
               | workers: - set : label?  strategy?  invalidate?
strategy     ::= strategy : ( random | platform | best_first )
invalidate   ::= invalidate : ( capacity_used n% | max_concurrent_invocations n | overload )
followup     ::= followup : ( default | fail )
```

Fig. 2. The syntax of tAPP.

```
- default:                  - couchdb_query:              - workers:
  - workers:                  - workers:                    - wrk:  near_DB_worker1
    - set:                      - wrk:  DB_worker1           - wrk:  near_DB_worker2
    strategy: platform         - wrk:  DB_worker2           strategy:  best_first
    invalidate: overload       strategy: random             invalidate: ↲
                               invalidate: capacity_used 50%    max_concurrent_invocations 100
                                                            followup: fail
```

Fig. 3. Example of a tAPP script.

Besides the `default` tag, the `couchdb_query` tag is used for those functions that access the database. The scheduler considers worker blocks in order of appearance from top to bottom. As mentioned above, in the first block (associated to `DB_worker1` and `DB_worker2`) the scheduler randomly picks one of the two worker labels and considers the corresponding worker invalid when it reaches the 50% of capacity. Here, the notion of capacity depends on the implementation (e.g., our OpenWhisk-based tAPP implementation in Sect. 4 uses information on the CPU usage to determine the load of invokers). When both worker labels are invalid, the scheduler goes to the next `workers` block, with `near_DB_worker1` and `near_DB_worker2`, chosen following a `best_first` strategy—where the scheduler considers the ordering of the list of `workers`, sending invocations to the first until it becomes invalid, to then pass to the next ones in order. The `invalidate` strategy of the block (applied to the single `wrk`) regards the maximal number of concurrent invocations over the labelled worker—`max_concurrent_invocations`, which is set to 100. If all the worker labels are invalid, the scheduler applies the `followup` behaviour, which is to `fail`. Users can define subsets of workers by specifying a label associated with the workers, e.g., `local` selects only those workers associated to the *local* label. The scheduling on worker-`set`s follows the same logic of block-level worker selection: it exhausts all workers before deeming the item invalid. Since worker-set selection/invalidation policies are distinct from block-level ones, we let users define the `strategy` and `invalidate` policies to select the worker in the set. For example, we can pair the above selection with a `strategy` and an `invalidate` options, e.g.,

```
- workers: - set: local strategy: random invalidate: capacity_used 50%
```

which tells the scheduler to adopt the random selection strategy and the capacity_used invalidation policy when selecting the workers in the *local* set. When worker-sets omit the definition of the selection strategy we consider the default one. When the invalidation option is omitted, we either apply that of the enclosing block or, if that is also missing, the default one. Summarising, given a policy tag, the scheduler follows the strategy (option) to select the corresponding blocks. A block includes three clauses.

The workers clause either contains a non-empty list of worker (wrk) labels, each paired with an optional invalidation condition, or a worker-set label (possibly blank, to select all workers) to range over sets of workers; workers sets optionally define the strategy and invalidate options to select workers within the set and declare them invalid.

The strategy clause defines the policy of item selection at the levels of *policy_tag*, *workers* block, and workers sets. tAPP supports three strategies: random, which selects items in a fair random manner; best_first, which selects items following their order of appearance; and platform, which selects items following the default strategy of the serverless platform—in our prototype, this corresponds to a co-prime-based selection.

The invalidate clause specifies when a worker (label) cannot host the execution of a function. When all labels in a block are invalid, we follow the defined strategy to select the next block until we either find a valid worker or exhaust all blocks. In the latter case, we apply the followup behaviour. Current invalidate options are: overload, where the worker lacks enough computational resources to run the function; capacity_used, where the worker reached a threshold percentage of CPU load; and max_concurrent_invocations, where the worker reached a threshold number of concurrent invocations. All invalidate options include the non-reachability of a worker.

Within a policy, the followup clause specifies what to do when all the blocks in a policy tag are invalid; either: fail, which drops the scheduling of the function; and default, which applies the default policy. Since the default block is the only possible "backup" tag used when all workers of a custom tag cannot execute a function (because they are all invalid), the followup value of the default tag is always set to fail.

To further detail the topological constraints of function execution scheduling, we have the *controller*. This is an optional, block-level clause that identifies which controllers in the current deployment we want to target to execute the scheduling policy of the current tag. Similarly to workers, we identify controllers with a label.

Users can label controllers and workers with the topological *zone* where they belong. When the designated controller is unavailable, tAPP can use this topological information to try to satisfy the scheduling request by forwarding it to some alternative controller. Indeed, a *controller* can have a topology_tolerance parameter, which specifies what workers an alternative controller can use. Specifically, all is the default and most permissive option and does not restrict the topology zone of workers; same constrains the function to run on workers in the same zone of the faulty controller (e.g., for data locality); **none** forbids the forward to other controllers.

```
- couchdb_query:
  - controller: DBZoneCtl
    workers:
      - set: local
        strategy: random
    topology_tolerance: same
  followup: default
```

As an example, we could use the topology zones and rewrite the previous tAPP script from Fig. 3 for the **couchdb_query** tag as shown on the left. In this way, we guarantee that the function will be executed always on the workers in the same zone of the database. Lastly, tAPP lets users express a selection strategy for policy blocks; as represented by the optional *strategy* fragment of the *tag* rule in tAPP's syntax. By default, when we omit to define a *strategy* policy for blocks, tAPP allocates functions following the blocks from top to bottom—i.e., **best_first** is the default policy. Here, for example, setting the **strategy** to **random** captures the simple load-balancing strategy of using randomness to uniformly distributing requests among the available controllers.

4   Supporting tAPP in OpenWhisk

We now discuss how we modified and extended OpenWhisk to support tAPP policies. In the following, we pair OpenWhisk with the popular and widely supported container orchestrator Kubernetes to orchestrate the deployment of the components.

Figure 1 depicts the architecture of our OpenWhisk extension, where we reuse the *Workers* and the *Kafka* components, we modify *Nginx* and the *Controllers* (light blue in the picture), and we introduce two new services: the *Watcher* and the *NFS Server* (in the highlighted area of Fig. 1). The modifications mainly regard letting Nginx and Controllers retrieve and interpret both tAPP scripts and data on the status of nodes, to forward requests to the selected controllers and workers. Concerning the new services, the Watcher monitors the topology of the Kubernetes cluster and collects its current status into the NFS Server, which provides access to tAPP scripts and the collected data to the other components. Below, we present the two new services, the changes to the existing OpenWhisk components, and how the proposed system supports live-reloading of tAPP configurations. We conclude with a description of the deployment procedure of the resulting prototype.

OpenWhisk Controller. To let the original OpenWhisk controller execute tAPP scripts, we extended the existing codebase of OpenWhisk. The component is written in Scala and it consists of a base **LoadBalancer** class which the vanilla OpenWhisk load balancer extends. To let OpenWhisk support tAPP scheduling policies, we introduced a new class that also extends the base one, called **ConfigurableLoadBalancer**. This class implements a parser and an engine that interprets tAPP scripts.

Watcher and NFS Server Services. We introduce the *Watcher* service to map tAPP-level information, such as zones and controllers/workers labels, to deployment-specific information, e.g., the name Kubernetes uses to identify computation nodes.

To realise the Watcher, we rely on the APIs provided by Kubernetes, which we use to deploy our OpenWhisk variant. In Kubernetes, applications are collections of services deployed as "pods", i.e., a group of one or more containers that must be placed on the same node and share network and storage resources. Kubernetes automates the deployment, management, and scaling of pods on a distributed cluster and one can use its API to monitor and manipulate the state of the cluster.

Our Watcher polls the Kubernetes API, asking for pod names and the respective *labels* and *zones* of the nodes (cf. Fig. 1), and stores the mapping into the *NFS Server*.

As shown in Fig. 1, Nginx uses the output of the Watcher to forward requests to controllers, allowing tAPP scripts to target controllers through their label rather than their specific pod identifier. Besides abstracting away deployment details, this feature supports dynamic changes to the deployment topology, e.g., when Kubernetes decides to move a controller pod at runtime on another node.

Moreover, the *NFS Server* works as the main injection point for tAPP scripts, both right after deployment and during the execution of the platform. When a new script is available on the *NFS Server*, the Controllers and Nginx obtain a copy, avoiding possible latencies due to fetching at function invocation. Future refinements can include the implementation of a dedicated API for the injection of scripts, removing the need for the *NFS Server*.

Nginx, OpenWhisk's Entry Point. Nginx forwards requests to all available controllers, following a hard-coded round-robin policy. To support tAPP, we change how Nginx processes incoming requests of function execution. We used *njs* (a subset of the JavaScript language that Nginx provides to extend its functionalities) for this integration.

Namely, we wrote an njs plug-in to analyse all requests passing through Nginx. The plug-in extracts any tag from the request parameters and compares it against the tAPP scripts. If the extracted tag matches a policy-tag, we interpret the associated policy, resolve its constraints, and find the related node label. The last step is translating the label into a pod name, done using the label-pod mapping produced by the Watcher service. Since Nginx manages all inbound traffic, we strived to keep the footprint of the plug-in small, e.g., we only interpret tAPP scripts and load the mappings when requests carry some tags and we use caching to limit retrieval downtimes from the NFS Server. From the user's point of view, the only visible change regards the tagging of requests. When tags are absent, Nginx follows the `default` policy or, when no tAPP script is provided, it falls back to the built-in round-robin.

Topology-Based Worker Distribution. We associate labels with pods via the topology labels provided by Kubernetes. These labels are names assigned to nodes that can describe the structure of the cluster by annotating their zones and attributes. In Fig. 1, we draw labels as boxes on the side of the controllers and workers.

Since OpenWhisk does not have a notion of topology, all controllers can schedule all functions on any available worker. Our extension unlocks a new design space that administrators can use to fine-tune how controllers access workers, based on their topology. At deployment, DevOps define the access policy used by all controllers. Our investigation led us to identify four topological-deployment access policies.

The *default* policy is the original one of OpenWhisk, where controllers have access to a fraction of all workers' resources. This policy has two drawbacks. First, it tends to *overload* workers, since controllers race to access workers in an uncoordinated manner. Second, it gives way to a form of *resource grabbing*, since controllers can access workers outside their zone, effectively taking resources away from "local" controllers.

The *min_memory* policy is a refinement of the *default* policy and it mitigates overload and resource-grabbing by assigning only a minimal fraction of the worker' resources to "foreign" controllers. For example, in OpenWhisk the resources regard the available memory for one invocation (in OpenWhisk, 256 MB). When workers have no controller in their topological zone or no topological zone at all, we follow the default policy. The *min_memory* policy has a drawback too: it can lead to scenarios where smaller zones quickly become saturated and unable to handle requests.

The *isolated* policy lets controllers access only co-located workers. This reduces overloading and resource grabbing but accentuates small-zone saturation effects.

The *shared* policy accesses primarily local workers and lets them access foreign ones after having exhausted the locals. This policy mediates between partitioning resources and efficient usage, but it can suffer from resource grabbing by remote controllers.

Controllers follow the policies declared in the available tAPP scripts and access topological information and tAPP scripts in the same way as described for Nginx. If no tAPP script is available, controllers resort to their original, hard-coded logic but prioritise scheduling functions on co-located workers.

Since the cluster's topology, its attributes, and the related tAPP scripts can change (e.g., to include a new node), we designed our prototype to dynamically support such changes, avoiding stop-and-restart downtimes. We implement this feature by storing a single global copy of the policies in the NFS Server, while we keep multiple, local copies in Nginx and each controller instance. When we update the reference copy, we notify Nginx and the controllers and let them handle cache invalidation and retrieval.

Deploying tAPP -based OpenWhisk The standard way to deploy OpenWhisk is by using the Docker images available for each component of the architecture—this lets developers choose the configuration that suits their deployment scenario, spanning single-machine deployments, where all the components run on the same node, and clustered (e.g., via Kubernetes) deployments, e.g., assigning a different node to each component. Since we modified the Controller component of the architecture, we built a new, dedicated Docker image so that it is generally available to be used in place of the vanilla controller.

5 Evaluation

We evaluate our prototype by comparing the performance of vanilla Open-Whisk and our tAPP-based variant under different benchmarks. We show that the overhead of running tAPP scheduling policies is negligible and that, in locality-bound scenarios, custom scheduling policies reduce function run times.

To obtain our empirical results, we devise two kinds of benchmarks. The first kind of benchmarks measures the overhead of the advanced features introduced by our prototype against the performance of vanilla OpenWhisk. The purpose of these "overhead" tests is to empirically quantify the impact of performance of the advanced, dynamic features introduced by tAPP in our prototype w.r.t. vanilla OpenWhisk. Since we want to focus on the performance of the platform, rather than the execution of the functions, we avoid tests that can introduce biases generated by data locality effects, i.e., those coming from the vanilla Open-Whisk accidentally choosing workers with a high-latency access to some data sources. The second kind of benchmarks focuses on "data-locality" effects and benchmarks the performance gain of topology-aware policies. The idea of these tests is to evaluate the performance gains that tAPP-based policies can provide, compared against the possible suboptimal scheduling of the vanilla version.

In what follows, we mark (**O**) overhead tests and (**D**) data-locality ones.

To perform a comprehensive comparison, we collected a set of representative serverless test applications, divided into ad-hoc and real-world ones. Ad-hoc tests stress specific issues of serverless platforms. Real-world tests are functions taken from publicly available, open-source repositories of serverless applications used in production and selected from the Wonderless [10] serverless benchmark dataset.

Ad-hoc Tests. Each ad-hoc test focuses on specific a trait: **hellojs (O)** implements a "Hello World" application and it provides an indication of the performance functions with a simple behaviour which parses and evaluates some parameters and returns a string; **sleep (O)** waits 3 s and benchmarks the handling of multiple functions running for several seconds and the management of their queueing process; **matrixMult (O)** multiplies two 100×100 matrices and returns the result to the caller, to measure the performance of handling functions performing some meaningful computation; **cold-start (O)** is a parameterless variant of **hellojs** that loads a heavy set of dependencies (42.8 MB) required and instantiated when the function starts; **mongoDB (D)** stresses the effect of data locality by executing a query requiring a document from a remote MongoDB database. The requested document is lightweight, corresponding to a JSON document of 106 bytes, with little impact on computation. This test focuses on the performance of accessing delocalized data; **data-locality (D)** encompasses both a memory- and bandwidth-heavy data-query function. It requests a large document (124.38 MB) from a MongoDB database and extracts a property from the returned JSON. This test witnesses both the impact of data locality w.r.t latency and bandwidth occupation.

All tests use Node.js 10 except those using MongoDB (v5), which use Node.js 12.

Real-World Tests. We draw our real-world tests from Wonderless [10]; a peer-reviewed dataset with almost 2000 projects automatically scraped from GitHub. The projects target serverless platforms like AWS, Azure, Cloudflare, Google, and OpenWhisk.

In a way, Wonderless reflects the current situation of serverless industrial adoption. The distribution of its projects is heavily skewed towards AWS-specific applications. Indeed, out of the 1877 repositories in the dataset, 97.8% are AWS-specific. Since we need the projects to work on OpenWhisk, we exclude most of them, leaving us with 66 projects which, unfortunately, sometimes carry limited information on their purpose and usage, they implement "Hello Word" applications, and have deployment problems. Thus, to select our real-world tests, we followed these exclusion criteria: *a)* the project must have a README.md file written in English with at least a simple description of the project's purpose. This filters out repositories that contain no explanation on their inner workings or a description of the project; *b)*the project works as-is, i.e., no compilation or execution errors; are thrown when deployed and the only modifications allowed for its execution regard configuration and environment files (i.e., API keys, credentials, and certificates). The reason for this rule concerns both the validity and reliability of the dataset, since fixing execution bugs could introduce biases from the researchers and skew the representativeness of the sample; *c)* the project must not use paid services (e.g., storage on AWS S3 or deployment dependent on Google Cloud Functions), which guarantees that the tests are generally available and easily reproducible; *d)* the project must represent a realistic use case. These exclude "Hello World" examples and boilerplate setups. The project must implement at least a function accepting input and producing an output as a result of either an internal transformation (such as code formatting or the calculation of a complex mathematical expression) or the interaction with an external service. This rule filters out all projects which do not represent concrete use cases.

The filtering led to the selection of three real-world tests:[2] **slackpost (O)**, from bespinian/k8s-faas-comparison, is a project written in Javascript, run on Node.js 12, and available for different platforms. It consists of a function that sends a message through the Slack API. While not complex, it is a common example of a serverless application that acts as the endpoint for a Slack Bot; **pycatj (O)**, from hellt/pycatj-web, is a project written in Python, run on Python 3.7, and it requires pre-packaged code to work. It consists of a formatter that takes

---

[2] For reproducibility, we provide the list of the rejection criteria applied to all 63 non-AWS discarded projects at [1].

an incoming JSON string and returns a plain-text one, where key-value pairings are translated in Python-compatible dictionary assignments. As a sporadically invoked web-based function, it represents an ordinary use case for serverless; **terrain (D)**, from terraindata/terrain, is a project written in Javascript and run on Node.js 12. The repository contains a serverless application that stress-tests a deployed backend. The backend is a traditional, non-serverless application deployed on a separate machine from the test cluster, which works as the target for this stress test. This is a common example of a serverless use case: monitoring and benchmarking external systems.

5.1   Test Environment

We used Apache JMeter to test and record the latency of our benchmarks, i.e., the time between the delivery of the request and the reception of the first response.

Configuration. The basic configuration for JMeter to run the ad-hoc tests uses 4 parallel threads (users), with a 10-s ramp-up time, i.e., the time needed to reach the total number of threads, and 200 requests per user. For some ad-hoc tests, we considered more appropriate a slight modification of the basic configuration. For the **sleep** test we use 25 requests per user since we deem it not necessary to have a larger sample size as the function has a predictable behaviour. The **cold-start** is meant to deliberately disregards the best practices of serverless development to showcase how the platform handles the cold start of "heavy" functions. For this reason, we throttle the invocations of these functions one every 11 min to let caches timeout—OpenWhisk's default cache timeout is 10 min. – and we use only 1 user performing 3 requests; this is enough to witness the effect on cache invalidation and initialisation times. Finally, due to the fact that the **data-locality** test is resource-heavy, we use only 50 repetitions for each of the 4 users; this is enough to witness data-locality effects.

We have a different configuration for each Wonderless test: **slackpost** has 1 user, 100 repetitions, and a 1-s pause, to account for Slack API's rate limits; **pycatj** has 4 parallel users, 200 repetitions, and a 10-s ramp-up time, akin to the default for ad-hoc tests; **terrain** has 1 user, 5 repetitions, and a 20-s pause, since the task is already a stress test and the amount of parallel computation on the node is high.

For each test with the exclusion of the previously mentioned **cold-start**, we execute 10 runs, removing and re-deploying the whole platform every 2 repetitions to avoid benchmarking specific configurations, e.g., bad, random configurations where vanilla OpenWhisk elects as primary a high-latency worker.

Cluster. For both reproducibility and reliability, we automatised all the levels of the deployment steps: the provisioning of the virtual machines (VMs) and both the deployment of Kubernetes and of (our extended version of) Open-Whisk on Google Cloud Platform via a Terraform and Ansible scripts. Once the Kubernetes cluster is up and running, we use the Helm package from

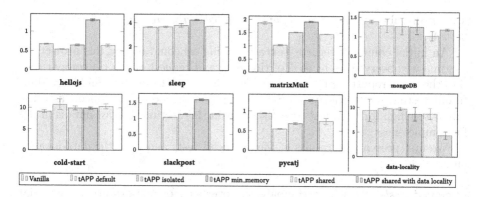

Fig. 4. Left: overhead tests (no data locality effects), average latency (bars) and standard deviation (barred lines) in seconds. Right: data-locality tests, average latency (bars) and standard deviation (barred lines) in seconds.

openwhisk-deploy-kube [2], that we forked to implement a tAPP-specific package for the installation with our custom controller image. This automatically deploys every component on a Kubernetes cluster and allows the user to parameterize the configuration of the deployment; specifically, we configure the deployment to select our tAPP-based controller image. The vanilla version os OpenWhisk is instead the one from OpenWhisk's official repository at https://github.com/apache/openwhisk-deploy-kube, commit 18960f.

We deployed both the vanilla and extended versions of OpenWhisk on a cluster of six virtual machines distributed across two regions (corresponding to two zone labels used in the deployment). We used a Kubernetes master node (not used as a computation node by OpenWhisk), along with one controller and one worker in the first region: *France Central*. The other controller and its two associated workers were in the second region: *East US*. All workers are *Standard_DS1_v2* Azure virtual machines, while the Kubernetes master node and both controllers are *Standard_B2s* Azure virtual machines. For the test, we also deployed two machines in the AWS region (*us-east*): a *t2.micro* EC2 instance for MongoDB and a *t2.medium* EC2 instance for the **terrain** backend. All machines (both on Azure and AWS) ran Ubuntu 20.04. To identify the best target for the data-locality tests, we measured the latency between the five (excluding the Kubernetes master node) cluster nodes and the two EC2 instances, which averages at 2 ms for machines located in *East US*, and 80ms for machines located in *France Central*. This identified the *East US* nodes as the optimal targets. The code used to deploy and run the tests is available at [2].

5.2 Results

We now present the results of running our tests on vanilla OpenWhisk and our prototype. In particular, we test our extension under all four topology-based worker distribution policies: *default, isolated, min_memory,* and *shared* (cf. Sect. 4).

An initial comment regards **terrain**. While we could deploy this project, at runtime we observed up to 60% of timeouts and request errors (in comparison, the other tests report 0% failure rate). This test is a real-world one and, according to our testing methodology (cf. Sect. 5), we use its code as-is. Since this error rate is too high for valid tests, we discard it in this section (its raw data is in [1], for completeness).

We first present the results of the overhead tests and then the data-locality ones.

Overhead Tests. To better compare the overhead of our extension w.r.t. the vanilla OpenWhisk one, we run the **hellojs, sleep, matrixMult, cold-start, slackpost,** and **pycatj** without a tAPP script. As a consequence, we also do not tag test functions, since there would be no policies to run against. As specified in Section 4, this makes our platform resort to the original scheduling logic of OpenWhisk, although it prioritises (and undergoes the overhead of) scheduling functions on co-located workers. These tests are therefore useful to evaluate the impact on performance of our four zone-based worker distribution policies, in comparison with the topology-agnostic policy hard-coded in OpenWhisk (cf. Section 2).

We report on the left of Fig. 4, in seconds, the average (bars) and the variance (barred lines) of the latency of the performed tests. For reference, we report in [1] all the experimental data. Since the standard deviation in the results is generally small, we concentrate on commenting on the results of the averages.

In the results, Vanilla OpenWhisk has better performance w.r.t. all our variants in the **sleep** and the **cold-start** cases, where all tested policies have similar performance. The latency in these tests does not depend on the adopted scheduling policies, but on other factors: the three-second sleep in **sleep**, the long load times in **cold-start**. While we expected a sensible overhead in both cases, we found encouraging results: the overhead of topology-based worker selection strategies is negligible—particularly in the **sleep**, where the *shared* policy almost matches the performance of vanilla OpenWhisk.

In the other four tests (**hellojs, matrixMult, slackpost,** and **pycatj**), the *default* worker distribution policy outperforms both vanilla OpenWhisk and the other policies. This policy combines the standard way in which OpenWhisk allocates resources (where each worker reserves the same amount of resources for each controller) and our topology-based scheduling approach (where each controller selects workers in the same zone and uses remote workers only when the local ones are overloaded). These results confirm that the latency reduction from topology-based scheduling compensates (and even overcomes) its overhead—in some cases, the performance gain is significant, e.g., **matrixMult** shows a latency drop of 44%.

We deem the good performance of our extension in these tests (spanning simple and more meaningful computation and real-world applications) a positive result. Indeed, we expected topology-based scheduling to mainly allay data locality issues, but we have experimentally observed significant performance improvements also in tests free from this effect.

We also note that the *min_memory* policy tends to perform the worst. To explain this fact, we draw attention to also the results of the *isolated* policy: both strategies can lead to saturated zones when faced with many requests, but they act differently with overloaded local workers. The *isolated* policy ignores remote workers and returns control to Nginx, which passes the invocation to a different controller. The *min_memory* policy instead tries to access remote workers with minimal resource availability, which can lead to higher latencies due to queuing and remote communications. The results of *default* and *shared* reinforce this conclusion: they increase resource sharing within the cluster and mitigate possible asymmetries (here, we had two workers in one zone and one in the other).

Data-Locality Tests. For the data-locality tests, we first run them without tagging functions and provide no tAPP script, thus comparing vanilla OpenWhisk and our extension on a common ground where the main difference between the two stands on the four distribution policies applied at deployment level and their overhead. Then, we ran the same tests (on our extension), but we tagged the functions and provided a tAPP script that favours executing functions on workers close to the data source.

We report on the right of Fig. 4, in seconds, the average (bars) and the variance (barred lines) of the latency of the data-locality tests **mongoDB** and **data-locality**—the full experimental data is in [1]. For brevity, we show, with the right-most bar on the right of Fig. 4, the results of the best-performing distribution policy (*shared*, see below) paired with the mentioned tAPP script.

As expected, in all tests our extension outperforms vanilla OpenWhisk, confirming previous evidence on data locality [12] and presenting useful applications of topology-aware scheduling policies for topology-dependent workflows.

In **mongoDB**, our extension outperforms vanilla OpenWhisk under all strategies, although it undergoes a higher variance. The small variance of vanilla OpenWhisk in this test is probably thanks to the light test query, which mitigates instances where vanilla OpenWhisk uses high-latency workers.

The results from **data-locality** confirm the observation above. There, the variance for vanilla OpenWhisk is larger—quantitatively, the variances of **mongoDB** for our extension stay below 0.5 s, while the variance of vanilla OpenWhisk in **data-locality** is 9-fold higher: 4.5 s. Here, the heavier test query strongly impacts the performance of those "bad" deployments that prioritise high-latency workers.

More precisely, the best performing strategies are *shared* for **mongoDB** and *min_memory* for **data-locality**. In the first case, since the query did not weigh too much on latency (e.g., bandwidth-wise), mixing local and remote workers favoured the *shared* policy, which, after exhausting its local resources, can freely access remote ones. In the second case, the *min_memory* policy performed slightly better than the *shared* one. We attribute this effect to constraining the selection of workers mainly to the local zone and resorting in minimal part to remote, higher-latency workers.

Given the results above, we performed the tAPP-based tests (right-most column on the right of Fig. 4) with the *shared* policy[3].

Compared to the tag-less *shared* policy, the tagged case in **mongoDB** is a bit slower, but more stable (small variance). In **data-locality** it almost halves the run time of the tag-less case.

These tests witness the trade-off of using tAPP-based scheduling to exploit data locality and the overhead of parsing the tAPP script: due to its many lightweight requests, **mongoDB** represents the worst case for the overhead, but the test still outperforms vanilla OpenWhisk (showing that the overhead is compensated by the advantages of our worker selection strategies); in **data-locality**, the heaviness of the query and the payload favours spending a small fraction of time to route functions to the workers with lower latency to the data source.

6 Related Work and Conclusion

Related Work. Many works tackle minimising serverless function invocation latency, often trying to optimise function scheduling [17,20].

One work close to ours is by Sampé et al. [19], where the authors propose to favour data locality by allocating functions to storage workers. The main difference with our proposal is that we designed tAPP to specify scheduling constraints on topologies, where data locality may emerge; contrarily Sampé et al. frame the problem as topologies induced by data-locality issues.

Broadening our scope, we find proposals like Banaei et al. [7], who present a scheduling policy that governs the order of invocation processing, depending on the availability of the resources they use; Abad et al. [3] who propose a package-aware technique that favours re-using the same workers for the same functions to cache dependencies; Suresh and Gandhi [23], who introduced a scheduling policy oriented by resource usage of co-located functions on workers; Steint [22] and Akkus et al. [4] who respectively present a scheduler based on game-theoretic allocation and on the interaction of sandboxing of functions and hierarchical messaging. Other works rely on the state and relations among functions to determine scheduling policies. Examples include scheduling functions within a single workflow as threads within a single process of a container instance, reducing overhead by sharing state among them [15]; using state by supporting both global and local state access, aiming at performance improvements for data-intensive applications [21]; associating each function invocation with a shared log among serverless functions [13].

Drawing a comparison between the above works and ours, by using tAPP, the user expresses explicitly topologies considered at scheduling time, while topologies emerge as implicit, runtime configurations in the other proposals.

---

[3] In **data-locality**, min_memory has a slightly lower average than *shared*, but the latter has both lower variance and maximal latency.

Conclusion. We presented a tAPP-based serverless platform implementation for the specification and execution of topology-aware serverless scheduling policies. We used the presented tool to show that topology-aware scheduling can improve the performance of serverless architectures. Indeed, our benchmarks have shown that in almost all the considered test cases, the tAPP-based solution outperforms the unmodified platform, making it suitable both for generic applications, and especially for locality-sensitive functions.

Regarding future work, we consider extending the support for tAPP to other serverless platforms, like OpenLambda, OpenFAAS, and Fission. We also plan to expand our range of tests: both to include other aspects of locality (e.g., sessions) and specific components of the platform (e.g., message queues, controllers), and new benchmarks for alternative platforms, to elicit the peculiarities of each implementation. Moreover, we plan to consider cloud-edge use cases, where both local and remote machines execute functions and may benefit from topology-aware optimisations that exploit data locality. Regarding tests, we remark on the general need for more platform-agnostic and realistic suites, to obtain fairer and thorough comparisons.

References

1. tAPP-based openwhisk extension (2022). https://github.com/mattrent/openwhisk
2. Repository of rejected projects from wonderless (2022). https://github.com/mattrent/openwhisk-deploy-kube
3. Abad, C.L., Boza, E.F., Eyk, E.V.: Package-aware scheduling of faas functions. In: Proceedings of ACM/SPEC ICPE, pp. 101–106. ACM (2018). https://doi.org/10.1145/3185768.3186294
4. Akkus, I.E., et al.: SAND: towards high-performance serverless computing. In: Proceedings of USENIX/ATC, pp. 923–935 (2018)
5. Anderson, J.C., Lehnardt, J., Slater, N.: CouchDB: the definitive guide: time to relax. " O'Reilly Media, Inc." (2010)
6. Armbrust, M., et al.: Above the clouds: a Berkeley view of cloud computing. University of California, Berkeley, Rep. UCB/EECS **28**(13), 2009 (2009)
7. Banaei, A., Sharifi, M.: Etas: predictive scheduling of functions on worker nodes of apache openwhisk platform. J. Supercomput. (2021). https://doi.org/10.1007/s11227-021-04057-z
8. Bernstein, D.: Containers and cloud: from lxc to docker to kubernetes. IEEE Cloud Comput. **1**(3), 81–84 (2014)
9. De Palma, G., Giallorenzo, S., Mauro, J., Trentin, M., Zavattaro, G.: A declarative approach to topology-aware serverless function-execution scheduling. In: 2022 IEEE International Conference on Web Services, ICWS 2022, Barcelona, Spain, July 11–15, 2022. IEEE (2022)
10. Eskandani, N., Salvaneschi, G.: The wonderless dataset for serverless computing. In: Proceedings of IEEE/ACM MSR, pp. 565–569 (2021). https://doi.org/10.1109/MSR52588.2021.00075
11. Hassan, H.B., Barakat, S.A., Sarhan, Q.I.: Survey on serverless computing. J. Cloud Comput. **10**(1), 1–29 (2021)
12. Hendrickson, S., Sturdevant, S., Harter, T., Venkataramani, V., Arpaci-Dusseau, A.C., Arpaci-Dusseau, R.H.: Serverless computation with openlambda. In: Proceedings of USENIX HotCloud (2016)

13. Jia, Z., Witchel, E.: Boki: stateful serverless computing with shared logs. In: Proceedings of ACM SIGOPS SOSP, pp. 691–707. ACM, New York, NY, USA (2021). https://doi.org/10.1145/3477132.3483541

14. Jonas, E., et al.: Cloud programming simplified: a Berkeley view on serverless computing. Technical report UCB/EECS-2019-3, EECS Department, University of California, Berkeley (2019)

15. Kotni, S., Nayak, A., Ganapathy, V., Basu, A.: Faastlane: accelerating function-as-a-service workflows. In: Proceedings of USENIX ATC, pp. 805–820. USENIX Association (2021)

16. Kreps, J., Narkhede, N., Rao, J., et al.: Kafka: a distributed messaging system for log processing. In: Proceedings of NetDB, vol. 11, pp. 1–7 (2011)

17. Kuntsevich, A., Nasirifard, P., Jacobsen, H.A.: A distributed analysis and benchmarking framework for apache openwhisk serverless platform. In: Proceedings of Middleware (Posters), pp. 3–4 (2018)

18. Oren Ben-Kiki, Clark Evans, I.d.N.: Yaml ain't markup language (yaml^{TM}) version 1.2 (2021). https://yaml.org/spec/1.2.2/

19. Sampé, J., Sánchez-Artigas, M., García-López, P., París, G.: Data-driven serverless functions for object storage. In: Proceedings of Middleware, pp. 121–133. ACM (2017). https://doi.org/10.1145/3135974.3135980

20. Shahrad, M., Balkind, J., Wentzlaff, D.: Architectural implications of function-as-a-service computing. In: Proceedings of MICRO, pp. 1063–1075 (2019)

21. Shillaker, S., Pietzuch, P.: Faasm: Lightweight isolation for efficient stateful serverless computing. In: Proceedings of USENIX ATC, pp. 419–433. USENIX Association (2020)

22. Stein, M.: The serverless scheduling problem and noah. arXiv preprint arXiv:1809.06100 (2018)

23. Suresh, A., Gandhi, A.: Fnsched: an efficient scheduler for serverless functions. In: Proceedings of WOSC@Middleware, pp. 19–24. ACM (2019). https://doi.org/10.1145/3366623.3368136

Coconut: Typestates for Embedded Systems

Arwa Hameed Alsubhi$^{(\boxtimes)}$ and Ornela Dardha

University of Glasgow, Glasgow, UK
a.alsubhi.1@research.gla.ac.uk, ornela.dardha@glasgow.ac.uk

Abstract. Typestate programming defines object states and actions to improve software safety by ensuring operations on objects follow the correct sequence. While its adoption in object-oriented languages has increased, limitations persist in the features supported. Typestates are particularly useful in embedded systems for operation sequencing, yet examples in this area are scarce. We introduce Coconut, a C++ tool that leverages typestate programming with templates for specifying typestates and combining static type checking and dynamic analysis to ensure proper class instance behaviour. It uniquely supports advanced programming features like branching, recursion, aliasing, concurrency, and optional typestate visualisation, facilitating idiomatic object-oriented programming with inheritance. Illustrating its effectiveness, we apply Coconut to actual embedded system projects, advancing the field by introducing a comprehensive set of features and practical examples for implementing typestate programming.

Keywords: Typestate · C++ · Embedded Systems

1 Introduction

Software development in critical sectors such as finance and healthcare necessitates thorough testing and maintenance to protect sensitive data and ensure human safety. A key aspect of this maintenance involves the use of protocols that dictate the sequence of operations for objects and help reduce errors, as highlighted by [49]. For example, in message-passing processes, establishing a connection is a prerequisite before any message transmissions can occur. While some protocols are straightforward, others in real-world systems are complex and challenging, requiring ongoing research to refine enforcement approaches.

Typestate analysis is one such approach that could effectively enforce specific sequences of operations on objects, thus managing and reinforcing protocols, as discussed by [54]. To illustrate further, consider the LightSwitch class shown in Fig. 1. The protocol dictates that the LightSwitch must not be turned on if it is already in the **on** state, nor turned off if it is in the **off** state. If the object ls in Fig. 2 attempts to call SwitchOn() twice without an intervening SwitchOff(), typestate analysis statically detects and prevents this protocol violation. For more details on how this analysis is enforced in Coconut, refer to Sect. 2.

© IFIP International Federation for Information Processing 2024
Published by Springer Nature Switzerland AG 2024
I. Castellani and F. Tiezzi (Eds.): COORDINATION 2024, LNCS 14676, pp. 219–238, 2024.
https://doi.org/10.1007/978-3-031-62697-5_12

```
1  class LightSwitch{
2  public:
3  void SwitchOn(){
4  std::cout<<"Switching On\n";
5  }
6  void SwitchOff(){
7  std::cout<<"Switching Off\n";
8  }
9  };
```

Fig. 1. LightSwitch Class

```
1  int main() {
2  LightSwitch ls;
3  (ls->*&LightSwitch::SwitchOn)();
4  (ls->*&LightSwitch::SwitchOff)();
5  return 0;
6  }
```

Fig. 2. LightSwitch Client Code

Leveraging the advantages of typestate, several new programming languages, such as Vault, Fugue, Plaid, and Obsidian, have been developed with a focus on integrating typestate as a key feature, as detailed in [18–20,51]. Additionally, tools like Mungo, Java Typestate Checker (JaTyC), and Papaya have been applied to object-oriented programming languages, such as Java or Scala, to facilitate typestate checking [5,10,32,34,41]. Although these projects leverage typestate checking to support various programming features, they still lack some critical capabilities. For example, most of these projects do not support inheritance, with the notable exception of JaTyC, which fully supports it [5]. Furthermore, many typestate-based projects either eliminate aliasing, such as Mungo [34], or impose limitations on it, like Plaid [3].

These limitations arise from several factors. For instance, aliasing can complicate the management of object typestates. This is because changes made by one alias can affect the state of the object as seen by another alias, leading to inconsistencies and undermining the accuracy of the object's current state analysis. Similarly, implementing typestate in programs that use inheritance is challenging because subclasses may introduce new methods and behaviours that do not align with the parent class's typestate. This can lead to a situation where the subclass's unique behaviours need separate enforcement mechanisms, adding complexity to the system design. To address these complexities, many typestate initiatives selectively focus on features that align with their core objectives, thus limiting their scope to ensure practical implementation that accommodates diverse needs. This project aims to provide such support by focusing on essential features that enhance the application of typestates across various scenarios.

In this paper, we examine the application of typestate analysis in embedded systems, such as medical devices, which require precise sequences of operations for reliable functionality. Given this requirement, typestate tools become valuable for addressing these operational needs in such systems. However, despite the growing interest in formal methods for verifying and validating embedded systems, such as [12,13,29–31], there is a noticeable lack of research on typestates in these systems. Formal methods such as Extended Finite State Machine (EFSM) [2] and Event-B [1] use states and events for system modelling. EFSM offers detailed behaviour modelling at a lower level, while Event-B supports multi-level system modelling. However, their complexity and resource demands pose challenges for systems with limited resources and constrained update processes. Typestate as mentioned in [40], offers a practical approach to behaviour representation and the ability to enhance code modularity. This modularity can improve the readability and maintainability of the codebase, thus simplifying coding and updating workflows [35].

This paper presents the Coconut tool, a C++ library with typestates. We selected C++ for this implementation due to its prominence in embedded systems and proven effectiveness in high-performance applications, as evidenced by [12,26,38,52]. C++20's brief inclusion of contract attributes-later removed-highlighted a gap in verifying object behaviour [16,46]. Typestates could address this, yet integrating them into C++ is challenging due to static reflection limitations and C++'s complex library creation process [11,55]. The existing ProtocolEncoder (ProtEnc) library offers typestate analysis but is limited by performance issues and restricted feature support, as highlighted in [53]. Our tool overcomes these limitations by applying distinct approaches in checking and analysing and offers more features beyond ProtEnc.

Contributions. The key contributions of this paper are as follows:

- **Typestate Analysis:** Coconut provides typestate templates for protocol definition and supports these with a comprehensive analysis to ensure class instances adhere to their protocols. Detects violations at compile-time and incorporates run-time assertions for enhanced robustness (Sect. 2).
- **Embedded Systems Case Studies:** We showcase the application of Coconut through case studies, such as the LightSwitch and Pillbox. The Pillbox case study is grounded in the actual deployment of the Pillbox system in a healthcare setting [12] (Sects. 2 and 3).
- **Comprehensive Programming Feature Set:** Coconut integrates a broad range of programming features, including branching, recursion, aliasing, concurrency, inheritance, and typestate visualisation. Coconut is the first tool to integrate these features comprehensively (Sect. 3).
- **Evaluation Study:** We conducted a comparative evaluation to benchmark Coconut's performance against three distinct case studies, each implemented in C++ and evaluated across different metrics (see Sect. 4). Furthermore, we tested each Coconut example to ensure its effectiveness in identifying bugs and enforcing typestate.

2   The Coconut Tool

This section explores the integration, system overview, template mechanics, and static and dynamic analysis capabilities of the Coconut tool.

2.1   Integration, Compatibility, and Usage

Coconut is a C++ library tailored for C++20 and later versions, offering specialised functionalities. It utilises CMake [33], a well-known cross-platform build

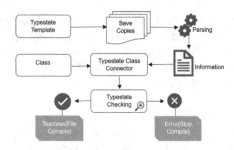

Fig. 3. Coconut Typestate Checking Process

system, to simplify the compilation process across various operating systems and environments. This integration facilitates compatibility with various external dependencies, such as the Boost library [15]. Coconut offers flexible integration into C++ projects, allowing developers to selectively include its header file based on their needs, thus enabling or bypassing its features accordingly. Comprehensive instructions for its installation and usage are available in its repository[1]. The library implements a type-safe state machine using template metaprogramming [43], Boost.Hana [14] and functional programming principles. It provides mechanisms to define states, transitions, and rules for a typestate, along with utilities for tracking instances and visualising the state machine's structure. This approach is particularly useful for compile-time checks and enforcing correct state transitions in a type-safe manner.

2.2 System Overview

Upon integrating the Coconut library, developers can specify behavioural protocols for their class objects using the provided templates. The system parses and analyses these templates to collect information about all possible states and permitted behaviours. As explained in Fig. 3, This data is passed to the `TypestateClassConnector`, which establishes a linkage between each class and its corresponding typestate, ensuring compliance with defined typestate guidelines throughout the codebase. The `State_Manager` class is responsible for typestate verification. It manages this by wrapping Pointers to Member Functions (PMFs) that are used to call class functions. These PMFs are accessed using operators like `.*` and `->*`. The `State_Manager` acts as a gatekeeper, employing a `constexpr` template function to check whether an object is in the correct state before it allows a function call to proceed. It verifies against the typestate rules stored in a tuple. If the function call aligns with the rules, the `State_Manager` updates the object's state in the tuple to reflect the new state. If a function call violates the rules, the checking process will detect this and stop the compilation of the program.

---

[1] https://zenodo.org/records/10853974.

```
1  BETTER_ENUM(LightSwitchState, int, OFF, ON);
2  using LightSwitchProtocol = Typestate_Template<
3  State<+LightSwitchState::OFF,&LightSwitch::SwitchOn,+LightSwitchState::ON>,
4  State<+LightSwitchState::ON,&LightSwitch::SwitchOff,+LightSwitchState::OFF>>;
```

Fig. 4. LightSwitch Typestate

2.3 Templates and State Management in Coconut

Coconut utilises the concept of *enumeration* by leveraging either built-in *enumeration* or the BETTER_ENUM library. The BETTER_ENUM library [6] enhances enum functionality by enabling conversions to and from strings, which aids in typestate visualisation. Moreover, it offers compile-time validation capabilities not available with built-in enums, often utilised in examples within our tool. Using templates, the typestate specification is defined as a Finite State Machine (FSM). This FSM is modelled through a template-based struct and implemented via template meta-programming [43], which allows for flexibility in accommodating various data types. This versatility enables the management of diverse classes, such as File and Sound, within the Coconut tool. States and transitions are expressed as follows:

- **Typestate_Template:** This template serves as the container for the FSM, utilising *variadic templates* [28] to accommodate an arbitrary number of state transitions.
- **State:** Each state transition is modelled as follows:
  - **Current_State:** Indicates the state the object is currently in.
  - **Pointer_To_Allowable_Function:** Defines the member function pointer that is allowed to transit the object from the Current_State to the Next_State.
  - **Next_State:** Specifies the state to which the object transitions after the function is called.
- **Wrapper Templates for State Transition Management**: Each class is connected with the Typestate_Template and wrapped by a manager that embeds typestate logic directly into the class structure. This wrapper generates code that uses the tuple stored in Typestate_Template to check typestate configurations within the Coconut framework. Upon instantiation, each class begins in a state defined by the current_state in the Typestate_Template. This ensures that the object begins its life-cycle from the correct state. The process of state transition checking is initiated whenever a state-changing method is called. If the transition is valid according to the Typestate_Template, the method is called, moving the object to its next state. If a transition is invalid, static assertions prevent compilation, while runtime assertions manage function calls in dynamic behaviours.

To demonstrate how templates function within the Coconut tool, consider the LightSwitch example mentioned in Sect. 1, as illustrated in Fig. 1. Initially, the typestates of the LightSwitch are defined in the `Typestate_Template`. This includes specifying permissible states and transitions between them as seen in Fig. 4. Following the specification, a wrapper transforms the LightSwitch class to incorporate these typestates. This setup integrates the logic necessary for state transitions directly into the structure of the class. In Fig. 2, upon instantiation, the `ls` is set to the OFF state, as defined by the first state entry in the **Typestate_Template**. When the `SwitchOn()` method is called, Coconut checks the typestate configurations stored in the tuple to verify if the transition to the ON state is permissible using `SwitchOn()`. If the transition is valid, the `ls` moves to the ON state and the program compiles successfully. If the `ls` in Fig. 2 in line 4 calls `SwitchOn()` the compilation will stop, enforced by static assertions.

2.4   Static and Dynamic Analysis in Coconut

In the Coconut tool, the code analysis starts with static analysis during the compilation phase. This involves checking that the code behaves correctly when typestate-related functions are called within `if-constexpr` conditions or loops. Static analysis ensures that these calls correctly manage state transitions based on the compile-time conditions and the defined rules, preventing potential logic errors before the program runs. Additionally, static analysis includes aliasing analysis, which tracks how multiple references to the same object might impact the object's state during these function calls when executed within a monolithic context. It also examines inheritance structures to ensure that derived classes adhere to the state management rules of their base classes.

After successful compilation, dynamic analysis takes over during code execution to manage conditions not addressed during the static phase. This includes handling `if-else` branches that respond to runtime conditions involving changes in internal state or effects of predefined variables. For example, a vending machine may enter a maintenance state triggered by internal diagnostics, which is checked at runtime. The dynamic aliasing part of the analysis examines how aliases affect an object's state through function calls in dynamic segments of the program, using a compositional approach. This analysis also supports concurrent method calls across multiple threads, ensuring alignment with type states.

Limitations and Future Work. Coconut's current limitations include a lack of support for dynamic data structures like arrays and linked lists, restricting its application in complex data manipulation. It also lacks full support for direct interactions with users or real-time data from external systems, such as processing live data feeds from sensors or streaming data from online services. Additionally, advanced concurrency challenges such as synchronisation, race conditions, and deadlocks. These areas are targeted for enhancement in future updates.

3   PillBox Case Study

This section demonstrates how our tool can be applied to a real-world scenario using the smart PillBox, an embedded medical system designed to ensure patients take their medications on time, as detailed in [12].

```
1   class PillBox {
2   public:
3       PillBox() {
4           DrawersBox = new std::vector<Drawer*>();
5       }
6       void Activate_PillBox() {
7           std::cout<<"PillBox is active now!\n";
8       }
9       void addDrawers(Drawer* d) {
10          DrawersBox->push_back(d);
11      }
12      Drawer* Process_System_Time(int h, int m) {
13          for (Drawer* d : *DrawersBox) {
14              if (h == d->get_the_hour() && m == d->get_minutes())
15                  { return d; }}
16          return nullptr;
17      }
18      void Deactivate_PillBox() {
19          std::cout<<"PillBox is Deactivated now!\n";
20      }
21      void Switch_ON(Drawer* d) {
22          redled.setRedLed("ON");
23          std::cout<<"It's time to take "<<d->get_pill_name()<<"!\n";
24      }
25      void Switch_OFF(Drawer* d) {
26          redled.setRedLed("OFF");
27          std::cout<<"Drawer with the pill "<< d->get_pill_name()<<" is
                closed\n";
28      }
29      void Blink(Drawer* d) {
30          redled.setRedLed("Blinking");
31          std::cout<<"Please close the drawer "<< d->get_pill_name() << "\n";
32      }
33  private:
34      std::vector<Drawer*>* DrawersBox;
35      RedLed redled;
36  };
```

Fig. 5. PillBox Class

3.1   PillBox Original vs Coconut Version

Remark 1. Before discussing the implementation of PillBox in Coconut, it is important to review the original deployment as described in [12] and the identified issues. PillBox is a programmable device that allows for the addition or removal of modular drawers and was originally modelled using the Asmeta framework [24], a model-based engineering platform which uses four hierarchical Abstract State Machines (ASM) to define system behaviours. Since ASM models cannot be executed directly on the hardware, translating these models into C++ code with the tool Asm2C++ [23] was crucial. The translated C++ code is used for debugging and validating system performance, which is unachievable with ASM alone. This translated code has significant hardcoding and extensive conditional statements, reflecting the complexities of the original ASM code and making it challenging to trace execution and reason about the code's behaviour. Furthermore, a new ASM model is required each time a drawer is added to the system, which currently only supports up to three drawers, leading to inefficiencies. Comparing the Coconut tool implementation with this setup is essential to understand how each manages the system. A small fragment of the code from the original implementation can be found in Appendix A.

Typestate Solution: In response to challenges identified in the original Pill-Box implementation [12], we propose a solution based on typestates facilitated by the Coconut tool. Typestates offer a structured framework for modelling PillBox behaviour, effectively addressing these challenges. By utilising typestates within Coconut, we establish a unified framework for the PillBox, regardless of the number of drawers. Unlike the original approach, which required separate modelling and validation for each level of the hierarchical structure using hardcoding, typestate specifications are defined once for the entire PillBox. This process simplifies the checking and verification of client code, reducing the complexity and redundancy associated with modelling and validating multiple scenarios compared to the original implementation using ASM, thus making it easy to trace execution and reason about the code's behaviour.

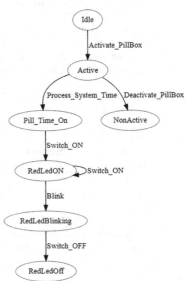

Fig. 6. PillBox State Machine

Now, we will demonstrate how Coconut implements typestates for the smart PillBox and see how typestate checking ensures the system functions correctly as illustrated in the state machine (Fig. 6). In the PillBox class (Fig. 5), multiple drawers hold pills with specific intake times, and a RedLed, initially off. Each drawer is represented as a class (Fig. 7), detailing the pill and its intake time. Similarly, the RedLed in the `PillBox` class is also a class (Fig. 8).

PillBox Typestate Description. Each `PillBox` instance starts in the (`Idle`) state. Upon activation, the `RedLed` switches on to indicate the time to take a pill from a specific `Drawer`. The `RedLed` remains illuminated until the patient opens the `Drawer` and retrieves the pill. After pill retrieval, the `RedLed` blinks to close the `Drawer`, then switches off. This sequence repeats for each `Drawer` when its corresponding pill time arrives. This typestate is expressed using **State** and

Typestate_Template, depicted in Fig. 9, and represented as an FSM in Fig. 6. To demonstrate, in Fig. 10, the `pillbox1` instance of the `PillBox` class is set to the `Idle` state when is created in line 12, as defined by the first state entry in the **Typestate_Template**. When the `Activate_PillBox()` method is called on `pillbox1`, Coconut checks the typestate configurations stored in the tuple to verify if the transition to the `Activated` state is permissible using `Activate_PillBox()`. If the transition is valid, `pillbox1` moves to the `Activate` state, and the program compiles successfully. However, if `pillbox1` attempts to call `Activate_PillBox()` again after line 16, the compilation will stop, enforced by static assertions. Note that methods outside the state machine, like `addDrawers`, are considered "anytime" methods and are not subject to typestate checks.

```
1  class Drawer {
2  public:
3      Drawer(std::string
4      pillName, int hour, int
           minute):
5      pillName_(pillName),
6      hour_(hour), minute_(minute) {}
7      std::string get_pill_name()
8      {return this->pillName_;}
9      int get_the_hour()
10     {return this->hour_;}
11     int get_minutes()
12     {return this->minute_;}
13 private:
14     std::string pillName_;
15     int hour_, minute_;
16 };
```

Fig. 7. Drawer Class

```
1  class RedLed {
2  public:
3      void setRedLed(std::string
           state)
4      {this->RedLedState = state;}
5  private:
6      std::string RedLedState;
7  };
```

Fig. 8. RedLed Class

3.2   Discussion of Programming Features

This section outlines Coconut's key features, including branching, recursion, aliasing, concurrency, and inheritance. These features play roles in decision-making, task simplification, maintaining consistent object states, supporting multi-threaded interactions, and enhancing code scalability. They are useful for developing maintainable software for complex systems like the smart PillBox, as illustrated by [21], which provides insights into various scenarios where such features are utilised in software development for complex systems.

Branching and Recursion. Coconut supports branching in programming, enabling objects to follow multiple paths within a program. For instance, as demonstrated in Fig. 10, when the `pillbox1` instance is in the (Active)

```
1  using PillBox_typestate = Typestate_Template<
2  State<+domain::Idle,&PillBox::Activate_PillBox,+domain::Active>,
3  State<+domain::Active,&PillBox::Process_System_Time,+domain::Pill_Time_On>,
4  State<+domain::Pill_Time_On,&PillBox::Switch_ON,+domain::RedLedON>,
5  State<+domain::RedLedON,&PillBox::Switch_ON,+domain::RedLedON>,
6  State<+domain::RedLedON,&PillBox::Blink,+domain::RedLedBlinking>,
7  State<+domain::RedLedBlinking,&PillBox::Switch_OFF,+domain::RedLedOFF>,
8  State<+domain::Active,&PillBox::Deactivate_PillBox,+domain::NonActive>>;
```

Fig. 9. PillBox Typestate Specification

```
1  static void OperateRedLed(PillBox& p, Drawer* d){
2      for(int i=0;i<5;i++){
3          (p->*&PillBox::Switch_ON)(d);
4      }
5      (p->*&PillBox::Blink)(d);
6      (p->*&PillBox::Switch_OFF)(d);
7  }
8  int main() {
9      Drawer* drawer1 = new Drawer("Panadol", 3, 50);
10     Drawer* drawer2 = new Drawer("Piriton Antihistamine", 8, 40);
11     constexpr bool EnableDrawersOperations = true;
12     PillBox pillbox1;
13     PillBox& ptr_pillbox1 = pillbox1;
14     pillbox1.addDrawers(drawer1);
15     pillbox1.addDrawers(drawer2);
16     (pillbox1->*&PillBox::Activate_PillBox)();
17     if constexpr (EnableDrawersOperations) {
18         Drawer* d = (pillbox1->*&PillBox::Process_System_Time)(3,50);
19         OperateRedLed(ptr_pillbox1, d);
20     }
21     else {
22         (pillbox1->*&PillBox::Deactivate_PillBox)();
23     }
24     return 0;
25 }
```

Fig. 10. PillBox Client Code

state, it can selectively choose which method to invoke. It can proceed with Process_System_Time() as shown in line 18, transitioning to the (Pill_Time_On) state, or it can call Deactivate_PillBox() to transition to the (NonActive) state. Coconut also supports loops, as illustrated in Fig. 10, where the for loop in line 2 continuously turns on a red LED with Switch_ON() and signals when to take a pill, repeating this process until the incrementer reaches 5.

Unrestricted Aliasing. Coconut analyses relationships between different variables and objects in the program. For instance, it analyses the relationships between `pillbox1`, `ptr_pillbox1` as seen in line 13 in Fig. 10, and any other variables that may reference the same `pillbox1` and aliases are directly linked to their respective instances and states. When `pillbox1` or `ptr_pillbox1` in lines 16 or 19 calls a function, Coconut checks this data against the predefined typestate. If it conforms, Coconut updates the instance's state, and this change is then reflected across all aliases.

Concurrency. In C++, concurrency and threading are managed using the `std::thread` class, which facilitates the execution of functions, function objects, or lambda expressions. Wrappers as discussed in Sect. 2, encapsulate typestate on objects. For concurrency, these wrappers use hidden `mutexes` to enforce exclusive execution of certain code blocks by one thread at a time, with runtime checks ensuring adherence to typestate for consistent state transitions. Consider the scenario in Fig. 10, where the main function executes two threads with distinct operations, as detailed in Fig. 11. Here, Coconut integrates `mutexes` within wrappers, employing runtime checks to enforce adherence to specific typestate rules, thus preventing state inconsistencies. For instance, if thread `t1` initiates system activation, it acquires a mutex, blocking thread `t2` from starting until `t1` completes and releases the mutex. Conversely, if `t2` starts first, encountering a non-activated system due to `t1` not having run yet, `t2`'s execution halts.

Inheritance. Coconut enforces typestate rules across superclasses and subclasses in line with the Liskov Substitution Principle (LSP) [36], ensuring that subclasses can seamlessly replace superclasses without impacting program functionality. It analyses four inheritance scenarios to ensure methods and behaviours

```
1  std::thread t1([&pillbox1]{
2      (pillbox1->*&PillBox::Activate_PillBox)();
3  });
4  std::thread t2([&pillbox1]{
5      Drawer* d = (pillbox1->*&PillBox::Process_System_Time)(3,50);
6  });
```

Fig. 11. Concurrency Example

conform to typestate requirements. Particularly in scenarios where both classes have typestates, Coconut ensures that subclasses adhere to the specifications of both their own class and their superclasses, as elaborated in the repository.

3.3   Coconut vs. State-of-the-Art Typestate-Based Tools

Coconut retains all previously discussed features and introduces an optional typestate visualisation feature. This feature helps developers represent typestates diagrammatically, improving clarity and understanding. Developers can use the `Visualise_TypestateTemplate<enum>` function which uses Graphviz [27] to visualise protocols and create diagrams, such as the one shown in Fig. 6. Before concluding this section, we summarise our programming feature contributions and compare them with other typestate-based tools, as shown in Table 1. Compared to other typestate-based projects, *Coconut manages to provide support for all discussed features*, unlike other tools that lack other features.

Table 1. Coconut vs typestate-based Projects Features. A checkmark in the table indicates the presence of a feature. Most of these features are implemented at compile time. However, features like Unrestricted Aliasing and Concurrency are offered at runtime, except for Concurrency in JaTyC21, which is offered at compile time.

	Branching	Recursion	Inheritance	Safe Aliasing	Unrestricted Aliasing	Concurrency	Visual
Mungo	✓	✓					
JaTyC21	✓	✓		✓		✓	
JaTyC22	✓	✓	✓				
DSI_Rust		✓					✓
Plaid	✓	✓		✓		✓	
Clara	✓	✓					
Plural	✓	✓		✓			
Papaya	✓	✓		✓	✓		
Accumulation	✓	✓		✓			
Fugue	✓	✓	✓	✓			
Obsidian	✓	✓		✓			
ProtEnc		✓		✓			
Coconut	✓	✓	✓	✓	✓	✓	✓

4   Evaluation Study

Benchmarks and Metrics. In our evaluation study, we aim to assess the performance of the Coconut tool, which applies typestate analysis, by comparing it with three distinct case studies. Initially, we evaluate the performance using a straightforward example of a LightSwitch embedded system as a baseline [8]. Next, we examine the PillBox embedded system, previously discussed in Sect. 3, which involves hardcoding and utilises an Abstract State Machine [12]. Finally, we compare Coconut's performance against an existing typestate-based tool, ProtEnc, implemented in C++ [53]. We have selected four key performance metrics for this analysis, which are:

- **Compilation Time (CT)**: Measures the time required to compile code.
- **Run Time (RT)**: Measures the duration of program execution.
- **Memory Usage (MU)**: Assesses the amount of execution memory usage.
- **Code Complexity**: Evaluates the complexity of the source code.

These metrics are selected to assess the software's efficiency, reliability, and maintainability, aspects that are particularly important in embedded system environments. Compilation and execution times reflect speed and efficiency, memory usage helps gauge resource optimisation, and code complexity provides insight into maintainability. These selected measures align with standard practices in embedded systems [42,45,48].

Process. We used a Python script with libraries like pandas, lizard, openpyxl, time, psutil, and Libclang17dev [17,25,37,39,44,56] to measure metrics such as compile time, runtime, and memory usage. Each script ran 100 times to find average results. For code complexity, we checked the number of tokens, lines of code (NLOC), and Cyclomatic complexity. *Notably, the original PillBox system heavily relied on runtime hardcoding and checks, using the Arduino library [4] to monitor data from an embedded device like system time and the RedLed status. To ensure a fair comparison with Coconut, which mainly checks at compile time without direct device access, we adjusted the PillBox to move all checks to compile time.* For data collection, we tested the modified system's compile time over 100 iterations, each processing unique parameters such as pill names, times (in hours and minutes), and the red LED status, mimicking real-world operations. We applied the same testing approach to the Coconut PillBox version to align with our goal of evolving Coconut into a typestate monitoring tool.

Results, Conclusion and Future Improvement After experimentation, as depicted in Fig. 12, we observed that Coconut incurs a higher compile-time overhead compared to other benchmarks. However, it exhibits slightly better performance in terms of runtime and memory usage. In assessing code complexity, Coconut achieves lower values for Cyclomatic complexity, NLOC, and token count than the other benchmarks. These lower complexity metrics suggest that code written with Coconut might be simpler and less complex, which can make it easier to understand and maintain. *Note that the results for Pillbox in the table refer to the modified version.* Additionally, the effectiveness of Coconut in identifying bugs was assessed through case studies, with detailed findings available

Metrics	LightSwitch Original	LightSwitch Coconut	PillBox Original	PillBox Coconut	ProtEnc Original	ProtEnc Coconut
Compile Time (Milliseconds)	850 ▼	2889 ▲	2200 ▼	3339 ▲	2713 ▼	3387 ▲
Run Time (Milliseconds)	27 ▲	13 ▼	18 ▲	12 ▼	11 ▲	9 ▼
Memory Usage (Kilobyte)	1778 ▲	1774 ▼	1805 ▲	1784 ▼	1818 ▲	1776 ▼
NLOC	25 ▲	24 ▼	201 ▲	105 ▼	84 ▲	48 ▼
Tokens	145 ▲	116 ▼	1355 ▲	743 ▼	461 ▲	309 ▼
Cyclomatic Complexity	3 ▲	2 ▼	21 ▲	19 ▼	6 ▲	5 ▼

Fig. 12. Metrics Results

in the Coconut repository. We plan to broaden our evaluation in the future to include more comprehensive case studies in embedded systems and to incorporate additional metrics and expand testing to include more complex scenarios.

5   Conclusion, Related and Future Work

Related Work. Typestate was introduced by Strom and Yemini [50] to enhance program reliability through compile-time semantic checks. This foundational concept focused on ensuring correct variable declaration and initialisation, setting the stage for future developments in typestate programming.

In the development of typestate in programming languages, projects like Vault [19], Fugue [20], and Plaid [3,51] played pivotal roles. These projects expanded typestate into programming languages or language extensions, allowing the definition of resource protocols or class states. This approach mirrors the strategies seen in Rust's Typestate Pattern Tool [47] and the ProtocolEncoder (ProtEnc) in C++ [53], which prioritise augmenting existing languages. Furthermore, the concept of session types, as explored in tools like Mungo, JaTyC, and Papaya [5,32,34], emphasises separate object protocol definitions and static class instance checking against these protocols.

Aliasing, where multiple references can be assigned to a single object, is treated differently across various typestate-oriented projects. Projects like Vault [19], Fugue [20], Plaid [3,51], and Plural [9] have developed unique constructs and modes to manage aliasing. Vault uses adoption and focus, creating linear and non-linear references to control access to objects. Fugue distinguishes between NotAliased and MayBeAliased modes, directly addressing the aliasing issue. Plaid and Plural introduce access permissions, blending aliasing and access control for the management of object references.

Supported Programming Features. Branching and recursion are seamlessly integrated into tools like Mungo [34] and Papaya [32], using language-specific statements for recursion management. Concurrency is uniquely tackled in typestate tools. Plaid [3] prioritises access permissions, while JaTyC21 [41] focuses on tracing state changes for safe concurrent computations. Inheritance, crucial in object-oriented programming, is addressed by JaTyC22 [5] and Fugue [20], allowing subclasses to extend superclasses' typestates.

Embedded Systems. Formal methods are essential in the verification and validation of embedded systems in healthcare and robotics. Bonfanti et al.'s systematic literature review highlighted this necessity in medical software development, ensuring human safety [13]. Such methods include the use of UML-B state machines and class diagrams to model and analyse the HD Machine for treating kidney failure [29], evaluating various states and transitions essential to its operation. In robotics, finite state machines have been demonstrated as effective approaches for controlling robot behaviour and performance [7,22]. For autonomous vehicles, a model integrating finite-state machine and reinforcement learning methods is highlighted, crucial in navigating cut-in situations [31]. Another model employs FSM to address the parking challenges faced by autonomous vehicles, utilising sensors and system requirements [30].

Conclusion and Future Work. To conclude, in this paper, we introduced the Coconut tool and discussed the usage of templates to define typestates for objects in C++. Our tool ensures the conformity of the typestate definitions on objects by conducting a thorough analysis and covering a full spectrum of programming features to date. We presented the architecture of the tool and showcased its support for different programming features through case studies in the embedded systems industry, to introduce and emphasise the importance of typestate as an approach for validating and verifying such systems. We assessed the Coconut tool through many tests for Coconut case studies, also we conducted an evaluation study with three benchmarks using four metrics. In future work, we aim to enhance Coconut by addressing its performance limitations. Our vision is to transform Coconut into a typestate monitoring tool capable of processing embedded device data, facilitating evaluation and comparison with actual embedded systems.

Acknowledgements. Supported by the UK EPSRC New Investigator Award grant EP/X027309/1 "Uni-pi: safety, adaptability and resilience in distributed ecosystems, by construction". Additionally, this work has partial support from the Royal Embassy of Saudi Arabia Cultural Bureau. We thank Simon Gay for his valuable comments on the paper.

A   PillBox Original Implementation

See Figs. 13, 14.

```
void pillbox_FULL::r_Main_seq() {
    for (auto _compartment : Compartment::elems)
        if (true) {
            if ((drugIndex[0][_compartment]
                    < (unsigned int) ((time_consumption[0][_compartment]).size())))) {
                { //par
                if (!opened[0][_compartment] & openSwitch[_compartment]) {
                    opened[1][_compartment] = true;
                }
                if (opened[0][_compartment] & !openSwitch[_compartment]) {
                    opened[1][_compartment] = false;
                }
                if ((redLed[0][_compartment] == OFF)) {
                    if ((time_consumption[0][_compartment][drugIndex[0][_compartment]]
                            < systemTime)) {
                        r_pillToBeTaken(_compartment);
                    }
                }
                if ((redLed[0][_compartment] == ON)
                        & !((systemTime - compartmentTimer[0][_compartment]) >= 1)
                        & opened[0][_compartment] & !openSwitch[_compartment]) {
                    r_pillTaken_compartmentOpened(_compartment);
                }
                if ((redLed[0][_compartment] == ON) & !opened[0][_compartment]
                        & openSwitch[_compartment]) {
                    r_compartmentOpened(_compartment);
                }
                [...]
```

Fig. 13. Code Snippet of PillBox from the original implementation in [12]

```
for (const auto& _compartment : Compartment::elems) {
    time_consumption[0].insert( { _compartment, [&]() { /*<--- caseTerm*/
        if(_compartment==compartment1)
        return std::vector<unsigned int> {1, 20, 30};
        else if(_compartment==compartment2)
        return std::vector<unsigned int> {40, 50, 60};
        else if(_compartment==compartment3)
        return std::vector<unsigned int> {9, 20, 30};
    }() });
    time_consumption[1].insert( { _compartment, [&]() { /*<--- caseTerm*/
        if(_compartment==compartment1)
        return std::vector<unsigned int> {1, 20, 30};
        else if(_compartment==compartment2)
        return std::vector<unsigned int> {40, 50, 60};
        else if(_compartment==compartment3)
        return std::vector<unsigned int> {9, 20, 30};
    }() });
}
systemTime = 0;
for (const auto& _compartment : Compartment::elems) {
    name[0].insert( { _compartment, [&]() { /*<--- caseTerm*/
        if(_compartment==compartment1)
        return "Tylenol";
        else if(_compartment==compartment2)
        return "Aspirine";
        else if(_compartment==compartment3)
        return "Moment";
    }() });
    name[1].insert( { _compartment, [&]() { /*<--- caseTerm*/
```

Fig. 14. Code Snippet of PillBox 2 from the original implementation in [12]

References

1. Abrial, J.R.: Modeling in Event-B: System and Software Design. Cambridge University Press, Cambridge (2010). https://doi.org/10.1017/CBO9781139195881
2. Alagar, V.S., Periyasamy, K.: Extended finite state machine. In: Specification of Software Systems. Springer, London (2011). https://doi.org/10.1007/978-0-85729-277-3_7
3. Aldrich, J., et al.: Permission-based programming languages (NIER Track). In: Proceedings of the 33rd International Conference on Software Engineering (ICSE), pp. 828–831. ACM (2011). https://doi.org/10.1145/1985793.1985915
4. Arduino: Arduino libraries (2024). https://www.arduino.cc/reference/en/libraries/
5. Bacchiani, L., Bravetti, M., Giunti, M., Mota, J., Ravara, A.: A Java typestate checker supporting inheritance. Sci. Comput. Program. **221**, 102844 (2022). https://doi.org/10.1016/j.scico.2022.102844
6. Bachin, A.: Better enums (2015–2019). http://aantron.github.io/better-enums/
7. Balogh, R., Obdržálek, D.: Using finite state machines in introductory robotics. In: Lepuschitz, W., Merdan, M., Koppensteiner, G., Balogh, R., Obdržálek, D. (eds.) RiE 2018. AISC, pp. 85–91. Springer, Cham (2019). https://doi.org/10.1007/978-3-319-97085-1_9
8. Barr, M.: Programming Embedded Systems in C and C++. O'Reilly (1999)
9. Bierhoff, K., Beckman, N.E., Aldrich, J.: Practical API protocol checking with access permissions. In: Drossopoulou, S. (ed.) ECOOP 2009. LNCS, vol. 5653, pp. 195–219. Springer, Heidelberg (2009). https://doi.org/10.1007/978-3-642-03013-0_10
10. Biffle, C.L.: The Typestate Pattern in Rust (2019). http://cliffle.com/blog/rust-typestate/
11. Bispo, J., Paulino, N., Sousa, L.M.: Challenges and opportunities in C/C++ source-to-source compilation. In: Bispo, J., Charles, H.P., Cherubin, S., Massari, G. (eds.) Proceedings of the 14th Workshop on Parallel Programming and Run-Time Management Techniques for Many-Core Architectures and 12th Workshop on Design Tools and Architectures for Multicore Embedded Computing Platforms (PARMA-DITAM 2023). Open Access Series in Informatics (OASIcs), vol. 107, pp. 2:1–2:15. Schloss Dagstuhl — Leibniz-Zentrum für Informatik (2023). https://doi.org/10.4230/OASIcs.PARMA-DITAM.2023.2
12. Bombarda, A., Bonfanti, S., Gargantini, A.: Developing medical devices from abstract state machines to embedded systems: a smart pill box case study. In: Mazzara, M., Bruel, J.-M., Meyer, B., Petrenko, A. (eds.) TOOLS 2019. LNCS, vol. 11771, pp. 89–103. Springer, Cham (2019). https://doi.org/10.1007/978-3-030-29852-4_7
13. Bonfanti, S., Gargantini, A., Mashkoor, A.: A systematic literature review of the use of formal methods in medical software systems. J. Softw. Evol. Process **30**(5), e1943 (2018). https://doi.org/10.1002/smr.1943
14. Boost Developers: Boost C++ libraries (Boost.Hana documentation). https://www.boost.org/doc/libs/1_84_0/libs/hana/doc/html/index.html
15. Boost Developers: Boost C++ libraries (2024). https://www.boost.org/
16. Caminiti, L.: Boost.Contract 1.0.0. https://www.boost.org/doc/libs/1_80_0/libs/contract/doc/html/index.html (2008–2019)
17. Clark, C., Kappert, E.: Openpyxl — a Python library to read/write Excel 2010 xlsx/xlsm files (2024). https://pypi.org/project/openpyxl/

18. Coblenz, M., et al.: Obsidian: typestate and assets for safer blockchain programming. ACM Trans. Program. Lang. Syst. **42**(3) (2020). https://doi.org/10.1145/3417516

19. DeLine, R., Fähndrich, M.: Enforcing high-level protocols in low-level software. SIGPLAN Not. **36**(5), 59–69 (2001). https://doi.org/10.1145/381694.378811

20. DeLine, R., Fähndrich, M.: Typestates for objects. In: Odersky, M. (ed.) ECOOP 2004. LNCS, vol. 3086, pp. 465–490. Springer, Heidelberg (2004). https://doi.org/10.1007/978-3-540-24851-4_21

21. Driscoll, P.J., Parnell, G.S., Henderson, D.L.: Decision Making in Systems Engineering and Management. Wiley, Hoboken (2022)

22. Estivill-Castro, V., Hexel, R.: Run-time verification of regularly expressed behavioral properties in robotic systems with logic-labeled finite state machines. In: Proceedings of the IEEE International Conference on Simulation, Modeling, and Programming for Autonomous Robots (SIMPAR), pp. 281–288. IEEE (2016), https://doi.org/10.1109/SIMPAR.2016.7862408

23. Formal Methods and SE Laboratory University of Milan, Formal Methods and Software Engineering Lab University of Bergamo: Asm2c++ (2006–2022). https://asmeta.github.io/download/asm2c++.html

24. Formal Methods and SE Laboratory University of Milan, Formal Methods and Software Engineering Lab University of Bergamo: Asmeta framework (2006–2022). https://asmeta.github.io/

25. Giampaolo, F.: psutil (2024). https://pypi.org/project/psutil/

26. Giftthaler, M., Neunert, M., Stäuble, M., Buchli, J.: The control toolbox — an open-source C++ library for robotics, optimal and model predictive control. In: Proceedings of the IEEE International Conference on Simulation, Modeling, and Programming for Autonomous Robots (SIMPAR), pp. 123–129. IEEE (2018). https://doi.org/10.1109/SIMPAR.2018.8376281

27. Graphviz Team: Graphviz (2021). https://www.graphviz.org/

28. Gregor, D., Järvi, J.: Variadic templates for C++. In: Proceedings of the ACM Symposium on Applied Computing (SAC), pp. 1101–1108. ACM (2007). https://doi.org/10.1145/1244002.1244243

29. Hoang, T.S., Snook, C., Ladenberger, L., Butler, M.: Validating the requirements and design of a hemodialysis machine using iUML-B, BMotion studio, and co-simulation. In: Butler, M., Schewe, K.-D., Mashkoor, A., Biro, M. (eds.) ABZ 2016. LNCS, vol. 9675, pp. 360–375. Springer, Cham (2016). https://doi.org/10.1007/978-3-319-33600-8_31

30. Hu, Y., et al.: Decision-making system based on finite state machine for low-speed autonomous vehicles in the park. In: IEEE International Conference on Real-time Computing and Robotics (RCAR), pp. 721–726 (2022). https://doi.org/10.1109/RCAR54675.2022.9872208

31. Hwang, S., Lee, K., Jeon, H., Kum, D.: Autonomous vehicle cut-in algorithm for lane-merging scenarios via policy-based reinforcement learning nested within finite-state machine. IEEE Trans. Intell. Transp. Syst. **23**(10), 17594–17606 (2022). https://doi.org/10.1109/TITS.2022.3153848

32. Jakobsen, M., Ravier, A., Dardha, O.: Papaya: global typestate analysis of aliased objects. In: Proceedings of the 23rd International Symposium on Principles and Practice of Declarative Programming (PPDP). ACM (2021). https://doi.org/10.1145/3479394.3479414

33. Kitware Inc.: Cmake (2024). https://cmake.org/

34. Kouzapas, D., Dardha, O., Perera, R., Gay, S.J.: Typechecking protocols with Mungo and StMungo. In: Proceedings of the 18th International Symposium on Principles and Practice of Declarative Programming (PPDP), pp. 146–159. ACM (2016). https://doi.org/10.1145/2967973.2968595

35. Kumar, B.: A survey of key factors affecting software maintainability. In: Proceedings of the International Conference on Computing Sciences, pp. 261–266 (2012). https://doi.org/10.1109/ICCS.2012.5

36. Liskov, B.H., Wing, J.M.: A behavioral notion of subtyping. ACM Trans. Program. Lang. Syst. **16**(6), 1811–1841 (1994). https://doi.org/10.1145/197320.197383

37. LLVM Developer Group: libclang-17-dev: Development package for Clang (2024). https://packages.debian.org/search?keywords=libclang-17-dev

38. Mayr, M., Salt-Ducaju, J.M.: A C++ implementation of a cartesian impedance controller for robotic manipulators (2022)

39. McKinney, W., et al.: pandas: powerful Python data analysis toolkit (2024). https://pandas.pydata.org/

40. Militão, F., Aldrich, J., Caires, L.: Substructural typestates. In: Proceedings of the ACM SIGPLAN Workshop on Programming Languages Meets Program Verification (PLPV), pp. 15–26. ACM (2014). https://doi.org/10.1145/2541568.2541574

41. Mota, J., Giunti, M., Ravara, A.: Java typestate checker. In: Damiani, F., Dardha, O. (eds.) COORDINATION 2021. LNCS, vol. 12717, pp. 121–133. Springer, Cham (2021). https://doi.org/10.1007/978-3-030-78142-2_8

42. Oliveira, M.F., Redin, R.M., Carro, L., Lamb, L.D.C., Wagner, F.R.: Software quality metrics and their impact on embedded software. In: Proceedings of the 5th International Workshop on Model-based Methodologies for Pervasive and Embedded Software (MOMPES), pp. 68–77. IEEE (2008). https://doi.org/10.1109/MOMPES.2008.11

43. Porkoláb, Z., Mihalicza, J., Sipos, A.: Debugging C++ template metaprograms. In: Proceedings of the 5th International Conference on Generative Programming and Component Engineering (GPCE), pp. 255–264. ACM (2006). https://doi.org/10.1145/1173706.1173746

44. Python Software Foundation: time — time access and conversions (2024). https://docs.python.org/3/library/time.html

45. Redin, R.M., et al.: On the use of software quality metrics to improve physical properties of embedded systems. In: Kleinjohann, B., Wolf, W., Kleinjohann, L. (eds.) DIPES 2008. ITIFIP, vol. 271, pp. 101–110. Springer, Boston (2008). https://doi.org/10.1007/978-0-387-09661-2_10

46. Reis, G.D., J. D. Garcia, J. Lakos, A.M., N. Myers, B.S.: Support for contract based programming in C++ (2018). https://open-std.org/JTC1/SC22/WG21/docs/papers/2018/p0542r5.html

47. Rust Language: The Embedded Rust Book (2018). https://docs.rust-embedded.org/book/static-guarantees/typestate-programming.html#typestate-programming

48. Sherman, T.: Quality attributes for embedded systems. In: Sobh, T. (ed.) Advances in Computer and Information Sciences and Engineering, pp. 536–539. Springer, Dordrecht (2008). https://doi.org/10.1007/978-1-4020-8741-7_95

49. Šimoňák, S.: Verification of communication protocols based on formal methods integration. Acta Polytechnica Hungarica **9**(4), 117–128 (2012). http://acta.uni-obuda.hu/Simonak_36.pdf

50. Strom, R.E., Yemini, S.: Typestate: a programming language concept for enhancing software reliability. IEEE Trans. Softw. Eng. **SE-12**(1), 157–171 (1986). https://doi.org/10.1109/TSE.1986.6312929

51. Sunshine, J., Naden, K., Stork, S., Aldrich, J., Tanter, E.: First-class state change in plaid. In: Proceedings of the ACM International Conference on Object Oriented Programming Systems Languages and Applications (OOPSLA), pp. 713–732. ACM (2011). https://doi.org/10.1145/2048066.2048122
52. TIOBE: TIOBE Index (2000–2023). https://www.tiobe.com/tiobe-index//
53. Tolmer, V.: Protenc library (2019). https://github.com/nitnelave/ProtEnc
54. Wang, J., Tepfenhart, W.: Formal Methods in Computer Science. Chapman and Hall/CRC (2019). https://doi.org/10.1201/9780429184185
55. Xiao, X., Balakrishnan, G., Ivančić, F., Maeda, N., Gupta, A., Chhetri, D.: Arc++: effective typestate and lifetime dependency analysis. In: Proceedings of the International Symposium on Software Testing and Analysis (ISSTA), pp. 116–126. ACM (2014). https://doi.org/10.1145/2610384.2610395
56. Yin, T.: Lizard: an extensible cyclomatic complexity analyzer (2024). https://pypi.org/project/lizard/1.8.7/

TRAC: A Tool for Data-Aware Coordination
(with an Application to Smart Contracts)

João Afonso[1], Elvis Konjoh Selabi[2,3] (ID), Maurizio Murgia[3(✉)] (ID),
António Ravara[1] (ID), and Emilio Tuosto[3] (ID)

[1] NOVA School of Science and Technology, Caparica, Portugal
[2] Università di Camerino, Camerino, Italy
[3] Gran Sasso Science Institute, L'Aquila, Italy
maurizio.murgia@gssi.it

Abstract. We propose TRAC, a tool for the specification and verification of coordinated multiparty distributed systems. Relying on finite-state machines (FSMs) where transition labels look like Hoare triples, TRAC can specify the coordination of the participants of a distributed protocol for instance an execution model akin blockchain smart contracts (SCs). In fact, the transitions of our FSMs yield guards, and assignments over data variables, and with participants binders. The latter allow us to model scenarios with an unbounded number of participants which can vary at run-time. We introduce a notion of *well-formedness* to rule out meaningless or problematic specifications. This notion is verified with TRAC and demonstrated on several case studies borrowed from the smart contracts domain. Then, we evaluate the performance of TRAC using a set of randomised examples, studying the correlations between the features supported and the time taken to decide well-formedness.

1 Introduction

We propose TRAC, a tool to support the coordination of distributed applications. The design of TRAC is inspired by the Azure initiative of Microsoft [32] which advocates the use of finite-state machines (FMSs) to specify the coordination of smart contract (SC for short). This idea is not formalised; in fact, Azure's FSMs are informal sketches aiming to capture the "correct" executions of SCs. For instance, the FSM for the simple market place (SMP) scenario borrowed from [33] (the textual description is ours):

Research partly supported by the EU H2020 RISE programme under the Marie Skłodowska-Curie grant agreement No 778233, by the PRIN 2022 PNRR project DeLiCE (F53D23009130001), by the MUR project PON REACT EU DM 1062/21, by the PRO3 MUR project Software Quality, "by the MUR dipartimento di eccellenza", and by PNRR MUR project VITALITY (ECS00000041), Spoke 2 ASTRA - Advanced Space Technologies and Research Alliance. This work is also partially funded by the Portuguese National Science Foundation projects NOVA LINCS (UIDB/04516/2020) and Smarty (2022.09138.PTDC).

I. Castellani and F. Tiezzi (Eds.): COORDINATION 2024, LNCS 14676, pp. 239–257, 2024.
https://doi.org/10.1007/978-3-031-62697-5_13

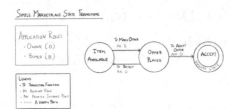

The FSM informally specifies a protocol coordinating the participants enacting the roles owner and buyer, from a *global* standpoint; we call *coordination protocol* such specification. A coordination protocol can be regarded as *global view* –in the sense of choreographies [22,25]– where the state of the protocol determines which operations are enabled. This resembles the execution model of monitors [24]. In fact, as in monitors, coordination protocols encapsulate a state that –through an API– concurrent processes can have exclusive access to. The API is basically a set of operations guarded by conditions set to maintain an invariant on the encapsulated state (in the SMP scenario the operations are MakeOffer, AcceptOffer, and Reject). The key differences between coordination protocols and monitors [24] is that in the former (*i*) participants are distributed and do not share memory, (*ii*) the invocation of an operation whose guards is not valid in the current state is simply ignored without preempting the caller, and therefore (*iii*) processes do not have to be awaken.

We aim to refine the approach of Azure so to enable algorithmic verification of relevant properties of data-aware coordination of protocols. In fact, as for monitors, the interplay among the operations that modify the state and the guards in the API can lead to unexpected behaviours when informal specifications are used. We illustrate this problem with some examples on the SMP example.

1. The sketch of SMP does not clarify if a participant can play more roles simultaneously; for instance, it is not clear if an owner must be a different instance than buyers.
2. The labels distinguish roles and instances (AR and AIR): in fact, it is assumed that there can be many instances of a same role. Scope and quantification of roles is not clear; for instance, a requirement specified in [33] reads "The transitions between the Item Available and the Offer Placed states can continue until the owner is satisfied with the offer made." This sentence does not clarify if, after a rejection, the new offer can be made by a new buyer or it must be the original one;
3. The sketch specify neither the conditions enabling operations in a given state nor how operations change the state of the contract's variables; should the price of the item remain unchanged when the owner invokes the Reject?

Contributions and Structure. Section 2 introduces *data-aware FSMs* (DAFSMs) to formalise coordination protocols. Roughly, DAFSMs allow specifications (*i*) to express conditions on how operations affect the state of the protocol and (*ii*) to explicitly declare the capabilities of participants. We propose *well-formedness* condition on DAFSMs to rule out erroneous coordination protocols.

The definition of DAFSMs is instrumental to our main contribution which is TRAC, a tool realising our model described in Sect. 3. We build on an initial proposal developed in [1].

The applicability of TRAC is demonstrated by showing how its features can specify and verify the SCs in [32]. Moreover, we discuss the performances of the TRAC with an experimental evaluation (cf. Sect. 4). Our experimental data and the source code of TRAC are available at https://github.com/loctet/TRAC. The reader is referred to the accompanying artefact paper [2] for detailed documentation, examples of usage, and implementation details of TRAC.

Related work and conclusions are given respectively in Sects. 5 and 6.

2   Data-Aware FSMs

In our model, protocols' *participants* cooperate through a *coordinator* according to their *role*. We let $\mathsf{p}, \mathsf{p}', \ldots$ denote *participant variables*, $\mathsf{R}, \mathsf{R}', \ldots$ denote *roles*, and $\mathsf{c}, \mathsf{c}', \ldots$ denote $\mathcal{C}$ *coordinator names*. Each coordinator name c has:

- A finite set $\mathcal{V}_\mathsf{c}$ of *data variables*; we let $\mathsf{c.x}, \mathsf{c.y}, \ldots$ range over $\mathcal{V}_\mathsf{c}$ and write $\mathsf{x}, \mathsf{y}, \ldots$ when the coordinator name is clear from the context. Each variables has an associated data type, e.g., Int, Bool, ...; we also allow usual structured data types like arrays.
- A set of *function names*, ranged over by $\mathsf{c.f}, \mathsf{c.f}', \ldots$. Function parameters, ranged over by $\mathsf{x}, \mathsf{y}, \ldots$, can be either data or participants variables; we allow functions to be applied to different lists of parameters.

An *assignment* takes the form $\mathsf{c.x} := \mathsf{e}$, where e is an expression.[1] The set $\mathcal{B}$ of assignments is ranged over by β while $B, B', \ldots$ range over finite subsets of $\mathcal{B}$ where each variable can be assigned at most once; moreover, we assume that all assignments in B are executed simultaneously. In every assignment $\mathsf{c.x} := \mathsf{e}$ data variables occurring in e must have the old qualifier to refer to their value before the assignments.[2] The set of *guards* $\mathcal{G}$, ranged over by $\mathsf{g}, \mathsf{g}', \ldots$, consists of constraints (i.e., boolean expressions) over data variables and function parameters. Parameter *declarations* are written as $\mathsf{x} : T$ or $\mathsf{p} : \mathsf{R}$ to respectively assign data type T to x and role R to p; we let $\mathcal{D}$ be the set of all declarations and d to range over $\mathcal{D}$. Lists of declarations are denoted by $\vec{\mathsf{d}}$ with the implicit assumption that the parameters in $\vec{\mathsf{d}}$ are pairwise distinct.

The set $\mathcal{P}$ of *qualified participants* consists of the terms generated by

$$\pi ::= \nu\, \mathsf{p} : \mathsf{R} \;\mid\; \mathsf{any}\, \mathsf{p} : \mathsf{R} \;\mid\; \mathsf{p}$$

---

[1] We borrow from Z3 a substantial subset of expressions over variables and parameters (barred participants parameters) whose syntax is standard and therefore omitted. We assume that expressions do not have side effects.

[2] We adapt the mechanism based on the old keyword from the Eiffel language [31] which, as explained in [30] is necessary to render assignments into logical formulae since e.g., $x = x + 1 \Leftrightarrow$ False. This will be used in Definition 5.

where both ν and any are binders. Intuitively, ν p: R specifies that variable p represents a fresh participant with role R while any p: R qualifies p as an existing participant with role R. With p we refer to a participant in the scope of a binder.

Before its formal definition (cf. Definition 1), we give an intuitive account of our model. We use FSMs as coordination protocols with a single coordinator c. The transitions of an FSM represent the call to functions exposed by the coordinator c performed by participants. Such calls may update the current control state (by means of state transitions) and the state of data variables (by mean of assignments). Access to functions can be restricted to some participants (using participants variables and modifiers), and the availability of a function may depend on the current control or data states (using guards). A protocol starts in the initial state of the FSM specifying where the initial state of variables is set by the creator of the coordinator; intuitively, the creator may be thought of as an object in object-oriented programming created by invoking a constructor.

Definition 1. *Let $2^{\mathcal{B}}_{\text{fin}}$ be the set of all finite subsets of $\mathcal{B}$ and $\mathcal{L} = \mathcal{G} \times \mathcal{P} \times \mathcal{F} \times \vec{\mathcal{D}} \times 2^{\mathcal{B}}_{\text{fin}}$ be the set of labels, ranged over by ℓ. A data-aware finite state machine (DAFSM for short) is a tuple $\mathcal{S} = (S, q_0, \rightarrow, F, c, \nu\, p: R, \vec{d_0}, B_0)$ where:*

- *$(S, q_0, \rightarrow, F)$ is an FSM over $\mathcal{L}$ (namely, S is finite set of states, $q_0 \in S$ is the initial state, $\rightarrow \subseteq S \times \mathcal{L} \times S$, and $F \subseteq S$ is the set of accepting states);*
- *$c \in \mathcal{C}$ is the coordinator name;*
- *for each transition label $(g, \pi, f, \vec{d}, B)$, if $c.x := e \in B$ then every data parameter occurring in e occurs in $\vec{d}$, e is well typed, and the data variables occurring in the guards of any of the transitions of $\mathcal{S}$ belong to $\mathcal{V}_c$;*
- *$\nu\, p: R$ binds p to the participant creating the coordinator;*
- *$\vec{d_0} \subseteq \vec{\mathcal{D}}$ is the coordinator's list of declarations, which we consider equivalent up-to α-renaming;*
- *$B_0 \subseteq_{\text{fin}} \mathcal{B}$ is a set of assignments (setting the initial values of the state variables).*

A path is a finite sequence of transitions $s_0 \xrightarrow{\ell_1} s_1 \cdots s_n \xrightarrow{\ell_n} s_{n+1}$ with $s_0 = q_0$.

The next example introduces a convenient graphical notation for DAFSMs in which guards on transitions are in curly brackets for readability; this notation is reminiscent of Hoare triples (guards are not to be confused with sets).

Example 1. Let $\ell_{\text{new}} = \{\text{offer} > 0\}\ \nu\ b: B \triangleright c.\text{makeOffer}(\text{Int} : \text{offer})\ \{c.\text{offer} := \text{offer}\}$ and $\ell_{\text{ext}} = \{\text{offer} > 0\}$ any $b: B \triangleright c.\text{makeOffer}(\text{Int} : \text{offer})\ \{c.\text{offer} := \text{offer}\}$. The DAFSMs below represents the SMP protocol of Sect. 1.

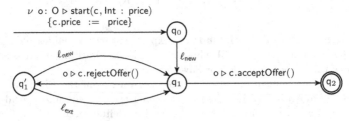

The initial state is q_0 and it is graphically represented by the source-less arrow entering it. The label[3] of this arrow represents the invocation from a new participant o with the owner's role O to the constructor for a coordinator c with a parameter price of type Int. The set of assignments is the singleton initialising the coordinator's variable c.price to price.

In q_0, the only enabled function is c.makeOffer(Int : offer); the first buyer b invoking this function with an actual parameter offer, satisfying the guard offer > 0, moves the protocol to state q_1 while recording the new offer in the coordinator state with the assignment c.offer := offer. Contextually, the state of the coordinator records that the caller b plays role B.

From state q_1 only the owner o can make the protocol progress by either accepting or rejecting the offer. In the former case, the protocol reaches the accepting state q_2 (graphically denoted with a doubly-circled node); in the latter case, the protocol reaches state q_1' where either an existing buyer or a new one can make further offers. ◇

Notably, the DAFSM of Example 1 refines the informal one in Sect. 1 by more precisely specifying that offers can arrive either from previous buyers or new ones (cf. item 2 in Sect. 1).

2.1 Well-Formedness of DAFSM

The restrictions in Definition 1 concern single transitions; however, DAFSMs can model meaningless and wrong behaviours, due to conditions spanning several transitions, e.g., free occurrences of participant variables, lack of participants of a role or inconsistent guards. Below we spell-out those constraints after motivating them with simple examples.

A first issue is the presence of free occurrences of participants names.

Example 2. The DAFSM

$$\xrightarrow{\nu\, o:\, O \triangleright start(c)} \boxed{s_0} \xrightarrow{p \triangleright c.f()} \boxed{s_1}$$

is syntactically erroneous since the participant variable p is not bound. ◇

In our model qualified participants of the form ν p: R and any p: R, and parameter declarations of the form p : R act as binders. In a DAFSM all occurrences of participant variable should be in the scope of a binder to be meaningful.

Definition 2. *A transition* $(s_1, g, \pi, c.f, \vec{d}, B, s_2)$ *binds* p *if and only if:*

$$\exists R : \pi = \nu\, p:\, R \quad \vee \quad \pi = any\, p:\, R \quad \vee \quad p:\, R \in \vec{d}$$

The occurrence of p *in a path* $\sigma = \sigma_1(s_1, g, p, c.f, \vec{d}, B, s_2)\sigma_2$ *is bound in* σ *if there is a transition in* σ_1 *binding* p *and it is bound in a DAFSM* S *if all the paths of* S *including the occurrence binding it. Finally,* S *is closed if all occurrences of participant variables are bound in* S.

---

[3] We may omit writing guards when they are True and assignments when they are empty as in the transitions from q_1.

Another problem arises when the role of a qualified participant is empty.

Example 3. If we bind the occurrence of p in the DAFSM of Example 2 with the binder any, we obtain the closed DAFSM

$$\mathcal{S}_2 = \quad \xrightarrow{\nu\, o\colon O \triangleright \mathsf{start(c)}} \underbrace{s_0} \xrightarrow{\mathsf{any}\ p\colon R \triangleright \mathsf{c.f()}} \underbrace{s_1}$$

However, we argue that $\mathcal{S}_2$ is ill-formed since R is necessarily empty in s_0. Hence no action is possible, and the execution gets stuck in the initial state. ◇

We now propose a simple syntactical check that avoids the problem of empty roles. Notice that a sound and complete procedure for empty roles detection subsumes reachability, which may be undecidable depending on the chosen expressivity of constraints and expressions.

Definition 3. *A binder expands* role R *if it is a qualified participant of the form* $\nu\, p\colon R$ *or a parameter declaration of the form* $p : R$. *A transition expands* role R *if its binder expands* role R. *A role* R *is expanded* in a path σ *if and only if:*

$$\sigma = \sigma_1(s_1, g, \mathsf{any}\ p\colon R, c.f, \vec{d}, B, s_2)\sigma_2 \implies \exists t \in \sigma_1 : t\ \textit{expands}\ R$$

A DAFSM $\mathcal{S}$ *expands a role* R *if every path of* $\mathcal{S}$ *expands* R. *Finally,* $\mathcal{S}$ *is* (strongly) *empty-role free* if $\mathcal{S}$ *expands every role in* $\mathcal{S}$.

Despite the quantification over the possibly infinite set of all paths, empty-role freedom can be decided by considering only *acyclic* paths, that is paths which contain at most one occurrence of each state. Clearly, there are only finitely many acyclic paths. Notice that $\mathcal{S}_2$ above is not empty-role free.

Finally, progress can be jeopardised if assignments falsify all the guards of the subsequent transitions, as in the next example.

Example 4. The DAFSM below is both closed and empty-role free, as the caller of c.f is o which is bound by the constructor, and there are no any modifiers.

$$\xrightarrow{\nu\, o\colon O \triangleright \mathsf{start(c)}\ \{c.x := 0\}} \underbrace{s_0} \xrightarrow{\{c.x > 0\}\ o \triangleright \mathsf{c.f()}} \underbrace{s_1}$$

Crucially, c.x > 0 will never be satisfied at run-time because c.x is initialised to 0 and never changed. So again every execution gets stuck in state s_0. ◇

Similarly to empty roles, detecting inconsistencies is undecidable at least for expressive enough constraints and expressions. We therefore devise a syntactic technique amenable of algorithmic verification. The idea is to check that every transition t, regardless of the "history" of the current execution, leads to a state which is either accepting or it has at least a transition enabled. This is intuitively accomplished by checking that the guard of t, after being updated according to the assignments of t, implies the disjunction of the guards of the outgoing transitions from the target state of t. Before formally introduce our notion of consistency, we need a few auxiliary definitions.

Definition 4. *For all states* s, *we define the* progress constraint g_s *as* True *when* s *is accepting, and otherwise as the disjunction of guards of the outgoing transitions of* s. *Let* c.x $\notin B$ *mean that for all* c.y $:= e \in B$, x *and* y *differ, and* old c.x *does not occur in expression* e.

The progress constraint *of an assignment set B is*

$$g_B = \bigwedge_{(c.x := e) \in B} c.x = e \wedge \bigwedge_{c.x \notin B} c.x = old\ c.x$$

In order to define our notion of consistency we need to work with closed formulae; for this reason we introduce universal and existential closures of logical propositions. Given a set of variables $X = \{x_1, \ldots, x_n\}$, we write $\forall X : \phi$ for the proposition $\forall x_1, \ldots, \forall x_n : \phi$, and likewise for $\exists X : \phi$.

In the following definition we assume for simplicity that each data parameter is declared at most once in the DAFSM; this assumption does not affect generality since data parameters can be alpha-converted.[4]

Definition 5. *A transition* $t = (s, g, \pi, c.f, \vec{d}, B, s')$ *is consistent if:*

$$\forall X : \exists Y : (g\sigma \wedge g_B) \implies g_{s'}$$

where $X = \{$c.x, old c.x $\mid$ c.x is a contract variables of c$\}$, Y *is the set of symbols for data parameters occurring in $\vec{d}$ or in any outgoing transition from* s', *and σ is the substitution such that $\sigma :$ c.x $\mapsto$ old c.x for all contract variables* c.x *of* c.
A DAFSM $\mathcal{S}$ is consistent *if so is every transition of $\mathcal{S}$.*

Non-determinism could be useful for some applications, but most of the time *determinism* is a desirable property (e.g., SCs are usually required to be deterministic [8]). Before the formal definition, we give a few examples illustrating how non-determinism may arise in DAFSMs.

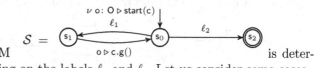

Example 5. The DAFSM is deterministic or not, depending on the labels ℓ_1 and ℓ_2. Let us consider some cases.

$\ell_1 = \ell_2 = $ o $\triangleright$ c.g() $\mathcal{S}$ is non-deterministic because a call to function c.f by o can lead either to s_1 or to s_2.

$\ell_1 = \nu$ p: R $\triangleright$ c.g() and $\ell_2 = $ any p: R $\triangleright$ c.g() $\mathcal{S}$ is deterministic intuitively because the next state is unambiguously determined by the caller of c.g: the protocol moves to s_1 or s_2 depending whether the call is performed by an existing or a new participant.

$\ell_1 = \{x \le 10\}$ o $\triangleright$ c.g(x : Int) and $\ell_2 = \{x > 10\}$ o $\triangleright$ c.g(x : Int) $\mathcal{S}$ is deterministic because guard x $\le$ 10 leading to s_1 and guard x $>$ 10 leading to s_2 are disjoint; therefore the next state is determined by the value of the parameter x, and every value enables at most one transition.

---

[4] TRAC actually suitably alpha-converts data parameters to meet this assumption.

Also, taking ℓ_1 as in the latter case and $\ell_2 = \{x \geq 10\}$ o▷c.g(x : Int) would make
S non-deterministic because the guards of ℓ_1 and of ℓ_2 are not disjoint therefore
the next state is not determined by the caller of c.g.   ◇

We now define a notion of *strong determinism*, which is decidable and can be
efficiently established. To this aim, we first define the binary relation $\# \subseteq \mathcal{P} \times \mathcal{P}$
as the least symmetric relation satisfying:

$$\nu \, p: R\#p', \quad \nu \, p: R\#\text{any } p': O, \quad \text{and} \quad R \neq O \implies \text{any } p: R\#\text{any } p': O \quad (1)$$

Intuitively, if $\pi_1 \# \pi_2$, then the participants in π_1 and π_2 *differ*. Indeed, the first
two item just say that a new participant is necessarily different from an existing
one. The third item says that two participant with different roles are necessarily
different (since we require that every participant can have at most one role).

We now define *strong determinism* which basically ensures that different
transitions calling the same function from a same participant have mutually
exclusive guards.

Definition 6. *A DAFSM is* (strongly) deterministic *if for all of its transitions*
$t_1 \neq t_2$ *from the same source state and calling the same function we have:*

$$(g_1 \wedge g_2) \implies (\pi_1 \# \pi_2)$$

where, for $i \in \{1, 2\}$, g_i *is the guard of* t_i *and* π_i *is the qualified participant of*
t_i.

Finally, we can formalise our notion of well-formedness.

Definition 7. *A DAFSM is* well-formed *when empty-role free, consistent, and*
deterministic.

Example 6. Consider the following well-formed DAFSM.

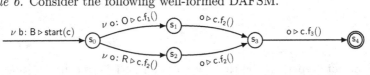

In fact, it is easy to see that all o is defined on each transition to and from
state s_3, there are no (undefined) variables, and that consistency trivially holds.
                                                                                      ◇

Example 7. The following DAFSM is not well-formed

$$\nu \, o: O \triangleright \text{start(c)} \{c.x := 1\} \quad s_0 \quad o \triangleright c.f_1() \quad s_1 \quad \{c.x > 0\} \, o \triangleright c.f_2() \quad s_2$$

in fact, the transition from s_0 violates Definition 5 since True does not imply
c.x > 0 hinting that the protocol could get stuck in state s_1. However, this never
happens because c.x is initially set to 1 and never changed, hence the transition
from s_1 would be enabled when the protocol lands in s_1.   ◇

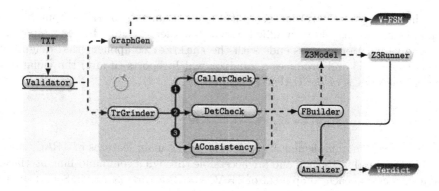

Fig. 1. The architecture of TRAC (Color figure online)

3   The Tool

We implement our model in TRAC. Specifically, TRAC renders DAFSMs in terms
of a DSL to specify DAFSMs and verify the well-formedness condition defined
in Sect. 2 relying on the SMT solver Z3. We present the architecture of TRAC in
Sect. 3.1 and some implementation details in Sect. 3.2.

3.1   Architecture

Figure 1 represents the architecture of TRAC which, for convenience, is com-
partmentalised into two principal modules: DAFSM parsing and visualisation
(yellow box) and TRAC's core (orange box). The latter module implements well-
formedness check (green box). Solid arrows represent calls between components
while dashed arrows data IO.

The flow starts Validator performing basic syntactic checks on a textual
representation[5] of DAFSMs and transforming the input in a format that simplifies the analysis of the following phases. Specifically, the output of Validator
can be passed (*i*) to GraphGen, a component yielding a visual representation
of DAFSMs (V-FSM output) and (*ii*) to the "transitions Grinder" TrGrinder
component (orange box) for well-formedness checking.

The component TrGrinder relays each transition of the DAFSM in input to
the components in the green box that perform the verification of well-formedness
according to Sect. 2; more precisely:

- CallerCheck (arrow ❶) that returns a boolean which is true if, and only if,
  the DAFSM is closed and strongly empty-role free;
- DetCheck (arrow ❷) that builds a Z3 formula which is true if, and only if,
  the state is strongly deterministic;
- AConsistency (arrow ❸) to generate a Z3 formula which holds if, and only
  if, the transition is consistent.

---

[5] Our DSL is immaterial here; it is described in the accompanying artefact submission.

The component `FBuilder` computes the conjunction of the output of the components above, yelding a `Z3Model`, which is then executed by the `Z3Runner`.

The verification process ends with the `Analizer` component that diagnoses the output of Z3 and produces a `Verdict` which reports (if any) the violations of well-formedness of the DAFSM in input.

3.2 Implementation

We now give some implementation details on the main features of TRAC which are implemented in Python and are accessible through a command-line interface. Here we focus on each component of TRAC's architecture; as said in Sect. 1, more implementation details can be found in [2].

The `Validator` processes the input which essentially lists transitions of a DAFSM expressed in the format of our DSL. For instance, the transition to make offers of Example 1 is rendered in our DSL as

```
S0 {_offer>0} b:B > c.makeOffer(int _offer) {offer := _offer} S1
```

Basically, `Validator` reads each transition in the file and extract participants, actions, states, preconditions, assignments and input parameters of the action. To inspect the DAFSM in input, TRAC relies on `GraphGen`[6] which creates a visual representation of graphs.

The DAFSM obtained by `Validator` is transformed by `TrGrinder` in an internal format suitable for the analysis. Iterating on the transitions, `TrGrinder` invokes different checker component by supplying them with the necessary data.

The first component invoked by `TrGrinder` is `CallerCheck` which takes in input a transition t and the (internal representation of the) DAFSM. If the caller of t is of the form p or any p: R, `CallerCheck` retrieves all acyclic paths[7] that, from the initial state, lead to t's source state, and then checks that every such path contains ν p: R or any p: R for some R (if the caller was p), or contains ν p: R (if the caller was any p: R). As soon as a path violates that condition, `CallerCheck` halts returning False otherwise True is returned. To avoid checking again a same path, the formula is saved and just retrieved when transitions with same same source and caller as t are considered.

The component `DetCheck` implements Definition 6. The component takes as inputs a transition t and the list $\mathcal{T}_t$ of transitions with source the target of t. The list is partitioned by grouping transitions that invoke the same function and whose qualified participants are not related by # (Eq. (1)). Let $\mathcal{F}_t$ be the set of all such partitions. For non-singleton partitions, `DetCheck` builds a Z3 formula which is true if, and only if, whenever the guard of a transition is true the guards of the other transitions are false. More precisely, an invocation of `DetCheck` with

---

[6] `GraphGen` is a wrap component that uses GraphStream [35] to generate the visual FSM (V-FSM).

[7] Crucially, the internal format produced by `TrGrinder` is instrumental for extracting acyclic paths using the `networkx` library [23].

parameters t and $\mathcal{T}_t$ returns a Z3 formula corresponding to

$$\Phi_{\text{DetCheck}} = \bigwedge_{F \in \mathcal{F}_t} \Phi(F)$$

where, assuming that $g_{t'}$ is the guard of a transition t', we set

$$\Phi(F) = \bigwedge_{t' \in F} \left(g_{t'} \implies \bigwedge_{t'' \in F,\ t'' \neq t'} \neg g_{t''} \right)$$

We hence apply DetCheck to every transition t and avoid double checking by keeping track of checked states.

Component AConsistency implements Definition 5. Using the formula of the formal definition "as is" however would be inefficient, because of the presence of universal quantification and many unnecessary variables and equations (those of the form c.x = old c.x). Universal quantification, as usual with SMT solvers, is dealt with by just removing quantifiers and negating the formula. The result of the checker will be negated again at the end. Unnecessary equations are removed as follows. Given a transition t and a list of outgoing transitions from its source, AConsistency scrutinises the pre-conditions and postconditions for shared state variables. When a variable is used in both conditions, AConsistency rename the occurrences of the variable in the pre-conditions by adding the _old suffix. Likewise, the suffix _old is added to state variables x occurring in the right-hand side of an assignment of the post-condition if x is assigned in the post-conditions. Subsequently, the assignments in the postconditions are transformed in a conjunction of equations representing the state update. Finally, AConsistency constructs a Z3 formula which ensures that given the pre-conditions and post-conditions bounded by input variables, at least one precondition of the outgoing transitions should be met.

From the outputs of each of the above components, FBuilder generates a single formula composed of the conjunction of all the formulae for each transition. After going through all transitions, FBuilder compiles all the generated Z3 formulas to build the Z3Model. After processing all transitions, FBuilder outputs a Python file containing the set of Z3 formulae, referred in Fig. 1 as the Z3Model. This model includes all the necessary libraries, variable declarations, and solver configurations to run the model and determine its satisfiability.

The component Z3Runner takes this Python file, executes it, and forwards the results to the Analizer. If the Z3Model is found to be satisfiable, it indicates that the DAFSM is well-formed; otherwise, it is deemed non-well-formed. This final output is the Verdict.

Finally, we remark that TRAC operates in two modes: a non-stop mode, which builds and evaluates the entire model (used for our experimental evaluation) and a stop mode, which halts immediately as soon as a violation of well-formedness if found.

4 Evaluation

We evaluate DAFSMs expressiveness and TRAC performance using two benchmarks. The first consists of the examples from the Azure BC workbench [32], showing how the DAFSMs (and the current version of TRAC) deals with simple, yet realistic, SCs also used in related work (e.g., [21]); the second contains randomly generated large examples to stress-test TRAC.

Table 1. Features in the Azure benchmark

	ICI	BI	PP	RR	MPR
Hello Blockchain	⊖	✓	⊖	⊖	⊖
Bazaar	×	✓	⊖	⊖	⊖
Ping Pong	×	✓	⊖	⊖	⊖
Defective Component Counter	⊖	✓	✓	⊖	⊖
Frequent Flyer Rewards Calculator	⊖	✓	✓	⊖	⊖
Room Thermostat	⊖	⊖	✓	⊖	⊖
Simple Marketplace	⊖	✓	⊖	↗	⊖
Asset Transfer	⊖	✓	✓	↗	⊖
Basic Provenance	⊖	✓	✓	↗	⊖
Refrigerated Transport	⊖	✓	✓	↗	↗
Digital Locker	⊖	✓	✓	↗	↗

Legend

✓: feature present in the example and TRAC successfully handles it
× : feature present but not supported by TRAC
⊖ : feature not present int to the example
↗ : feature present and TRAC supports it with some workarounds

These examples exhibit a variety of features that are essential for the representation of SCs. We consider a significant range of features in our analysis, including inter-contracts interactions (ICI), joining of new participants by-invocation (BI) or by participant passing (PP), role revocation (RR), and the possibility for a participant to assume multiple roles (MPR). Our aim is to assess to what degree TRAC can model these features, present in illustrative expressive examples in the literature on SCs. Our findings are outlined in Table 1.[8] Notably, TRAC covers most of the features and the only limitation is that TRAC does not support yet inter-contracts interactions (ICI column). Notably, we could approximately model the examples with RR and MPR using some workarounds. In particular, in all the examples featuring RR revocation was performed on singleton roles, that is roles that can be played by at most one participant at a time. Moreover, every revocation is followed by a re-assignment of the role to a participant. We therefore modelled this situation using a participant variable for the role. So, $\nu\, p : R$ simultaneously assigns role to p, and revokes R from the

---

[8] Commonplace features such as multiple participants and multiple roles are present in all the examples and supported by TRAC.

previous participant holding it. This has the drawback that the role cannot be reassigned to a participant formerly holding it. For MPR, in the examples considered the participant with multiple roles was at most one. We could therefore add explicit moves for that participant only to emulate it having two roles.

We now turn our attention to the performance of TRAC, using a benchmark of randomly generated DAFSMs. More precisely, we evaluated TRAC using a data set of 135 DAFSMs[9] randomly generated according to the following process.[10] Let $\mathsf{rand}(i, j)$ be a random number between number i and $j \geq i$ (we let $\mathsf{rand}(i) = \mathsf{rand}(1, i)$). We fix a maximal number of participants $p \in \mathsf{rand}(2, 10)$, of functions $f \in \mathsf{rand}(10, 20)$, and of data variables $v \in \mathsf{rand}(50)$. For each $s \in \{10, 20, 30\}$ and for each $s \leq t \leq 3s$ such that $t \mod 5 = 0$ we generate five DAFSMs, each having s states, by iterating the following steps until all nodes are connected and t transitions have been generated:

- create $\mathsf{rand}(2, 5)$ transitions with the current state as source and randomly selected target nodes not connected yet (if any, otherwise the targets are selected randomly on the whole set of nodes);[11]
- for each of the transitions a qualified participants and an operation with a number of parameters are randomly selected according to $\mathsf{rand}(p)$, $\mathsf{rand}(0, f)$, and $\mathsf{rand}(0, v)$.

We measured the performance of DetCheck, AConsistency, and CallerCheck by averaging the running time over ten executions of each generated DAFSM. The experiments were conducted on a Dell XPS 8960, 13th Gen Intel Core (9-

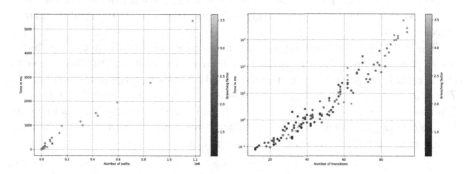

Fig. 2. CallerCheck time against of number paths (left) and transitions (right, y-axis in logaritmic scale)

---

[9] Number fixed to obtain graphs with a few dozens states but increasing number of transitions and qualified participants.

[10] The parameters (fixable as script inputs) were set in order to obtain sufficiently large DAFSMs (covering cases with millions of paths) while maintaining the execution time below one hour.

[11] We do not spell out the details of the random generation of guards and assignments – they are immaterial for the performance of DetCheck, AConsistency, and FBuilder.

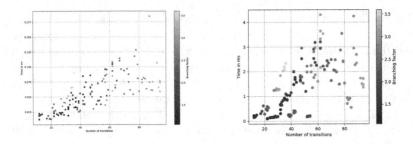

Fig. 3. DetCheck (left) AConsistency (right) time against number of transitions

13900K) with 32 cores and 32GB RAM running Linux 6.5.0-17-generic (Ubuntu 23.10, 64bit). The results are reported in the following plots that we now discuss.

The evaluation results presented in Fig. 2 shows the execution time taken for CallerCheck against the number of paths in the model: as the number of paths increases with the number of transitions of the FSM, the outcome confirms that times to check closedness and empty-role freeness is exponential in the number of transitions. Interestingly, even in the cases with more that 10^6 paths, CallerCheck terminates the analysis in less that 6 seconds.[12]

Figure 3 shows the results of our analysis for DetCheck and AConsistency. The left plot in Fig. 3 hints that the execution time of DetCheck linearly grows with the number of transitions. Figure 3 right shows that the time to run AConsistency is too low to allow any conclusion.

These plots result from initial investigations of the performances of the main components of TRAC.[13] Further analysis is require to correlated number of transitions and time.

The complexity of checking well-formedness is dominated by CallerCheck, which is exponential in the number of transitions since CallerCheck has to check a path property. Indeed, the complexity of other components depends by Z3 performance, which is acceptable unless guards contain (nested) quantifiers. Studying the complexity of Z3 is not our goal here: our experiments focus on the source of complexity of TRAC, which shows good performances even for experiments with high number of paths (cf. Fig. 2).

5   Related Works

The literature on models of coordination is vast. We restrict our comparison to tool-supported approaches within three categories: FSM-based models, formal

---

[12] To improve the readability of the left plot of Fig. 2 we did not include two DAFSMs whose number of paths was higher more than a factor of 20 that other instances. This is not necessary for plot on the right, which in fact includes all the generated DAFSMs, since there we use a logarithmic scale.

[13] Further, more systematic, experiments are needed to lead to broader conclusions.

language models, and domain-specific languages for SCs. We compare DAFSMs with other coordination models as well as with approaches specific to SCs.

Coordination models of distributed systems based on extensions of FSMs with (fragments) of first-order logic have appeared in the literature. Notably data-aware version of BIP and REO have been studied in [16,37]. As in DAFSMs, data can be accessed and modified as part of an interaction in both BIP and REO. A difference with our model is that interactions can involve more participants and updates are local to the participants of interactions. This also applies to recent models based on asserted communicating finite-state machines [36,38].

Choreography automata [3] and their extension with assertions [19] are global specifications for communicating systems behind Corinne [34] and CAScr [20]. Both these tools are designed to check well-formedness conditions different than ours (resp. those in [3] and in [19]) and neither of them supports multiple instances of roles. Assertions in CAScr are not guards; they express rely-guarantee conditions between the sender and the receiver of interactions. In the same vein, CAT [5] is an automata-based tool for the verification of communication protocols. Based on *contract automata* [4,6,7], CAT is not data-aware and its contracts purely regard the communication interface of participants (which are also fixed).

Protocol languages that advocates a programming style based on FSMs to specify SCs are FSolidM framework [28,29] and SMARTSCRIBBLE [17]. The former relies on model checking CTL formulae to verify safety and liveness properties (including deadlock-freedom). The automata have a global state, represented by contract, input, and output variables, and transitions are guarded by boolean conditions on these variables. The tool has been extended to feature code generation and interaction verification between multiple SCs [26]. This progress marked a substantial improvement in detecting common vulnerabilities such as re-entrancy attacks and fallback errors.

The interaction patterns programmable with SMARTSCRIBBLE [17] correspond to FSMs. The tool extracts Plutus code[14] from valid protocol descriptions, leaving to the developer the task to fill in the application logic. Automatic code generation (a feature we aim to) greatly accelerates developing time, and guarantee correct-by-construction code (in what concerns the interaction patterns).

Participants are first-class citizens in DAFSMs while FSolidM encodes them with variables and SMARTSCRIBBLE identifies participants with roles which are fixed statically. Also, SMARTSCRIBBLE does not support assertions.

An application of Event-B to SCs generating automatically Solidity code appeared in [39]. There is no report on the validation of the tool with benchmarks.

A parallel line of research explores the use of BC technology to audit choreographic programs [11,12]. Roughly, the idea is to generate Solidity contracts from models expressed as BPMN [22], so that the contracts' trace the execution of their choreography. Notably, [13] is an extension of [12] which allows multiple participants to play the same role. This line of work has fairly different goals

---

[14] Plutus is the programming language to develop SCs to the Cardano BC.

than ours: its aim is to exploit BC immutability to record the execution in a secure way. Our approach instead concerns modelling and verifying distributed applications coordinated by a FSM, possibly implemented as an SC.

The previous tools take a "top-down approach" – propose an abstraction to (rigorously) define formal models of computations. In several cases, SCs code is automatically generated from (correct) specifications. The next proposals, Obsidian [10] and Stipula [14,15,27], embed the definition of the FSM in the contracts' programming language. Both are inspired by *typestates* [40] and their use in programming languages [18]: states are explicit entities with a defined API; invocations to an operation of the API of a state possibly update of the variables of the program and yield to (possibly) another state. In this respect, the execution model of both languages is quite similar to DAFSMs.

Obsidian uses typestates and linear types [41] to control "assets" (critical resources of SCs). Safe, yet flexible, aliasing is ensured with an ownership type system [9]. Two case studies shows usability of Obsidian in "real-world" scenarios.

Stipula focuses on legal contracts and provides a strict discipline to guarantee *liquidity*: no asset remains frozen forever.

The Azure repository has been used as a benchmark in [21] where solidity code is annotated with assertions. There the Contractor toolkit extracts from the annotate code data-aware abstractions (akin to FSMs). Such abstraction can then be validate with respect to user-defined properties. The main strength of Contractor is the possibility to automatically construct sound models, while its main drawback is that it does not directly support multi object protocols.

6   Conclusions and Future Works

This paper proposes DAFSMs, a data-aware coordination model for orchestrated computation applicable to the description of multiparty protocols. The key novelties are: 1. support for multiple participants, organised by roles, which can dynamically join a protocol; 2. assertions used to describe protocol states and control how (parametrised) actions change it;3. a notion of well-formed models and a checking algorithm; 4. a tool for describing systems with DAFSMs, visualising them as FSMs, and checking well-formedness.

The usual limits of over-approximating approaches apply to TRAC; for instance, TRAC will report that the DAFSM of Example 7 is not well-formed, even though it is sound. Our approach does not support features such as role revocation and inter-contract interactions that are sometimes used in e.g., smart contracts.

We are currently working on generalisations of the model to allow role revocation. In scope of future work is to define a model-checking approach to support safety and liveness property analysis. Also, a possible evolution of TRAC is to add suggestions to help designers to address "incompleteness" of models; for instance, TRAC could flag a warning if outgoing transitions of a state do not cover some cases. Other interesting lines of work are code generation and extraction of DAFSMs from actual SC programs. A deeper analysis of the performances should also be conducted on more case studies and possibly refining the random generation of DAFSMs.

Acknowledgements. The authors thank the anonymous reviewers for their comments and Franco Raimondi for his tips on Z3.

References

1. Afonso, J.: Mechanisms for modeling and validation of smart contracts. Master's thesis, Departamento de Informática, NOVA School of Science and Technology (2023). Advisor: António Ravara
2. Afonso, J., Konjoh Selabi, E., Murgia, M., Tuosto, E., Ravara, A.: Artefact submission for paper #8 of COORDINATION 2024 (2024). https://doi.org/10.5281/zenodo.10996456
3. Barbanera, F., Lanese, I., Tuosto, E.: Choreography automata. In: Bliudze, S., Bocchi, L. (eds.) COORDINATION 2020. LNCS, vol. 12134, pp. 86–106. Springer, Cham (2020). https://doi.org/10.1007/978-3-030-50029-0_6
4. Basile, D., ter Beek, M.: Contract automata library. Sci. Comput. Program. **221**, 102841 (2022). https://doi.org/10.1016/J.SCICO.2022.102841
5. Basile, D., Degano, P., Ferrari, G.-L., Tuosto, E.: Playing with our CAT and communication-centric applications. In: Albert, E., Lanese, I. (eds.) FORTE 2016. LNCS, vol. 9688, pp. 62–73. Springer, Cham (2016). https://doi.org/10.1007/978-3-319-39570-8_5
6. Basile, D., ter Beek, M.: A runtime environment for contract automata. In: Chechik, M., Katoen, J., Leucker, M. (eds.) FM 2023. LNCS, vol. 14000, pp. 550–567. Springer, Cham (2023). https://doi.org/10.1007/978-3-031-27481-7_31
7. Basile, D., ter Beek, M., Pugliese, R.: Synthesis of orchestrations and choreographies: bridging the gap between supervisory control and coordination of services. Log. Methods Comput. Sci. **16**(2) (2020). https://doi.org/10.23638/LMCS-16(2:9)2020
8. Buterin, V.: Ethereum: a next generation smart contract and decentralized application platform (2014). https://ethereum.org/whitepaper
9. Clarke, D., Östlund, J., Sergey, I., Wrigstad, T.: Ownership types: a survey. In: Clarke, D., Noble, J., Wrigstad, T. (eds.) Aliasing in Object-Oriented Programming. Types, Analysis and Verification. LNCS, vol. 7850, pp. 15–58. Springer, Heidelberg (2013). https://doi.org/10.1007/978-3-642-36946-9_3
10. Coblenz, M.J., et al.: Obsidian: typestate and assets for safer blockchain programming. ACM Trans. Program. Lang. Syst. **42**(3), 14:1–14:82 (2020). https://doi.org/10.1145/3417516
11. Corradini, F., Marcelletti, A., Morichetta, A., Polini, A., Re, B., Tiezzi, F.: Chorchain: a blockchain-based framework for executing and auditing BPMN choreographies. In: BPM (PhD/Demos). CEUR Workshop Proceedings, vol. 3216, pp. 132–136. CEUR-WS.org (2022)
12. Corradini, F., Marcelletti, A., Morichetta, A., Polini, A., Re, B., Tiezzi, F.: Engineering trustable and auditable choreography-based systems using blockchain. ACM Trans. Manag. Inf. Syst. **13**(3), 31:1–31:53 (2022). https://doi.org/10.1145/3505225

13. Corradini, F., Marcelletti, A., Morichetta, A., Polini, A., Re, B., Tiezzi, F.: Blockchain-based execution of BPMN choreographies with multiple instances. Distributed Ledger Technol. Res. Pract. (2023). https://doi.org/10.1145/3637555

14. Crafa, S., Laneve, C.: Liquidity analysis in resource-aware programming. In: Tarifa, S.L.T., Proença, J. (eds.) FACS 2022. LNCS, vol. 13712, pp. 205–221. Springer, Cham (2022). https://doi.org/10.1007/978-3-031-20872-0_12

15. Crafa, S., Laneve, C., Sartor, G., Veschetti, A.: Pacta sunt servanda: legal contracts in *Stipula*. Sci. Comput. Program. **225** (2023). https://doi.org/10.1016/J.SCICO.2022.102911

16. Dokter, K., Jongmans, S.S., Arbab, F., Bliudze, S.: Combine and conquer: relating BIP and Reo. J. Logic Algebraic Methods Program. **86**(1), 134–156 (2017). https://doi.org/10.1016/j.jlamp.2016.09.008

17. Falcão, A., Mordido, A., Vasconcelos, V.T.: Protocol-based smart contract generation. In: Matsuo, S., et al. (eds.) FC 2022. LNCS, vol. 13412, pp. 555–582. Springer, Cham (2022). https://doi.org/10.1007/978-3-031-32415-4_34

18. Garcia, R., Tanter, É., Wolff, R., Aldrich, J.: Foundations of typestate-oriented programming. ACM Trans. Program. Lang. Syst. **36**(4), 12 (2014). https://doi.org/10.1145/2629609

19. Gheri, L., Lanese, I., Sayers, N., Tuosto, E., Yoshida, N.: Design-by-contract for flexible multiparty session protocols. In: Ali, K., Vitek, J. (eds.) 36th European Conference on Object-Oriented Programming (ECOOP 2022). Leibniz International Proceedings in Informatics (LIPIcs), vol. 222, pp. 8:1–8:28. Schloss Dagstuhl – Leibniz-Zentrum für Informatik, Dagstuhl, Germany (2022). https://doi.org/10.4230/LIPIcs.ECOOP.2022.8

20. Gheri, L., Lanese, I., Sayers, N., Tuosto, E., Yoshida, N.: Design-by-contract for flexible multiparty session protocols (artifact). Dagstuhl Artifacts Ser. **8**(2), 21:1–21:5 (2022). https://doi.org/10.4230/DARTS.8.2.21

21. Godoy, J., Galeotti, J.P., Garbervetsky, D., Uchitel, S.: Predicate abstractions for smart contract validation. In: Proceedings of the 25th International Conference on Model Driven Engineering Languages and Systems, MODELS 2022, pp. 289–299. ACM (2022). https://doi.org/10.1145/3550355.3552462

22. Object Management Group: Business Process Model and Notation. http://www.bpmn.org

23. Hagberg, A.A., Schult, D.A., Swart, P.J.: Exploring network structure, dynamics, and function using networkx. In: Varoquaux, G., Vaught, T., Millman, J. (eds.) Proceedings of the 7th Python in Science Conference, Pasadena, CA USA, pp. 11–15 (2008)

24. Hansen, P.: Operating System Principles. Prentice-Hall, Hoboken (1973)

25. Kavantzas, N., Burdett, D., Ritzinger, G., Fletcher, T., Lafon, Y.: Working Draft 17 December 2004. http://www.w3.org/TR/2004/WD-ws-cdl-10-20041217

26. Keerthi Nelaturu, A.M., et al.: Correct-by-design interacting smart contracts and a systematic approach for verifying erc20 and erc721 contracts with verisolid. IEEE Trans. Dependable Secure Comput. **20** (2023). https://doi.org/10.1109/TDSC.2022.3200840

27. Laneve, C.: Liquidity analysis in resource-aware programming. J. Log. Algebraic Methods Program. (2023)

28. Mavridou, A., Laszka, A.: Designing secure ethereum smart contracts: a finite state machine based approach. In: Meiklejohn, S., Sako, K. (eds.) FC 2018. LNCS, vol. 10957, pp. 523–540. Springer, Heidelberg (2018). https://doi.org/10.1007/978-3-662-58387-6_28

29. Mavridou, A., Laszka, A., Stachtiari, E., Dubey, A.: Verisolid: correct-by-design smart contracts for ethereum. In: Goldberg, I., Moore, T. (eds.) FC 2019. LNCS, vol. 11598, pp. 446–465. Springer, Cham (2019). https://doi.org/10.1007/978-3-030-32101-7_27

30. Meyer, B.: Introduction to the Theory of Programming Languages. Prentice-Hall, Hoboken (1990)

31. Meyer, B.: Eiffel: The Language. Prentice-Hall, Hoboken (1991). http://www.eiffel.com/doc/#etl

32. Microsoft: The blockchain workbench (2019). https://github.com/Azure-Samples/blockchain/tree/master/blockchain-workbench

33. Microsoft: Simple marketplace sample application for azure blockchain workbench (2019).   https://github.com/Azure-Samples/blockchain/tree/master/blockchain-workbench/application-and-smart-contract-samples/simple-marketplace

34. Orlando, S., Pasquale, V.D., Barbanera, F., Lanese, I., Tuosto, E.: Corinne, a tool for choreography automata. In: Salaün, G., Wijs, A. (eds.) FACS 2021. LNCS, vol. 13077, pp. 82–92. Springer, Cham (2021). https://doi.org/10.1007/978-3-030-90636-8_5

35. Pigné, Y., Dutot, A., Guinand, F., Olivier, D.: Graphstream: a tool for bridging the gap between complex systems and dynamic graphs (2008)

36. Pombo, C., Suñé, A., Tuosto, E.: A dynamic temporal logic for quality of service in choreographic models. In: Ábrahám, E., Dubslaff, C., Tarifa, S. (eds.) ICTAC 2023. LNCS, vol. 14446, pp. 119–138. Springer, Cham (2023). https://doi.org/10.1007/978-3-031-47963-2_9

37. Qin, X., Bliudze, S., Madelaine, E., Hou, Z., Deng, Y., Zhang, M.: SMT-based generation of symbolic automata. Acta Informatica **57**, 627–656 (2020). https://doi.org/10.1007/s00236-020-00367-6

38. Senarruzza Anabia, D.: Bisimulación de Data-aware Communicating Finite State Machines con propiedades en las acciones. Master's thesis, Departamento de Computación, Facultad de Ciencias Exactas y Naturales, Universidad de Buenos Aires (2023). advisors: Carlos G. Lopez Pombo and Hernán C. Melgratti

39. Singh, N.K., Fajge, A.M., Halder, R., Alam, M.I.: Formal verification and code generation for solidity smart contracts. In: Distributed Computing to Blockchain, pp. 125–144. Elsevier (2023). https://doi.org/10.1016/B978-0-323-96146-2.00028-0

40. Strom, R.E., Yemini, S.: Typestate: a programming language concept for enhancing software reliability. IEEE Trans. Software Eng. **SE-12**(1), 157–171 (1986). https://doi.org/10.1109/TSE.1986.6312929

41. Wadler, P.: Linear types can change the world! In: Programming Concepts and Methods: Proceedings of the IFIP Working Group 2.2, 2.3 Working Conference on Programming Concepts and Methods, p. 561. North-Holland (1990)

ScaFi-Blocks: A Visual Aggregate Programming Environment for Low-Code Swarm Design

Gianluca Aguzzi$^{(\boxtimes)}$, Roberto Casadei , Matteo Cerioni, and Mirko Viroli

Alma Mater Studiorum – Universitá di Bologna, Cesena, Italy
{gianluca.aguzzi,roby.casadei,mirko.viroli}@unibo.it,
matteo.cerioni2@studio.unibo.it

Abstract. Swarm programming is focused on the design and implementation of algorithms for large-scale systems, such as fleets of robots, ensembles of IoT devices, and sensor networks. Writing algorithms for these systems requires skills and familiarity with programming languages, which can be a barrier for non-expert users. Even if visual programming environments have been proposed for swarm systems, they are often limited to specific platforms or tasks, and do not provide a high-level programming model that can be used to design algorithms for a wide range of swarm systems. Therefore, in this paper, we propose a low-code swarm programming environment, called ScaFi-Blocks, which allows users to design and implement swarm algorithms visually.

ScaFi-Blocks is based on the ScaFi aggregate computing framework, which provides a high-level programming model for the design of distributed algorithms. Aggregate computing is based on the concept of field-based coordination, and it allows users to design algorithms by composing simple building blocks, which motivates the design of the proposed artefact. The environment is designed to be user-friendly and to support the design of a wide range of collective applications. In this paper, we present the architecture of ScaFi-Blocks, discuss its features and capabilities, and provide a preliminary evaluation of the programming environment based on a case study featuring articulated swarm behaviour.

Keywords: field-based coordination · low-code · visual programming · aggregate computing · swarm robotics · macroprogramming

1 Introduction

Swarm programming is an emergent approach for devising collective algorithms within extensive, decentralized systems like swarms of robots, IoT device ensembles, and sensor networks. The intrinsic complexity and dynamic nature of such systems present challenges in articulating desired collective behaviours succinctly and effectively. Traditional device-centric programming paradigms fall short in addressing the needs of large-scale system design, amplifying the cognitive load

© IFIP International Federation for Information Processing 2024
Published by Springer Nature Switzerland AG 2024
I. Castellani and F. Tiezzi (Eds.): COORDINATION 2024, LNCS 14676, pp. 258–276, 2024.
https://doi.org/10.1007/978-3-031-62692-5_14

and widening the gap between the programmers' intentions and the achievable solutions [38]. To mitigate these issues, several solutions that shift the focus from individual devices to collective behaviours have been proposed. Among these, macroprogramming [17] and automatic design [26] stand out as prominent directions. Macroprogramming models, particularly *aggregate computing* [8], treat collectives as first-class entities simplifying the devising of collective behaviours. Conversely, automatic design employs techniques like evolutionary robotics [27] and multi-agent reinforcement learning [28] to navigate the vast design space of swarm algorithms, which might be infeasible to explore manually. However, both avenues demand substantial expertise and/or a deep programming knowledge, posing barriers to entry for non-specialists. Furthermore, designing algorithms for swarm systems remains a daunting task due to the inherent complexity, high cognitive load, and susceptibility to errors. In related fields, low-code solutions (i.e., environments that allow users to design applications with minimal coding), especially those employing *visual programming* [39,45] environments, have been proposed to lower these barriers and reduce cognitive load, facilitating the design of applications in a more intuitive and accessible manner.

For such reasons, this paper introduces *ScaFi-Blocks*, a low-code swarm programming environment that leverages visual programming to *democratize* the development of swarm algorithms. Building on the ScaFi [20] aggregate computing framework and Blockly visual programming library[1], ScaFi-Blocks enables users to visually compose algorithms using simple, yet powerful, building blocks. This approach not only lowers the entry barrier for utilizing the ScaFi framework but also supports the development of a broad spectrum of collective applications with reduced cognitive effort and error proneness thanks to the compositional nature of aggregate computing. In the following, we outline the architecture of ScaFi-Blocks, discuss its distinctive features and capabilities, and present a preliminary evaluation through a case study some common field-based coordination algorithms. This contribution fills a notable gap in the literature by providing a visual low-code programming environment specifically designed for swarm systems, thereby facilitating broader access and innovation in the field of swarm programming.

2 Background

2.1 Visual Programming and Low-Code Engineering

Visual programming refers to programming approaches based on the use and arrangement of graphical elements [21,33,41,48], in contrast with traditional programming approaches based on textual programs. Visual programming approaches are mainly motivated by (i) pedagogical reasons, namely to help beginners learn the basics of programming (cf. Scratch [5]), and (ii) methodological and practical reasons, beyond education, primarily to support end-users and domain experts to create and tailor applications [33]. Indeed, visual programming can help to (i) reduce the entry barrier to tools, through simplified

---

[1] https://developers.google.com/blockly.

notation, (ii) reduce the cognitive load, by simplifying the presentation of relevant information, (iii) reduce the likelihood of errors, through suitable constraints to the arrangements of visual elements, and (iv) foster the collaboration between domain experts and programmers, through a notation that the former group of users can more easily understand.

A related concept and keyword to visual programming is *low-code*, namely the idea and practice of enabling the development of applications with limited source code writing [44]. Therefore, visual programming is a means for achieving low-code or even *no-code* [47]. As in visual programming, the focus is both on empowerment of non-programmers and productivity in terms e.g. of proper collaboration with domain experts [9]. Typical approaches followed by visual and low-code platforms or environments [9] to achieve their goals include supporting data management, workflow management, and providing integrated development environments (IDEs).

2.2   Swarm Engineering

Engineering swarms is a significant research challenge [12] that is related to finding effective ways to express a global behaviour able to solve problems or provide services in a possibly complex environment. Swarm design methods can be classified into two main classes of approaches [12,16]: (i) *automatic* design methods, where algorithms are used to learn or synthesise behaviours (e.g. as driven by signals like rewards or fitness metrics—cf. multi-agent reinforcement learning [14] and evolutionary robotics [49]); and (ii) *manual* design methods, where algorithms are implemented by the designers using a classical iterative, incremental, trial-and-error process, often supported by specific *domain-specific languages (DSLs)* [3,43]. In this work, we focus on the latter kind of approaches, namely on what can be referred to as *swarm programming* [3,43].

Swarm programming can be considered under the umbrella of *macroprogramming* [17], the abstract paradigm of expressing the macro-level or collective behaviour in systems featuring multiple interacting components. In this context, various kinds of concrete approaches and corresponding languages have been proposed, featuring different kinds of macro-level abstractions capturing, e.g., space-time structures (cf. SpatialViews [40] and field-based coordination [36,51]), collective communication (cf. attribute-based communication [1] and SCEL [23]), dynamic groups of devices (cf. *ensembles* [1,23]), and distributed values (e.g., *computational fields* [36,51]).

Specifically to swarm programming, a further distinction is sometimes made between (i) *task orchestration languages*, where task descriptions are used by centralised entities to give instructions to the swarm members (such as in TeCoLa [32], Dolphin [35], Maple-Swarm [31], PARoS [24], Resh [15]), and (ii) *decentralised swarm programming languages*, which instead focus on the definition of the control program of the swarm members, either by a traditional, node-level (e.g., multi-agent oriented programming [10]) or a more macroscopic perspective (e.g., MacroSwarm, Buzz).

Additionally, recurrent types of collective and self-organising behaviour have been described under the form of *patterns* [12,25,42,50], then sometimes also provided as corresponding DSL constructs for swarms as in *MacroSwarm* [3] or *Buzz* [43]. The ability of designing swarm behaviour through *compositions* of patterns, or *blocks* of collective behaviour, is a powerful feature. This is often provided by task-orchestration languages, which however generally provide centralised implementations, whereas it is most interesting when supported by decentralised swarm programming languages.

2.3 Aggregate Computing

Aggregate computing [51] is an approach for programming collective adaptive and self-organising systems such as swarms.

System Model. Aggregate computing assumes a system of computing *devices* able to exchange messages with *neighbours*. A device is assumed to be equipped with *sensors* and *actuators*, their only interface with the environment. Also, each device has a *buffer* for storing the most recent message of its neighbours.

Execution Model. Aggregate computing generally adopts an execution strategy that resembles the local, decentralised, repetition-based dynamics of self-organisation [11,18]. Each device computes at *asynchronous sense–compute–interact rounds*, namely a round consists of three main steps:

1. *sense*: the device gathers all the relevant information from its local context, which includes the most recent and *not-expired* messages from neighbours and the environment state (as sampled by sensors);
2. *compute*: the device evaluates the aggregate program (see next) against its local context, resulting in an *output* and a coordination message called an *export*;
3. *interact*: the device interacts with its environment, by *broadcasting* the export to all its neighbours (a step needed to support collective coordination) and performing *actuations* as dictated by the output of the program.

Notice that the model does not fix a number of details such as the concrete neighbouring relationship, scheduling strategy for rounds, message expiration, communication technology etc. Indeed, such details can be fine-tuned specifically to the application scenario at hand and even dynamically at the middleware level to achieve non-functional tradeoffs. Many of such details are not required for understanding the paradigm, and specifically for this paper, and are actually addressed by research such as [18,19].

Programming Model. The *aggregate program* is what defines the collective behaviour and is evaluated at the compute step by all the devices. An aggregate program is expressed as a composition of functions of computational fields.

A *computational field* [36,51] is a map from devices to values, and the main abstraction of aggregate computing, which is formalised in terms of calculi of computational fields or variants thereof [6,51]. The details of field calculi and their constructs are beyond the scope of this paper, which instead is about low-code programming. What is more important to understand, is that computational fields provide a denotation of collective inputs, collective outputs, and collective results (of expression evaluation). For instance, having all the devices in the system read their temperature sensor yields a field of temperatures; also, by relating this field to the field of their positions in space, the system provides a map of the temperatures in an environment. Also, to control a swarm, we can use fields of actuations; for instance, collective movement can be represented as a field of velocity vectors. Similarly, the evaluation of a local Boolean expression by all the devices in the system results in a Boolean field mapping each device to a truth value to denote, e.g., what are the sinks of a distributed collection process, or the leaders of the swarm. Another use of fields is for supporting *interaction* in the system: a device may process information from its neighbours in terms of a so-called *neighbouring field*, which maps each neighbour to their corresponding value for a given expression. So, for instance, the neighbouring field of temperature readings allows a device to access the temperatures in its surroundings.

A collective behaviour can be expressed as a function from fields to fields, whose body is an expression involving fields. Internally, such function may also use neighbouring fields to support communication; hence, a function becomes a *block* or *reusable component* that embeds all is needed to realise some collective-level behaviour. Also, crucially, functional composition can be used to express more complex collective behaviours in terms of simpler ones.

Example: Gradient. The gradient is one of the most fundamental self-organisation building blocks. It is the computation of the field of numbers denoting the minimum distances from source nodes. Such a computation can be encapsulated as a function from the Boolean field of sources to the numeric field of distances. Invoking a gradient, then, requires each device to evaluate it in each one of its rounds, and to share with neighbours the information dictated by such block. A simple implementation of the gradient is as follows: the source outputs a null distance, whereas the other devices output the minimum value over the neighbouring field of gradients augmented with the distances to those neighbours. The repeated evaluation of such logic results in a self-stabilising gradient that will eventually converge to the stable (i.e. non-changing) correct field once the environment gets stable.

Toolchain. An aggregate computing toolchain includes languages, middlewares (including simulators), and development environments. A prominent toolchain implementation is ScaFi [7,20], which includes a Scala-internal DSL for writing aggregate programs, an internal simulator, and other tools. Among the tools, we mention ScaFi-Web [2], which is a web-based development environment that streamlines the experimentation with the language with an accessible frontend and a set of pre-defined programs and scenarios. To date, there exist no visual or low-code implementations for aggregate computing. This work provides ScaFi-Blocks, by extending ScaFi-Web with a support for block-based visual programming.

3   ScaFi-Blocks

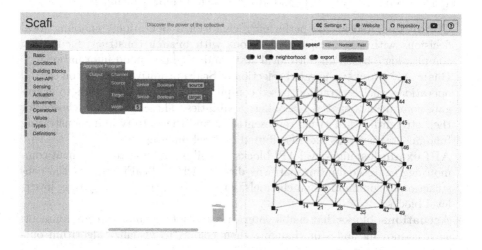

Fig. 1. The ScaFi-Blocks visual programming environment

ScaFi-Blocks (Fig. 1) is a visual programming environment that leverages Blockly, a web-based visual programming library developed by Google. The page is divided into three main areas:

- The toolbox, which contains the building blocks that can be used to design algorithms (the left part in the picture).
- The workspace, where the user can design the algorithm by dragging and dropping the building blocks from the toolbox (the central part).
- The simulation area, where the user can execute the algorithm and visualize the behaviour of the swarm (the right part).

ScaFi-Blocks is seamlessly integrated with ScaFi-Web, a robust web-based platform designed for the creation and execution of aggregate computing algorithms. This integration fosters an intuitive and accessible means for users, particularly those without extensive expertise in aggregate computing, to engage with and understand the core principles of this computational paradigm. Indeed, ScaFi-Blocks exposes some of the most common building blocks of the ScaFi framework, allowing users to compose algorithms visually, and creating some of the most idiomatic field-based coordination algorithms and then execute them on the ScaFi-Web platform. Simplifying the design of algorithms in this manner not only reduces the cognitive load and error proneness but also fosters collaboration, allowing non-expert users to contribute to the design of algorithms.

3.1 Features

Core Blocks: ScaFi-Blocks introduces a suite of core building blocks designed to encapsulate the essential principles of the ScaFi framework, making aggregate computing concepts accessible and intuitive. These blocks include:

- **Conditions:** blocks for performing conditional operations, enabling local decisions with `mux` or spatial decisions with `branch` construct, facilitating complex logic based on both local state and neighbourhood information.
- **Basic AC blocks:** a curated selection of ScaFi primitives focused on spatial operations, such as gradient-based computation, to introduce users to aggregate computing's spatial reasoning capabilities. These blocks are chosen for their straightforward visual representation and their utility in demonstrating fundamental patterns like distributed channel building.
- **API examples:** high-level API blocks that illustrate how to implement common aggregate computing patterns directly within ScaFi, such as the construction of communication channels, without the need for composing lower-level blocks.
- **Actuations:** blocks that enable interaction with the simulation environment, such as moving nodes or changing their colour, to visualize algorithm outcomes and dynamics.
- **Sensing:** blocks designed to gather information from the environment or the node itself, including sensing boolean conditions or retrieving node identifiers, essential for context-aware computing.

Movement API: The movement API within ScaFi-Blocks provides a high-level abstraction for controlling node mobility in the simulated environment. This API allows users to specify movement strategies and behaviours, such as flocking or pattern formation, directly through visual blocks. This approach simplifies the integration of dynamic behaviours into aggregate algorithms, making the exploration of mobile sensor networks and robotic swarms more accessible.

Simulated Environment: ScaFi-Blocks is complemented by a simulated environment that acts as a virtual testbed for swarm algorithms. This environment supports the execution of ScaFi-Blocks programs, allowing users to observe the emergent behaviours of their algorithms in real time. It is equipped with features to simulate various conditions, including node movement and local actuation, offering a rich platform for experimentation and learning.

Code Generation: a key feature of ScaFi-Blocks is its ability to generate executable ScaFi code from the visual blocks. This code-generation process not only bridges the gap between visual programming and textual code but also serves as an educational tool, enabling users to learn ScaFi syntax and concepts through direct comparison. The generated code can be exported and run within the ScaFi ecosystem, facilitating a smooth transition from visual design to practical implementation.

Blockly Workspace Session: at the core of the ScaFi-Blocks interface is the Blockly workspace, a flexible and interactive area where users can assemble their algorithms. The workspace session is designed to be intuitive, supporting drag-and-drop composition, real-time feedback, and session saving/loading functionalities. This ensures a user-friendly experience, encouraging experimentation and iterative design processes. The Blockly workspace is instrumental in making aggregate computing concepts tangible, allowing users to visualize and manipulate the building blocks of their algorithms cohesively and engagingly.

4 ScaFi-Blocks Design and Implementation

4.1 Design Principles

The ScaFi-Blocks environment is crafted around several core principles aimed at enhancing *usability, learning,* and *engagement*:

User-Friendly Interface: at its heart, ScaFi-Blocks is engineered to be intuitive, employing a drag-and-drop interface for algorithm design. This method significantly lowers the cognitive load and potential for errors, making the system accessible to non-experts and encouraging collaborative algorithm development.

Rapid Feedback Loop: recognizing the importance of immediate feedback in swarm programming, ScaFi-Blocks should ensure users receive instant execution results in a simulated environment. This feature, inspired by environments such as Scratch and Snap, is crucial for understanding the effects of algorithmic modifications, thus accelerating the learning process for the ScaFi framework and its paradigms.

Knowledge Transfer: to bridge the gap between visual and textual programming, ScaFi-Blocks automatically translates visual designs into ScaFi code. This functionality is pivotal for users to grasp underlying concepts and learn the ScaFi syntax through direct comparison, promoting a deeper understanding of algorithm structures.

Compositional Approach: reflecting the essence of aggregate computing, ScaFi-Blocks emphasizes the composition of complex algorithms from simple building blocks. This design principle showcases the framework's power to create sophisticated behaviours from basic elements, aligning with the compositional nature of aggregate computing.

Minimalist Design: ScaFi-Blocks adopts a minimalist approach, providing a curated set of building blocks that simplify the design process while encapsulating the framework's complexity. This strategy allows users to concentrate on algorithmic logic rather than the intricacies of the ScaFi framework or field calculus.

Engagement and Fun: Finally, ScaFi-Blocks is designed to be both enjoyable and educational, offering an interactive experience that makes learning the ScaFi framework an engaging adventure. Users can experiment within a simulated environment, discovering and visualizing fascinating behaviours and dynamics.

Together, these principles guide the development of ScaFi-Blocks, ensuring it serves as an accessible, educational, and enjoyable tool for both newcomers and experienced users in the field of swarm programming.

4.2   Architecture

The architecture of ScaFi-Blocks is delineated in Fig. 2, illustrating its dual-component structure:

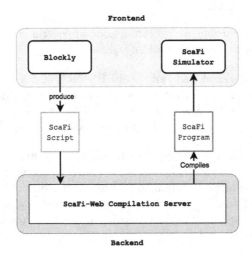

Fig. 2. The architecture of ScaFi-Blocks.

- **frontend:** this component constitutes the visual programming interface alongside the execution engine that runs compiled ScaFi programs;
- **backend:** it processes ScaFi-Web scripts, compiling them into a format executable by the frontend.

A typical workflow in ScaFi-Blocks involves the following steps:

1. the user designs an algorithm using the visual interface. Blockly then converts this visual representation into a textual format, adhering to predefined specifications (refer to the Blockly documentation[2] for further details).
2. This textual representation is forwarded to the backend, where it is compiled into an executable format for the frontend.
3. Finally, the compiled program is relayed back to the frontend for execution.

4.3   Implementation Details

ScaFi Blocks represents a significant enhancement to ScaFi Web by integrating the Blockly library as an alternative to the conventional textual editor. This integration facilitates a more interactive and visual programming experience. The setup process for a Blockly environment in a new scenario encompasses several key steps:

1. **Defining new blocks:** for each new block, it is essential to specify its characteristics, including the block's name, the number of inputs it requires, its colour, and the type of result it produces. These details are typically organized and stored in a JSON file, facilitating easy management and configuration.
2. **Describing the toolbox:** the toolbox is a critical component of the Blockly interface, acting as a categorization system for the blocks. It organizes the blocks into categories, making them accessible from the Blockly editor's menu (refer to Fig. 1). This organization aids users in finding the appropriate blocks for their programming tasks.
3. **Defining generators:** generators are functions that, given a block, produce the corresponding string representation for that block, and determine the order of evaluation within the global expression. These generators convert Blockly's visual blocks into executable ScaFi code, suitable for running in the designated environment.

The implementation of block generators is predominantly achieved through JavaScript. However, to facilitate integration with ScaFi Web, the translation process is handled via Scala.js[3] in this case. Specifically, a class is defined for each block type, encapsulating a strategy (i.e., a generator) to generate the ScaFi code corresponding to that block. Blocks are categorized into two main types:

- **Unit blocks:** these blocks do not yield a result and, as such, cannot be connected to other blocks. An example within our context is the output block, which acts as a terminal point for a block sequence.
- **Value blocks:** in contrast, value blocks produce a result and can be attached to other blocks as inputs or outputs. These blocks are fundamental for constructing meaningful sequences of operations.

---

[2] https://developers.google.com/blockly/guides/create-custom-blocks/blockly-developer-tools.

[3] https://github.com/cric96/ScaFi-Blocks.

To illustrate, consider the implementation of the *sense* block, which is designed to interact with sensors:

The Scala.js code snippet below outlines the class definition for this block type:

```
class SenseBlockType extends ValueBlockType:
    override def name: String = "sense"
    override def order: Order = Orders.ORDER_ATOMIC
    override def fieldNames: Seq[String] = Seq()
    override def inputNames: Seq[String] = Seq("TYPE", "SENSOR_NAME")
    override def generator: Generator = (block) =>
        val _type = Blockly.ScaFi.valueToCode(block, "TYPE", Orders.NONE)
        val sensorName = Blockly.ScaFi.valueToCode(block, "SENSOR_NAME", Orders.NONE)
        val code = s"sense[${_type}](${sensorName})"
        (code, Orders.NONE)
```

In this code snippet, the generator function is particularly noteworthy. It utilizes the `Blockly.ScaFi.valueToCode` method to extract and transform the values associated with the `"TYPE"` and `"SENSOR_NAME"` inputs into the appropriate ScaFi code snippet. Consequently, when the *sense* block is used within the Blockly editor, it results in the generation of ScaFi code resembling:

```
sense[TYPE]("SENSOR_NAME")
```

This approach, whereby each block type is associated with a specific class that defines its behaviour and code generation logic, enables the seamless translation of visual programming constructs into executable ScaFi code.

5   Walkthrough

In this section, we discuss three comprehensive examples that can be implemented with the system we developed that demonstrate all the functionalities of the developed system, which are the *gradient*, the *channel*, and *flocking*. These examples are shown in images Fig. 3, Fig. 5, and Fig. 6, each with the following two parts:

- the first line shows the implementation through Blockly;
- the last line shows a run of the simulation at three different time instants.

Gradient Example: One of the most idiomatic blocks in aggregate programming, it allows computing the distance from areas classified as sources. It is a foundational block because, on top of it, other spatio-temporal constructs such as the channel can be built. The gradient, in ScaFi, is part of a library block described in the following manner:

```
def gradient(source: Boolean, metric: Metric): Double
```

Thus, to call it, it is typically described in the following way:

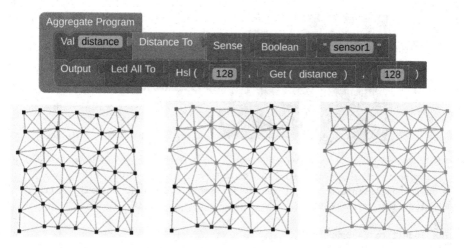

Fig. 3. The distance block example.

```
gradient(sense("source"), nbrRange)
```

Here, we wanted to hide the complexity of passing a metric to calculate this data structure, so we hid this step and allowed the developer to define only the source. Perception was also captured with a block ("**sense**" in the example) to which the name of the sensor and the desired type are passed. Furthermore, here we have made the system colour itself using the output as a saturation value and using the actuations exposed by ScaFi web. To do this and make the code more readable, we relied on a variable that was then used in evaluating the HSL value.

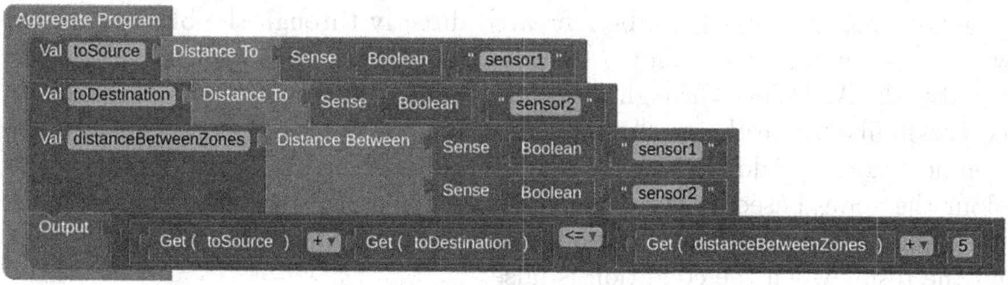

Fig. 4. The channel block built with ScaFi-Blocks.

Channel Example: This block produces a spatial structure that connects an area marked as a source and an area marked as a destination. This structure is capable of *self-heal*, so in cases of changes in topology, the system finds another stable configuration where the channel reforms following the shortest path between

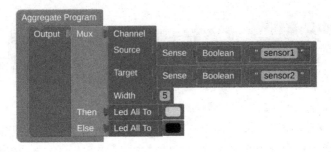

```
1
2  //using StandardSensors, BlockG, Actuation
3  mux(channel(sense[Boolean]("sensor1"), sense[Boolean]("sensor2"), 5)) {
4     ledAll to "#ffff00"
5  }{
6     ledAll to "#000000"
7  }
```

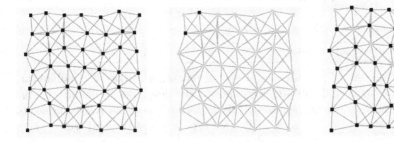

Fig. 5. The channel example, in the second line the code shown in the "show code" block.

these zones. The channel can be recreated directly through the blocks exposed by our system (see, for example, Fig. 4). But in this case, we have also made available the API block through the ScaFi system. Moreover, ScaFi Blocks offers the possibility to see the generated code using "show block" (second line in the reference figure). Additionally, to colour the gradient, we have conditions to colour the nodes based on the channel's value. To do this, we used the mux block which accepts three blocks, the condition, the result when the condition is true, and the result when the condition is false.

Flocking Example: To also show the system's ability to perform actuations, we integrated a small example in which we show how it is possible to move nodes using flocking policies as described by Reynolds [46]. This part of the library derives from ScaFi web and allows moving the nodes according to a velocity vector. In this case, the library is much more complex and requires several parameters to be configured.

Here is an example of minimalism: in this case, the flock has been summarized in a single block that actually translates into the following code:

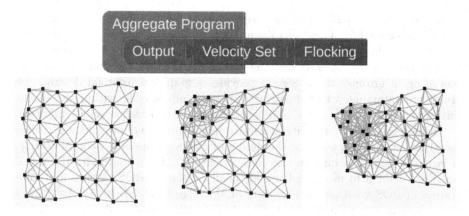

Fig. 6. A simple example of flocking implemented through ScaFi-Blocks.

```
//using StandardSensors, AdvancedFlock, BlockG, FlockLib, Movement2D, BlockT, CustomSpawn,
// Actuation, BlocksWithGC, BlockS
velocity set FlockBehaviour(attractionForce = 0.001, alignmentForce = 0.1,
    repulsionForce = 0.5,separationDistance = 10.0,
).run()
```

All the variables in this case distracted the developer against the intent, which was to describe a flock of nodes. Finally, to effectively perform the movement, the program must return the `velocity set` block, which, in the ScaFi web, is a block that sets the velocity of the nodes and is used to move the nodes in the simulation environment.

6 Related Work

There exist some recent reviews on visual programming, most notably on its application for end-user development [33], on the foundations of low-code [9], and on the comparison of visual and textual approaches for education [41]. There are also reviews/applications on the use of visual/low-code environments for distributed computing, e.g., on orchestration of distributed computations in the Internet of Things (IoT) [48], on the development of multiagent systems [34], on low-code IoT engineering [29], and on the human-computer interaction with social robots [21].

In the literature, the majority of works for visual and end-user robot programming focus on individual robots [4,21,52]. A few visual approaches, however, have also been proposed specifically for multi-robot systems and swarms. One approach is *FaMe (BPMN-driven FrAmework for Multi-robot systEms development)* [22], which adopts the *Business Process Modelling Notation (BPMN)* standard, and specifically its collaboration diagrams, and targets the ROS 2 platform. FaMe supports reusable behaviour and distributed execution. In this work, we focus primarily on collectives, whereas FaMe targets more heterogeneous composites [37]. The *Multi-Agent script Programming Language for multi-potent Ensembles (Maple-Swarm)* [31] is an approach that extends the concept of hierarchical task networks for defining partial plans, also leveraging the abstraction of agent groups. Maple-Swarm provides a graphical frontend designer for visual programming, which however somewhat mixes code within the blocks corresponding to swarm tasks, and hence cannot be regarded as a low-code tool.

Other proposals in the literature are less related and provide, e.g., some visual or low-code support for the design of single robots or ad-hoc platforms, or visual languages lacking any low-code orientation. For instance, in [13], visual DSLs are defined to promote low-code configuration of ROS2 setups and integration of ROS with message brokers at the edge or cloud. In *SeSAm* [30], a visual programming environment is combined with agent-based simulation, but the visual language follows a quite "high-code", imperative style not promoting compositionality of behaviours and usability.

7   Conclusions

In this paper, we have presented ScaFi-Blocks, a novel low-code swarm programming environment that leverages the visual programming paradigm to democratize the development of swarm algorithms. By building upon the ScaFi aggregate computing framework, ScaFi-Blocks offers a user-friendly interface that simplifies the design and implementation of distributed algorithms for swarm systems. The environment lowers the entry barrier for non-expert users and facilitates a broader engagement with swarm programming.

Through a detailed discussion of the design principles, architecture, and features of ScaFi-Blocks, we have demonstrated its potential to foster innovation and collaboration in the field of swarm programming. The examples of gradient, channel, and flocking algorithms illustrated in this paper underscore the practicality and versatility of ScaFi-Blocks in enabling the design of sophisticated swarm behaviours with minimal coding effort. This preliminary work has outlined the foundation and capabilities of ScaFi-Blocks, a novel low-code environment for swarm programming. Looking ahead, our future research will focus on a comprehensive evaluation of ScaFi-Blocks through user studies and case studies. Specifically, we aim to identify the target user group for this tool, examining the prerequisite knowledge required for its effective use. Additionally, while the design principles of ScaFi-Blocks have been methodologically followed, comparative evaluations with similar approaches remain unaddressed. We plan to expand our evaluation to include aspects such as usability, learning curves, and user engagement, enhancing the overall effectiveness of the environment. Moreover, we also plan to extend the programming environment with additional features and building blocks, e.g., by leveraging the MacroSwarm library [3], further enhancing its capabilities and usability.

Acknowledgment. This work was supported by the Italian PRIN project "Common-Wears" (2020 HCWWLP) and the EU/MUR FSE PON-R&I 2014-2020.

References

1. Abd Alrahman, Y., De Nicola, R., Loreti, M.: Programming interactions in collective adaptive systems by relying on attribute-based communication. Sci. Comput. Program. **192** (2020). https://doi.org/10.1016/j.scico.2020.102428
2. Aguzzi, G., Casadei, R., Maltoni, N., Pianini, D., Viroli, M.: SCAFI-WEB: a web-based application for field-based coordination programming. In: Damiani, F., Dardha, O. (eds.) COORDINATION 2021. LNCS, vol. 12717, pp. 285–299. Springer, Cham (2021). https://doi.org/10.1007/978-3-030-78142-2_18
3. Aguzzi, G., Casadei, R., Viroli, M.: MacroSwarm: a field-based compositional framework for swarm programming. In: Jongmans, S.S., Lopes, A. (eds.) COORDINATION 2023. LNCS, vol. 13908, pp. 31–51. Springer, Cham (2023). https://doi.org/10.1007/978-3-031-35361-1_2
4. Ajaykumar, G., Steele, M., Huang, C.: A survey on end-user robot programming. ACM Comput. Surv. **54**(8), 164:1–164:36 (2022). https://doi.org/10.1145/3466819
5. Armoni, M., Meerbaum-Salant, O., Ben-Ari, M.: From scratch to "real" programming. ACM Trans. Comput. Educ. **14**(4), 25:1–25:15 (2014). https://doi.org/10.1145/2677087
6. Audrito, G., Casadei, R., Damiani, F., Salvaneschi, G., Viroli, M.: Functional programming for distributed systems with XC. In: 36th European Conference on Object-Oriented Programming, ECOOP 2022. LIPIcs, vol. 222, pp. 20:1–20:28. Schloss Dagstuhl - Leibniz-Zentrum für Informatik (2022). https://doi.org/10.4230/LIPIcs.ECOOP.2022.20
7. Audrito, G., Casadei, R., Damiani, F., Viroli, M.: Computation against a neighbour: addressing large-scale distribution and adaptivity with functional programming and scala. Logical Methods Comput. Sci. **19**(1) (2023). https://lmcs.episciences.org/10826
8. Beal, J., Pianini, D., Viroli, M.: Aggregate programming for the internet of things. Computer **48**(9), 22–30 (2015)
9. Bock, A.C., Frank, U.: In search of the essence of low-code: An exploratory study of seven development platforms. In: ACM/IEEE International Conference on Model Driven Engineering Languages and Systems Companion, MODELS 2021 Companion, pp. 57–66. IEEE (2021). https://doi.org/10.1109/MODELS-C53483.2021.00016
10. Boissier, O., Bordini, R.H., Hubner, J., Ricci, A.: Multi-agent Oriented Programming: Programming Multi-agent Systems Using JaCaMo. MIT Press, Cambridge (2020)
11. Bonabeau, E., Dorigo, M., Théraulaz, G.: Swarm Intelligence: From Natural to Artificial Systems. Santa Fe Institute Studies in the Sciences of Complexity, Oxford university press, Oxford (1999)
12. Brambilla, M., Ferrante, E., Birattari, M., Dorigo, M.: Swarm robotics: a review from the swarm engineering perspective. Swarm Intell. **7**(1), 1–41 (2013). https://doi.org/10.1007/s11721-012-0075-2
13. Brouzos, R., Panayiotou, K., Tsardoulias, E.G., Symeonidis, A.L.: A low-code approach for connected robots. J. Intell. Robotic Syst. **108**(2), 28 (2023). https://doi.org/10.1007/S10846-023-01861-Y
14. Busoniu, L., Babuska, R., Schutter, B.D.: A comprehensive survey of multiagent reinforcement learning. IEEE Trans. Syst. Man Cybern. Part C **38**(2), 156–172 (2008). https://doi.org/10.1109/TSMCC.2007.913919

15. Carroll, M., Namjoshi, K.S., Segall, I.: The Resh programming language for multirobot orchestration. In: IEEE International Conference on Robotics and Automation, ICRA 2021, pp. 4026–4032. IEEE (2021). https://doi.org/10.1109/ICRA48506.2021.9561133

16. Casadei, R.: Artificial collective intelligence engineering: a survey of concepts and perspectives. Artif. Life **29**(4), 433–467 (2023). https://doi.org/10.1162/ARTL_A_00408

17. Casadei, R.: Macroprogramming: concepts, state of the art, and opportunities of macroscopic behaviour modelling. ACM Comput. Surv. **55**(13s), 275:1–275:37 (2023). https://doi.org/10.1145/3579353

18. Casadei, R., Dente, F., Aguzzi, G., Pianini, D., Viroli, M.: Self-organisation programming: a functional reactive macro approach. In: IEEE International Conference on Autonomic Computing and Self-Organizing Systems, ACSOS 2023, pp. 87–96. IEEE (2023). https://doi.org/10.1109/ACSOS58161.2023.00026

19. Casadei, R., Fortino, G., Pianini, D., Placuzzi, A., Savaglio, C., Viroli, M.: A methodology and simulation-based toolchain for estimating deployment performance of smart collective services at the edge. IEEE Internet Things J. **9**(20), 20136–20148 (2022). https://doi.org/10.1109/JIOT.2022.3172470

20. Casadei, R., Viroli, M., Aguzzi, G., Pianini, D.: ScaFi: a Scala DSL and toolkit for aggregate programming. SoftwareX **20**, 101248 (2022). https://doi.org/10.1016/j.softx.2022.101248

21. Coronado, E., Mastrogiovanni, F., Indurkhya, B., Venture, G.: Visual programming environments for end-user development of intelligent and social robots, a systematic review. J. Comput. Lang. **58**, 100970 (2020). https://doi.org/10.1016/J.COLA.2020.100970

22. Corradini, F., Pettinari, S., Re, B., Rossi, L., Tiezzi, F.: A BPMN-driven framework for multi-robot system development. Robotics Auton. Syst. **160**, 104322 (2023). https://doi.org/10.1016/J.ROBOT.2022.104322

23. De Nicola, R., Loreti, M., Pugliese, R., Tiezzi, F.: A formal approach to autonomic systems programming: the SCEL language. ACM Trans. Auton. Adapt. Syst. **9**(2), 7:1–7:29 (2014). https://doi.org/10.1145/2619998

24. Dedousis, D., Kalogeraki, V.: A framework for programming a swarm of UAVs. In: 11th PErvasive Technologies Related to Assistive Environments Conference (PETRA'18), Proceedings, pp. 5–12. ACM (2018). https://doi.org/10.1145/3197768.3197772

25. Fernandez-Marquez, J.L., Serugendo, G.D.M., Montagna, S., Viroli, M., Arcos, J.L.: Description and composition of bio-inspired design patterns: a complete overview. Nat. Comput. **12**(1), 43–67 (2013). https://doi.org/10.1007/S11047-012-9324-Y

26. Francesca, G., Birattari, M.: Automatic design of robot swarms: achievements and challenges. Front. Robot. AI **3**, 29 (2016). https://doi.org/10.3389/FROBT.2016.00029

27. Francesca, G., Brambilla, M., Brutschy, A., Trianni, V., Birattari, M.: Automode: a novel approach to the automatic design of control software for robot swarms. Swarm Intell. **8**(2), 89–112 (2014)

28. Hüttenrauch, M., Sosic, A., Neumann, G.: Deep reinforcement learning for swarm systems. J. Mach. Learn. Res. **20**, 54:1–54:31 (2019). http://jmlr.org/papers/v20/18-476.html

29. Ihirwe, F., Ruscio, D.D., Mazzini, S., Pierini, P., Pierantonio, A.: Low-code engineering for internet of things: a state of research. In: MODELS 2020: ACM/IEEE

23rd International Conference on Model Driven Engineering Languages and Systems, Companion Proceedings, pp. 74:1–74:8. ACM (2020). https://doi.org/10.1145/3417990.3420208

30. Klügl, F.: Sesam: visual programming and participatory simulation for agent-based models. In: Multi-Agent Systems - Simulation and Applications, pp. 477–507. Computational Analysis, Synthesis, and Design of Dynamic Systems, CRC Press / Taylor & Francis (2009). https://doi.org/10.1201/9781420070248.CH16

31. Kosak, O., Huhn, L., Bohn, F., Wanninger, C., Hoffmann, A., Reif, W.: Mapleswarm: programming collective behavior for ensembles by extending HTN-planning. In: Margaria, T., Steffen, B. (eds.) ISoLA 2020 Part II. LNCS, vol. 12477, pp. 507–524. Springer, Cham (2020). https://doi.org/10.1007/978-3-030-61470-6_30

32. Koutsoubelias, M., Lalis, S.: TeCoLa: a programming framework for dynamic and heterogeneous robotic teams. In: Proceedings of the 13th International Conference on Mobile and Ubiquitous Systems: Computing, Networking and Services (MobiQuitous 2016), pp. 115–124. ACM (2016). https://doi.org/10.1145/2994374.2994397

33. Kuhail, M.A., Farooq, S., Hammad, R., Bahja, M.: Characterizing visual programming approaches for end-user developers: a systematic review. IEEE Access 9, 14181–14202 (2021). https://doi.org/10.1109/ACCESS.2021.3051043

34. Lemée, J., Burattini, S., Mayer, S., Ciortea, A.: Domain-expert configuration of hypermedia multi-agent systems in industrial use cases. In: Agmon, N., An, B., Ricci, A., Yeoh, W. (eds.) Proceedings of the 2023 International Conference on Autonomous Agents and Multiagent Systems, AAMAS 2023, London, United Kingdom, 29 May 2023 - 2 June 2023, pp. 2499–2501. ACM (2023). https://doi.org/10.5555/3545946.3598981, https://dl.acm.org/doi/10.5555/3545946.3598981

35. Lima, K., Marques, E.R.B., Pinto, J., Sousa, J.B.: Dolphin: a task orchestration language for autonomous vehicle networks. In: 2018 IEEE/RSJ International Conference on Intelligent Robots and Systems, IROS 2018, pp. 603–610. IEEE (2018). https://doi.org/10.1109/IROS.2018.8594059

36. Mamei, M., Zambonelli, F., Leonardi, L.: Co-fields: a physically inspired approach to motion coordination. IEEE Pervasive Comput. 3(2), 52–61 (2004). https://doi.org/10.1109/MPRV.2004.1316820

37. Masolo, C., Vieu, L., Ferrario, R., Borgo, S., Porello, D.: Pluralities, collectives, and composites. In: Formal Ontology in Information Systems - Proceedings of the 11th International Conference, FOIS 2020. Frontiers in Artificial Intelligence and Applications, vol. 330, pp. 186–200. IOS Press (2020). https://doi.org/10.3233/FAIA200671

38. Mone, G.: Rise of the swarm. Commun. ACM 56(3), 16–17 (2013)

39. Myers, B.A.: Visual programming, programming by example, and program visualization: a taxonomy. In: Proceedings of the SIGCHI Conference on Human Factors in Computing Systems, CHI 1886, pp. 59–66. ACM (1986). https://doi.org/10.1145/22627.22349

40. Ni, Y., Kremer, U., Stere, A., Iftode, L.: Programming ad-hoc networks of mobile and resource-constrained devices. In: Proceedings of the 2005 ACM SIGPLAN Conference on Programming Language Design and Implementation. PLDI05, ACM (2005). https://doi.org/10.1145/1065010.1065040

41. Noone, M., Mooney, A.: Visual and textual programming languages: a systematic review of the literature. J. Comput. Educ. 5(2), 149–174 (2018). https://doi.org/10.1007/s40692-018-0101-5

42. Oh, H., Shirazi, A.R., Sun, C., Jin, Y.: Bio-inspired self-organising multi-robot pattern formation: a review. Robot. Auton. Syst. **91**, 83–100 (2017). https://doi.org/10.1016/J.ROBOT.2016.12.006

43. Pinciroli, C., Beltrame, G.: Swarm-oriented programming of distributed robot networks. Computer **49**(12), 32–41 (2016)

44. Pinho, D., Aguiar, A., Amaral, V.: What about the usability in low-code platforms? A systematic literature review. J. Comput. Lang. **74**, 101185 (2023). https://doi.org/10.1016/J.COLA.2022.101185

45. Ray, P.P.: A survey on visual programming languages in internet of things. Sci. Program. **2017**, 1231430:1–1231430:6 (2017). https://doi.org/10.1155/2017/1231430

46. Reynolds, C.W.: Flocks, herds and schools: A distributed behavioral model. In: Stone, M.C. (ed.) Proceedings of the 14th Annual Conference on Computer Graphics and Interactive Techniques, SIGGRAPH 1987, Anaheim, California, USA, July 27-31, 1987. pp. 25–34. ACM (1987). https://doi.org/10.1145/37401.37406

47. Rokis, K., Kirikova, M.: Challenges of low-code/no-code software development: a literature review. In: Nazaruka, E., Sandkuhl, K., Seigerroth, U. (eds.) BIR 2022. LNBIP, vol. 462, pp. 3–17. Springer, Cham (2022). https://doi.org/10.1007/978-3-031-16947-2_1

48. Silva, M., Dias, J.P., Restivo, A., Ferreira, H.S.: A review on visual programming for distributed computation in IoT. In: Paszynski, M., Kranzlmüller, D., Krzhizhanovskaya, V.V., Dongarra, J.J., Sloot, P.M.A. (eds.) ICCS 2021. LNCS, vol. 12745, pp. 443–457. Springer, Cham (2021). https://doi.org/10.1007/978-3-030-77970-2_34

49. Trianni, V.: Evolutionary Swarm Robotics - Evolving Self-Organising Behaviours in Groups of Autonomous Robots, Studies in Computational Intelligence, vol. 108. Springer, Heidelberg (2008). https://doi.org/10.1007/978-3-540-77612-3

50. Viroli, M., Audrito, G., Beal, J., Damiani, F., Pianini, D.: Engineering resilient collective adaptive systems by self-stabilisation. ACM Trans. Model. Comput. Simul. **28**(2), 16:1–16:28 (2018). https://doi.org/10.1145/3177774

51. Viroli, M., Beal, J., Damiani, F., Audrito, G., Casadei, R., Pianini, D.: From distributed coordination to field calculus and aggregate computing. J. Log. Algebraic Methods Program. **109** (2019). https://doi.org/10.1016/j.jlamp.2019.100486

52. Weintrop, D., et al.: Evaluating coblox: a comparative study of robotics programming environments for adult novices. In: Proceedings of the 2018 CHI Conference on Human Factors in Computing Systems. CHI 2018, ACM (2018). https://doi.org/10.1145/3173574.3173940

Visualisation of Collective Systems with Sequit and Sibilla

Nicola Del Giudice$^{(\boxtimes)}$ ⓘ, Federico Maria Cruciani, and Michele Loreti ⓘ

University of Camerino, Via Madonna delle Carceri, 9, 62032 Camerino, Italy
{nicola.delgiudice,michele.loreti}@unicam.it,
federicomar.cruciani@studenti.unicam.it

Abstract. The analysis of Collective Systems involves the usage of several tools and techniques for addressing the different intricacies typical of this kind of system. One of these techniques is the simulation that, starting from a quantitative model of the system under analysis, is used to generate a set of possible computations. Typically, these data are used to perform statistical analyses and to infer performance measure. However, being able to represent results in an effective manner is crucial to help users to understand the meaning of collected simulation data. In this paper, we introduce Sequit a tool that, integrated with Sibilla, permits rendering in a 2D or 3D environment the evolution of a set of agents. A simple example, based on a flock behaviour, is used in the paper to show the use of Sibilla and Sequit.

Keywords: Collective Systems · Agent Simulation · Realtime Visualisation

1 Introduction

Several tools and techniques can be used to support design and analysis of Collective Systems (CS) [14] to address the intricacies typical of this kind of systems. One of the approaches is the one based on simulation: given a quantitative model representing the behaviour of the system under investigation, a set of *runs* are generated to perform *statistical analysis* and infer *performance measures*. However, when simulation is used, is also useful to represent the evolution of a *simulation run* in an *effective way*. In [29], the authors stress the attention on *how* simulations should be represented, highlighting the fact that poor visualisation may be counterproductive. To strengthen the importance of visualisation, the authors of [5] individuate different issues during the process, which starts from the data collection and ends with the representation of knowledge.

Visualisation methods can range from more static ones to more complex replays. This distinction depends on the level of detail one is interested to achieve. On the one hand, statistical analyses can be represented in terms of plots, charts, or diagrams. This is useful when working on quantitative analyses which require the study of trends and average evolution of systems [17]. In the other case,

© IFIP International Federation for Information Processing 2024
Published by Springer Nature Switzerland AG 2024
I. Castellani and F. Tiezzi (Eds.): COORDINATION 2024, LNCS 14676, pp. 277–294, 2024.
https://doi.org/10.1007/978-3-031-62697-5_15

visualisation is based on graphical solutions. These are used in various application domains, like robotics [19] or ecology [21], and usually exploit graphics processing power rather than the CPU. Plotting a graph is an easier task than creating a real-time visualisation tool. Many libraries already exist, starting from the well-known Python Matplotlib [28], and they can support different types of analysis.

In this paper, we introduce Sequit, a tool that, integrated with Sibilla [11], permits rendering in 2D and 3D environments the evolution of a set of agents. Sibilla is a modular tool, developed in Java, that supports statistical analysis of quantitative models that can be described by using different specification languages. Indeed, one of the main features of Sibilla is that it is not focused on a single specification language while it is possible to integrate new specification languages. To support tracing and visualisation of Sibilla models, a new module is introduced.

The approach proposed in this paper is based on the use of *Unity* technologies to deliver a lightweight and ready-to-use player that can be easily operated by everyone. A Sibilla module has been also developed to trace simulation runs and to produce data that can be visualised by Sequit. Thanks to the use of a simple file format, the proposed tool can be used also as a standalone solution, without the need to interact with Sibilla.

A simple running example, based on a flock behaviour [25], is used to show the use of Sibilla and Sequit, examining the obtained results with a playthrough of the tools.

The remaining parts of the paper are divided as follows. In Sect. 2 few related works are discussed. In Sect. 3, we give a glimpse of Sibilla while the flock example is presented in Sect. 4. The implementation of the new module is explained in Sect. 5, while we see it in action in Sect. 6. Finally, in Sect. 7 some final remarks together with possible future developments are discussed.

2 Related Works

Many approaches that use 3D simulation already exist in the literature. These tools may vary in architecture and each one is specialised in its own way of representing the agents. Here, we would like to point out some existing solutions that may be useful to understand the general overview of the topic.

The first platform we would like to cite is *AnyLogic* [13,23], a proprietary software used in multiple domains (from healthcare to risk events or even transportation) for simulation. AnyLogic is a programming and simulation environment based on Java language. The tool focuses mainly on agent-based and business simulations, but it can be used also in other contexts. In addition, many existing libraries are natively available, like those for simulating pedestrians or railing systems.

Likewise, *StarLogo TNG (The Next Generation)* [6], and the newer, web-based version *StarLogo Nova*, is a proprietary tool (in this case owned by MIT). It relies on visual scripts to ease the development of agent-based systems. As the name may suggest, the tool is derived from *StarLogo* [24], an agent-based language, which in turn is inspired by *LOGO*[1]. However, StarLogo TNG has been discontinued and the last update for the Nova version dates back to 2021 (at the time of writing).

Moving to open source solutions, *GAMA* [8,27], an "agent-oriented" tool based on Eclipse, is an interesting choice. The platform relies on a specialised agent language, called *GAML* (GAma Modeling Language), which allows even non-expert users to declare agent species and give them a behaviour. GAMA provides a user interface to write and run agent models, and also 3D displays to render simulations. Moreover, the simulator is interactive, meaning that the user is able to inspect the entities, interact with the display, and more.

Gazebo [1,15] is also an open-source software, even if it is more oriented to Multi-Robot Systems and robotic simulations. It integrates *ROS* (Robotic Operating System) to model systems and uses *DART* as a physics engine. Gazebo allows the user to interact with the tool via different interfaces (command line, web, and graphical) and can be extended with other tools or even graphical plugins.

A recent solution is the one given by the authors of [4]. In this paper, a graphical user interface is presented to support *FCPP* [3] (Field Calculus implemented in C++), an efficient library for working with aggregate programming. The authors state the necessity of a more readable solution and not limited to numeric statistical information. For these reasons, the proposed tool aims to provide an interactive real-time visualiser for representing aggregate systems in a 3D fashion. The tool aims also to ease the user experience and allow control and interaction with the simulation. Another solution in the context of *field-based computations* is *Alchemist* [22]. This is a tool developed for collective systems and, especially, chemical-oriented scenarios, and results are plotted with Python libraries. This tool has been used to model and trace different CAS scenarios. For instance, in [2], the tool has been used to model a swarm scenario.

The usage of common Game Engines (GE), such as *Unity* or *Unreal Engine*, for simulating agent-based systems has been also questioned in [18]. Here the authors propose a roadmap for integrating GEs and said systems, exploiting the features of the first ones. These should be used not only for the rendering properties but also for the eventual features that may derive from this union. In fact, we can already find some plugins that can be used in pairs with Unity3D to perform crowd simulation. For example, the authors of [30] take advantage of BDI architectures, while in [12] a plugin to use the *Menge* framework with the GE is presented.

All the approaches mentioned above are based on a *specialised* solution that is specific for a language/framework. On the contrary, Sequit aims to provide a solution that is not focused on a specific approach. Indeed, our tool can be easily integrated in many contexts. The single requirement is to have a *.csv* file containing the values to trace.

---

[1] The LOGO manual can be found at https://dspace.mit.edu/handle/1721.1/6226.

3   Sibilla in a Nutshell

As we said, the developed module has been conceived with the necessity of having a ready-to-use offline simulator able to replicate the agents' traces. These can be easily and in a relatively rapid way produced using a distributed and dedicated tool. In this section, we will briefly see what is Sibilla and the available specification languages, with a focus on YODA, a language for specifying agent-based models.

3.1   Sibilla Architecture

Sibilla[2] is a modular tool developed in Java aiming to provide a common set of functionalities to support formalisation and analysis of different Collective Adaptive Systems (CAS). These are considered large groups of interactive heterogeneous entities and, due to their nature and referring domain, they may vary in specification and interactions. Sibilla is built by keeping in mind this necessity, allowing the integration of new languages, and currently, the tool is equipped with APIs for 1) *system simulation*, 2) *transient analysis via statistical model checking*, and 3) *modelling different CASs.*

The framework is based on a modular architecture and is composed of three layers. The first one is the *Back-end*, which provides the fundamental classes of Sibilla. This layer is, in turn, composed of three components. The *Models* component is responsible for those classes and interfaces describing stochastic processes and is also responsible for the classes for integrating specification languages in Sibilla. The *Simulation* component is used to sample model paths, which are possible computations of a model, and extract necessary measures and collect statistical information. The *Analysis* component allows the extraction of data from the simulations to perform quantitative analyses of systems using statistical inference techniques.

The *Front-end* layer offers the interfaces to allow interaction between Sibilla and the final user. The tool can be used in three different ways. First of all, a user can run and simulate a model using the *Command Line Interpreter* (called Sibilla Shell) to perform basic operations. A Python front-end has been also implemented using the *Pyjnius* library, which simplifies the communications with Java, allowing to plot paths using packages like Mathplotlib. Sibilla can be also integrated with other Java solutions, thanks to the Java APIs and the Runtime class.

Finally, the *Runtime* layer coordinates the communication between the back-end and the front-end layers. It acts as a controller, if the Model-View-Controller pattern is considered, and is structured in modules. These are called to select and upload the corresponding specification language that should be used.

The Trace Command. Compared to previous versions of Sibilla, we provide a new runtime command to represent single agent paths easily. Usually, the simulation

---

[2] The tool is available on GitHub at https://github.com/quasylab/sibilla.

process of a system with the tool requires the user to define the simulation parameters, such as the deadline, the time interval and the times the simulation will be repeated. Then the model is simulated and the available measures are collected. However, this procedure does not consider every attribute of the agent, thus we can not appreciate any meaningful change in the state (e.g. the agent has reached its goal or has changed a behavioural attribute). With the `trace` command, we can capture every attribute. We will see how we can use this input in Sect. 6.

3.2 YODA

Currently, Sibilla supports the specification and simulation of four different CAS languages: *Language of Interactive Objects* (LIO) [16], *Language of Population Models* (LPM) [7], *Simple Language for Agent Modelling* (SLAM), and *Yet anOther agent Description lAnguage* (YODA). Here, we would like to introduce the reader to YODA. In fact, this is the language we used to model the example described in the next section and from which we derived the agent traces that will be visualised in Sequit.

YODA [10] is a Multi-Agent specification language that permits the description of the behaviour of each agent and the dynamics of the enclosing environment. The language has been conceived with the idea that the agent may not have direct access to external information and thus may not be able to update itself directly. To overcome this necessity, we depute the environment, promoting it to a *"first-class citizen"* [31] and stressing the relationship between agents and the enclosing environment.

The language is equipped with a formalism, allowing a user to understand which are the constraints that should be followed while designing the model, and a grammar that can be used to specify systems. In YODA, an agent is defined in terms of: a *state*, what the agent intrinsically knows; a *information set*, external data about the agent; an *observation set*, what the agent perceives; a set of *actions*, changing the agent state; and a *behaviour*, for deciding how the agent will act. On the other hand, the environment is composed of two main functions. The first one, the *sensing* function, is responsible for updating the observations of each agent, while the other, the *dynamics* function, updates the external information. YODA[3] can be used to specify a wide range of case scenarios, from multi-robot systems, where agents move and interact with each other, to flocks, which is used as a running example for this paper. YODA provides an agent specification language permitting the description of the behaviour of each agent and the dynamics of the enclosing environment. The latter has a major role in the language and it is responsible for updating the external information of the agent.

4 A Running Scenario: Flock Behaviour

Agent-based specifications vary in the domain, objectives and other characteristics. From more elementary models, like simple robots moving around, to more

---

[3] More details are available at https://github.com/quasylab/sibilla/wiki/YODA.

complex Multi-Agent Systems (MAS), like the flock, all should operate inside a physical environment and have spatial references for our purposes. To show the functionalities of Sequit, we decided to use a known example: the *Flock Behaviour*.

The model was developed originally by Reynolds in [25] and later seen and improved in [9], for example. This model considers a group of birds (or boids, as Reynolds called them) roaming around. Typically, these agents move in a certain direction, given an acceleration, from an origin point. However, birds adopt three types of policy to avoid collisions: alignment, cohesion, or separation. In the first case (Fig. 1a), each agent aligns itself according to its neighbours' direction. When adopting the cohesion (Fig. 1b), a bird tries to keep a short distance from each other, meaning that it will estimate the future position of its neighbour and turn towards it. Finally, in the separation policy (Fig. 1c), birds try to avoid collision with each other by distancing themselves.

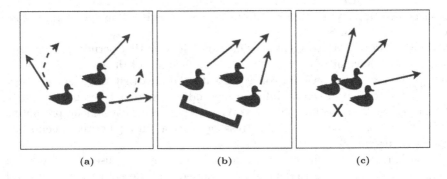

(a)   (b)   (c)

Fig. 1. The three policies of a flock

The flock behaviour used as an example in Sequit is a reinterpretation of Reynolds's original model. First of all, the birds are free to move without caring about possible obstacles in the environment. Then, the bird movement is based on a mean point calculated on the mean position of every available agent. The decision is made considering two main conditions: the position and the distance. Regarding the first condition, each agent is informed about the actual position of the mean point concerning its position. In the other case, the bird observes the distance from said point. After these two variables are observed, the agent decides if it has to distance itself, get closer, or maintain the direction. For simplicity reasons in reading the model, we omitted the steering factor of the bird, meaning that the bird immediately turns in the chosen direction. The full model specification can be found on the GitHub repository of Sibilla. The produced traces of this model are the ones we are going to use in Sect. 6.

In Listing 1.1, we display a snippet of the YODA specification of a flock. Given the parameters we want to use in the model (in this case, the number of available birds and two distances), we define the Bird using the components seen

```
param nbirds = 10; param maxDist = 2; param minDist = 1;
param speed = 1;

agent Bird =
  state :
    real angle = 0.0;
  features :
    real x = 0.0; real y = 0.0;
  observations :
    real meanX = 0.0; real meanY = 0.0;
    bool isTooFar = false; bool isTooClose = false;
  actions :
    moveA [ angle <- U[0.0, 90.0]; ]
    moveB [ angle <- U[90.0, 180.0]; ]
    moveC [ angle <- U[180.0, 270.0]; ]
    moveD [ angle <- U[270.0, 360.0]; ]
    maintain [ angle <- angle; ]
  behaviour :
    when isTooFar && ((meanX < 0.0) && (meanY < 0.0)) -> [moveC:1]
    ...
    orwhen isTooClose && ((meanX < 0.0) && (meanY < 0.0)) -> [moveA:1]
    ...
    otherwise [ maintain : 1]
end

environment :
  sensing :
    Bird [
      meanX <- mean Bird.x - it.x;
      meanY <- mean Bird.y - it.y;
      isTooFar <- sqrt (((mean Bird.x - it.x)^2)+((mean Bird.y - it.y)
      ^2)) > maxDist;
      isTooClose <- sqrt (((mean Bird.x - it.x)^2) + ((mean Bird.y - it.
      y)^2)) < minDist;
    ]
  dynamic :
    Bird [
      x <- x + speed*sin(angle);
      y <- y + speed*cos(angle);
    ]
end

configuration Main :
  for o sampled distinct nbirds time from U[0, nbirds] do
    Bird [ x = o; y = o; ]
  endfor
end
```

Listing 1.1. Flock Scenario Specification

before. The agent state is composed of an `angle`, which, as the name suggests, defines the angle orientation. Instead, the features refer to the coordinates x and y of the bird. Because our variant of the model considers the distance from the mean point of the flock, we include the position(`meanX` and `meanY`) of it and if the bird is too close (`isTooClose`) or too far (`isTooFar`) from it in the observations. The actions describe the movement in the four dials, e.g., if the action `moveA` is performed, the agent updates its direction with a value between 0 and 90. The behavioural rules are based on the distance from the mean point of the flock and where it is located, meaning that if the bird is too far from it and it is in the third dial, the bird will perform `moveA`, for example.

The environment declaration considers the sensing function and dynamics function. In the sensing, we update each observation of each bird agent: the mean coordinates are based on the mean value deducted from the position of every bird, while the boolean variables are calculated by comparing the absolute distance with maxDist and minDist. In the dynamics, we simply need to update the position of the agent by summing the original position with the shift obtained from the trigonometric equation multiplied by the speed of the birds that, for the sake of simplicity, we assume the same for all the elements of the flock.

Finally, the configuration allows to initialise the birds. The name of the configuration Main will be used in the simulation phase and it is described in Sect. 6.1.

5   Implementation

While Sibilla has been developed using Java and takes advantage of computational efficiency, from the graphical point of view, we want a more complete and well-structured solution that can host simulation visualisation. For this reason, we rely on the well-known Game Engine *Unity*[4], which is a real-time environment used not only in gaming, but also in movie making, architecture, and automotive. The term real-time describes images' rendering frequency and the possibility of dynamically interacting with the application. As a Game Engine, it serves as a convergence point of different developing aspects, allowing assets to interact with each other. In this section, we discuss how the module is implemented. We will see how the classes and available game objects work in order to replay the simulation traces of each agent.

5.1   Module Architecture

In Unity, classes and objects are included in what are technically called *Game Objects* (GO). These are the foundations for scenes (the environment where actions take place) and *"act as a container for functional components which determine how the Game Object looks, and what the Game Object does."*[5] A GO can be everything that belongs to a single scene and can range from a 3D model to a camera, or even the user interface. Our solution has been developed in a single scene including the necessary GOs. They are represented as three invisible GOs allowing the management of the simulation. These are: *Button Manager*, *Game Manager*, and *Simulation Manager*. Moreover, we included a set of utility classes to read files. Figure 2 shows an overview of the architecture and how each component interacts with each other or with external resources.

Button Manager. This object manages how the user can directly interact with the tool using the available buttons. The added script contains the invoked methods when a button is pressed. This GO is connected with the Game Manager, the

---

[4] Full site at https://unity.com/.
[5] https://docs.unity3d.com/Manual/class-GameObject.html.

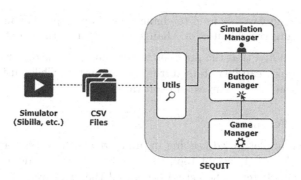

Fig. 2. Sequit Architecture

Simulation Manager, and the Camera object (which has two modes described in the next section).

Game Manager. The Game Manager is a common object used while developing applications within an engine. Usually, it manages and coordinates the interactions between the user and the game, e.g. by showing the collected points or the remaining life of the player. In this case, the Game Manager is used to navigate between the interfaces and eventually print on the display possible messages. Its main task, however, is to stop, resume, and change the velocity of the simulation, by exploiting Unity's libraries.

Simulation Manager. In the tool, we provide a GO called Simulation Manager that, differently from the other two, is responsible for instantiating the acting agents. The Simulation Manager takes advantage of a custom interface called `IAgentController`. This is used to implement the controllers for 2D and 3D agents, which in both cases should be able to change shape and colour and proceed into the next step.

Utils. The Utils namespace contains the utility classes for reading and interpreting the .csv files. Starting from two custom interfaces (`IFileReader` and `IStepsController`), two classes have been developed: the `CsvFileReader` class and the `FileStepsController` class. The first one is responsible for reading the table and is based on the .NET native class `StreamReader`. In fact, apart from the constructor, we take advantage of the existing library to perform the reading of lines. The other class is used to check the correctness of each line parsed by the reader and to scroll up and down the data table. To represent said line of the given file, the class `Step` has been implemented. It consists of five variables representing the information that the agent controller can use to move or visually inform of a state change. These are:

- **Time**, a float variable to measure the time steps;
- **Position**, a Vector3 variable used to move the agent in the space;
- **Rotation**, a Vector3 variable used to rotate the agent in a certain direction;

- **Shape**, a string variable used to change the shape (sprite or model);
- **Color**, a string variable used to change the colour of the agent.

It should be noted that the previous format must be the one used in the .csv file. This file format can be obtained from our main tool Sibilla, using the `trace` command, or from other sources and software.

5.2   Module Features

Sequit has been implemented keeping in mind what can be the basic needs of a common user. As a lightweight tool, its objective is to provide a solution that can be used immediately. The actual version of the visualiser has the following functionalities: *two degrees of freedom* for the camera, *controlling* the simulation and adding *2D* and *3D agents*. In this section, we discuss said features.

Switching Cameras. Our solution permits the user to visualise the replay of traces from two points of view. Using the corresponding button, the user can switch between the two camera modes, shown in Fig. 3: *eagle-eye* and *rotatory*. In the first case (Fig. 3a), we put the camera above the plane where the agents operate to have a better comprehension of 2D cases. Using this type of camera, the user can navigate with WASD/Arrow keys and with the mouse wheel can move away to have a better view of the scene or get closer to appreciate the details. The other type of camera (Fig. 3b) uses the same keys, even if the movement is focused around a focal point. This kind of camera can be useful for inspecting 3D scenarios.

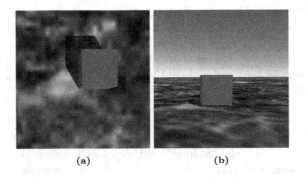

(a)   (b)

Fig. 3. The two different available cameras

Simulation Control. The agents move in the scene according to the provided trace. However, one may be interested in understanding how the entities are located in the environment at a certain moment. For this reason, the visualiser implements a method that, using basic Unity constructs, stops (and obviously resumes) the time and allows us to inspect the situation. In the same way, it is also possible to speed up or slow down the visualisation. The actual velocity of the simulation is displayed in the user interface.

Generating Agents. The fulcrum of the visualiser is the possibility to load the traces and generate the agents. Sequit provides a form where it is possible to configure the visualisation as the user desires. Initially, it is necessary to state if we want to generate 2D agents (as sprites) and 3D agents (as models). Independently of the type, we can specify the directory path containing the .csv files in the text field. The final step is to choose an optional preloaded plain among those available. Once we press the generation button, the visualiser reads the provided data and generates an entity for each available file. The agents will start moving right after the data has been loaded correctly.

6   Visualising the Running Scenario

In this section, we will show how the flock example introduced in Sect. 4 can be visualised by using Sequit. In order to obtain the traces representing the behaviour of involved agents, the tool Sibilla is used. As already said, we would like to remark that the use of Sequit is not limited to Sibilla, but we only need to have a valid set of *.csv* files representing the behaviour of involved agents. A short guide can be found in the Sequit repository[6].

6.1   Generating System Traces

The first step to visualise system traces consists of selecting the model of interest and using Sibilla to generate a simulation run. For the sake of simplicity, in this paper, we omit all the steps needed to setup Sibilla (all the documentation is available on the GitHub repository of the tool referenced above) and we jump right into the list of commands to use. In the example, we have used the Sibilla shell and the simulation script of Listing 1.2.

```
module "yoda"               /* Load YODA model */
load "flock.yoda"           /* Load system specification */
init "Main"                 /* Set initial configuration */
deadline 100                /* Set simulation deadline */

trace "flock.trc" in "./traces/flock"
                            /* Trace and save results */
```

Listing 1.2. List of commands to start simulating the flock

We need first of all to select the specification language to use (in our case YODA) by using command module"yoda". After that, by using the command load , the file containing the YODA model to simulate is loaded. Moreover, we have to set the initial configuration (via the command init "Main") and the *deadline* of the simulation, that is the time horizon of the simulation. Finally, we can generate the simulation traces by using the command trace. This command

---

[6] https://github.com/quasylab/Sequit.

takes two parameters: the specification of the data to trace and the folder where collected values will be saved. As a result, we will obtain a *.csv* file for each agent initialised in the system under consideration, containing the collected info described in Sect. 5.

An example of trace specification is reported in Listing 1.3. This file defines how the values needed for the visualisation can be computed from agents' attributes and consists of a sequence of assignments. Assigned values refer to position (x, y and z), direction, shape, and colour. Values are computed via expressions that can contain agent attributes. We can observe that the same data, like for instance the coordinates, can be omitted when an attribute with the same value is declared in the agents. A conditional block, based on the statement **when**, can be used to select different values according to a list of conditions. For instance, in our case, the colour used to depict an agent depends on the attributed `isTooFar` and `isTooClose`.

```
direction = angle;
shape = bird;
colour = {
    when isTooFar: blue;
    when isTooClose: red;
    otherwise: yellow;
}
```

Listing 1.3. An example of tracing specification

6.2   Visualising the Flock

Once we obtain the simulation traces from our model, we can load them into Sequit. When Sequit is executed a simple user interface is provided to start the visualisation or to quit the application (see Fig. 4). By pressing the button *Start*, the dialogue of Fig. 5 is provided, which can be used to select the kind of model to render (2D or 3D), the directory where the simulation traces can be loaded, and the *plane* to use as a background.

When all the needed parameters have been provided, the visualisation can be started by pressing the button *Generate Agents*. The tool instantiates all the agents that start moving according to the info saved on the loaded traces.

A button bar placed at the bottom of the visualisation window can be used to control the visualisation (see Fig. 6). On the left, we can find the buttons that can be used to *start/pause* the video and to control the *playback speed*, which can be used to slow down or speed up the video. On the other side, the buttons that control the camera, as described in Sect. 5.2, are placed.

In our example, we have used the 2D configuration, the "Sky" plane, and the eagle-eye view camera. We can observe that, as we specified in Listing 1.3, the birds appear in a different colour depending on the distance from the mean point of the flock: blue if it is too far, red if too close, and yellow if it is at the

Fig. 4. The starting screen of Sequit

Fig. 5. The initial interface with the agent form

right distance range. In Fig. 7, instead, we present a screenshot of a time instant where all the birds are far from the mean point. As we can see, here all the birds are coloured blue, which that they need to get closer, according to the specified behaviour.

The result of a simulation can be seen in the available demo video[7]. The overall simulation process has been performed on a MacBook Air, with an M1 CPU and 16GB of memory. Considering 100 time units per simulation, the production of agents' traces, which has been performed with Sibilla, required on an average of 10 simulations: 221 ms with 5 birds, 456 ms with 50 birds, and 4 s and 565 ms with 500 birds. Sequit was not visibly affected by the amount of loaded traces. It is possible to assess the capacity of the visualiser by loading the five hundred entities (as shown in Fig. 8) that can be also found in the provided links on GitHub.

---

[7] All materials are at http://quasylab.unicam.it/sibilla/sequit/.

Fig. 6. The Flock at the beginning of the simulation

Fig. 7. The Flock after a while

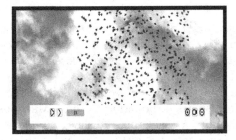

Fig. 8. A Flock of 500 birds

7   Conclusions

In this paper, we introduced Sequit, a tool for visualising agent traces. We have also shown how the tool Sibilla and the specification language YODA can be used to generate these traces. However, thanks to the use of a simple *.csv* format, other tools can be used to produce the trajectories representing the agents' behaviour.

Our proposal has been conceived with the idea of having a lightweight and ready-to-use offline simulator that everyone can easily operate. We discussed the architecture of the visualiser, which is based on three different Unity Game Objects, each with its own responsibilities, and a utility namespace to read files. We also provided a general overview of the features provided by our tool. Finally, a simple case scenario based on flock behaviour has been used to show the workflow that, starting from a YODA specification permits generating the simulation traces and visualising the results.

7.1 Future Works

For the future developments of Sequit, we are planning to introduce more functionalities designed to improve the user experience. First, we would like to add the possibility of having a third degree of freedom for the camera. More specifically, it could be interesting to have a camera mode that follows a specific agent during its trace execution. This agent could be selected either via the simulation window (by a click) or via appropriate queries depending on the agent attributes.

For what concerns the visualisation control, we would like to implement a controllable progress bar to scroll between time instants of the simulation, along with some shortcut buttons for restarting and rewinding the agents. At the moment, the application is built to support Windows, macOS, and Linux distributions, but we would like to provide an additional build supporting WebGL [20]. This will make it more accessible even for those who may not be able to run it as a local solution.

In order to improve the optimisation and usability of Sequit, we are considering two major implementations. In the first case, we would like to explore and add Unity *DOTS*[8] technology. This is based on the *ECS* (Entity-Component-System) paradigm and it is considered as "*a combination of technologies and packages that delivers a data-oriented design approach to building games in Unity*". This means that data relies on a single function instead of having an object-oriented approach. DOTS could be used to represent those systems requiring many, identical entities, like Population Models. The second major improvement we are planning is the development of a *Unreal Engine*-based version of Sequit. While the actual version is lightweight and does not require much effort from the user, there are some limitations from a flexibility and openness point of view due to the engine's architecture and compiler choice (C# compiled to C++). Instead, Unreal Engine [26] projects are compiled directly in C++, allowing the user to customise the application extensively. An Unreal Engine version could permit a more straightforward process, immediately connecting Sibilla with Sequit.

References

1. Agüero, C.E., et al.: Inside the virtual robotics challenge: simulating real-time robotic disaster response. IEEE Trans. Autom. Sci. Eng. **12**(2), 494–506 (2015). https://doi.org/10.1109/TASE.2014.2368997
2. Aguzzi, G., Casadei, R., Viroli, M.: Macroswarm: a field-based compositional framework for swarm programming. In: Jongmans, S., Lopes, A. (eds.) COORDINATION 2023. LNCS, vol. 13908, pp. 31–51. Springer, Cham (2023). https://doi.org/10.1007/978-3-031-35361-1_2

---

[8] https://unity.com/dots.

3. Audrito, G.: FCPP: an efficient and extensible field calculus framework. In: IEEE International Conference on Autonomic Computing and Self-Organizing Systems, ACSOS 2020, Washington, DC, USA, 17–21 August 2020, pp. 153–159. IEEE (2020). https://doi.org/10.1109/ACSOS49614.2020.00037
4. Audrito, G., Rapetta, L., Torta, G.: Extensible 3D simulation of aggregated systems with FCPP. In: ter Beek, M.H., Sirjani, M. (eds.) COORDINATION 2022. LNCS, vol. 13271, pp. 55–71. Springer, Cham (2022). https://doi.org/10.1007/978-3-031-08143-9_4
5. Banks, J., Chwif, L.: Warnings about simulation. J. Simul. **5**(4), 279–291 (2011). https://doi.org/10.1057/JOS.2010.24
6. Begel, A., Klopfer, E.: Starlogo TNG: an introduction to game development. J. E-Learn. **53**(2007), 146 (2007)
7. Bortolussi, L., Hillston, J., Latella, D., Massink, M.: Continuous approximation of collective system behaviour: a tutorial. Perform. Eval. **70**(5), 317–349 (2013). https://doi.org/10.1016/J.PEVA.2013.01.001
8. Caillou, P., Gaudou, B., Grignard, A., Truong, Q.C., Taillandier, P.: A simple-to-use BDI architecture for agent-based modeling and simulation. In: Jager, W., Verbrugge, R., Flache, A., de Roo, G., Hoogduin, L., Hemelrijk, C.K. (eds.) Advances in Social Simulation 2015. Advances in Intelligent Systems and Computing, vol. 528, pp. 15–28. Springer, Cham (2015). https://doi.org/10.1007/978-3-319-47253-9_2
9. De Nicola, R., Stefano, L.D., Inverso, O., Valiani, S.: Modelling flocks of birds from the bottom up. In: Margaria, T., Steffen, B. (eds.) ISoLA 2022, Part III. LNCS, vol. 13703, pp. 82–96. Springer, Cham (2022). https://doi.org/10.1007/978-3-031-19759-8_6
10. Del Giudice, N., Loreti, M.: YODA: Yet anOther agent Description lAnguage. In: Casadei, R., et al. (eds.) IEEE International Conference on Autonomic Computing and Self-Organizing Systems Companion, ACSOS-C 2022, Virtual, CA, USA, 19–23 September 2022, pp. 82–87. IEEE (2022). https://doi.org/10.1109/ACSOSC56246.2022.00038
11. Del Giudice, N., Matteucci, L., Quadrini, M., Rehman, A., Loreti, M.: Sibilla: a tool for reasoning about collective systems. In: ter Beek, M.H., Sirjani, M. (eds.) COORDINATION 2022. IFIP Advances in Information and Communication Technology, vol. 13271, pp. 92–98. Springer, Cham (2022). https://doi.org/10.1007/978-3-031-08143-9_6
12. Diamanti, M., Vilhjálmsson, H.H.: Extending the menge crowd simulation framework: visual authoring in unity. In: Martinho, C., Dias, J., Campos, J., Heylen, D. (eds.) IVA 2022: ACM International Conference on Intelligent Virtual Agents, Faro, Portugal, 6–9 September 2022, pp. 30:1–30:3. ACM (2022). https://doi.org/10.1145/3514197.3549698
13. Emrich, S., Suslov, S., Judex, F.: Fully agent based modellings of epidemic spread using AnyLogic. In: Proceedings of EUROSIM, pp. 9–13 (2007)
14. Hölzl, M.M., Rauschmayer, A., Wirsing, M.: Engineering of software-intensive systems: state of the art and research challenges. In: Wirsing, M., Banâtre, J., Hölzl, M.M., Rauschmayer, A. (eds.) Software-Intensive Systems and New Computing Paradigms - Challenges and Visions. LNCS, vol. 5380, pp. 1–44. Springer, Heidelberg (2008). https://doi.org/10.1007/978-3-540-89437-7_1
15. Koenig, N.P., Howard, A.: Design and use paradigms for gazebo, an open-source multi-robot simulator. In: 2004 IEEE/RSJ International Conference on Intelligent Robots and Systems, Sendai, Japan, 28– 2 October 2004, pp. 2149–2154. IEEE (2004). https://doi.org/10.1109/IROS.2004.1389727

16. Le Boudec, J., McDonald, D.D., Mundinger, J.: A generic mean field convergence result for systems of interacting objects. In: Fourth International Conference on the Quantitative Evaluaiton of Systems (QEST 2007), 17–19 September 2007, Edinburgh, Scotland, UK, pp. 3–18. IEEE Computer Society (2007). https://doi.org/10.1109/QEST.2007.8

17. Loreti, M., Hillston, J.: Modelling and analysis of collective adaptive systems with CARMA and its tools. In: Bernardo, M., Nicola, R.D., Hillston, J. (eds.) SFM 2016. LNCS, vol. 9700, pp. 83–119. Springer, Cham (2016). https://doi.org/10.1007/978-3-319-34096-8_4

18. Mariani, S., Omicini, A.: Game engines to model MAS: a research roadmap. In: Santoro, C., Messina, F., Benedetti, M.D. (eds.) Proceedings of the 17th Workshop "From Objects to Agents" co-located with 18th European Agent Systems Summer School (EASSS 2016), Catania, Italy, 29–30 July 2016. CEUR Workshop Proceedings, vol. 1664, pp. 106–111. CEUR-WS.org (2016)

19. de Melo, M.S.P., da Silva Neto, J.G., da Silva, P.J.L., Teixeira, J.M.X.N., Teichrieb, V.: Analysis and comparison of robotics 3d simulators. In: 21st Symposium on Virtual and Augmented Reality, SVR 2019, Rio de Janeiro, Brazil, 28–31 October 2019, pp. 242–251. IEEE (2019). https://doi.org/10.1109/SVR.2019.00049

20. Parisi, T.: WebGL - Up and Running: Building 3D Graphics for the Web. O'Reilly, Sebastopol (2012)

21. Pettit, C., Bishop, I., Sposito, V., Aurambout, J.P., Sheth, F.: Developing a multiscale visualisation framework for use in climate change response. Landscape Ecol. **27**, 487–508 (2012)

22. Pianini, D., Montagna, S., Viroli, M.: Chemical-oriented simulation of computational systems with ALCHEMIST. J. Simulation **7**(3), 202–215 (2013). https://doi.org/10.1057/JOS.2012.27

23. Possik, J.J., et al.: A distributed simulation approach to integrate anylogic and unity for virtual reality applications: case of COVID-19 modelling and training in a dialysis unit. In: Cecilia, J.M., Martinez, F.J. (eds.) 25th IEEE/ACM International Symposium on Distributed Simulation and Real Time Applications, DS-RT 2021, Valencia, Spain, 27–29 September 2021, pp. 1–7. IEEE (2021). https://doi.org/10.1109/DS-RT52167.2021.9576149

24. Resnick, M.: Starlogo: an environment for decentralized modeling and decentralized thinking. In: Tauber, M.J. (ed.) Conference on Human Factors in Computing Systems: Common Ground, CHI 1996, Vancouver, BC, Canada, 13–18 April 1996, Conference Companion, pp. 11–12. ACM (1996). https://doi.org/10.1145/257089.257095

25. Reynolds, C.W.: Flocks, herds and schools: a distributed behavioral model. In: Stone, M.C. (ed.) Proceedings of the 14th Annual Conference on Computer Graphics and Interactive Techniques, SIGGRAPH 1987, Anaheim, California, USA, 27–31 July 1987, pp. 25–34. ACM (1987). https://doi.org/10.1145/37401.37406

26. Shannon, T.: Unreal Engine 4 for Design Visualization: Developing Stunning Interactive Visualizations, Animations, and Renderings. Addison-Wesley Professional, Boston (2017)

27. Taillandier, P., et al.: Building, composing and experimenting complex spatial models with the GAMA platform. GeoInformatica **23**(2), 299–322 (2019). https://doi.org/10.1007/S10707-018-00339-6

28. Tosi, S.: Matplotlib for Python developers. Packt Publishing Ltd (2009)

29. Vernon-Bido, D., Collins, A.J., Sokolowski, J.A.: Effective visualization in modeling & simulation. In: Diallo, S.Y., Tolk, A. (eds.) Proceedings of the 48th Annual

Simulation Symposium, ANSS 2015, part of the 2015 Spring Simulation Multi-conference, SpringSim 2015, Alexandria, VA, USA, 12–15 April 2015, pp. 33–40. SCS/ACM (2015)

30. Wai, S.K., WaiShiang, C., bin Khairuddin, M.A., Bujang, Y.R.B., Hidayat, R., Paschal, C.H.: Autonomous agents in 3D crowd simulation through BDI architecture. JOIV Int. J. Inform. Visual. **5**(1), 1–7 (2021)

31. Weyns, D., Omicini, A., Odell, J.: Environment as a first class abstraction in multiagent systems. Auton. Agents Multi Agent Syst. **14**(1), 5–30 (2007). https://doi.org/10.1007/S10458-006-0012-0

Implementing a Message-Passing Interpretation of the Semi-Axiomatic Sequent Calculus (SAX)

Adrian Francalanza[1] , Gerard Tabone[1(✉)] , and Frank Pfenning[2]

[1] University of Malta, Msida, Malta
{adrian.francalanza,gerard.tabone}@um.edu.mt
[2] Carnegie Mellon University, Pittsburgh, PA, USA
fp@cs.cmu.edu

Abstract. We present language implementation based on a formulation of sessions types for message-passing programs in terms of an adjoint intuitionistic logic. This logical formulation can naturally describe asynchronous concurrency and can handle linear, affine, multicast and replicated types. This allows the resulting language to express a variety of common programming idioms such as service replicable, broadcast communication and message cancellations within the same programming, while still guaranteeing safety. Our tool consists of a type-checker and an interpreter. It is implemented in the Go language, leveraging its concurrency features in order to investigate the implementability of the operational interpretation proposed by the adjoint logic formulation. We assess the performance of our concurrent interpreter and show that it scales adequately to the number of concurrent processes executed.

Keywords: behavioural types · concurrency · language implementation

1 Introduction

The Semi-Axiomatic Sequent Calculus (SAX) [10,27] is a logical framework that blends features of the sequent calculus with axiomatic presentations of intuitionistic logic, replacing non-invertible rules by corresponding axioms. The framework has been shown to elegantly handle a variety of substructural modalities such as linear, affine, multicast and replication within one uniform formalism. SAX also induces a natural operational interpretation in terms of active and passive parallel processes that interact *asynchronously*. Numerous variants of such an interpretation have been studied for a variety of computational models, ranging from shared memory concurrency [10], futures [31], and message-passing

This work has been supported by the Security Behavioural APIs project (No: I22LU01-01) funded by the UM Research Excellence Funds 2021 and the Tertiary Education Scholarships Scheme (Malta). This work is also supported by the BehAPI project funded by the EU H2020 RISE of the Marie Skłodowska-Curie action (No: 778233).

© IFIP International Federation for Information Processing 2024
Published by Springer Nature Switzerland AG 2024
I. Castellani and F. Tiezzi (Eds.): COORDINATION 2024, LNCS 14676, pp. 295–313, 2024.
https://doi.org/10.1007/978-3-031-62697-5_16

concurrency [30]. Every proposed interpretation is shown to observe standard requirement such as progress and preservation, in addition to other operational properties such as confluence and deadlock-freedom.

This paper focusses on the message-passing operational interpretation of SAX, and investigates the *implementability* of the proposed operational model. Concretely we build a type-checker that automates the verification of process terms modelling session type specifications [20], according to the substructural type system developed in the aforementioned paper. This gives us a language for expressing *safe* message-passing concurrency that departs from the strict linearity constraints: we can flexibly express a variety of common programming idioms such as replicable services broadcast communication and message cancellations. We also build an interpreter that executes typed programs according to the concurrent reduction semantics given in [30]. Our interpreter targets the Go programming language which natively supports message-based concurrency via channels and goroutines [11]. More precisely, our implementation supports two execution options (using unbuffered and buffered channels respectively) which allows us to better asses the implementability of the asynchronous semantics proposed.

Structure and Contribution. After reviewing the static and dyamic semantics of our language (Sect. 2) we outline the design decisions leading to our type-checker (Sect. 3). This is followed by a discussion on the implementation of the interpreter (Sect. 4). We finally evaluate our implementation in Sect. 5. The accompanying tool, called GRITS, is available at https://github.com/gertab/Grits (archived [35]).

2 SAX for Message-Passing Concurrency

The asynchronous message-passing language proposed by Pruiksma et al. [30] centers around the intuitionistic judgement Eq. (1) below. It defines an interface specification for process P, asserting that it *provides* the behaviour described by the proposition B on the channel denoted by variable y, assuming that some $Q_1, \ldots, Q_k$ processes (to which it is *client*) each provide a behaviour described by A_i on channel x_i respectively.

$$x_1 : A_1, \ldots, x_k : A_k \vdash P :: (y : B) \tag{1}$$

At runtime, the variables $x_1, \ldots, x_k, y$ in Eq. (1) are instantiated to dynamically-allocated channel names $a_1, \ldots, a_k, b$, resulting in the process arrangement of Fig. 1. The behaviour described by the channel propositions in Eq. (1) have a dual interpretation. Process R in Fig. 1 is a *client* on channel b whereas processes $Q_1, \ldots, Q_k$ *provide* on channels $a_1, \ldots, a_k$ to which process P is a client. In the sequel, we let identifiers $u, v, w, \ldots$ range over both names, $a, b, c, d, \ldots$ and variables $x, y, z, \ldots$.

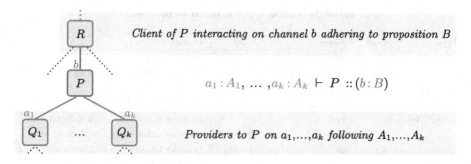

Fig. 1. Hierarchical structure of processes, from P_2's perspective

Types. Channel propositions are *session types*, expressed as linear logic connectives [4] indexed by a specific *mode* of truth, m (which is elided when implicit).

$$A^m, B^m \in \text{Type} ::= A^m \otimes B^m \quad | \; A^m \multimap B^m \quad | \; \oplus \{l : A_l^m\}_{l \in L} \quad | \; \&\{l : A_l^m\}_{l \in L}$$
$$| \; \mathbf{1}^m \qquad | \; t^m \qquad | \; \uparrow_m^n A^m \qquad | \; \downarrow_n^m A^m$$
$$m, n, o \in \text{Mode} ::= \mathsf{l} \; (linear) \quad | \; \mathsf{a} \; (affine) \quad | \; \mathsf{m} \; (multicast) \quad | \; \mathsf{r} \; (replicable)$$

A tensor, $A^m \otimes B^m$, represents the *sending* of channel of type A^m along with the continuation channel of type B^m. Implication, $A^m \multimap B^m$, is its dual, representing the *receipt* of a channel A^m with the continuation of type B^m. A labelled n-ary sum-type, $\oplus\{l : A_l^m\}_{l \in L}$, represents the *internal choice* from a range of labels $l \in L$ transferred along with the continuation channel having type A_l, whereas the *external choice*, $\&\{l : A_l^m\}_{l \in L}$, receives such a label $l \in L$ and continuation channel at type A_l. The unit type, $\mathbf{1}^m$, and the recursion variable, t^m, are standard; a collection of *contractive* [16] equi-recursive type definitions, $t^m = A^m$, is assumed.

All logical connectives combine types at the *same mode*, except upshifts, $\uparrow_m^n A^m$ and downshifts, $\downarrow_n^m A^m$. Four modes are considered, representing the possible combinations of contraction and weakening. This induces a mode preorder, $m \succeq n$ (see axioms below), whenever m has *more* substructural properties than n.

$$\mathsf{r} \succeq \mathsf{m} \qquad \mathsf{r} \succeq \mathsf{a} \qquad \mathsf{m} \succeq \mathsf{l} \qquad \mathsf{a} \succeq \mathsf{l}$$

whereas linear and replicable are bottom and top elements, affine allows only weakening whereas multicast only permits contraction. Shifts, are subject to the following mode ordering constraints: $\uparrow_n^m A^n$ and $\downarrow_n^m A^m$ require that $m \succeq n$.

Syntax. Our process syntax follows closely the one in [30]. The constructs inducing interaction (*i.e.,* send, select, close and cast) are all *asynchronous* (*i.e.,* without any continuation process). Forwarding, spawning, splitting and dropping are structural constructs (the latter two are implicit in [30]). The processes assume

Table 1. Session types mapped to processes

Type	Cont.	Process	Cont.	Description
c: $A \otimes B$	-	send $c\langle a,d \rangle$	-	provider sends $a : A$, $d : B$ on c
		$\langle x,y \rangle \leftarrow$ recv $c; P$	$P\,[{}^{a,\,d}/_{x,\,y}]$	client receives $a : A$, $d : B$ on c
c: $A \multimap B$	$d : B$	$\langle x,y \rangle \leftarrow$ recv $c; P$	$P\,[{}^{a,\,d}/_{x,\,y}]$	provider receives $a : A$, $d : B$ on c
		send $c\langle a,d \rangle$	-	client sends $a : A$, d on c
c: $\oplus\{l : A_l\}_{l \in L}$	-	$c.k\langle d \rangle$	-	provider selects $k \in L$ with $d{:}A_k$ on c
		case $c\,(l\langle y \rangle \Rightarrow P_l)_{l \in L}$	$P_k\,[{}^d/_y]$	client branches to $k \in L$ with $d{:}A_k$ on c
c: $\&\{l : A_l\}_{l \in L}$	$d : A_k$	case $c\,(l\langle y \rangle \Rightarrow P_l)_{l \in L}$	$P_k\,[{}^d/_y]$	provider branches to $k \in L$ with $d{:}A_k$ on c
		$c.k\langle d \rangle$	-	client selects $k \in L$ with $d{:}A_k$ on c
c:$\downarrow_n^m A^m$	-	cast $c\langle d \rangle$	-	provider upshifts to $d : A^m$ on c
		$y \leftarrow$ shift $c; P$	$P\,[{}^d/_y]$	client upshifts to $d : A^m$ on c
c:$\uparrow_n^m A^n$	-	$y \leftarrow$ shift $c; P$	$P\,[{}^d/_y]$	provider downcasts to $d : A^n$ on c
		cast $c\langle d \rangle$	-	client downcasts to $d : A^n$ on c
c:$\mathbf{1}$	-	close c	-	provider terminates on c
		wait $c; P$	P	client receives termination on c

a collection of named process definitions $p(\overline{x}) = P$ which are invoked using $p(\overline{u})$ (where p ranges over process names).

$$
\begin{aligned}
P, Q \in \text{PROC} ::= \ &\text{send } u\langle v,w \rangle & \textit{(send)} & \quad | \ \langle x,y \rangle \leftarrow \text{recv } u; P & \textit{(receive)} \\
& | \ u.l\langle v \rangle & \textit{(select)} & \quad | \ \text{case } u\,(l\langle y \rangle \Rightarrow P_l)_{l \in L} & \textit{(branch)} \\
& | \ \text{close } u & \textit{(close)} & \quad | \ \text{wait } u; P & \textit{(wait)} \\
& | \ \text{cast } u\langle v \rangle & \textit{(cast)} & \quad | \ x \leftarrow \text{shift } u; P & \textit{(shift)} \\
& | \ \text{fwd } u\ v & \textit{(forward)} & \quad | \ x \leftarrow \text{new } P; Q & \textit{(spawn)} \\
& | \ \langle x,y \rangle \leftarrow \text{split } u; P & \textit{(split)} & \quad | \ \text{drop } u; P & \textit{(drop)} \\
& | \ p(\overline{u}) & \textit{(call)} &
\end{aligned}
$$

Three *synchronous* processes (*i.e.*, receive, branch and shift) together with spawn and split, bind variables in the respective continuation processes (*e.g.* receive binds variables x and y in P). To facilitate the mechanisation of typechecking, we follow Sano et al. [32], Crary [7] and require every bound variable to be used linearly (exactly once) in the binding scope. Process spawning, *i.e.*, $x \leftarrow$ new $P; Q$, partially breaks this syntactic constraint and allows x to be used linearly in P and in Q to generate a more standard formulation of the CUT rule (see below).

Type System. Based on Eq. (1), the SAX type system for static and runtime terms[1] takes the form Eq. (2) and observes *mode independence*: $\forall i \in 1..k \ . \ m_i \geq$

---

[1] Static terms are closed (*i.e.*, no free variables) and do not contain any names.

n.

$$u_1 : A_1^{m_1}, \ldots, u_k : A_k^{m_k} \vdash P :: (v : B^n) \tag{2}$$

Type environments, Γ, range over sequences of antecedents, $u_i : A_i^{m_i}$, subject to exchange. The structural rules are fairly standard, augmented with mode considerations. *E.g.* CUT (below) embodies computation via the interaction between the spawning (client) process, Q, and the spawnee (provider), P, via the dynamically allocated channel x. To preserve mode independence, all antecedent modes typing P should be ordered w.r.t. the mode of channel x, $\Gamma \succeq m$, which should also preserve independence w.r.t. the channel that Q provides on, $m \succeq n$. Rules DRP and SPL explicitly link weakening and contraction to structural terms.

$$\frac{}{u : A^m \vdash \mathsf{fwd}\, wu :: (w : A^m)} \;\text{ID} \qquad \frac{\Gamma \succeq m \succeq n \quad \Gamma \vdash P :: (x{:}A^m) \quad \Gamma', x{:}A^m \vdash Q :: (u{:}B^n)}{\Gamma, \Gamma' \vdash x \leftarrow \mathsf{new}\, P; Q :: (u : B^n)} \;\text{CUT}$$

$$\frac{m \in \{\mathsf{a},\mathsf{r}\}\, \Gamma \vdash P :: (w{:}B^n)}{\Gamma, u{:}A^m \vdash \mathsf{drop}\, u; P :: (w{:}B^n)} \;\text{DRP} \qquad \frac{m \in \{\mathsf{m},\mathsf{r}\}\, \Gamma, x{:}A^m, y{:}A^m \vdash P :: (w{:}B^n)}{\Gamma, u{:}A^m \vdash \langle x, y \rangle \leftarrow \mathsf{split}\, u; P :: (w{:}B^n)} \;\text{SPL}$$

There is a left and right rule for every logical connective. Crucially, in SAX, right rules of positive connectives and left rules of negative connectives are axioms, capturing the asynchronous nature of the constructs inducing interaction. We detail the typing rules for the tensor and implication connectives below and outline the relationship for the remaining connectives in Table 1.

$$\frac{}{u : A^m, v : B^m \vdash \mathsf{send}\, wuv :: (w : A^m \otimes B^m)} \;\otimes\text{R} \qquad \frac{\Gamma, x : A^m, y : B^m \vdash P :: (w : C^n)}{\Gamma, u : A^m \otimes B^m \vdash \mathsf{recv}\, uxy P :: (w : C^n)} \;\otimes\text{L}$$

$$\frac{\Gamma, x{:}A^m \vdash P :: (y{:}B^m)}{\Gamma \vdash \mathsf{recv}\, wxy P :: (w{:}A^m \multimap B^m)} \;\multimap\text{R} \qquad \frac{}{u{:}A^m, w{:}A^m \multimap B^m \vdash \mathsf{send}\, wuv :: (v{:}B^m)} \;\multimap\text{L}$$

For completeness, we list below the remaining rules used by the type system. The environment Σ is fixed and left implicit; it stores the typing information for all process definitions. For a comprehensive discussion of these rules, see [30].

$$\frac{\Sigma(p) = \overline{y : A^m} \vdash P :: (x : B^n)}{u : \overline{A^m} \vdash p(w, \overline{u}) :: (w : B^n)} \;\text{CALL} \qquad \frac{}{\cdot \vdash \mathsf{close}\, w :: (w : 1^m)} \;\text{1R} \qquad \frac{\Gamma \vdash P :: (w : A^n)}{\Gamma, u : 1^m \vdash \mathsf{wait}\, u; P :: (w : A^n)} \;\text{1L}$$

$$\frac{l \in L}{u : A_l^m \vdash w.l\langle u \rangle :: (w : \oplus\{l : A_l\}_{l \in L}^m)} \;\oplus\text{R} \qquad \frac{\Gamma, y_l : A_l^m \vdash P_l :: (w : B^n) \quad \text{for each } l \in L}{\Gamma, u : \oplus\{l : A_l\}_{l \in L}^m \vdash \mathsf{case}\, u\, (l\langle y_l \rangle \Rightarrow P_l)_{l \in L} :: (w : B^n)} \;\oplus\text{L}$$

$$\frac{\Gamma \vdash P_l :: (y_l : A_l^m) \quad \text{for each } l \in L}{\Gamma \vdash \mathsf{case}\, w\, (l\langle y_l \rangle \Rightarrow P_l)_{l \in L} :: (w : \&\{l : A_l\}_{l \in L}^m)} \;\&\text{R} \qquad \frac{l \in L}{u : \&\{l : A_l\}_{l \in L}^m \vdash u.l\langle w \rangle :: (w : A_l^m)} \;\&\text{L}$$

$$\frac{\Gamma \vdash P :: (y : A^n)}{\Gamma \vdash y \leftarrow \mathsf{shift}\, w; P :: (w :\uparrow_n^m A^n)} \;\uparrow\text{R} \qquad \frac{}{u :\uparrow_n^m A^n \vdash \mathsf{cast}\, u\langle w \rangle :: (w : A^n)} \;\uparrow\text{L}$$

$$\frac{}{u : A^m \vdash \mathsf{cast}\, w\langle u \rangle :: (w :\downarrow_n^m A^m)} \;\downarrow\text{R} \qquad \frac{\Gamma, x : A^m \vdash P :: (w : B^o)}{\Gamma, u :\downarrow_n^m A^m \vdash x \leftarrow \mathsf{shift}\, u; P :: (w : B^o)} \;\downarrow\text{L}$$

Table 2. Abstract and concrete mapping for types

Abstract Types	Concrete Types	Abstract Types	Concrete Types
$A \otimes B$	A * B	1	1
$A \multimap B$	A -* B	t	t
$\oplus\{l : A_l\}_{l \in L}$	+{l1 : A1, ...}	$\uparrow_m^n A^m$	m /\n A
$\&\{l : A_l\}_{l \in L}$	&{l1 : A1, ...}	$\downarrow_n^m A^m$	m /\n A
$t^m = T$	type t = m T	l, a, m, r	lin, aff, mul, rep

Runtime. Closed processes execute concurrently by interacting on names assigned to channels. A running process takes the form

$$\mathsf{prc}(N; a; P)$$

The channel on which process P provides is referred to *externally* (by other processes) via the set of names $N = \{b_1, \ldots, b_n\}$ (a unique name per reference), and *internally* by P using name a (prc acts as a name binder for a in P). P may in turn contain other names to refer to channels provided by other processes. The semantics is given in terms of reduction rules; we use "$\_$" in lieu of names, a, or sets of names, N, when irrelevant (and unchanged between redex and reduct).

(CUT) $\mathsf{prc}\left(\_; \_; x \leftarrow \mathsf{new}\ P; Q\right) \longrightarrow \mathsf{prc}\left(\{b\}; c; P\left[{}^c/x\right]\right), \mathsf{prc}\left(\_; \_; Q\left[{}^b/x\right]\right)$

(SND) $\mathsf{prc}\left(\{a\}; b; \mathsf{send}\ b\langle c,d\rangle\right), \mathsf{prc}\left(\_; \_; \langle x,y\rangle \leftarrow \mathsf{recv}\ a; P\right) \longrightarrow \mathsf{prc}\left(\_; \_; P\left[{}^{c,\,d}/x,y\right]\right)$

(RCV) $\mathsf{prc}\left(\{a\}; b; \langle x,y\rangle \leftarrow \mathsf{recv}\ b; P\right), \mathsf{prc}\left(\_; d; \mathsf{send}\ a\langle c,d\rangle\right) \longrightarrow \mathsf{prc}\left(\_; d; P\left[{}^{c,\,d}/x,y\right]\right)$

For instance, CUT spawns a new process $P\left[{}^c/x\right]$ while allocating two names, one internal, c, and one external, b (used by the spawning process Q) to refer to the channel provided by the spawnee $P\left[{}^c/x\right]$. SND describes the sending by a provider on a channel known by a client via the (external) name a; since communication is asynchronous, the provider terminates after the interaction. Dually, RCV describes the receipt of a message by a process providing on a channel known externally via name a. See Pruiksma et al. [30] for details.

3   Static Type-Checker

We implement a tool called GRITS, that defines a language for describing message-passing programs that satisfy SAX type specifications and runtime, and execute them. It is implemented in Go [11] and is publicly available on GitHub [35].

Programs are written in a syntax similar to the one in Sect. 2, with a few minor discrepancies. Types are written with the syntax mapping in Table 2.

Moreover processes are allowed to refer to the name of the channel they provide on via the keyword `self`.[2] The structure of a GRITS program follows the general structure outlined below. It starts with a series of type declarations, line 1, followed by a series of *named* process template declarations, line 3, and a single main process that starts the computation, line 5.

```
1   type t = m A                      // t^m = A^m
2   ...
3   let p(x1:A1,...,xk:Ak):B = P
    // p(x1,...,xk) = P  with  x1:A1,...,xk:Ak ⊢ P :: (self:B)
4   ...
5   exec q()
```

Typechecking follows closely the typing rules outlined in Sect. 2. Its automation is facilitated by the fact that most typing rules are syntax directed. The only exception is rule CUT; its premises require the analysis to statically guess:

1. the type associated to the channel x provided by the spawned process P
2. how to split the antecedents across the two premises

GRITS solves the first issue by allowing spawning to include type information and be written as $x : A \leftarrow \text{new } P; Q$. The second issue is solved by limiting the typing of P to analytic cuts (snips [10]). Concretely, the syntax of P is limited to either asynchronous constructs (*i.e.*, send, select, close and cast) or process calls, since the antecedents in their (axiom) typing rules are precisely determined from the structure of the term. More complex variations for P can always be packaged as a separate process definition and then used via a process call.

Expressivity. The program excerpt below is adapted from [30, Ex. 10]. The `map` process declaration takes two parameters: a map (`f`) and the original list of numbers (`l`). The mapping function `f` is declared at a *replicable mode* since it will be copied and used over each element of the list. Since the list elements are linear numbers, the map has to first shift to linear mode before it is applied.

```
1   type nat = lin +{zero : 1, succ : nat}
2   type listNat = lin +{cons : nat * listNat, nil : 1}
3   type mapType = lin /\ rep (nat -* nat)
```

The type declarations `nat` and `listNat` define natural number and lists recursively, whereas `mapType` defines the type of a replicable map function.

```
4   let map(f:mapType, l:listNat):listNat =
5       case l (
6         cons<l'> => <curr, l''> <- recv l';
7             <f', f''> <- split f;   // map channel 'f' copied
8             fl : lin (nat -* nat) <- new cast f'<self>;
9             curr_upd : nat <- new send fl<curr, self>;
10            k'' : listNat <- new map(f'', l'');
11            k' : nat * listNat <- new send self<curr_upd,k''>;
12            self.cons<k'>
13        | nil<l'> => drop f;        // map channel 'f' unused
14            self.nil<l'>
15      )
16
```

---

[2] Processes fully observe the linearity syntactic constraint since, in $x \leftarrow \text{new } P; Q$, variable x is used linearly in Q exclusively, but not in P which uses `self` instead.

```
17  let mapByInc() : mapType  =
18      s <- shift self;
19      <toAdd, result> <- recv s;
20      self.succ<toAdd>                    // increment by one 'succ'
```

In the **cons** case of the **map** definition, the process creates two copies of the replicable mapping process (line 7) before downcasting one to **lin** and applying it to the current element of the list (lines 8, 9). The remaining lines apply the map recursively to the tail of the list and reconstruct a new list with the mapped values. In the **nil** case, the mapping process is left unused (line 13). From lines 17 to 20 a replicable mapping process is defined behaving as a successor.

```
21  let main() : listNat =      // main process
22      l : listNat <- new simpList();
23      f : mapType <- new mapByInc();
24      map(f, l)
25
26  exec main() // launch main process
```

The main process initialises a **nat** list process (code elided), launches a replicable mapping process, and spawns a client **map** process to the former two.

```
27  prc[l] : listNat = simpleList()
28  prc[f] : mapType = mapByInc()
29  prc[b] : listNat = map(f, l)
    // f:mapType, l:listNat ⊢ map(f, l) :: (self : listNat)
```

For debugging and modelling purposes, GRITS allow the execution to start from a particular snapshot, instead of having to launch all execution from one root process. The alternative launching code above describes three processes that are already running in parallel providing on channels named l, f and b (lines 27–29).

```
30  assuming l : listNat    // instead of  prc[l] : listNat = simpleList()
31  prc[f] : mapType =  mapByInc()
32  prc[b] : listNat = map(f, l)
```

GRITS also allows programs to be developed compositionally, by eliding parts of the computation. For instance, line 30 in the excerpt above does *not* specify the precise code of the process providing at channel l, instead describing its interface specification. This still permits the program to be typechecked.

Bank Service Example. The services offered by a hypothetical bank are formalised by the affine type **bankType** (lines 1 to 2 below). Two choices are initially offered: a **login** option and another one for general queries (**gen_query**) regarding opening times (details omitted). A **login** request is answered by either an **auth** (authenticated) or an **not_auth** response; the latter response allows the user to retry logging again. An authenticated user can initiate a transaction. For this, the interaction must shift into linear mode ($\uparrow_\textsf{l}^\textsf{a}$ **transaction**) to force transaction termination; the labels **start** and **finish** delimit a (*dummy*) transaction.

```
1  type bankType = aff &{ login      : authType
2                         gen_query : ... }
3  type authType = aff +{ auth      : lin /\ aff transaction,
4                         not_auth : bankType }
5  type transaction = lin +{ start : +{ finish : 1 } }
```

The behaviour dictated by the type **bankType** is implemented and typechecked using GRITS. The **bank** process waits to receive either a **login** or **gen_query** label (line 7). An authenticated user (line 8) is handled by **authService()** (line 8), where a shift (into linear mode, line 13) is performed before executing the transaction (lines 14–16).

```
6   let bank() : bankType =
7       case self (
8           login<s>      => auth <- new authService();
9                            self.auth<auth>
10          | gen_query<s> => ...
11      )
12  let authService() : lin /\ aff transaction =
13      s' <- shift self;              // handle transaction in linear mode
14      s'' : lin 1 <- new close self;
15      s''' : lin +{finish : 1} <- new self.finish<s''>;
16      self.start<s'''>
```

The execution launched below models an *indecisive* user (**user1**, line 17), who initiates an interaction but promptly cancels it (line 18); this is permitted by the **bankService**'s affine mode.

```
17  prc[bankService] : bankType = bank()
18  prc[user1] : lin 1 = drop bankService;
19                       close self
```

Conversely, a different user (**user2**, line 22) requests a login and waits to be authenticated (line 24). After shifting modes (line 25), the interaction with **bankService** proceeds in linear mode (lines 25–30).

```
20  prc[user2] : lin 1 =
21      print _attempt_login_;                          //stdout notification
22      b : authType <- new bankService.login<self>;
23      case b (
24          authenticated<b'> =>
25              t :
    transaction <- new cast b'<self>; //cannot drop t (linear)
26                  case t (
27                      start<t'> =>  case t' (
28                                      finish<t''> => wait t''; close self
29                                  )
30                  )
31          | not_authenticated<b'> => drop b'; close self
32      )
```

4   Runtime Interpreter

Typechecked programs are executed by an interpreter that leverages the concurrency features of the Go language. Every process is mapped to a goroutine that provides on a dedicated channel. This one-to-one mapping of concurrency units allows us to better assess the implementability of the proposed model.

Copy Semantics. *Contractible* processes (*i.e.*, in multicast or replicable mode) can be *assigned* multiple names using $\langle x, y \rangle \leftarrow$ split $u; P$. The following reduction rules achieve this in two steps (the suggestive name ι is used to denote the internal name of the channel provided, analogous to the keyword self).

$$\text{(SPL)} \qquad \mathsf{prc}\,(\{a\};\ \iota;\ \langle x,y\rangle \leftarrow \mathsf{split}\ b; P) \quad \longrightarrow \quad \begin{array}{l} \mathsf{prc}\,(\{c,d\};\ \iota;\ \mathsf{fwd}\ \iota\ b)\,, \\ \mathsf{prc}\,(\{a\};\ \iota;\ P\,[^{c,\,d}/_{x,\,y}]) \end{array}$$

$$\text{(FWD)} \qquad \mathsf{prc}\,(\{b\};\ \iota;\ P)\,,\ \mathsf{prc}\,(N;\ \iota;\ \mathsf{fwd}\ \iota\ b) \quad \longrightarrow \quad \mathsf{prc}\,(N;\ \iota;\ P)$$

Rule SPL generates two new names for the name being duplicated, connecting them via *forwarding*, which then reacts with the process providing on the name being duplicated to increase its set of external names, rule FWD.

$$\text{(DUP)} \quad \mathsf{prc}\,(\{a,b\};\ \iota;\ P) \quad \longrightarrow \quad \begin{array}{l} \mathsf{prc}\,(a;\ \iota;\ P\sigma_1)\,,\ \mathsf{prc}\,(b;\ \iota;\ P\sigma_2)\,, \\ \big\{\mathsf{prc}\,(\{c\sigma_1,c\sigma_2\};\ \iota;\ \mathsf{fwd}\ \iota\ c)\big\}_{c\in\mathbf{fn}(P)\backslash\{\iota\}} \end{array}$$

$$\text{where } P \neq \mathsf{fwd}\ \_\ \_ \ \text{ and } \mathbf{rename}(\mathbf{fn}(P)\setminus\{\iota\}) = \langle\sigma_1,\sigma_2\rangle$$

Processes with multiple names are given a *copy* semantics. Rule DUP generates a process copy P for each of the two name references a and b. By the hierarchical arrangement resulting from typechecking, process P is the root of a tree of processes that need to be duplicated as well. This is done in two steps. For every reference P has towards its clients (*i.e.*, immediate children), rule DUP generates two new (unique) names using $\mathbf{rename}(\mathbf{fn}(P)\setminus\{\iota\}) = \langle\sigma_1,\sigma_2\rangle$ (σ_1 and σ_2 are maps from names to names) and renames the two copies of P accordingly, *i.e.*, $P\sigma_1$ and $P\sigma_2$. Moreover, for *every* (externally) renamed name in P, $c \in \mathbf{fn}(P)\setminus\{\iota\}$, it creates a forwarding associating it to its renaming, $c\sigma_1$ and $c\sigma_2$. This results in a downwards chain of duplications to all child (provider) processes.

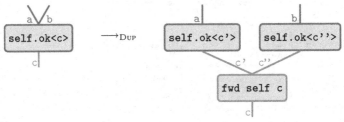

For example, a process self.ok<c> (depicted above), which is multiply referenced by the names a and b, is split into two copies where each copy renames the client reference name c to c' and c''. A corresponding forwarding process is also created to propagate the copying to the client process with name c via a combination of the rules FWD and DUP.

$$\text{(GRC)} \qquad \mathsf{prc}\,(\emptyset;\ \iota;\ P) \quad \longrightarrow \quad \big\{\mathsf{prc}\,(\emptyset;\ \iota;\ \mathsf{fwd}\ \iota\ a)\big\}_{a\in\mathbf{fn}(P)\backslash\{\iota\}} \qquad \text{where } P \neq \mathsf{fwd}\ \_\ \_$$

Dually, unreferenced processes, *i.e.*, $N = \emptyset$, trigger a cascading garbage collection procedure to its clients via forwarding; rule GRC above. Corresponding this reduction discipline, processes executing non-structural commands (*e.g.* rules SND and RCV) only become active *when* they are referenced by a *single* name.

Synchronous and Asynchronous Implementations. In a hierarchically organised soup of processes that are typechecked according to a SAX specification, messages can flow in two directions: either from a provider (bottom process) to its client (top process) or vice versa. For example, in a RCV reduction (diagram below, left), messages flow *downwards* from a client, while in a SND reduction (below, right), messages flow *upwards* towards the client.[3]

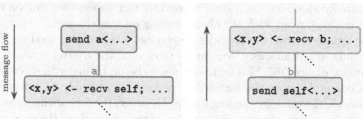

Although direct interactions between matching processes (*e.g.* send $u\langle v, w\rangle$ with $\langle x, y\rangle \leftarrow$ recv $u; P$ processes) are straightforward to implement, the possibility of having proxy processes mediating via forwarding (in order to alter the hierarchical structure) complicate the implementation of the communication protocol for the interpreter. Our interpreter offers two implementations to support our study: a synchronous setup, where Go channels are *unbuffered*, and an asynchronous setup with *buffered* channels.

Synchronous. The synchronous setting employs *two* Go channels per provider. A *data channel* is used for non-structural interactions such as send, (label) select and cast (see rules SND and RCV above). In addition, a *control channel* is dedicated to structural interactions such as splitting and garbage-collection, which are all conducted via forwarding (see rules SPL and GRC above and Table 1). The implementation then makes use of the Go `select` construct to interact on either of these channels depending on the surrounding process context.

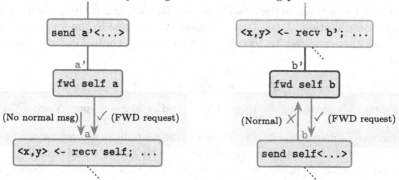

Consider a variant of the previous two send and recv examples with a forward process in between. In both the left and right cases, the fwd process is executed uniformly by the interpreter: it sends a channel name on the control channel indicating to the respective provider underneath it the name of the (new) data

---

[3] Other non-structural reductions (*e.g.* label branching and shifting) behave similarly.

channel to listen on (instead of the existing one). In the left scenario, a client attempts to send a message downwards on channel a'; since the process providing on a' (the fwd process) is not ready to receive on the (synchronous) Go channel, the communication blocks. Conversely, the recv process providing on channel a waits for messages on *both* data and control channels. The fwd process does not communicate on the data channel, but instead sends on the control channel. This eventually succeeds, generating a provider recv process waiting on channel a', which can now react with the client sending on this channel.

In the right scenario, the provider on channel b is ready to send on the data channel while, simultaneously, waiting to receive on the control channel, resulting in a *mixed choice* [26]. This turns out *not* to be problematic in a synchronous setting. Concretely, since the forwarding process is not ready to receive on the data channel b, the message sending blocks. However, the forwarding process successfully sends a forwarding request on the control channel, as the send provider process on channel b is ready to accept it, completing a FWD reduction.

Asynchronous. In a setup with buffered channels (where sending does not require a *handshake* from the other channel endpoint), the execution strategy for the

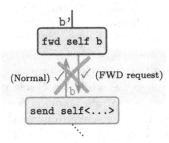

right hand scenario discussed above *fails*. In an asynchronous setting (depicted on the side), data messages will be sent *upwards*, in the opposite direction of the forwarding requests (which are sent downwards). Since neither are blocking, both sending of messages will succeed in reaching the respective channel buffer. Nevertheless, neither message will eventually be read off this buffer, leading to two deadlocked processes.

One compositional solution to this problem is *not* to use a uniform forwarding behavior. In an asynchronous setting, our interpreter categorises the forward construct into two: an *active* (fwd^{A}) or *passive* forward (fwd^{P}), aligning with message flow direction. Apart from localising the change to the forwarding construct, this change allows us to collapse the data and control channels and just use one.

$$(\text{FWD}_{\text{P}}) \quad \text{prc}\left(b;\ \gamma;\ P^+\right),\ \text{prc}\left(N;\ \iota;\ \text{fwd}^{\text{P}}\ \iota\ b\right),\ \longrightarrow\ \text{prc}\left(N;\ \gamma;\ P^+\right)$$

$$(\text{FWD}_{\text{A}}) \quad \text{prc}\left(b;\ \gamma;\ P^-\right),\ \text{prc}\left(N;\ \iota;\ \text{fwd}^{\text{A}}\ \iota\ b\right),\ \longrightarrow\ \text{prc}\left(N;\ \gamma;\ P^-\right)$$

When messages flow upwards, *i.e.*, messages originate from a provider sending on the data channel (P^+ ranges over send $u\langle v, w\rangle$, $u.l\langle v\rangle$, close u and cast $u\langle v\rangle$), they may interact with a *passive* forwarding process. This forwarding process passively waits for incoming messages before reducing to a P^+ processes themselves (FWD$_{\text{P}}$). Conversely, when a synchronous process (P^- includes the remaining non-structural constructs) expects incoming messages from a client, it may interact with an *active* forwarding process. Similar to the synchronous case, *active* forwards initiate the interaction by sending a forwarding request message (FWD$_{\text{A}}$). Examples of passive and active forward processes are depicted below.

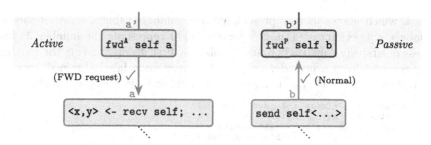

In [28, 29], different versions for the forward processes are also explored, depending on the *polarity* of the forwarded channels. From an implementation perspective this is similar to how we infer the direction of message flow, where messages flowing *upwards* use positive channels (and passive forwards), while messages flowing *downwards* use negative channels (and active forwards). The information the channel polarities is obtained from the associated types in Sect. 2.

5 Evaluation

The objective of this study is to evaluate the implementability of the proposed asynchronous message-passing interpretation for SAX. Sections 3 and 4 provide evidence that this can be accomplished using a concurrent implementation. This section assesses whether this implementation is satisfactory in terms of its ability to scale with the number of spawned processes, thereby utilising any underlying multicore architecture.

Setup. In order to measure the scalability of our implementation, we make use of SAX TOOL [27], which is the only other existing implementation of a message-passing interpretation for SAX. The fact that we can express common programs in both GRITS and SAX TOOL allows us to use the latter as a baseline for comparing runtime performance. Although SAX TOOL is a pedagogic tool with limited focus on performance, it was developed using Standard ML: programs are executed in a sequential setup which does not exploit any underlying parallel architecture. In contrast, the implementation discussed in Sect. 4 maintained a one-to-one mapping to goroutines. Our evaluation utilises two inherently concurrent programs that can be parameterised to scale with the number of running processes. We compare the respective execution time executed over GRITS (using synchronous and asynchronous semantics), against SAX TOOL. All experiments were carried out on a Apple M2 Pro (10-core) CPU machine with 16GB of memory, running Go 1.21.6 on macOS 14. The respective readings are reported in the two graphs of Fig. 2.

Natural Number Doubling. A program that can be interpreted both in GRITS and SAX TOOL is a number doubling procedure (adopted from [27]). It is defined as a process definition, `double`, that consumes a number and provides another number doubled in value. We reuse the unary natural number type `nat` from

Sect. 3, which allows us to represent natural numbers using a series of successor labels, *e.g.* +{succ: +{succ: +{zero: 1}}} represents the number 2. The
process recursively constructs a new number by first deconstructing the number
being received from a provider (x), and for every succ label obtained, two are
sent instead (lines 5–6), recursing until the number is fully exhausted (line 3).

```
1    type nat = lin +{zero : 1, succ : nat}
2    let double(x : nat) : nat =
3        case x ( zero<x'> => self.zero<x'>
4              | succ<x'> => h <- new double(x');
5                            d : nat <- new d.succ<h>;   // first succ
6                            self.succ<d>                // second succ
7        )
```

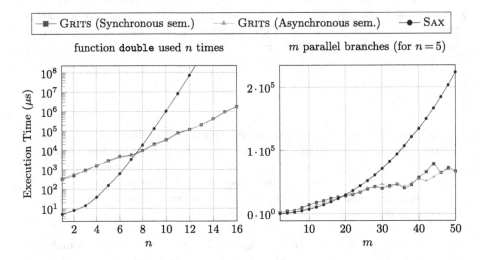

Fig. 2. Performance benchmarks comparing the different semantic implementations
(from Sect. 4) with SAX TOOL. The *execution time* axis for the left graph is *logarithmic*,
while the right one uses normal axis.

Sequential Doubling. For the first evaluation scenario, we invoke double multiple
times in sequence, producing a natural number with an exponential size. *E.g.*,
for the process providing on n1 representing the number one (line 8) we double
twice "in sequence" (lines 13 and 14) to obtain the final value of 4 ($= 1 \times 2^2$).

```
8    prc[n1] : nat = // Produces the natural number 1, i.e. succ(zero)
9        t : 1 <- new close t;
10       z : nat <- new z.zero<t>;
11       self.succ<z>
12   prc[b] : nat =
13       d1 <- new double(n1);
14       d2 <- new double(d1); // double used twice
15       fwd self d2
```

The evaluation varies the number of times (n) the doubling function is
repeated, to produce a number with exponential size ($= 2^n$). The results are
reported in Fig. 2 (left), showing the time taken (μs) by the interpreter to

finish executing. The GRITS concurrent implementation initially performs less efficiently for smaller programs ($n \leq 7$). This behavior is attributed to the overhead incurred when spawning new threads with a very short lifespan. However, as the program size increases, it exhibits better scalability, outperforming SAX TOOL.

Concurrent Doubling. The second evaluation scenario induces more parallelism. It invokes the aforementioned sequential doubling procedure, fixed at $n = 5$, for m times *concurrently*, generating a forest-like structure with m *parallel* trees. The benchmark results (Fig. 2, right) show a similar trend, with SAX TOOL outperforming our implementation for smaller programs, but the situation reversing for larger programs. We even observe that the execution of the GRITS concurrent implementation appears to grow linearly for the readings taken.

Results. Despite limiting our experiments to the testing sizes of $1 \leq n \leq 16$ and $2 \leq m \leq 50$, the readings from both graphs in Fig. 2 exhibit a clear trend. This allows us to extrapolate and conclude that the proposed model of Pruiksma et al. [30] can be implemented adequately in concurrent fashion in order to be able to scale. Although the asynchronous implementation of Sect. 4 suggests that the proposed model can also be implemented in a distributed setting where processes are dispersed across different locations, we cannot draw conclusive evidence as to how this performs in relation to the synchronous variant. This might stem from the fact that the SAX model uses short-lived processes which might perform very little work before terminating. For instance, instead of spawning a process just to send a single message, a more efficient way would be to send a message sequentially from an existing process.

Threats to Validity. The experiment setup could have suffered from limited *granularity control*, which is generally difficult to automate [37]. Our results rely on Go's handling of concurrency to maximise the underlying parallel hardware. We did not consider higher process numbers to avoid the risk of running into stack overflows once certain system limits are hit; this would have been caused by our implementation design, where each reduction is performed via a function call, and by Go's lack of support for tail-recursion optimisation [17]. Our choice of experiment programs could have also introduced biases. Similarly, our choice for a baseline, namely SAX TOOL, could have also affected our scalability assessments.

6   Related Work

We mainly compare our work with other implementations based on the Curry-Howard interpretation [4] of intuitionistic linear logic. This induces a hierarchical structuring of concurrent processes, thereby avoiding the need to use type duality inherent in binary session type implementations [15, 20, 25, 33], or type projections, in the case of multiparty session types [12, 21, 22, 24].

To our knowledge, the only implementation based on the semi-axiomatic sequent calculus is SAX TOOL [27], used to establish a baseline in Sect. 5. At the time of writing, SAX TOOL only support linear modes, and the mode-shifting programs in Sect. 3 cannot be expressed. Internally, SAX TOOL relies on a sequential implementation in Standard ML to simulate concurrency, while GRITS uses native concurrency primitives to contend with the intricacies of the copy semantics discussed in Sect. 4.

Das et al. [9] introduce Rast, a language integrating session types with arithmetic refinements. It embeds assertions within the types to also account for a program execution's work and span. Similar to SAX TOOL, Rast follows a sequential interpretation. Additionally, Das et al. extended the work to obtain Nomos [8], which applies resource-aware session types to smart contracts.

Instead of developing bespoke languages, other projects integrate intuitionistic session types over existing languages. Ferrite [6] extends the SILL calculus [28,36] with process sharing [3] mechanisms to introduce shared session types as a Rust library. CC0 [34,38], a session-based extension of C0, adopts asynchronous message-passing semantics. It offers a Go back end using goroutines for processes and channels for message passing. For this variant, CC0 uses separate channels for bidirectional communication, which was not needed in our tool due to SAX's model. The Go runtime version was compared and shown to outperform a separate C-based implementation, where more heavyweight *pthreads* were used for concurrent processes.

Polite by Lakhani et al. [23] adopts a form of adjoint modalities to control type polarities, similar to SILL's approach to message flow reversal [28]. Since our channels are single-use, shifting allows us to seamlessly transition between modalities. Nomos [8] and Ferrite [6] use modes and shifts to obtain exclusive access to shared processes. Similar to the handling of forwarding in an asynchronous implementation, discussed in Sect. 4, the work in [8,9,28,31] adopt forwarding behavior based on polarity. Other frameworks, such as SILL and SILLs [3], utilise global substitutions for forwarding, a strategy unsuitable for our decentralised implementation. An adaptation of SILL is also used by Caires and Toninho [5] to study a fully sequential and deterministic evaluation strategy.

7   Conclusion

We investigate the implementability of the message-passing interpretation of SAX proposed in previous work [30]. This is conducted by building the tool GRITS, the first type-checker and interpreter to *fully* handle message-passing programs satisfying SAX specifications. The interpreter executes programs in decentralised fashion, leveraging concurrency features from the Go language such as *goroutines*. Our empirical evaluation leads us to conclude that SAX's [30] proposed model is not based on any infeasible assumptions that might prevent it from being implemented in a concurrent fashion.

Future Work. We plan to expand on the SAX semantics by integrating notions of shared processes [3,6,8] that co-exists alongside replicated processes with a copy semantics. Another planned extension is to consider the actor model [2,19] as an interpretation for SAX. Finally, we would like to investigate the use of SAX as a basis for the systematic instrumentation of detection monitors [13], partial-identity monitors [18] and enforcement monitors [1] for added assurances related to the temporal properties of program data; the SAX proof system can also be leveraged to enhance verdict explainability when property violations are detected [14].

References

1. Aceto, L., Cassar, I., Francalanza, A., Ingólfsdóttir, A.: Bidirectional runtime enforcement of first-order branching-time properties. Log. Methods Comput. Sci. **19**(1) (2023)
2. Agha, G.A.: ACTORS - A Model of Concurrent Computation in Distributed Systems. Artificial Intelligence. MIT Press, Cambridge (1990)
3. Balzer, S., Pfenning, F.: Manifest sharing with session types. Proc. ACM Program. Lang. **1**(ICFP), 37:1–37:29 (2017)
4. Caires, L., Pfenning, F.: Session types as intuitionistic linear propositions. In: Gastin, P., Laroussinie, F. (eds.) CONCUR 2010. LNCS, vol. 6269, pp. 222–236. Springer, Heidelberg (2010). https://doi.org/10.1007/978-3-642-15375-4_16
5. Caires, L., Toninho, B.: The session abstract machine. In: Weirich, S. (ed.) ESOP 2024. LNCS, vol. 14576, pp. 206–235. Springer, Cham (2024). https://doi.org/10.1007/978-3-031-57262-3_9
6. Chen, R., Balzer, S., Toninho, B.: Ferrite: a judgmental embedding of session types in rust. In: Ali, K., Vitek, J. (eds.) 36th European Conference on Object-Oriented Programming, ECOOP 2022, 6–10 June 2022, Berlin, Germany. LIPIcs, vol. 222, pp. 22:1–22:28. Schloss Dagstuhl - Leibniz-Zentrum für Informatik (2022)
7. Crary, K.: Higher-order representation of substructural logics. In: ICFP, pp. 131–142. ACM (2010)
8. Das, A., Balzer, S., Hoffmann, J., Pfenning, F., Santurkar, I.: Resource-aware session types for digital contracts. In: 34th IEEE Computer Security Foundations Symposium, CSF 2021, Dubrovnik, Croatia, 21–25 June 2021, pp. 1–16. IEEE (2021)
9. Das, A., Pfenning, F.: Rast: a language for resource-aware session types. Log. Methods Comput. Sci. **18**(1) (2022)
10. DeYoung, H., Pfenning, F., Pruiksma, K.: Semi-axiomatic sequent calculus. In: FSCD. LIPIcs, vol. 167, pp. 29:1–29:22. Schloss Dagstuhl - Leibniz-Zentrum für Informatik (2020)
11. Effective Go: Effective Go - The Go Programming Language (nd). https://go.dev/doc/effective_go#sharing
12. Fowler, S.: An Erlang implementation of multiparty session actors. In: Bartoletti, M., Henrio, L., Knight, S., Vieira, H.T. (eds.) Proceedings 9th Interaction and Concurrency Experience, ICE 2016, Heraklion, Greece, 8-9 June 2016. EPTCS, vol. 223, pp. 36–50 (2016)
13. Francalanza, A.: A theory of monitors. Inf. Comput. **281**, 104704 (2021)
14. Francalanza, A., Cini, C.: Computer says no: verdict explainability for runtime monitors using a local proof system. J. Log. Algebraic Methods Program. **119**, 100636 (2021)

15. Francalanza, A., Tabone, G.: Elixirst: a session-based type system for Elixir modules. J. Log. Algebraic Methods Program. **135**, 100891 (2023)
16. Gay, S.J., Hole, M.: Subtyping for session types in the pi calculus. Acta Informatica **42**(2–3), 191–225 (2005)
17. Golang GitHub: Golang GitHub issue #22624 (2017). https://github.com/golang/go/issues/22624
18. Gommerstadt, H., Jia, L., Pfenning, F.: Session-typed concurrent contracts. J. Log. Algebraic Methods Program. **124**, 100731 (2022)
19. Hewitt, C., Bishop, P.B., Steiger, R.: A universal modular ACTOR formalism for artificial intelligence. In: Nilsson, N.J. (ed.) Proceedings of the 3rd International Joint Conference on Artificial Intelligence, Standford, CA, USA, 20–23 August 1973, pp. 235–245. William Kaufmann (1973)
20. Honda, K.: Types for dyadic interaction. In: Best, E. (ed.) CONCUR 1993. LNCS, vol. 715, pp. 509–523. Springer, Heidelberg (1993). https://doi.org/10.1007/3-540-57208-2_35
21. Honda, K., Yoshida, N., Carbone, M.: Multiparty asynchronous session types. J. ACM **63**(1), 9:1–9:67 (2016)
22. Lagaillardie, N., Neykova, R., Yoshida, N.: Implementing multiparty session types in rust. In: Bliudze, S., Bocchi, L. (eds.) COORDINATION 2020. LNCS, vol. 12134, pp. 127–136. Springer, Cham (2020). https://doi.org/10.1007/978-3-030-50029-0_8
23. Lakhani, Z., Das, A., DeYoung, H., Mordido, A., Pfenning, F.: Polarized subtyping. In: Sergey, I. (ed.) ESOP 2022. LNCS, vol. 13240, pp. 431–461. Springer, Cham (2022). https://doi.org/10.1007/978-3-030-99336-8_16
24. Neykova, R., Yoshida, N.: Multiparty session actors. Log. Methods Comput. Sci. **13**(1) (2017)
25. Padovani, L.: A simple library implementation of binary sessions. J. Funct. Program. **27**, e4 (2017)
26. Palamidessi, C.: Comparing the expressive power of the synchronous and asynchronous pi-calculi. Math. Struct. Comput. Sci. **13**(5), 685–719 (2003)
27. Pfenning, F.: Lecture notes on Semi-Axiomatic Sequent Calculus (2023). Course notes for Substructural Logics (15-836). Accompanying tool available from https://www.cs.cmu.edu/~fp/courses/15836-f23/resources.html
28. Pfenning, F., Griffith, D.: Polarized substructural session types. In: Pitts, A. (ed.) FoSSaCS 2015. LNCS, vol. 9034, pp. 3–22. Springer, Heidelberg (2015). https://doi.org/10.1007/978-3-662-46678-0_1
29. Pfenning, F., Pruiksma, K.: Relating message passing and shared memory, proof-theoretically. In: Jongmans, S., Lopes, A. (eds.) COORDINATION 2023. LNCS, vol. 13908, pp. 3–27. Springer, Cham (2023). https://doi.org/10.1007/978-3-031-35361-1_1
30. Pruiksma, K., Pfenning, F.: A message-passing interpretation of adjoint logic. J. Log. Algebraic Methods Program. **120**, 100637 (2021)
31. Pruiksma, K., Pfenning, F.: Back to futures. J. Funct. Program. **32**, e6 (2022)
32. Sano, C., Kavanagh, R., Pientka, B.: Mechanizing session-types using a structural view: enforcing linearity without linearity. Proc. ACM Program. Lang. **7**(OOPSLA2), 374–399 (2023)
33. Scalas, A., Yoshida, N.: Lightweight session programming in scala. In: Krishnamurthi, S., Lerner, B.S. (eds.) 30th European Conference on Object-Oriented Programming, ECOOP 2016, 18–22 July 2016, Rome, Italy. LIPIcs, vol. 56, pp. 21:1–21:28. Schloss Dagstuhl - Leibniz-Zentrum für Informatik (2016)

34. Silva, M.E.P., Florido, M., Pfenning, F.: Non-blocking concurrent imperative programming with session types. In: Cervesato, I., Fernández, M. (eds.) Proceedings Fourth International Workshop on Linearity, LINEARITY 2016, Porto, Portugal, 25 June 2016. EPTCS, vol. 238, pp. 64–72 (2016)

35. Tabone, G.: Grits: Implementing a Message-Passing Interpretation of the Semi-Axiomatic Sequent Calculus (Sax) (artefact for Coordination'24) (2024). https://doi.org/10.5281/zenodo.10837897, https://github.com/gertab/Grits

36. Toninho, B., Caires, L., Pfenning, F.: Higher-order processes, functions, and sessions: a monadic integration. In: Felleisen, M., Gardner, P. (eds.) ESOP 2013. LNCS, vol. 7792, pp. 350–369. Springer, Heidelberg (2013). https://doi.org/10.1007/978-3-642-37036-6_20

37. Westrick, S., Fluet, M., Rainey, M., Acar, U.A.: Automatic parallelism management. In: Proceedings of the ACM on Programming Languages, vol. 8, pp. 1118–1149 (2024)

38. Willsey, M., Prabhu, R., Pfenning, F.: Design and implementation of Concurrent C0. In: Fourth International Workshop on Linearity, pp. 73–82. EPTCS 238 (2016)

SEArch: An Execution Infrastructure for Service-Based Software Systems

Carlos Gustavo Lopez Pombo[1]($\boxtimes$) ⓘ, Pablo Montepagano[2],
and Emilio Tuosto[3] ⓘ

[1] Centro Interdisciplinario de Telecomunicaciones, Electrónica, Computación y Ciencia Aplicada, Universidad Nacional de Río Negro - Sede Andina and CONICET, San Carlos de Bariloche, Argentina
cglopezpombo@unrn.edu.ar
[2] Departamento de Computación, Facultad de Ciencias Exactas y Naturales, Universidad de Buenos Aires, Buenos Aires, Argentina
[3] Gran Sasso Science Institute, L'Aquila, Italy

Abstract. The shift from monolithic applications to composition of distributed software initiated at the start of the 21st century, is based on the vision of *software-as-service*. This vision, found in many technologies such as RESTful APIs, advocates globally available services cooperating through an infrastructure providing (access to) distributed computational resources. Choreographies can support this vision by abstracting away local computation and rendering interoperability with message-passing: cooperation is achieved by sending and receiving messages. Following this choreographic paradigm, we develop SEArch, after Service Execution Architecture, a language-independent execution infrastructure capable of performing transparent dynamic reconfiguration of software artefacts. Choreographic mechanisms are used in SEArch to specify interoperability contracts, thus providing the support needed for automatic discovery and binding of services at runtime.

1 Introduction

In the past two decades the paradigm generally known as *Service-Oriented Computing* (SOC) has become predominant in software development. This paradigm comprises many variants such as—among others—cloud computing, fog and edge computing, and many forms of distributed computing associated with what is

Research partly supported by the EU H2020 RISE programme under the Marie Skłodowska-Curie grant agreement No 778233. The authors acknowledge the support of the PRO3 MUR project Software Quality, and PNRR MUR project VITALITY (ECS00000041), Spoke 2 ASTRA - Advanced Space Technologies and Research Alliance. The authors thank Ignacio Vissani for his indispensable contributions to the design of SEArch and the anonymous reviewers for their comments.
C. G. Lopez Pombo—On leave from Instituto de Ciencias de la computación CONICET–UBA and Departamento de Computación, Facultad de Ciencias Exactas y Naturales, Universidad de Buenos Aires.

I. Castellani and F. Tiezzi (Eds.): COORDINATION 2024, LNCS 14676, pp. 314–330, 2024.
https://doi.org/10.1007/978-3-031-62697-5_17

known as the *Internet of Things*.[1] Key to service-oriented computing is the possibility of dynamically and automatically search and combine distributed and heterogeneous computational resources exposed as services interacting over an existing communication infrastructure. This vision of software systems is partially present in applied technologies, such as RESTful APIs (that foster the API Economy by supporting dynamic reconfiguration); however, to the best of our knowledge, full automation of service-discovery is not supported.

Our main contribution is an infrastructure to support automatic discovery of services. To this end, we represent both provision and requirement contracts as *communicating finite-state machines* [1]; this allows us (*i*) to foster heterogeneity by abstracting away implementation details and (*ii*) to support automatic discovery of services through a mechanism based on bisimilarity [2], so providing a semantic notion of compatibility between provision and requirement contracts. We rely on choreographic approaches [3] which propose an interaction mechanism by conceptually separating the local computations of the components from their communication aspects. Under this approach, interoperability is understood at a more abstract level decoupled from any computational aspect. Within choreographic approaches, message-passing systems advocate sending and receiving of messages over communication channels as a simple cooperation mechanism. *Asynchronous Relational Networks* (ARNs) [4] yield a formalisation of the elements of an interface theory for service-oriented software architectures. More precisely, ARNs are a formal orchestration model based on hypergraphs whose hyperedges are interpreted either as processes or as communication channels. The nodes (or points) that are only adjacent to process hyperedges are called *provides-points*, while those adjacent only to communication hyperedges are called *requires-points*: the former constitute the interface through which a service exports its functionality while the latter yield the interface through which an activity expects a certain service to provide a functionality. In the operational semantics of ARNs given in [5] actions performed by a component can dynamically trigger an automatic and transparent process of discovery and binding of a compliant service. The composition of ARNs (i.e., how binding is viewed from a formal perspective) is obtained by "fusing" provides-points and requires-points, subject to a certain compliance check between the contracts associated to them. Later, [6] used *communicating finite state machines* (CFSM) [1] as a formal language for determining service interoperability automatically.

More recently, [7] has proposed data-aware CFSMs, an extension of CFSMs with *assertions*, namely first-order formulae associated to the communication actions. Besides, [7] has introduced a bisimulation relation for data-aware CFSMs and implemented an algorithm for checking bisimilarity of data-aware CFSMs. In this setting, given participants A and B, and a first order formula $\alpha(x)$, where x is a free variable, an action $AB!y\langle v\rangle \mid \alpha(x)$ is interpreted as: participant A <u>sends to</u> participant B a message of type y with value v <u>guaranteeing</u> that $\alpha(v)$ holds. Dually, $AB?y\langle v\rangle \mid \alpha(x)$ is interpreted as participant A <u>receives from</u> participant B a message of type y with value v <u>assuming</u> that $\alpha(v)$ holds. The rationale behind

---

[1] Although the terminology has evolved, SOC is still widely used.

data-aware CFSMs is that assertions act as functional contracts predicating over the data exchanged by the components that participate in the communication.

In this work we introduce the language-independent execution infrastructure SEArch, after Service Execution Architecture, based on the operational semantics given to ARNs and the interoperability and functional compliance criterion supported by data-aware CFSMs. In particular, we give the architecture of SEArch (Sect. 2) and its main implementation details (Sect. 3). Also, we showcase SEArch on an on-line business cart (Sect. 4). In Sect. 5 we draw some conclusions and discuss further lines of research.

2   A Conceptual View of SEArch

There is a wide range of service-oriented architectures (SOAs) dictating design principles for SOC, each one with its own idiosyncrasy [8–11]. We embrace those that hinge on three main concepts: a *service provider*, a *service client*, and a *service broker*. The latter handles a *service repository*, a catalogue of service descriptions searched for in order to discover services required at runtime. In fact, the service broker is instrumental to the *discovery* of services according to a contract and of their *binding*, the composition mechanism that permits to "glue" services together at runtime as advocated by some SOAs.

To support SOC, SEArch offers a mechanism for populating registries and composing service-based applications. Registering a service is, in principle, very simple: the service provider sends the service broker a request for registering a service attaching a (signed) package containing the contract and the unique resource identifier (URI) of the provided service.

The execution process of a service-based system in SEArch is significantly more complex. Figure 1 depicts the workflow. When launched, a component registers its communication channels to its *middleware*, each of which has its corresponding contract formalised as a set of data-aware CFSMs, one for each requires-point. This is required because the middleware has to mediate the communication with other components. In fact, when the component of a running application, say C, tries to interact with another component, the middleware C, say M, captures the attempt and checks whether the communication session for that communication channel has been created. If no such session exists, the dynamic reconfiguration process is triggered as follows:

1. M sends the service broker the contract of the communication channel;
2. for each data-aware CFSM R in the contract, the service broker queries the service repository for candidates;
3. the service repository returns a list of candidates in the form $\langle \text{Pr}, u \rangle$, where Pr is a data-aware CFSM and u is the URI of the service[2]; the broker checks whether the provision contract Pr is compatible with the requirement contract R, which is done by resorting to bisimilarity check;

---

[2] SEArch is parametric in the implementation of the service repository so we assume it is not capable of checking compliance using behavioural contracts. We only rely on its capability of returning a list of candidates, obtained by using potentially more efficient and less precise criteria, for example, an ontology.

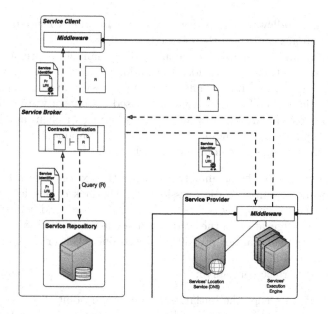

Fig. 1. Service execution procedure in SEArch

4. once the service broker has found services satisfying all the requirement contracts, it returns the set of URIs to M;
5. M opens a communication with the middleware of each service returned by
   the provider requiring the execution of the corresponding service.

Then, M sends to or receives from the middleware of the partner component
the actual message; and the execution process proceeds. Notice that during the
execution new requirements might crop up; for instance, because some brokered
services need further services.[3] This will initiate a new brokerage phase to discover the newly required services. The schematic view discussed before establishes several requisites over the implementation of middleware and the service
broker. We organise the discussion by considering these elements and their role
in the execution architecture:

The middleware provides a private and a public interface. The former implements functionalities accessible by service clients and service providers. The public interface implements the capabilities needed for interacting with service brokers and other middlewares.

The private interface consists of:

- **RegisterApp** to register a service and expose it in the execution infrastructure. This functionality opens a bidirectional (low level) communication chan-

---

[3] This implies that a service may have one or more required-points associated to
communication channels of its own.

nel with the middleware that will remain open in order to support the (high level) communication with other services.

- **RegisterChannel** to register communication channels expressing requirements. This functionality provides the middleware with the relevant information for triggering the reconfiguration of the system and managing the communications. The functionality can be used by any software artefact running in the host, regardless of whether it is a service or client application.
- **AppSend/AppRecv** to communicate with partner components
- **CloseChannel** to close a communication channel.

The reader should note the asymmetry between the existence of a function for explicitly closing a communication session, and the lack of one for opening it. The reason for this asymmetry resides in that, on the one hand, transparency in the dynamic reconfiguration of the system is a key feature of SEArch but, on the other hand, it is in general not possible to determine whether a communication session will be used in the future.

The public interface consists of:

- **InitChannel** to accept the initiation of a point-to-point (low-level) communication channel. This operation allows the broker to initiate the communication infrastructure that will connect the service executing behind their middleware to the other participants in a communication session being setup.
- **StartChannel** to receive notifications about point-to-point communication channels. This operation formally notifies the middleware that the brokerage of participants according to a communication channel description was successful and the communication session has been properly setup.
- **MessageExchange** to exchange messages between middlewares.

Figure 2 shows the application infrastructure and how buffers are used to provide point-to-point communication with external services. Within the infrastructure, it is possible to identify the structural design of the middleware.

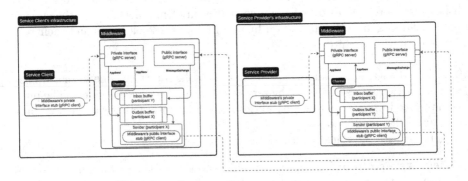

Fig. 2. Point-to-point communication between a service client and a service provider.

The service broker exposes only two functionalities in a public interface:

- **BrokerChannel** to issue requests for brokerage. This operation allows a middleware to request for the brokerage of a communication channel, and the subsequent creation of a communication session to let services interact.
- **RegisterProvider** to issue requests for the registration of a service provider. This operation is the external counterpart of the functionality **RegisterApp** through which the middleware provides the service providers the possibility of being offered as services available in the execution infrastructure.

Figure 3 shows the sequence diagram offering a high level view of the process of registration of a service to the service broker.

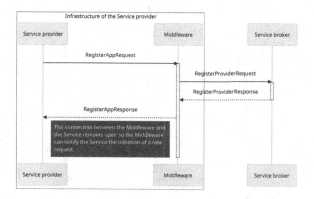

Fig. 3. Sequence diagram of the process of registration of a service.

Figure 4 shows the brokerage process of a communication channel given the interfaces of the middleware and the service broker, detailed above in this section.

The process of brokering a communication channel for building a session (cf. Fig. 4) is significantly more complex. The service client uses the communication channel in the message **AppSend** (step ❸). Concurrently, the middleware begins the brokerage process by sending the contract to the service broker (step ❹) and enqueues the message while acknowledging the service client with a message of type **AppSendRespond** (step ❺). If the service client has to receive a message (**AppRecv**), the middleware captures the attempt triggering the brokerage and going through the same process for initiating the communication session. In this case, the service client will remain blocked until the expected message arrives.

The service broker, upon receiving the contract, queries the service repository for candidates and executes the compliance checks. Each compliance check can be too costly so the service broker implements a cache for storing precomputed positive results.

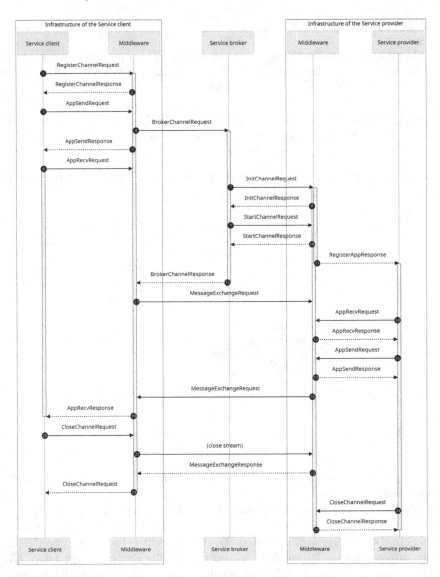

Fig. 4. Sequence diagram of the process of brokerage of a communication channel.

After choosing concrete providers for the participants in the contract, the service broker performs two successive rounds of message exchanges with the chosen service provider. In the first round, a message of type `InitChannelRequest` is sent (step ❼) to tell the middlewares that a communication session involving its service provider is being initiated; the message also contains the URIs of all the other participants in the communication session. At the same time, this message allows the service broker to verify that the provider is indeed online.

Upon receipt of this message, a middleware must accept incoming messages for this channel and enqueue them for the eventual reception by the service provider. If all the service providers respond successfully with a message of type InitChannelResponse (step ⑧), then the service broker performs a second round with a message of type StartChannelRequest (step ⑨), to confirm that the communication session has been initiated.

After receiving both initialization messages, the middleware sends the service provider a message of type RegisterAppResponse (step ⑪) containing the UUID of the new communication session. Then, each service provider can start communicating over this session according to its contracts. Once a session is initiated, the middlewares establish unidirectional streams with each other to send messages. In Fig. 4 the middleware of the service client opens a stream with the other middleware by sending a message of type MessageExchange (step ⑬). After the service provider has received the message (steps ⑭– ⑮), it sends a message (steps ⑯ – ⑰) forcing the middleware of the service provider to establish a stream in the opposite direction (step ⑱).

Finally, the service client can close the channel by sending a message of type CloseChannelRequest (step ⑳) to its middleware, closing the stream used to communicate with the middleware of the service provider.

3 Implementation

The main objective of SEArch[4] is to provide transparent integration of services offering abstractions for the interoperability of heterogeneous software artefacts. This is mainly achieved by the middleware featured by SEArch, which mediates all the interactions between software components. To this end, we implemented the lower layer of the communication infrastructure over gRPC[5], Protocol Buffers[6]. The former is a high-performance RPC framework offering an easy and scalable solution to the problem of microservices integration; the latter is a typed and structured data packet serialisation format, used as an interface description language, which provides a high-level solution for system level communication.[7] Both gRPC and Protocol Buffers aim to provide a general tool for developing communication infrastructures between systems. For this reason, there are compilers that interpret message and service definitions from Protocol Buffer .proto files, and generate code in a wide variety of programming languages for manipulating those messages with native classes and types.[8]

---

[4] Available at https://github.com/pmontepagano/search.

[5] Available at https://grpc.io.

[6] Available at https://protobuf.dev/.

[7] Although widely used, HTTP is not an ideal option for SEArch due to two severe limitations: HTTP supports request-response and it has no native support for typed messages (schemas).

[8] Until July of 2023 gRPC and Protocol Buffers officially supports C# / .NET, C++, Dart, Go, Java, Kotlin, Node, Objective-C, PHP, Python and Ruby among others; https://grpc.io/docs/languages/.

We implemented SEArch in Go [12], a language with native support for channel-based concurrency (goroutines) and gRPC. Such flexibility is of particular relevance to us as it provides a high degree of portability, especially in order to cope with the heterogeneity of the computational resources available, that could be integrated to the SEArch ecosystem.

As stated above, we adopt CFSMs to model contracts for interoperability; more specifically, we use an implementation in Go of CFSMs[9] which we extended with a bisimilarity test. Test for bisimilarity is used by SEArch service brokers as interoperability compliance criterion when selecting service providers. There exist extensions of the CFSMs enabling their use for describing functional aspects of participants [7] and quality-of-service non-functional aspect [13], but they had not yet been added to `nickng/cfsm` so, for the sake of this presentation, the compliance check will only reflect interoperability. Choosing Go as a programming language was key for building a solution satisfying the most important hypothesis of the computational model; the order of messages is preserved. This hypothesis is vital to the correctness of a message-passing communicating system, thus it becomes an important constraint of the implementation. Channels in Go are similar to Unix pipes, being thread-safe FIFO queues. This, together with the use of an RPC of type stream, allowed for the implementation of inbox and outbox buffers for each participant, together with a sender routine in charge of processing the Outbox; also providing a simple implementation for `MessageExchange` and `AppRecv` which essentially act as enqueue and dequeue operations, respectively.

In general, testing bisimilarity of CFSMs is computationally costly, resulting in a bottleneck. To tackle this problem the service broker features a cache associating lists of compliant services to requirement contracts. The implementation consists of a very simple schema shown in Fig. 5 done as an *object-relational mapping* (ORM) in `ent`[10], a simple and powerful entity framework specifically designed for Go. Whenever a requirement contract produces a miss in the cache table, or when the service repository returns candidates that have not been

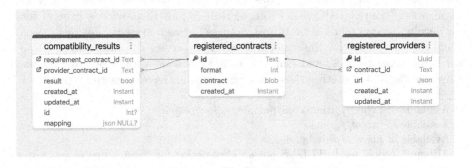

Fig. 5. ORM schema definition for the cache.

---

checked, the compliance checks are performed concurrently by launching separate goroutines[11]. For the moment, the concurrent execution of compliance checks only profits from parallelism locally (multi-core and multi-CPU servers) but it provides no support for multi-server architectures like clusters, cloud computing, etc.

4 An Online Shop

This section shows a case study where an online shop relies on a third party payment service. The application involves three participants: a client (developed in Java), a seller (a backend server developed in Python), and a payment service (developed in Go). Figure 6 shows an abstract view of the three components where contracts are represented by the gray boxes (The source code of these components can be found at https://github.com/pmontepagano/search/examples/credit-card-payments). The rotated V-shape box represents the client's communication channel specified by the contracts ClientApp, Srv, and PPS, where the latter two are to be interpreted as requirements to be fulfilled by other participants. The contracts of seller and payment service are to be interpreted as provisions by the corresponding services.

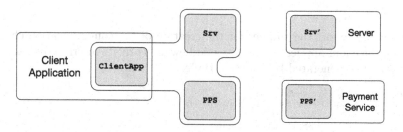

Fig. 6. A view of Client (left), seller (top right), and payment service (bottom right)

We now detail each component.

4.1 Client Application

As said, the client component is implemented in Java. We focus on how channel registration and communication are rendered in the client.

The communication channel of the client consists of the CFSMs in Fig. 7. This specification dictates that ClientApp starts by sending a PurchaseRequest to the seller (Srv) and, after receiving the TotalAmount from the seller, the client sends CardDetailsWithTotalAmount to the payment server (PPS); then the purchase is completed as shown in Fig. 7. The other CFSMs behave accordingly.

---

[11] The library conc (available at https://github.com/sourcegraph/conc) was used to prevent leaks (routines that execute indefinitely).

```
 1   .outputs ClientApp
 2   .state graph
 3   q0 Srv ! PurchaseRequest q1
 4   q1 Srv ? TotalAmount q2
 5   q2 PPS ! CardDetailsWithTotalAmount q3
 6   q3 PPS ? PaymentNonce q4
 7   q4 Srv ! PurchaseWithPaymentNonce q5
 8   q5 Srv ? PurchaseOK q6
 9   q5 Srv ? PurchaseFail q7
10   .marking q0
11   .end
12
13   .outputs Srv
14   .state graph
15   q0 ClientApp ? PurchaseRequest q1
16   q1 ClientApp ! TotalAmount q2
17   q2 ClientApp ? PurchaseWithPaymentNonce q3
18   q3 PPS ! RequestChargeWithNonce q4
19   q4 PPS ? ChargeOK q5
20   q4 PPS ? ChargeFail q6
21   q5 ClientApp ! PurchaseOK q7
22   q6 ClientApp ! PurchaseFail q8
23   .marking q0
24   .end
25
26   .outputs PPS
27   .state graph
28   q0 ClientApp ? CardDetailsWithTotalAmount q1
29   q1 ClientApp ! PaymentNonce q2
30   q2 Srv ? RequestChargeWithNonce q3
31   q3 Srv ! ChargeOK q4
32   q3 Srv ! ChargeFail q5
33   .marking q0
34   .end
```

Fig. 7. Communication channel specification

Below we report the snippet for the creation of the communication channel between the client application and its middleware's private interface by resorting the Java stubs generated by Protocol Buffer.

```
1  import io.grpc.ManagedChannelBuilder;
2  import ar.com.montepagano.search.v1.PrivateMiddlewareServiceGrpc;
3
4  // Get the stub to communicate with the middleware
5  ManagedChannel channel = ManagedChannelBuilder.forTarget(
6    "middleware-client:11000").usePlaintext().build();
7  PrivateMiddlewareServiceGrpc.PrivateMiddlewareServiceBlockingStub stub =
8    PrivateMiddlewareServiceGrpc.newBlockingStub(channel);
```

Relying on the snippet above, the next one shows how the client registers the communication channel to the middleware:

```
1  RegisterChannelRequest request = RegisterChannelRequest.newBuilder().setRequirementsContract(
2    contract).build();
3  RegisterChannelResponse response = stub.registerChannel(request);
4  var channelId = response.getChannelId();
```

The object `contract`, passed to the function `SetRequirementsContract`, is an instance of the Java class `GlobalContract` (automatically generated from Protocol Buffer type), built from the specification in Fig. 7.

The snippet shown below exhibits the client application invoking the middleware's operation `AppSendRequest` for sending a message `PurchaseRequest` (see line 3 of Fig. 7) to participant `Srv` over the channel identified by `channelId` (the channel identifier is received at the moment of the registration of the communication channel, see line 6 of channel registration snippet).

```
1   // Send PurchaseRequest with each item quantities and the shipping address
2   Map<String, Integer> items = new HashMap<>();
3   for (int selectedBook : selectedBooks) {
4       String bookTitle = bookTitles[selectedBook - 1];
5       if (items.containsKey(bookTitle)) {
6           items.put(bookTitle, items.get(bookTitle) + 1);
7       } else {
8           items.put(bookTitle, 1);
9       }
10  }
11  var body = ByteString.copyFromUtf8(String.format(
12      "{\"items\": %s, \"shippingAddress\": \"%s\"}",
13      gson.toJson(items), shippingAddress));
14  var msg = AppMessage.newBuilder().setType("PurchaseRequest").setBody(body).build();
15  var sendreq = AppSendRequest.newBuilder().setChannelId(
16      channelId).setRecipient("Srv").setMessage(msg).build();
17  var sendresp = stub.appSend(sendreq);
18  if (sendresp.getResult() != Middleware.AppSendResponse.Result.RESULT_OK) {
19      System.out.println("Error sending PurchaseRequest. Exiting...");
20      System.exit(1);
21  }
```

Analogously, the snippet below shows the client application invoking the middleware's operation **AppRecvRequest** for receiving a message **TotalAmount** (see line 4 of Fig. 7), from participant **Srv**, also over the channel identified by **channelId**.

```
1   var recvreq = Middleware.AppRecvRequest.newBuilder().setChannelId(
2       channelId).setParticipant("Srv").build();
3   var recvresp = stub.appRecv(recvreq);
4   if (!recvresp.getMessage().getType().equals("TotalAmount")) {
5       System.out.println("Error receiving TotalAmount. Exiting...");
6       System.exit(1);
7   }
8   var total_amount = gson.fromJson(recvresp.getMessage().getBody().toStringUtf8(), double.class);
9   System.out.println("Total amount: " + total_amount);
```

4.2   Required Services

The seller's server application was developed in Python; the following snippet exhibits the procedure for registering the backend server through a gRPC channel received as parameter.

```
1   from lib.search import v1 as search
2
3   async def main(grpc_channel):
4       stub = search.PrivateMiddlewareServiceStub(grpc_channel)
5       registered = False
6       logger.info("Connected to middleware. Waiting for registration...")
7       async for r in stub.register_app(
8           search.RegisterAppRequest(
9               provider_contract=search.LocalContract(
10                  format=search.LocalContractFormat.LOCAL_CONTRACT_FORMAT_FSA,
11                  contract=PROVIDER_CONTRACT,
12              )
13          )
14      ):
15          if registered and r.notification:
16              logger.info(f"Notification received: {r.notification}")
17              # Start a new session for this channel.
18              asyncio.create_task(session(grpc_channel, r.notification))
19          elif not registered and r.app_id:
20              # This should only happen once, in the first iteration.
21              registered = True
22              logger.info(f"App registered with id {r.app_id}")
23          else:
24              logger.error(f"Unexpected response: {r}. Exiting.")
25              break
26
27      grpc_channel.close()
```

The process starts on line 4 by opening a communication channel through the middleware's private interface, by resorting the Python stubs generated by Protocol Buffer. Then, the middleware's operation `RegisterAppRequest` is invoked with a local contract (i.e., a CFSM described as a single finite state machine like the ones shown in Fig. 7). The result of the process depends on whether the service has been already registered or not; if the service has been properly registered by the broker, the latter will return an application identifier for the middleware to be able to refer to the service in its local host. Line 18 shows the asynchronous invocation to the function `session` which implements the server.

We omit the details of the Go implementation of the payment service because they are analogous to the seller implementation.

5   Conclusions, Related, and Future Work

In this work we combined well-established languages and tools from the fields of service-oriented architectures, language semantics, and behavioural types to develop SEArch. The execution infrastructure of SEArch hinges on ARNs and has a complete operational semantics (see [5, Sec 4]). Behavioural types, more specifically CFSMs, were used as interoperability contracts that can be automatically analysed, thus providing the means for checking service compliance with respect to a requirement contract. This last feature provides an answer to the problem of automatic service discovery at runtime. A careful selection of tools allowed us to implement a middleware and a service broker that jointly provide transparent creation and deletion of communication sessions, according to high-level behavioural contracts. This yields a general dynamic reconfiguration mechanism for this type of service-based software artefacts.

The infrastructure of SEArch is in a functional prototype stage and, consequently, the implementation leaves room for many extensions. Some of them are related to different aspects of scalability, for example, the current implementation features a service repository coupled to the implementation of the service broker. An alternative, and more scalable, design might implement the repository as a separate agent, allowing horizontal scaling of the role and separating the registration process from the broker service. This might also enable the broker to access multiple repositories. Another hurdle for scalability resides in the centralised implementation of the compliance check in the service broker; separating the analysis of contracts as a service used by the broker might allow implementation over clusters of computers that might even perform off-line checks for precomputing the content of the cache we proposed, and implemented, to make the brokering more efficient.

From Fig. 1 it is easy to observe that choosing a service relies on abstract notions of provision and requirement contract. As we mentioned in Sect. 1, CFSMs have been extended with both functional information and quality-of-service non-functional information, making QoS-enriched Data-aware CFSMs a type of contract fit for describing many aspects relevant for both, service compliance and service selection. We plan to implement both extensions, and their associated verification algorithms, within ChorGram [14,15].

To the best of our knowledge, the only other implementations of execution infrastructures for service-based software artifacts are commercial products, for instance [9–11]. All these platforms focus on improving the integration and scalability of systems within the organisation. While binding is done transparently as in SEArch, they do not provide any mechanism for automatic and dynamic discovery of services and much less a semantic compliance such as the one featured by SEArch.

A key feature of SEArch is the semantic compliance mechanism adopted in the brokerage process. This is paramount to support the actual automatic and dynamic composition of services implemented in different languages with a mechanism based on behavioural contracts that is still lacking in other infrastructures for SOAs [16]. Unlike industry, academia has considered semantic compliance based on behavioural theories [17–21]. We are not aware of any infrastructure based on these theories that allow the composition of services implemented in actual programming languages. The compliance mechanism featured by SEArch relies on bisimilarity of CFSMs, but does not encompass behavioural refinement or subtyping relations (as those studied in [17–21]). Extending SEArch with such mechanisms that would make our infrastructure more flexible is left for future work. An interesting line of work is also to embed in SEArch other compliance mechanisms based on different types of contracts, and their associated tools. Some options are tools like CAT [22] which is based on *contract automata* [23–25] or contract-oriented middlewares like the one in [26,27] which supports timed behavioural types or the one in [28], which is based on contract-oriented primitives. Recently, tools for inferring behavioural specifications from code have been proposed. For instance, KmcLib [29] extracts CFSMs from Ocaml code, the tool in [30] infers behavioural types from Java code, and ChorEr [31] extracts choreography automata [32] from Erlang code, while Contractor[12] is a tool that extracts automata models from C programs. Composing these tools with SEArch opens the possibility of smoothly integrating services to our infrastructure.

Lastly, the correct execution of software system in SEArch requires that the implementation of service providers honours the contract they expose. This may not hold for incorrect implementations or in adversarial settings where malicious providers could be present. In this work we adopted an approach in which the act of invoking the middleware's operation `RegisterAppRequest`, and consequently triggering the invocation of the service broker's operation `RegisterProviderRequest` makes the provider fully responsible for any inconsistency that might occur during execution. However, SEArch does not provide any mechanism for assigning the blame. Detecting these types of violations can be attained statically (e.g., with approaches like the one in [33,34] or using behavioural contracts to synthesise a program skeleton which, after the implementation, could be statically analysed by tools akin to Dafny [35]. However, runtime verification is required when code cannot be analysed (e.g., third-party components). In particular, one can use monitors capable of auditing the communication session, according to the global contract specifying the communication

---

[12] Available at http://lafhis.dc.uba.ar/dependex/contractor/Welcome.html.

channel. Under this view, it is paramount to provide analysis tools for the development of services in order to ensure compliance between the implementation and the provision contract. Extending SEArch for runtime verification is scope for future work.

References

1. Brand, D., Zafiropulo, P.: On communicating finite-state machines. J. ACM **30**(2), 323–342 (1983)
2. Milner, R.: Communication and Concurrency. International Series in Computer Science. Prentice Hall, Hoboken (1989)
3. World Wide Web Consortium: Web services description language (WSDL) version 2.0 part 1: Core language. https://www.w3.org/TR/wsdl20/
4. Fiadeiro, J.L., Lopes, A.: An interface theory for service-oriented design. Theoret. Comput. Sci. **503**, 1–30 (2013)
5. Vissani, I., Pombo, C.G.L., Ţuţu, I., Fiadeiro, J.L.: A full operational semantics for asynchronous relational networks. In: Codescu, M., Diaconescu, R., Ţuţu, I. (eds.) WADT 2015. LNCS, vol. 9463, pp. 131–150. Springer, Cham (2015). https://doi.org/10.1007/978-3-319-28114-8_8
6. Vissani, I., Lopez Pombo, C.G., Tuosto, E.: Communicating machines as a dynamic binding mechanism of services. In Gay, D., Alglave, J. (eds.) Proceedings of 8th International Workshop on Programming Language Approaches to Concurrency- and Communication-cEntric Software, PLACES. Electronic Proceedings in Theoretical Computer Science, vol. 203, pp. 85–98, April 2016
7. Anabia, D.N.S.: Bisimulación de data-aware communicating finite state machines con propiedades en las acciones. Master's thesis, Departamento de Computación, Facultad de Ciencias Exactas y Naturales, Universidad de Buenos Aires (2023). Advisors: Carlos G. Lopez Pombo and Hernán C. Melgratti
8. MuleSoft: 8 principles of service-oriented architecture (2022). https://blogs.mulesoft.com/digital-transformation/soa-principles/
9. IBM: What is service-oriented architecture (SOA)? (2024). https://www.ibm.com/topics/soa
10. Microsoft: Service-oriented architecture (2022). https://learn.microsoft.com/en-gb/dotnet/architecture/microservices/architect-microservice-container-applications/service-oriented-architecture
11. Oracle: Oracle SOA suite (2024). https://www.oracle.com/middleware/technologies/soasuite.html
12. Donovan, A.A., Kernighan, B.W.: The Go Programming Language. Addison-Wesley Professional Computing Series. Addison-Wesley Publishing Co., Inc., Boston (2015)
13. Lopez Pombo, C.G., Martinez Suñé, A.E., Tuosto, E.: A dynamic temporal logic for quality of service in choreographic models. In: Ábrahám, E., Dubslaff, C., Tarifa, S.L.T. (eds.) ICTAC 2023. LNCS, vol. 14446, pp. 119–138. Springer, Cham (2023). https://doi.org/10.1007/978-3-031-47963-2_9
14. Lange, J., Tuosto, E., Yoshida, N.: River publishers series in automation, control and robotics. In: A Tool for Choreography-Based Analysis of Message-Passing Software, pp. 125–146. River Publisher (2017)
15. Coto, A., Guanciale, R., Lange, J., Tuosto, E.: ChorGram: tool support for choreographic development (2015). https://bitbucket.org/eMgssi/chorgram/src/master/

16. Achir, M., Abdelli, A., Mokdad, L., Benothman, J.: Service discovery and selection in IoT: a survey and a taxonomy. J. Netw. Comput. Appl. **200**, 103331 (2022)
17. Bravetti, M., Zavattaro, G.: A theory of contracts for strong service compliance. Math. Struct. Comput. Sci. **19**(3), 601–638 (2009)
18. Castagna, G., Padovani, L.: Contracts for mobile processes. In: CONCUR (2009)
19. Castagna, G., Gesbert, N., Padovani, L.: A theory of contracts for web services. ACM Trans. Program. Lang. Syst. **31**(5) (2009)
20. Castagna, G., Gesbert, N., Padovani, L.: A theory of contracts for web services. In Necula, G.C., Wadler, P. (eds.) Proceedings of the 35th ACM SIGPLAN-SIGACT Symposium on Principles of Programming Languages, POPL 2008, San Francisco, California, USA, 7–12 January 2008, pp. 261–272. ACM (2008)
21. Fantechi, A., Gnesi, S., Lapadula, A., Mazzanti, F., Pugliese, R., Tiezzi, F.: A logical verification methodology for service-oriented computing. ACM Trans. Softw. Eng. Methodol. **21**(3) (2012)
22. Basile, D., Degano, P., Ferrari, G.-L., Tuosto, E.: Playing with our CAT and communication-centric applications. In: Albert, E., Lanese, I. (eds.) FORTE 2016. LNCS, vol. 9688, pp. 62–73. Springer, Cham (2016). https://doi.org/10.1007/978-3-319-39570-8_5
23. Basile, D., ter Beek, M.: Contract automata library. Sci. Comput. Program. **221**, 102841 (2022)
24. Basile, D., ter Beek, M.H., Pugliese, R.: Synthesis of orchestrations and choreographies: bridging the gap between supervisory control and coordination of services. Logical Methods Comput. Sci. **16**(2) (2020)
25. Basile, D., ter Beek, M.: A runtime environment for contract automata. In: Chechik, M., Katoen, J., Leucker, M. (eds.) FM 2023. LNCS, vol. 14000, pp. 550–567. Springer, Cham (2023). https://doi.org/10.1007/978-3-031-27481-7_31
26. Bartoletti, M., Cimoli, T., Murgia, M., Podda, A., Pompianu, L.: Contract-oriented programming with timed session types. In: Gay, S., Ravara, A. (eds.) Behavioural Types: From Theory to Tools, pp. 27–48. River (2017)
27. Bartoletti, M., Cimoli, T., Murgia, M., Podda, A.S., Pompianu, L.: A contract-oriented middleware. In: Braga, C., Ölveczky, P.C. (eds.) FACS 2015. LNCS, vol. 9539, pp. 86–104. Springer, Cham (2016). https://doi.org/10.1007/978-3-319-28934-2_5
28. Atzei, N., Bartoletti, M., Murgia, M., Tuosto, E., Zunino, R.: Contract-oriented design of distributed applications: a tutorial. In: Gay, S., Ravara, A. (eds.) Behavioural Types: From Theory to Tools. Automation, Control and Robotics, pp. 1–26. River (2017)
29. Imai, K., Lange, J., Neykova, R.: Kmclib: automated inference and verification of session types from OCaml programs. In: TACAS 2022. LNCS, vol. 13243, pp. 379–386. Springer, Cham (2022). https://doi.org/10.1007/978-3-030-99524-9_20
30. Vasconcelos, C., Ravara, A.: From object-oriented code with assertions to behavioural types. In: Seffah, A., Penzenstadler, B., Alves, C., Peng, X. (eds.) Proceedings of the Symposium on Applied Computing, SAC 2017, Marrakech, Morocco, 3–7 April 2017, pp. 1492–1497. ACM (2017)
31. Genovese, G.: ChorEr: un analizzatore statico per generare Automi Coreografici da codice sorgente Erlang. Master's thesis, University of Bologna (2023)
32. Barbanera, F., Lanese, I., Tuosto, E.: Choreography automata. In: Bliudze, S., Bocchi, L. (eds.) COORDINATION 2020. LNCS, vol. 12134, pp. 86–106. Springer, Cham (2020). https://doi.org/10.1007/978-3-030-50029-0_6
33. Bartoletti, M., Scalas, A., Tuosto, E., Zunino, R.: Honesty by typing. Logical Methods Comput. Sci. **12**(4) (2016)

34. Bartoletti, M., Scalas, A., Tuosto, E., Zunino, R.: Honesty by typing. In: Beyer, D., Boreale, M. (eds.) FMOODS/FORTE -2013. LNCS, vol. 7892, pp. 305–320. Springer, Heidelberg (2013). https://doi.org/10.1007/978-3-642-38592-6_21

35. Leino, K.R.M.: Dafny: an automatic program verifier for functional correctness. In: Clarke, E.M., Voronkov, A. (eds.) LPAR 2010. LNCS (LNAI), vol. 6355, pp. 348–370. Springer, Heidelberg (2010). https://doi.org/10.1007/978-3-642-17511-4_20

Author Index

© IFIP International Federation for Information Processing 2024
Published by Springer Nature Switzerland AG 2024
I. Castellani and F. Tiezzi (Eds.): COORDINATION 2024, LNCS 14676, pp. 331–332, 2024.
https://doi.org/10.1007/978-3-031-62697-5

Printed in the United States
by Baker & Taylor Publisher Services